Art, politics and dissent

MANCHESTER
UNIVERSITY PRESS

Art, politics and dissent

Aspects of the art left
in sixties America

FRANCIS FRASCINA

Manchester University Press

MANCHESTER AND NEW YORK

distributed exclusively in the USA by St. Martin's Press

Published by Manchester University Press
Oxford Road, Manchester M13 9NR, UK
and Room 400, 175 Fifth Avenue, New York, NY 10010, USA
http://www.man.ac.uk/mup

Distributed exclusively in the USA by
St. Martin's Press, Inc., 175 Fifth Avenue, New York,
NY 10010, USA

Distributed exclusively in Canada by
UBC Press, University of British Columbia, 6344 Memorial Road,
Vancouver, BC, Canada V6T 1Z2

British Library Cataloguing-in-Publication Data
A catalogue record for this book is available from the British Library

Library of Congress Cataloging-in-Publication Data
Frascina, Francis.
    Art, politics, and dissent: aspects of the art left in sixties America / Francis Frascina.
        p. cm.
    Includes bibliographical references and index.
    ISBN 0–7190–4468–5 (hb) — ISBN 0–7190–4469–3 (pbk.)
    1. Art—Political aspects—United States—History—20th century.   I. Title.
N72.P6 F73 1999
701'.03'097309046 21—dc21   99–044155

ISBN 0 7190 4468 5 *hardback*
        0 7190 4469 3 *paperback*

First published 1999

06 05 04 03 02 01 00 99   10 9 8 7 6 5 4 3 2 1

Typeset in Apollo with Rotis
by Graphicraft Limited, Hong Kong
Printed in Great Britain
by Bookcraft (Bath) Ltd, Midsomer Norton

Contents

List of plates   *page* vii

Introduction: researching alternative histories of the art left   1

1   'We Dissent': the Artists' Protest Committee and
    representations in/of Los Angeles   15

2   '"There" and "Here"', '"Then" and "Now"': the Los Angeles
    Artists' Tower of Protest (1966) and its legacy   57 – 96.

3   Angry Arts, the Art Workers' Coalition and the politics
    of 'otherness'   108 – 148

4   My Lai, *Guernica*, MoMA and the art left, New York 1969–70   160 – 199.

    Conclusion: culture wars and the American left   209 – 229.

Index   235

Plates

1 The J. Paul Getty Museum, Malibu, California, January 1996. (Photograph: Francis Frascina) *page* 1

2 Intersection of Sunset Boulevard and La Cienega Boulevard, West Hollywood, Los Angeles, December 1995. Original Site of 'Artists' Tower of Protest', 1966. (Photograph: Francis Frascina) 2

3 View of La Cienega Boulevard from Sunset Boulevard, West Hollywood, Los Angeles, December 1995. View from Original Site of 'Artists' Tower of Protest', 1966. (Photograph: Francis Frascina) 3

4 The *Los Angeles Free Press*, 3:9 (4 March 1966), front page. (Photograph provided by Irving Petlin) 5

5 Seventh Avenue and Times Square, Manhattan, New York, April 1994: 'GORAZDE'. (Photograph: Francis Frascina) 9

6 Seventh Avenue and Times Square, Manhattan, New York, April 1994: 'SERBS'. (Photograph: Francis Frascina) 10

7 Seventh Avenue and Times Square, Manhattan, New York, April 1994: 'NIXON'. (Photograph: Francis Frascina) 11

8 Times Square, Manhattan, New York, April 1994: 'CK' and 'SONY'. (Photograph: Francis Frascina) 12

9 Times Square, Manhattan, New York, April 1994: 'US ARMED FORCES RECRUITING CENTER'. (Photograph: Francis Frascina) 13

10 The Artists' Protest Committee, 'A CALL FROM THE ARTISTS OF LOS ANGELES', 1965, offset lithographic black and white poster, 22 × 15 inches. (Photograph provided by Irving Petlin) 22

11 The Artists' Protest Committee, 'STOP WE DISSENT', May 1965, placard, 18 × 14 inches. (Copy provided by Charles Brittin) 30

12 'Artists Protest Vietnam War', cover of *Art in America*, November/December 1971, with photograph of 'Artists' Tower of Protest' in construction by Charles Brittin. 69

13 Art Workers' Coalition/Peter Brandt/From an interview with Paul Meadlo by Mike Wallace/Photograph R. L. Haeberle, *Q. And babies? A. And babies*, 1970, offset lithographic colour poster, 25 × 38 inches. (Copy of poster provided by Irving Petlin) 171

Introduction: researching alternative histories of the art left

WE DISSENT:
OUR FOREIGN POLICIES IN VIETNAM AND DOMINICAN REPUBLIC ARE AGGRESSIVE AND DANGEROUS. WE HEREBY COMMIT OUR- SELVES TO A FOREIGN POLICY WHICH WILL REMOVE OUR TROOPS FROM VIETNAM AND DOMINICAN REPUBLIC NOW!!! (Artists' Pro- test Committee, 'STOP, WE DISSENT', *Los Angeles Free Press*, May 1965)[1]

Now struggling with political forms, pot, acid, 'black power', techno- logy, conservation all of which would carry liberation of old wormy white-spirit energy and the clarification of sick autocratic ambivalence towards woman. (Carolee Schneemann, 'Divisions and Rubble at Judson, 1967', in Jon Hendricks (ed.), *Manipulations*, Judson, New York, 1967)[2]

1 The J. Paul Getty Museum, Malibu, California, January 1996.

Specific images of two sites signify major aspects of the research for this book. Both are located in Los Angeles, the West Coast parallel to what Raymond Williams called the 'City of Emigrés and Exiles itself, New York'.[3] The first image, familiar to many art historians, is the J. Paul Getty Museum, Malibu, on the outskirts of Los Angeles, photographed in early January 1996 (Plate 1). Six thousand miles from the sites of classical Greece and Rome, the Getty Museum is a meticulous recreation of a first-century AD Roman country house, Villa dei Papiri, which stood outside the city of Herculaneum overlooking the bay of Naples. Construction began in 1971 and it opened to the public in January 1974.

The museum, including its research centre, is one of seven programmes of the John Paul Getty Trust, a private operating foundation devoted to the visual arts. It has enormous financial backing. This museum is full of Greek and Roman antiquities, pre-twentieth-century European paintings, sculptures, drawings, illuminated manuscripts, decorative arts and nineteenth- and twentieth-century European and American photographs. High security, a booking system for visits and all of the idyllic control of cultural selection confirms its status within the paradoxical character of modern museums. A new much larger Getty Centre for the History of Art and the Humanities and a museum, twice the size of the present one,

2 Intersection of Sunset Boulevard and La Cienega Boulevard, West Hollywood, Los Angeles, December 1995. Original Site of 'Artists' Tower of Protest', 1966.

opened in 1997 just down the freeway. While the new Centre was being built, the research institution was described, in the Getty *Calender* (winter 1995–6), as a 'think tank that gathers researchers from different disciplines and stimulates them to communicate with each other in ways they otherwise wouldn't'. The phrase 'think tank', has often been used to describe the RAND (Research ANd Development) Corporation, a research institution, a few miles down the coast at Santa Monica, with similarly high levels of financial backing and security. Here, since 1948 when RAND became a corporation with the help of various sources of funding including a grant of $1 million from the nascent Ford Foundation, researchers from different disciplines have been, and are, provided with resources to stimulate them to communicate with each other to propose theoretical models on a variety of topics. With a major influence on strategic military planning since the Second World War and particularly during the 1960s, the RAND Corporation's role in the escalation of United States action in Southeast Asia led artists to picket the Corporation's building in 1965. In Los Angeles the institutions of 'culture' have long been connected to those other institutions in southern California that, in various ways, serve the industrial military complex of the United States.

3 View of La Cienega Boulevard from Sunset Boulevard, West Hollywood, Los Angeles, December 1995. View from Original Site of 'Artists' Tower of Protest', 1966.

The museum as archive, repository, container, guardian of the canon of cultural approval is one of the conventional sites for art and design history. The museum is, for many researchers, a site of abundance, of plenitude, of pleasure. It provides an array of objects for study, inter-pretation and explanation. From a variety of specialising perspectives, it is a confirmation of 'presence' with more than enough potential for cultural historians to provide critical texts on 'absence'. With the John Paul Getty Museum we have intimate relationships between corporate capital, the oil business, the power of family dynasties in the United States, possessive individualism and obsessive accumulation. This spectacular *re-creation*, in Malibu, of a mythical antiquity is not many miles away from the realities of a significant otherness, the district of Watts, a heartland of economic deprivation and racist oppression in central Los Angeles.[4] In August 1965, a few years before the Getty re-creation was begun, Watts was in flames, in protest; an urban parallel to the rural centres of Civil Rights campaigns in the South. This was less than two months after the Artists' Protest Committee in Los Angeles had targeted the RAND Corporation, the recently opened Los Angeles County Art Museum and 'art gallery row' on North La Cienega Boulevard, in a series of protests primarily against United States military action in Vietnam.

My second site will be less familiar and is, in many ways, the anti-thesis of my first. Only a few miles away in West Hollywood, Los Angeles, this site is seemingly *unspectacular* (Plates 2, 3). Photographed a few days before the first image, the Getty Museum, it is no less a place of abundance, of plenitude, of the pleasure of historical specificity. But the conventional 'presence' of museum culture – legitimation and memorial – is absent. That which was at this site in February 1966 is no longer there, no longer exists. At noon on Saturday 26 February 1966, the 'Artists' Tower of Protest', or 'Peace Tower', at the junction of La Cienega and Sunset Boulevards, was dedicated with speeches by the artist Irving Petlin, ex-Green-Beret Master-Sergeant Donald Duncan, writer Susan Sontag, and the releasing by children of six white doves to symbolise peace (Plate 4). Including work by 418 artists, this collective memorial had to be defended night and day against attacks by those who regarded such manifestations as un-American and at best a collusion with the 'Communist menace' in Vietnam. Several of the defenders of the Tower were young men from Watts for whom 'Selma, Alabama' and 'South Vietnam' were inextricably connected. In June 1965, two months before the outburst of dissent in Watts, the journal *Ramparts* observed that American neo-colonialist ambitions were mirrored by injustice and oppres-sion at home. The people of Vietnam were being treated as 'niggers' in United States plans for Southeast Asia: 'They are destined to die as unre-corded and unlamented as died the thousands of Negro Americans who waged but one sort of war: that of trying to live as human beings.'[5]

LOS ANGELES FREE PRESS

LOCAL NEWS & REVIEWS

TELEGRAM FROM JEAN-PAUL SARTRE

A GREEN BERET & SUSAN SONTAG ON VIETNAM

157 PLACES TO GO THIS WEEK -PAGE 16

10¢

Building A Tower For Peace

VOL. 3, #9 (ISSUE #85)   COPYRIGHT. 1966   THE LOS ANGELES FREE PRESS   MARCH 4, 1966   654-4618   10¢ (15¢ OUTSIDE OF LOS ANGELES)

INTERNATIONALLY IMPORTANT ART EXHIBIT PLAYED DOWN BY L.A.'S PRESS, RADIO, TV

John Wilcock

Last Saturday, the Artists' Tower of Protest at the corner of La Cienega and Sunset was dedicated with speeches by artist Irving Petlin, ex-Green Beret Master Sergeant Donald Duncan, writer Susan Sontag, and the releasing by children of six white doves to symbolize peace.

Hundreds gathered at the site to participate in the events which are reported fully elsewhere in this issue, with complete transcriptions of the speeches of both Duncan and Sontag and a report of the beating which volunteer Tower guard Jim Gallagher suffered at the hands of a sailor.

By the previous Wednesday, almost 400 pictures had arrived at the site—two-foot square painted panels—and a couple of volunteers sat atop the 15-foot scaffolding and began to nail them in place. A girl who'd fallen off the scaffolding the previous day and sprained her ankle came along on crutches to watch.

There were some standouts: Roy Lichtenstein's mushroom cloud—white on a blue dotted background—was prominently displayed; and a naive, officer-type blindly saluting while his eyes were blindfolded with an American flag (this by Patrick Blackwell) drew attention. One picture showed a red octopus, that symbol that obsesses the

(Continued on Page 5)

4 The *Los Angeles Free Press*, 3:9 (4 March 1966), front page.

There were thousands of visitors to the Artists' Tower of Protest which was significantly 'other' both to art institutions, such as the Los Angeles County Art Museum, and to the creative institutions of corporate capital, such as the RAND Corporation. Some visitors drove up from the galleries along La Cienega Boulevard having seen recent exhibitions of artists active in the Tower project, for example Mark di Suvero, Irving Petlin and Judy Gerowitz (Judy Chicago). Others came to see what artists associated with the radical Ferus Gallery and 'Beat Culture', such as Wallace Berman, Jess (Collins) and Jay de Feo, were doing with Abstract Expressionists, Pop Artists and realists from the Works Progress Administration (WPA) era of the 1930s. Some of them were recipients of Wallace Berman's *Semina*, an alternative manifestation to the world of art journals such as *Artforum*, then with its offices above the Ferus Gallery. Other visitors included Ken Kesey and his 'Merry Pranksters' with their Day-Glo bus travelling around the West Coast conducting public 'acid-tests', accompanied by amplified rock music, strobe lights and free-form dance. Yet others were Marines from San Diego wanting to smash the whole thing down. Within weeks of the dedication of the Tower, Ed Kienholz's retrospective at the new Los Angeles County Art Museum opened amidst massive controversy about pornography and censorship. Thousands flocked to the Museum, and the art press expressed its indignation about the interference in the rights of the artist. The Tower, on the other hand, was neglected by the same journals. Art, politics and dissent mixed in paradoxical ways.

A year later, in January–February 1967, in New York 'Angry Arts Week' crossed cultural demarcations. Dissent was manifest in street theatre, film collage, performance, events and in alternative spaces. *The Collage of Indignation*, in the Loeb Student Centre, New York University, was a collective expression by over a hundred artists visited, again, by thousands. Part of it, a Mark Morrel construction incorporating the United States flag, was censored by the authorities. Angry Arts entered the streets and many participants wished for its legacy to remain in that symbolic space. Later in the year one of them destroyed *The Collage* in order to subvert the appropriation and commodification of the work by museum culture. As with performances and events, such as Carolee Schneemann's *Snows*, which was part of Angry Arts, the production and meanings of *The Collage* has to be 'reconstructed' to be retrieved from disparate and various sources. One of these is 'memory'. The 'memories' of particular participants; the 'memories' of files, archives and the alternative perspectives of publications such as the *Los Angeles Free Press*. The Artists' Tower of Protest, the public activities of Artists and Writers Protest in Los Angeles in 1965, Angry Arts and, in 1969, the formation of the Art Workers' Coalition do not reside in the canonical processes of journals, museums, galleries, critics and art dealers.

Aims

There are three broad aims of this book. The first is to provide case studies of specific moments of dissent in two metropolitan centres in the United States during the 1960s and the opening months of the 1970s. These case studies are *not* intended to constitute a comprehensive history of all expressions of dissent. My more modest aim is to consider some of the collective projects marginalised in dominant histories, by institutionalised processes of legitimation. These projects involved artists, critics and intellectuals in the period defined by the major escalations of military intervention by the United States in Vietnam. In this sense I am concerned with the underrepresented in existing histories, but the 'underrepresented' is not specifically focused on, say, gender or multiculturalism but on instances of the relationships between collective action and critiques of institutional processes and power. This is not, therefore, primarily a book about individuals, though there are several who figure prominently as historically active figures.

My second aim is to consider some of the contradictions and paradoxes within aspects of what may be called the 'art left' based in Los Angeles in the early and mid-1960s and in New York from the mid- to late 1960s. Again, these are designed to constitute 'alternative landmarks' in the established terrain of art and cultural histories. It is hoped that these 'alternative landmarks' will act for readers of other established histories as sources of illumination and, potentially, as correctives.

My third broad aim is to add to the existing archaeology of knowledge of the period with a research methodology informed by a range of interdisciplinary emphases. In conducting the research for the book it was clear that the strengths and dilemmas of 'oral history' were to be as central as the richness and limitations of archives. There are the stored records classified by archivists in institutions (libraries, special collections, museums) and those in private holdings; the holdings of individuals' memories, triggered by an interview, or those in files and boxes long ago closed and, as it were, in waiting for an inquisitive historian or cultural archaeologist. On shelves and rolls of microfilm there are also the 'archives', selective and politicised, of public record: newspapers, journals and magazines.

From one point of view this book is a series of detailed discussions of tangled moments and events. The texture of that detail is crucial if generalisations and the ironing out of paradoxes and contradictions are to be avoided. From another point of view, the chapters of this book constitute an anthology of texts, of theorised recoveries of aspects of the 1960s. In that sense they are examples of methodologies with a base, a starting point, in the social histories of art. As a work of history, selections and emphases are both the limits and the transgressions that make contributions to knowledge possible. This book, not by an American, is written by someone for whom Ellis Island, at the tip of Manhattan, has powerful meanings; meanings consciously and unconsciously manifest through migrant peasant families. My interests are rooted in marginalisation, in the products of dislocation and the construction of identities through the interchange of official ideologies and the demands of subcultural contingencies.

The four case studies that constitute the main sections of this book are inseparable from reconsideration of the processes of memory and loss, the historical roots of paradox and contradiction in the 1960s seemingly severed by the draw of dominant spectacular commodities in the 1990s. Remembering, recalling, narrating are processes with responsibilities both to the past and to the present. The responsibilities include care in reclaiming, in rubbing the grime away from, the textured grain of 'then' as distinct from official representations: memorials codified, pristine and normalised.[6]

The politics of remembering

My initial images of the J. Paul Getty Museum and the intersection of Sunset Boulevard and La Cienega Boulevard represent strands in the tangled process of reclaiming, of remembering. This process can be conveyed by another image, another representation: at the southern entrance to Times Square, New York, on 22 April 1994 (Plate 5). This location is a walk away from MoMA, where museum visitors can repeat the expected monadic experience of involuntary aesthetic engagement, encounters with for example Jasper Johns's *Flag*, or Jackson Pollock's *Number One, 1948*. Such gallery experiences extend the weekend leisure experience of the culture consumer. Investment in cultural capital is both actual in terms of trustees and benefactors and vicarious for ordinary visitors for whom the contained experience is no less an act of faithful communion. But this expectation has not always been shared, as the actions of the Art Workers' Coalition in 1969 and 1970 exemplify.

The viewing subject of the photograph is placed on Seventh Avenue, Manhattan, in the midst of spectacular abundance: the vertical signifiers of modern metropolitan life and finance. Signs of United States corporate capital in particular and global financial interests in general produce both the world of the character Gordon Gekko in Oliver Stone's *Wall Street* and the realities of economic extremes. In front of the viewer there is the enormous sublime scale of a black and white image, over 50 feet high, of a woman posing in denims. To the readers of magazines from *Just Seventeen* to *Vogue*, where the cult of personality is inextricably linked to consumption of manufactured fad, the woman is removed from anonymous shape to identifiable 'Kate Moss', a name associated with all

5 Seventh Avenue and Times Square, Manhattan, New York, April 1994: 'GORAZDE'.

that is signified by the term 'supermodel'. Here viewers' references range around the idealised representation of the female form as thin or skinny, with all of the ways in which anorexia or bulimia are possibly connected to the 'real' or 'imagined' perfectible 'body'. Here, too, the body of Kate Moss is a parallel to the normalised body of academic nudes displayed for regularised consumption in nineteenth-century sites and now enshrined in museums and galleries.

In the constant updates on the lives of supermodels such a represented body is also associated with the publicised lives of actors and musicians. With Kate Moss in 1994 it was Johnny Depp, seen in films such as *Platoon*, *Edward Scissorhands* and *What's Eating Gilbert Grape?*, with all of the fantasised fictions constructed by the limitless artificiality of media personalities. A particular body shape, the name Kate Moss and a commodity name, CK, with particular status is signified to the consumer of the image without need of the words (Calvin Klein). Either side of this image of the legitimated female body are two words in different formats. These convey to the readers of magazines and newspapers, and viewers of television news, two other worlds of this street-culture map. First, on the neon news strip around the base of the skyscraper, there is a constant headline update. The word GORAZDE slips past. And if any spectator is in doubt, the word SERBS quickly replaces it in the neon narrative (Plate 6). In April 1994 the Muslim town of Gorazde, in former Yugoslavia, was besieged by Serbian forces. In the constant reports

6 Seventh Avenue and Times Square, Manhattan, New York, April 1994: 'SERBS'.

different 'bodies' could possibly come into the minds of newsreaders; those of males and females, adults and children, who are in the midst of brutal conflict. And the informed spectator may range from a cascade of memories of the past year's reports of mass rapes, mutilation, ethnic cleansing, nationalism; the role of Western powers in relation to the civil war; the legacy of the collapse of Communism and the move to the free market; the Western powers' intervention in the 1991 Gulf War where oil reserves were an issue in contrast to the reliance on sanctions, embargoes and threats here. Placed in New York City the spectator might also speculate on debates about the lack of direct action by the United States in Bosnia in contrast to its active role in the Gulf War in 1991. Economic, ethnic and natural resource issues (oil) become relevant. For those from a particular generation, some of whom protested down the avenues of Manhattan in the 1960s, 1994 was the twenty-fifth anniversary of the revelations about the My Lai massacre: murder, rape, mutilation and the bodies of dead babies documented in Ron Haeberle's photographs published in *Life* magazine in December 1969.

Such potential memories are not far fetched. As the word SERBS passes out of the neon's headlines, the name NIXON blurs past (Plate 7). Medical bulletins on the former President Nixon, terminally ill, mixed with the other headlines from Bosnia.[7] NIXON conjures up a number of references: he had been an anti-Communist hawk in the late 1940s and

7 Seventh Avenue and Times Square, Manhattan, New York, April 1994: 'NIXON'.

1950s as supporter of the political right and then as Vice-President during the early Cold War years of the 1950s; he had made his name in the Alger Hiss case, pursuing a demolition of a mixture of class status and political otherness; was narrowly defeated by John F. Kennedy in 1960; elected as President in 1968 but forced to resign in 1974, the first President to do so, in the wake of evidence of corruption known as the Watergate scandal. He was also responsible for the escalation of the Vietnam War with the bombing of Cambodia in 1970 and presided over attacks aimed both at the television networks, for their news reports on anti-war events, and at student protestors, most infamously the killing by the National Guard of four students demonstrating at Kent State University against United States action in Vietnam and Cambodia in April 1970.

Here, on Seventh Avenue, a contrast with the changing neon text is another word on a static vertical sign: WOODSTOCK. On the left of the photograph, the word evokes resonances with the era of Nixon's presidency. In August 1969, the Woodstock Music and Art Fair, at Bethel in New York State, represented the Utopian vision of hippie 'flower power' and peaceful protest against the Vietnam War. In April 1994, recent press coverage of plans to celebrate the twenty-fifth anniversary of the 1969 original Music and Art Fair had produced another WOODSTOCK characterised by nostalgia and myth.

As spectators walk up Seventh Avenue into Times Square itself, the spectacle wraps around all of the repositioned gazes (Plate 8). The neon

8 Times Square, Manhattan, New York, April 1994: 'CK' and 'SONY'.

news strip continues around the building updating the insatiable production of news headlines moving as commodity, alongside those of
temperature and the prices of shares on the stock market. Another static
large-scale *Birth of Venus* image, with a recommendation to *BE SAFE IN
'94 PROTECT YOURSELF*, is below an enormous Sony television screen
with a constant moving flow. And then the potential connections shift as
both the Sony Corporation and the neon update the mobile spectator
with images and texts. The spectator moves and the 50-foot image of
'Kate Moss' becomes clearly fused with the product name of Calvin Klein.
Is this a relentless extension of what Carolee Schneemann called in 1967
a 'sick autocratic ambivalence towards woman'? Another shift and the
viewer is brought home to the US Armed Forces Recruiting Centre where
'Kate Moss' is looking straight back at any gaze (Plate 9). Times Square is
no less a memorial site with the constants each year being the updated
CK billboard, the neon news and the Sony screen.

Within this plethora of stimuli and consumption, the signs GORAZDE,
NIXON, WOODSTOCK can be lost to memory. In 1969 in the wake of
Woodstock, many in both the 'silent majority' and the 'counter-culture'
had forgotten Nixon's early Cold War participation. Yet, hawkish anti-
Communism and an antipathy to all that he regarded as inconsistent
with 'American ideals and principles'[8] made him a particular figure within
the haunted memories of those in the Old Left who recalled in 1969 and

9 Times Square, Manhattan, New York, April 1994: 'US ARMED FORCES RECRUITING CENTER'.

1970 the legacy of McCarthyism. In 1994, in Times Square, that memory too was potentially obscured, distracted by the spectacular site and the imminent *recovery* of 'President Nixon' in the obituaries and the eulogy by President Clinton.

The broader process of obscuration, of memory loss, that I am concerned with in this book can be illustrated by returning to my initial images from Los Angeles. Imagine that the Getty Museum's re-creation of selected Roman 'ideals and principles' has been placed over, covers, the fractured 'Pax Americana' that is signified by the absent memorial of protest at the junction of La Cienega and Sunset Boulevards. While the Artists' Tower of Protest was being organised in December 1965, an editorial in *Ramparts* was devoted to such a 'Pax Americana'. The editorial confronts readers with the context of Vietnam, 'which we are now destroying', Latin America, now 'locked into the American way of life', and Africa, currently 'our sporting ground':

> Blinded by success, made heady by our unlimited power, we have entered a new age that is predicated upon our rules of the game . . . Once Rome was master of the world. *Pax Romana*. Rome fell to the barbarians.
>
> Once Nazi Germany, in its spasm of megalomania, threatened to master the world. Pax Germanica. A thousand years shrank to a miserly twelve.
>
> Now America is master of the world and tentative possessor of even the stars. Pax Americana.[9]

Notes

1   Artists' Protest Committee, 'STOP, WE DISSENT', *Los Angeles Free Press*, 2:20 (14 May 1965), two-page advertisement, 6–7. A consistent style for apostrophes has been used (except in quotations) throughout this book in the names of this and similar groups, though the groups themselves were not always consistent in this respect.

2   Carolee Schneemann, 'Divisions and Rubble at Judson, 1967', in Jon Hendricks (ed.), *Manipulations* (New York, Judson, 1967), a series of texts and images without pagination contained in an envelope.

3   Raymond Williams, 'When Was Modernism', in *The Politics of Modernism: Against the New Conformists*, edited and introduced by Tony Pinkney (London, Verso, 1989), p. 34.

4   For an instance of a discussion of the realities of Watts interrupting the discussions of high art, see Mike Davis in 'A Double Funeral', in *Sunshine & Noir: Art in L.A. 1960–1997* (Humlebaek, Denmark, Louisiana Museum of Modern Art, 1997), pp. 153–9.

5   'Editorial: Our "Niggers" in Asia', *Ramparts*, 4:2 (June 1965), 4.

6   Recent examples of such 'care' include Meta Mendel-Reys, *Reclaiming Democracy: The Sixties in Politics and Memory* (New York and London, Routledge, 1995) and Marita Sturken, *Tangled Memories: The Vietnam War, the Aids Epidemic, and the Politics of Remembering* (Berkeley, Los Angeles and London, University of California Press, 1997). In different ways the work of Noam Chomsky, James Young and James Clifford has addressed the effects of erasure in normalised histories. The relationship between 'war and memory' in relation to 'Vietnam' was importantly addressed in the 1980s by books such as Reece Williams (ed.), *Unwinding the Vietnam War: From War Into Peace* (Seattle, Real Comet Press, 1987).

7   Nixon died on 22 April 1994, with newspaper reports and obituaries following on the next and subsequent days. For example see the front page of *The New York Times*, 23 April 1994, where 'Nixon', 'Serbs' and 'Gorazde' cohabit. President Clinton's 'Statement on Nixon's Death' which signalled the character of 'official memory' appears on p. 13.

8   Letter from Richard Nixon to Charles Plant (18 July 1949) in Hudson Walker Papers [Archives of American Art (AAA) Roll 0352, Frame 666]. See my Conclusion for further discussion.

9   'Editorial: Pax Americana', *Ramparts*, 4:8 (December 1965), 4.

1 'We Dissent': the Artists' Protest Committee and representations in/of Los Angeles

Introduction

The mythical status of Los Angeles has been in constant production and transformation. For many it is LotusLand, LaLaLand, a city in which the visual arts are governed by a 'sunshine muse', a pursuit of hedonistic indifference to politics and social injustice. Reliance on the urban freeway and the monadic insularity of the all-consuming and polluting car has, further, led writers to refer to the city as the 'ecology of evil'. In 1972, Peter Plagens used this latter phrase to characterise the substance of the city often conventionally represented by the images of succulent palm trees and glistening chrome.[1] His incisive article in the pages of *Artforum*, based in New York since June 1967 but first published in San Francisco in 1962 and then in Los Angeles from October 1965, provided a necessary corrective to the image of Los Angeles as the unproblematic product of a 1960s boom; an image of a consumerist dream come true, in which artists, art patrons and new museums constructed the elements of a rival centre to New York – a centre of 'pop chic' and technological bravura.

Plagens's 'Ecology of Evil' was an important landmark, with arguments and analyses which were further developed by Mike Davis in his *City of Quartz: Excavating the Future in Los Angeles*, published in 1990.[2] However, two years after his socio-cultural critique of Los Angeles, and representations of it, Plagens published *Sunshine Muse: Contemporary Art on the West Coast*, which is a more conventional history of the visual culture of the city.[3] Although Plagens, a Los-Angeles-based critic in the 1960s, provides a first-hand account of art and artists, *Sunshine Muse* is devoid of the perspectives and methodology that characterise his earlier article. Not only are examples of events and works produced by, for instance, the Artists Protest Committee in 1965 and 1966 absent, but also the politics of both recent and contemporary counter-culture and the activist side of Los Angeles visual culture are neglected.[4] This difference between Plagens's article and his book is not an unexpected paradox. It is, rather, a significant characteristic of transformations and developments in intellectual activity in the United States since the Second World

War. A parallel on the East Coast is the writings of Max Kozloff, who also wrote extensively for *Artforum*. An activist in anti-Vietnam-War protests and author of articles, particularly in *The Nation*, on events such as *The Collage of Indignation* in 1967, Kozloff published in 1970 *Renderings: Critical Essays on a Century of Modern Art*, which, he acknowledges, represents an unconscious editing-out of many of his more politicised pieces.[5] Both in Los Angeles and in New York, artists and intellectuals engaged with relationships between art, culture and politics in paradoxical, if not contradictory ways.

My aim, in this and the next linked chapter, is to excavate part of the art community's past in Los Angeles in the mid-1960s. In 1965, in the midst of the Johnson administration's first hundred days, legislation for the progressive reforms of the 'Great Society' was being passed at home, while abroad there was a major escalation of the war in Vietnam and United States interventions variously pursued in the Dominican Republic and Indonesia. Consumerist expectations, increasing affluence for some groups and support for progressive legislation was matched by a growing collective dissent, most intensely focused on United States foreign policy and interventions. The year 1965 was also a major one for Civil Rights, in which the interconnections between racism, economic oppression and social inequalities produced struggles and protests with one urban irruption in the heart of Los Angeles itself: the 'Watts Riots' in the August of that year. The range of critical responses to these contemporary events demonstrate the difficulties and problems of articulating political consciousness within a post-McCarthyite culture hostile to such utterances. Artists and intellectuals were, like many other groups, caught up in the dilemmas of these situations and in finding ways of combining a broad historical understanding of postwar developments with effective responses to new developments with which they disagreed. Their dissent was manifest both through the 'non-compliance' of members of a burgeoning counter-culture[6] at odds with the moral, social, sexual and political norms of Cold War America and through organised interventions by artists, writers and intellectuals who called for Americans 'to end your silence'. It is an example of the latter which I want to examine as a specific instance: the work of the Artists' Protest Committee, a large collective formed in 1965 and active throughout that year in a variety of projects, the most spectacular completed in early 1966.

The persistence of memory

At noon on Saturday 26 February 1966, the Artists' Tower of Protest, or Peace Tower,[7] at the junction of La Cienega and Sunset Boulevards, Los Angeles, was dedicated with speeches by the artist Irving Petlin, ex-Green-Beret Master-Sergeant Donald Duncan, writer Susan Sontag, and the 'releasing by children of six white doves to symbolize peace'.[8] The Tower, designed and built under the direction of the sculptor Mark di Suvero and the architect Kenneth H. Dillon, was a steel octahedron, tetrahedron, and double tetrahedron tensional configuration painted yellow and purple. It was 58 feet 4 inches high and surrounded by 418 two-foot-square works by individual artists.[9] These were attached four-deep high above the ground on a continuous hundred-foot-long billboard wall, which stretched either side and in a U shape behind the Tower. Those participating artists named as 'illustrious' by the organisers in a fund-raising letter were: Elaine de Kooning, Herbert Ferber, Sam Francis, Judy Gerowitz, Lloyd Hamrol, Roy Lichtenstein, Robert Motherwell, Lee Mullican, Ad Reinhardt, Larry Rivers, Jim Rosenquist, Mark Rothko, Frank Stella, George Segal, Jack Zajac, Philip Evergood, George Sugarman, Claes Oldenburg, Cesar, Karel Appel, Jean Helion, Leon Golub.[10] Organised by the Artists' Protest Committee, the specific site, structure, installation and relationship between elements constituted the 'work' which no longer exists except in fragments: mostly contemporary visual and verbal representations and the accounts of participants.[11] The definition of what constituted the 'work' was and is contentious. For many participants, the production and duration of display of the Artists' Tower of Protest was an 'event', with the Tower and all of the 418 panels representing the antithesis of conventional notions of 'art' and its commodification.

After three months of protecting the Tower, twenty-four hours a day, against attacks and counter-protests the Artists' Protest Committee had to contend with the landlord of the rented site refusing to renew the lease. The subsequent fate of the 'work' is as revealing about the period as are the struggles of its production and protection. Apart from how to continue the project until the end of the war in Vietnam, there were debates and differences about whether the various elements, together or separately, should or could be regarded as 'art' at all. This debate about the 'art' object was especially problematic given contemporary cultural emphases on the persona of the individual artist and the art market boom in postwar American paintings.[12] At one point, organisers attempted to relocate the Tower in the garden of the nearby Pasadena Art Museum and store the panels. The then acting Director of the Museum, Walter Hopps, recalls:

> A variety of suggestions were discussed as to where the Tower might be put. As to putting it in Pasadena I was very much in favour, but I knew what a terrible idea the trustees would think it was. They didn't entertain the idea seriously. I don't think it was ever brought formally to a yes or no.
>
> One location that was discussed was a beautiful grassy site on the hill in front of the Center for the Study of Democratic Institutions at Santa Barbara. It was offered fervently to them. You never heard of such a runaround in your life. The Institute for Policy Studies in Washington said they'd take it

and erect it in Washington. Eventually rather than have the hassle of ship-ping it, it was decided to break it up.[13]

In 1966, Hopps was struggling with the Pasadena trustees' discomfort with his radical reputation first forged as founder of the Ferus Gallery in Los Angeles in 1957 and then as a curator of innovative exhibitions at the Museum. In 1965, too, he had been embroiled in the complications of the activities of the United States Information Agency (USIA) in promot-ing United States values through the exhibition of the work of national artists at the VIII Bienal de São Paulo, Brazil. Hopps selected and organ-ised the United States exhibition for the Pasadena Museum chosen to represent the country.[14] Petlin also recalls the complex efforts to secure an alternative site, including plans to airlift the Tower by helicopter to Pasadena or to the Centre for the Study of Democratic Institutions at Santa Barbara, Hopps and the collector Ed Janss being instrumental.[15] Hopps was also in negotiations with the Institute for Policy Studies in Washington, a relatively left-wing 'think tank'. Eventually, the frame of the tower was cut up into one-foot pieces, their ends clipped and then compressed into individual 'pillows' for those present at the dismant-ling. The two-foot-square panels were wrapped in brown paper and sold anonymously in a lottery organised by the Los Angeles Peace Centre, raising about $12,000.[16]

The history of the production and the reception of the Tower is sig-nificant not least because of its status as a collective work, as a 'monu-ment' and as an interventionist 'event'. However, in dominant accounts and institutions of 'modern art' such aspects make the Tower of marginal interest: it no longer exists to be curated, conserved and exhibited; it was prompted by political protest, even 'tendency'; its collective pro-duction remainders paradigmatic issues of authenticity and authorship; its first context was a 'counter-culture' which was critical of those institu-tions dedicated to the preservation of official and consensual cultural values. In 1966, it was these very areas of 'marginal interest' that pro-vided the bases of alternative, even oppositional possibilities. Then, meas-ures of the sign value of the Tower included the relative effectiveness, the appropriateness, the creative power of the 'work' as a representation of artists' and intellectuals' response to currently pressing social and political issues. Importantly, in the early Cold War it was the first and, on this scale, only time when artists in Los Angeles realised the power of political co-operation in the production of art.[17] Prior to 1965, the vari-ous strands of artistic activity in southern California were apolitical with respect to the conventional institutions and traditions of political activ-ity.[18] There did exist a small, highly influential social and cultural nexus of artists and poets in Los Angeles and San Francisco, in the 1950s and early 1960s, whose politics were rooted in the legacies of bohemia and the avant-garde of Dada and Surrealism and transformed by a specific counter-cultural formation. These artists are often associated with what has been called 'Beat Culture'. Recent historical and political recovery of such artists' work can be signalled, initially, by citing the title of a publication, from 1992, *Wallace Berman: Support the Revolution*, which is part of a larger body of recent literature on the period.[19] Some of the 'Beat Culture' artists, including Berman, participated in the Tower partly because for them the 'dissent' it represented was not determined by institutional or careerist interests. This was important for such artists, who regarded this manner of collective dissent as crucial both to the anti-war movement and to a critique of the capitalist fascination with the cult of artistic persona characteristic of the gallery and the museum system.

The Tower, the activities of the Artists' Protest Committee and many parallel events on the East Coast, have become marginalised, made absent even, in many texts that purport to offer an alternative to conventional histories. A recent example is Thomas Crow's *The Rise of the Sixties: American and European Art in the Era of Dissent 1955–69* (1996), which ignores the Tower and other compatible events, artists and works that do not conform to the assumptions and methodologies of a minimally revised modernist canon.[20] There are several possible reasons for the absences which I wish to explore in the body of this text. One of them, I think, is the product of a contradictory strata in the political, social and cultural life of many American intellectuals on the left. For instance, Max Kozloff, active in the 1960s and early 1970s both as critic, on journals such as *Artforum* and *The Nation*, and as anti-war protestor, has looked back on the period in mixed ways. In 1973, transfixed by the crisis of the Vietnam War, he published a ground-breaking essay, 'American Painting During the Cold War'.[21] Although Kozloff draws upon revisionist studies and exposés of the cultural role of the CIA, such as that by Christopher Lasch in 1967, he still concentrates on the cultural politics of canonical works. He does not discuss events, protests and interventions (in some of which he was active), and only briefly mentions the Tower, in which he participated, mistakenly dating it as 1965 and claiming that Robert Rauschenberg secretly financed much of the project.[22] By 1992, Kozloff was even more cool about the 'anti-war or anti-establishment protests of American artists', thinking that it is a 'modest subject than can easily be exaggerated'.[23] His retrospective view indicates the ways in which leftist intellectuals for whom the cultural value of the art work itself is pre-eminent can become ambivalent if not self-censorious about events, activities and processes that were the result of responding to particular political and historical moments. Such a view is not shared by other participants in the Tower, and importantly the persistence of their memories is neither uncritical nor nakedly utopian.

The formation of the Artists' Protest Committee and the origins of the Tower

First news of the project was made public in a letter to the *Los Angeles Free Press*, on 26 November 1965, from Irving Petlin: 'The need to discover some unique, distinctive manner in which we as artists could express our protest against the drift of American foreign policy in Vietnam has been a primary source of discussion since the formation of the Artists' Protest Committee . . .' Support for a plan to build an 'Artists' Protest Tower' now needed 'a plot of land on which such a tower could be built'.[24] Readers were asked for help in donating or locating the required land. Two months later, the project and its confirmed location were reported as part of Grace Glueck's 'Art Notes' in *The New York Times* (30 January 1966), followed by 'Tower Against the War' in the Editorials of *The Nation*.[25] The juxtaposition of Glueck's discussion with a review by Hilton Kramer of Mark di Suvero's major exhibition at the Park Place Gallery, New York, signified differences, if not cultural contradictions, in notions of 'revolt' which ran through the period.[26] One was differences in the notion of 'revolt' as political or as aesthetic. Glueck evokes the former in naming di Suvero as the designer of the Tower, the politics of which are clearly signalled by the report and the quotations from Petlin: '"We expect hostility and are warning artists that their work may be destroyed . . . peace in Vietnam will give us the happy task of dismantling it, or perhaps [it will stand] as an enduring reminder of the tradition of artists who speak out against injustice in the world."'[27] Kramer, on the other hand, does not mention di Suvero's role in the Tower project, concentrating solely on the gallery sculptures. He claims that di Suvero 'seems to me to be the most significant new American sculptor' and draws attention to those characteristics of his work containable within the ideology of 'taste' and 'aesthetics of medium':

> there is something not only staggering, even offensive, in the size of the individual pieces, but something emphatically impolite in the way the artist persists in constructing a really monumental image out of materials so little adorned with the conventional facilities of sculptural ornament. The rough wooden beams, iron chains, and painted steel sections of Mr. di Suvero's giant constructions lie well beyond the perimeter of taste established by the more sedate open-form metal sculpture of the 1950's. In relation to the glittering surfaces of the latter, so suitable to expensive interiors and self-satisfied feeling, Mr di Suvero has seemed to be leading a peasant revolt in the esthetics of his medium.[28]

Ironically, much of what Kramer has to say could be applied to the Tower, which included painted metal sections and chains as essential to the tensional construction, but such an application would necessitate a view of a 'peasant revolt' in the *politics* rather than 'the esthetics of his medium'.

Within weeks of Petlin's letter in the *Los Angeles Free Press*, there appeared a striking 20 by 28 inch black and white poster, 'A Call From the Artists of Los Angeles', produced by Hardy Hanson for the Artists' Protest Committee, 'inviting a thousand of the most prominent artists in the world to join in the construction of the ARTISTS TOWER AGAINST THE WAR IN VIETNAM' (Plate 10).[29] The top half of the poster was dominated by an image of a Vietnamese family – mother, father and two children – followed by a 'partial list of supporting artists'. This list of sixty names included artists, writers, critics, curators and gallery owners.[30] The lower half of the poster provided information on the project and details of how to participate printed in five languages: English, Italian, German, Spanish and French. It stated:

> We artists today, each day, attempt to summon creative energy in an atmosphere polluted with the crime, the moral decay that is the reality of the war in Vietnam. It is no longer possible to work in peace.
>
> We, as artists consider the construction of the Tower Against the War in Vietnam as the most appropriate method to register our protest against the continuing senseless slaughter in Vietnam. This action will make our voice heard as no debate, no demonstration, no newspaper advertisement could. Here we speak in a manner native to us as artists.

Concern with the effects of debate, demonstration and newspaper advertisement was specific to the recent experiences of the Artists' Protest Committee. Some of this is indicated in a following paragraph from the poster:

> The Artists Protest Committee was formed in May 1965 as a spontaneous action on the part of artists in Los Angeles who wanted to actively participate in the ferment of dissent that had gripped the American cultural community faced with the escalation of the war in Vietnam. Demonstrations were organised in Los Angeles during the Spring and Summer of 1965. Simultaneously similar groups banded together for the same reasons in New York and elsewhere. Now the time has come for an act that is truly international in scope.

Two groups, with major roots in New York, had been formed, more or less at the same time, in early 1965, to discuss the possibilities of collective protest against the war in Vietnam.[31] 'Artists and Writers Dissent' was largely a writers' group, and 'Artists Protest' was primarily made up of painters. On 18 April, Easter Sunday, Writers and Artists Protest sponsored a large-format protest statement in *The New York Times*, entitled 'End Your Silence' and signed by 407 writers and artists and 'many other signatures were received too late to be included'.[32] The prime movers were writers linked to the *Nation*, in particular the poet Denise Levertov and the novelist Mitchell Goodman, who were co-secretaries of Writers and Artists Protest. A group of painters, including Rudolf Baranik,

10 The Artists' Protest Committee, 'A CALL FROM THE ARTISTS OF LOS ANGELES', 1965, offset lithographic black and white poster, 22 × 15 inches.

Elaine de Kooning, Ad Reinhardt and Anthony Toney, who were also preparing their own statement, joined this protest. In due course the groups merged under the title 'Writers and Artists Protest' which, after a brief time, became 'Artists and Writers Protest'. Ironically, 'End Your Silence' was placed by *The New York Times* below a report on 'The C.I.A. and How it Grew' detailing some of the Agency's covert activities.[33] Two pages later another call for the ending of the bombing in Vietnam, a cease-fire and unconditional negotiations was published in a large advertisement, '16,916 Protestant Clergymen Say – INITIATE NEGOTIATIONS NOW!' by the Clergymen's Emergency Committee for Vietnam.[34] A further indication of the intensity of these months is the front page of the same edition of *The New York Times*, which has as one of its lead reports: 'Johnson Refuses to Halt Bombings; Again Asks Talks', with the text of his previous day's speech on p. 2. This contrasts with, on the base of the page, '15,000 White House Pickets Denounce Vietnam War', including photograph, reporting a picket of the White House, on 17 April, organised by Students for a Democratic Society (SDS), and including Women Strike for Peace, Student Nonviolent Coordinating Committee (SNCC) and several Civil Rights organisations.[35]

Under the title 'Artists' Protest', a letter, dated 3 June 1965, was sent out from New York to potential friends and supporters inviting their participation in a second protest in *The New York Times*: 'The undersigned artists, writers and people in the theater world have joined together in protest against continuation of the present American policy in Vietnam and Central America [Dominican Republic] . . . we feel it is urgent to speak out again, and more loudly, with the addition of many more voices, to help arouse the conscience of our country.' The letter asked for a signature on an attached permission form and donation of '$10 (or more) to help pay for the ad, which we expect will include the names of at least 500 people'.[36] Two reasons for a second protest in *The New York Times*, so soon after the statement in the newspaper on 18 April, were the United States invasion of the Dominican Republic in late April and signals of an impending escalation of action in Vietnam, such as the blanket approval of $700 million of extra funds by Congress in May. A fear of escalation proved correct. In December 1964, United States troops amounted to approximately 23,300; by the end of 1965 the figure was 184,314. The period from March to July 1965 saw both an increase in military numbers and effectively a decision for war in Vietnam. After National Security Action Memorandum (NSAM) 328, signed on 6 April, an additional eighteen to twenty thousand military support forces, two marine battalions and one marine air squadron were sent and the President approved a 'change of mission' for all Battalions 'to permit their more active use'.[37] With his approval of another hundred thousand troops the President had, by the time of his press conference on 28 July (when he made public only fifty thousand), overseen an eightfold increase in troops since March.

In the midst of this, sufficient support was received to go ahead with the second 'Artists' Protest' in *The New York Times*. The statement, titled 'End Your Silence!', appeared on Sunday 27 June with 579 names of 'painters and sculptors, writers and editors, musicians and theater artists of the United States'.[38] Underneath the names, there was a further endorsement: 'The Artists Protest Committee of Los Angeles, representing two hundred working artists, expresses its full support for the above statement.' The second and third paragraph stated:

> A decade ago, when the people of Vietnam were fighting French colonialism, the artists and intellectuals of France – from Sartre to Mauriac, from Picasso to Camus – called on the French people's conscience to protest their leaders' policy as immoral and to demand an end to that dirty war – 'la sale guerre.' Today we in our own country can do no less.
>
> Our President must be made aware that his words of 'peace' will not be heard above the din of the bombs falling on Vietnam; that his concern for 'freedom' in South Vietnam is mocked by eleven years' maintenance there of brutal police régimes assisted by American money, American guns, and finally . . . American blood.

The statement went on to protest against United States involvement in both Vietnam and the Dominican Republic insisting that the 'leaders' of the nation were 'violating international law, the charter of the UN, and, indeed, the spirit of our own constitution'. It emphasised that their leaders' plans for United States hegemony 'for a "Pax Americana"' would inevitably lead 'not to peace but to death and destruction. They must accept the fact that they have no more right in Vietnam than did the French colonialists before them; further, that their intrusion in Latin America is justifiably interpreted, both abroad and here at home, as aggression.' The signatories' call for all citizens of the nation to join with them, to 'End Your Silence!', was followed by 'British Artists' Protest', a full-page statement, in *The New York Times* on Sunday 1 August 1965, welcoming the 'U.S. Artists' Protest and their statement of June 27th . . . We too must end our silence.' The statement continued:

> We must insist that, as co-chairman and signatory of the 1954 Geneva Agreement, Britain should now honour her obligations under that Agreement. Her Majesty's Government must do everything in its power to bring about the implementation of the articles of the Geneva Agreement, which include the provision of free elections in South Vietnam and full independence for the elected Government to negotiate the withdrawal of foreign forces and reunification with the North.[39]

A week before, on Sunday 25 July, a full-page counterblast to the 'End Your Silence!' statements appeared in *The New York Times* from the neoconservative institution Freedom House, based in New York. 'The Silent Centre Must Speak Up!' cited the recent advertisement 'signed by several hundred "artists" and seeking to persuade the country to abandon the defense of South Vietnam'. It went on to claim that the list 'included the names of avowed Communists' but 'more noteworthy is the long list of others who are not Communists and have nevertheless added their signatures; believing that they are striking a blow for "peace," they have allowed themselves to be become parties to an insidious propaganda campaign'.[40] Freedom House then offered a six-point 'Credo of Support for our national purpose in Vietnam' and included a large reproduction of a letter from Lyndon B. Johnson, dated 19 July, warmly welcoming the 'Credo'. Readers of The New York Times would have found two pages later a very different advertisement sponsored by 'Businessmen's Committee on Vietnam' which consisted of 'A Letter to Lyndon B. Johnson' expressing 'concern about the danger of an escalating war in Vietnam . . . We are also fearful that escalation, at some point, will slip beyond the present level of warfare into the nuclear holocaust that has been threatening mankind.'[41] Signed by 110 'businessmen', the open letter echoed many other statements such as the full-page one by the National Committee for a SANE Nuclear Policy, 'The winner of World War III [will be the cockroach]', which called for an end to the war in Vietnam before it escalated to a nuclear war.[42]

The invitation to participate in the Tower suggested that the voice of artists could not be heard effectively in such newspaper advertisements. It also suggested that 'debate' and 'demonstration' were similarly limited in effect. Again, this was based on recent experiences. Irving Petlin, like Leon Golub and Nancy Spero, had lived in Paris in the late 1950s and 1960s when intellectuals needed to find ways to circumvent institutional failures to protest effectively against French colonialism. Petlin had, for example, witnessed the drafting, in the back of a Parisian art gallery, of the 'Manifesto of 121' signed by French intellectuals in 1960 advocating 'insubordination' to France's colonial war in Algeria. In 1965, Petlin, then teaching at the University of California Los Angeles (UCLA), attempted to mobilise artists in protest against what he, and others, regarded as the early stages of an immoral, dirty and shameful United States parallel to French activity in Algeria and, prior to 1954, in Indochina.[43] Los Angeles had traditionally been a city without organised political activity, at least not in comparison to European cities and not even to that which characterised New York. San Francisco was marginally different, with protests against the Un-American Activities Committee of the United States Congress, but it was, arguably, the small bohemian community of California that fostered values of liberty and dissent taken up by the New Left in the 1960s.[44] On the other hand, there was a politicised character to the postwar economy of southern California which was military and science-based. California Institute of Technology (Cal Tech), in Pasadena, provided a focus that produced the Los Angeles aerospace industry. As Mike Davis argues:

> Nowhere else in the country did there develop such a seamless continuum between the corporation, laboratory and classroom as in Los Angeles, where Cal Tech via continuous cloning and spinoff became the hub of a vast wheel of public-private research and development that eventually included the Jet Propulsion Laboratory, Hughes Aircraft (the world center of airborne electronics), the Air Force's Space Technology Laboratory, Aerojet General (a spinoff of the latter), TRW, the Rand Institute, and so on.[45]

Ferus and the politics of the Los Angeles art community

Two major observations loomed large in Petlin's conversations with like-minded artists, poets, playwrights and intellectuals about protests against United States involvement in Vietnam in the heartland of military and profit-driven southern California. First, there was no institutional support for protest or for the use and display of visual culture in a critical and politicised way. Second, high culture was an important activity, process and pleasure for its participants and collectors, many of whom were in the military and science-based corporations and institutes. Could artists subject this high culture to a shudder, or even more fundamentally remove it from its lovers? Petlin was aware that one way of finding out whether Los Angeles artists were prepared to engage in such debate and potential action was to test the attitudes of those who had been associated with the Ferus Gallery. Opened by Ed Kienholz and Walter Hopps in 1957, on La Cienega Boulevard, it was regarded in the late 1950s and early 1960s as *the* avant-garde artists' gallery of the West Coast. Within a year and a half of opening, Hopps found a new partner, Irving Blum, with commercial experience, and moved the gallery to 'a perfectly designed Beverly Hills setting' across the street.[46] In 1962 Hopps became curator and soon acting director of the small Pasadena Museum of Art, where he held Duchamp's first museum retrospective in October 1963. Hopps had cultivated the Arensbergs, collectors of Cubist, Dadaist and Surrealist works and major patrons of Duchamp, who had a home in the Hollywood hills. With the Ferus Gallery he provided a base for the mix of such commercial and collecting interests with the work and social networks of Beat Culture, particularly the circle around Wallace Berman. The Ferus Gallery provided Berman's public debut, in 1957, resulting in his conviction and fine for obscenity. In July 1962, it had given Warhol his first major exhibition. The artists around the Ferus Gallery, who were committed to a variety of modernist traditions and subcultures (ranging from Beat to hotrod, motorcycle and deer hunting), included John Altoon, Larry Bell, Billy Al Bengston, Robert Irwin, Ed Kienholz,

Craig Kauffman, Allen Lynch, John Mason, Ed Moses, Ken Price, Ed Ruscha and Peter Voulkos.[47] For those linked to the Beat movement, around Wallace Berman, an open, interracial and sexually libertarian culture was advocated. This was distinct from the community who saw themselves more self-consciously as professional artists and, therefore, as part of a 'Ferus group'. These artists were described by the poet David Meltzer, who knew both circles well, as 'lumberjacks' because of their shirts and personas:

> They were much more the professional artists . . . Male display and male competition. They would be the contingency in the lumberjack shirts, and then you'd have the Berman contingency, the ethereal, exotic creatures . . . There was a great giving of work to each other in the [Berman] group. There was much more cross-pollination than in the lumberjack camps – they rubbed shoulders, but they were into cars, talking paint – clean some brushes, get back to work.[48]

Blum, too, recalls the effect of the macho artists obsessed by motor-cycling and surfing.[49] By mid-1965, Los Angeles artists from the Ferus Gallery singled out for promotion were Bell, Bengston and Irwin. They, along with Judd, Newman, Poons and Stella, had been chosen by Hopps for the USIA exhibition at the VIII Bienal de São Paulo. And, in the second special article by Alan Solomon in *The New York Times* on art in California, Bell, Bengston and Irwin were characterised as the 'repres-entatives of the new cool geometric American art' with three posed photo-graphs and Bell described as the 'philosopher with the cigar'.[50] These Los Angeles artists, along with Kauffman and Altoon, were given regular shows by Ferus, with Kauffman showing in March–April and Bell in October–November 1965. Kienholz showed in both the Ferus and Dwan Galleries.

Petlin recalls that, in conversation with Craig Kauffman in spring 1965, it was decided to call a meeting of artists to discuss the war in Vietnam. The venue was to be the Dwan Gallery, which had opened in Westwood in 1960 with John Weber joining it in 1962. Although there was no way of predicting who would turn up, it was thought that the views of two of the various types of Los-Angeles-based artists, con-nected to the Ferus Gallery and with links to the Dwan Gallery network, would be a good indication: Ed Kienholz and Larry Bell. The former was regarded as a potential supporter because of the apparently politicised nature of his work. In 1963 (June–July), the Dwan Gallery included in its Kienholz exhibition *The Illegal Operation* (1962), on the subject of back-street abortion, and *National Banjo on the Knee Week* (1963), with ambiguous national references including the United States flag. In 1964 (September–October), the Dwan Gallery showed his 'Three Tableaux' (*The Birthday, While Visions of Sugar Plums Danced in their Heads*, and *Back Seat Dodge – '38*, all 1964), with strong sexual and social signifiers.

Kienholz was also known as a ferocious and strong-minded character; one of the Ferus group 'lumberjacks'. Larry Bell, on the other hand, produced abstract sculptures that became associated with emphases on materials, shape and structure in early Minimalist and systems work. He was also regarded as a more 'ethereal' personality whose career had developed rapidly in the previous year. Petlin phoned both to test the potential response to the call for a meeting of artists. Kienholz was adamantly negative and pro-war, mainly as a solidarity with blue-collar Marines; it was not until later in the 1960s with for example *The Portable War Memorial* and *The Eleventh Hour Final* (both 1968) that Kienholz's view of the war changed. Although this was something of a surprise to Petlin, as Walter Hopps recalls: 'Kienholz . . . was a kind of libertarian anarchist: he wasn't in any sense leftwing, and he was totally sceptical of any political party.'[51] Irving Blum recalls Kienholz's work as having 'an excessively moral edge and overtone' and his personality as 'a kind of fascist temperament'[52] influenced by his frontier and hunting background leading him to have 'a complete arsenal wherever he has lived. He's had rifles, shotguns, pistols, hand grenades, one thing or another.'[53] Kienholz has talked about his Republican background, his love for his country, and claimed that 'I'm probably apolitical because I think that politics stink'.[54] He also recalls not talking about politics much in the late 1950s and early 1960s in Los Angeles. Larry Bell, on the other hand, was very positive and supportive of the proposals.

The meeting was called on 2 May with, according to the *Los Angeles Free Press*, seventy-five artists attending and an organising 'committee including Charles Mattox, Mike Steiner, Craig Kaufman [sic], Larry Bell, Richard Klix, Ervin [sic] Petlin and Dejon Dillon'.[55] John Weber, of the Dwan Gallery, took photographs; Phil Leider and John Coplans, from *Artforum*, came but insisted that they had to 'stay on the sidelines'.[56] Whilst their reasons may have been a wish not to offend the conservative views of the journal's publisher, Leider did report on the meeting and subsequent events in the July issue of *Frontier*.[57] He recalls a 'group of fifty artists':

> They had gathered by word of mouth, by telephone, by casual meetings in the street: Each artist found that the sense of oppression which recent events had bred in him was shared by his fellows. The meeting lacked leadership and direction, but, astonishingly, one by one the invariable issues which had paralysed liberal causes for years were overcome . . . A committee of some eight artists was elected to work out a program of protest events.[58]

A second meeting was called for the following Wednesday at the Dwan Gallery, which 'could barely contain the several hundred artists, art students and related persons who attended'.[59] Dissension was at a minimum, funds to cover the committee's expenses were raised without difficulty and by the end with 'extraordinary efficiency . . . a disorganized meeting of several hundred individualistic novices had dispatched the most touchy and entangled pieces of political business'.[60] Petlin recalls that the discussions at the Dwan Gallery centred on basic issues: how to begin to alert the public to implications of the escalation of American involvement in Vietnam? how to act with no funding and with no institutional support? One set of proposed strategies was to think of the ideas of the 'space', the 'theatre', the disposable and transitory life of the streets.[61] La Cienega Boulevard provided a particular street culture; in the late 1950s and early 1960s the area was a tenderloin district full of prostitutes, gay bars and the signifiers of a Los Angeles art boom with galleries for both tyro and experienced collectors and spectators. The art boom was an emergent phenomenon that could be targeted. What if this high-culture presence could be taken away as a vivid protest? Could a denial of cultural pleasure draw attention to the realities of political and military behaviour?

The artists decided on a series of events over one weekend which formed part of other protests in the community:

> perhaps one of the most exciting and new developments is the activity planned by the Los Angeles art community this weekend starting with a White-Out protest on Johnson's Vietnam policy at most of the La Cienega Blvd. art galleries on Saturday, May 15 from 10am to 5:30pm . . . On Sunday May 16, there will be an art community vigil at the new County Art Museum on Wilshire Blvd. from 1 to 3pm. On Monday night from 7:30 to 9:30pm on La Cienega Blvd. between Melrose Ave and Sunset Blvd. there will be a Happening/Protest in the galleries and on the streets.[62]

'We Dissent': 'Stop Escalation'

In the same issue of the Los Angeles Free Press, the Artists' Protest Committee placed a double-page advertisement with 174 signatories (Plate 11).[63] At the top was a six-rung black ladder leading into infinity with the word 'STOP' at its base, followed by 'WE DISSENT' and 'WE HEREBY COMMIT OURSELVES TO A FOREIGN POLICY WHICH WILL REMOVE OUR TROOPS FROM VIETNAM AND DOMINICAN REPUBLIC NOW!!!' Six 'Realities' follow, which state: that the constant use of force cannot be used to stop the process of transition and turmoil throughout the world nations; that we support the right of all people to express popular demand by revolution, as in the origins of the United States republic; that the actions of the United States were destroying the United Nations and Organizations of American States, created to settle disputes and keep the peace; that the responsibilities for world peace must be discharged through the United Nations; that the struggle for freedom 'at home' is weakened and made hypocritical by irresponsible tactics abroad; that military intervention is 'evil, immoral and illegal . . . a betrayal of our own ideals'. Significantly, too, item number 5 states that 'Selma and Santo Domingo are Inseparable', thereby drawing a parallel between

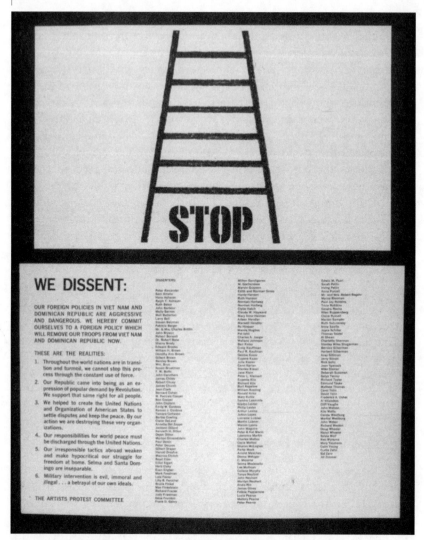

11 The Artists' Protest Committee, 'STOP WE DISSENT', May 1965, placard, 18 × 14 inches.

United States foreign intervention and domestic repression on 'bloody Sunday' (7 March 1965), when Alabama state troopers and local lawmen violently attacked a six-hundred-strong column of Civil Rights marchers at Selma (led by leaders of Student Nonviolent Coordinating Committee (SNCC) and Southern Christian Leadership Conference (SCLC)). Reports filled the media and resulted in further protests around the country; for example, Charles Brittin reported in the *Los Angeles Free Press*, 'Massive Climax to a Week of Civil Rights Protests in Los Angeles', detailing with photos the six-thousand-strong demonstration on 13 March.[64]

The Artists' Protest Committee's 'WE DISSENT' advertisement stated that 'Several hundred members of the city's painting colony met at the Dwan Gallery in Westwood to map out the [threefold] protest' against American policy in Vietnam and the Dominican Republic 'under the slogan "Stop Escalation."'. The 'White-Out' in a dozen or more La Cienega galleries would entail covering all the paintings on display with a wide strip of paper bearing the 'Stop Escalation' symbol of the protest (the black ladder and STOP on its base). The 'ladder of escalation' printed on card was designed to signify both a withdrawal of culture, covering the exhibits, and a source of protest, resistance to the threat of an escalation of the war in Vietnam.[65] 'White-Out' has multiple signifiers: it can suggest a post-nuclear explosion; it can imply the effects of white power; white is the Vietnamese symbol of death and mourning; and in this sense a 'white-out' of culture. On 'Sunday at 1p.m., soberly dressed artists in the hundreds will picket the new Los Angeles County Museum on Wilshire Blvd., all carrying "Stop Escalation" placards', which were large printed versions of the advert in the *Los Angeles Free Press*. On Monday night in a 'picket protest . . . artists plan to stage a traffic-stopping "walk-across" La Cienega using only marked crosswalks and fully complying with the law'. As Irving Blum recalls, the Monday night art walk, with twelve to fifteen galleries open on La Cienega north of Melrose Avenue, was a major social and cultural event.[66] Cultural managers in Los Angeles were fancying that the city was capable of challenging New York as a polar alternative art centre on the West Coast. The Monday night art walk with the galleries lit and open to the hundreds and thousands of visitors was an important signifier of the city's cultural aspirations, which were signalled also by the recent opening of the new Los Angeles County Museum of Art, with the then largest gallery floor space in the country. This weekend, like earlier ones, also saw other major protests in Los Angeles, mostly 'Teach-Ins' and 'Teach-Outs' at colleges and universities.

march by galleries + museums

As the *Los Angeles Free Press* reported, the threefold event was 'an unprecedented protest of the Los Angeles community' with 'more than a thousand artists and their friends' participating. Yet only this newspaper covered the full story in 'White-Out Blacked-Out: Protest by Art Community Gets Silent Treatment'.[67] As Phil Leider noted in the July issue of *Frontier*, the success of the three-stage demonstration astonished everyone, but there was considerable disappointment over the 'press blackout'.[68] The 'White-Out' saw La Cienega Boulevard, between Melrose and Santa Monica, plastered with the STOP ('Stop Escalation') signs: including parking meters, lamp-posts and telegraph poles. The great majority of the galleries posted the signs in their windows; those that were dubious simply closed and allowed the artists to cover the door and windows with their posters. Galleries, including Felix Landau and

David Stuart, covered their paintings and sculptures with white paper bearing the 'Stop Escalation' symbol of the protest. One gallery with a two-person show included an artist opposed to the White-Out, so only half the gallery included the protest. Not all artists supported the event. For example, Billy Al Bengston was opposed to the Ferus Gallery participating, saying that with the war going on all the people in Orange County had money to buy his art.[69] Orange County was a conservative area with people making money from military-related industries in southern California.

The participation of galleries and artists in such a political act was not only novel for those not noted for such acts, but also, as Petlin recalls, very 'moving'. The symbol was crucial. Petlin, and others, predicted that the escalation of ground warfare in Vietnam would lead to half a million troops being deployed and an emphasis on generational, racial and class warfare: the young, poor and educationally deprived with many African-Americans.[70] Leider reported that visitors were astonished to find galleries 'whited-out with the anti-bombing, anti-interventionist protest'.[71] According to the *Los Angeles Free Press*, unfortunately La Cienega was largely deserted during this Saturday afternoon. However, the next day thousands of visitors saw and spoke to the more than a 'hundred artists' conducting a silent vigil at the entrance to the new County Art Museum. Holding 'Stop Escalation' placards, the artists handed out copies of the Artists' Protest Committee's two-page 'We Dissent' advertisement. Leider reports that there were '500 or so artists' in sombre black dress in a silent stand-in with the knowledge and co-operation of many museum personnel who had participated in the preparatory meetings. The solid black mass of suits and dresses somewhat changed as museum visitors and other artists, wearing other colours and only just learning of the event, joined in the protest: 'The artists stood. Police cars parked at the curb. Press representatives came, saw and printed nothing. At a precise, prearranged time, a truck drew up at the curb, the artists deposited their protest signs in the truck and dispersed.'[72]

The culmination of the weekend was the gathering of an estimated one thousand demonstrators, most carrying posters calling for an end to the bombing and for the UN to take charge in Vietnam, protesting along 'gallery row' on La Cienega Boulevard. These artists, art students and supporters participated in a form of law-abiding protest, occasionally bursting into the chant 'Stop the war, stop the war, stop the war', particularly suited to the car culture of Los Angeles:

> Forming a peaceable line two blocks in length and several persons wide, the demonstrators kept circulating between two crosswalks several hundred yards apart. With such large numbers crossing, traffic piled up for several blocks. The process was repeated when they reached the crossing at the other end of their beat.[73]

Several radio and television crews were present, and the demonstration ended with most of the marchers signing a huge roll of paper, laid out on the sidewalk, which was submitted to the government. The police, in large numbers, requested the demonstrators to stop crossing the Boulevard and issued several minor tickets. Two incidents also threw into question the attitude of the police. A sports car roared into the crossing demonstrators causing panic and carrying several people with it, including two who had to be taken to hospital with minor injuries. Several people, including Petlin, chased the car several hundred yards. At Melrose Avenue, he saw a motorcycle cop who confirmed seeing the fleeing car: 'Petlin, still carrying posters, explained what had happened and asked to use the radio to report the incident. The cop replied "You can just take that [poster] and stick it up your ass," and refused to help in any way.' The second incident involved a seventeen-year-old girl hauled struggling into a police car by two policemen, apparently for obstructing traffic: 'Her banner said simply "peace."'[74] Again at a pre-arranged time the demonstration ended.

The phrase 'ladder of escalation' had a particular currency at the time. Although 'escalation', using the metaphor of the escalator, had been used in the late 1950s to mean the 'controlled exchange of ever larger weapons in war, leading to the destruction of civilization',[75] the 'ladder of escalation' was first coined in 1962 by Herman Kahn in *Thinking the Unthinkable*. He used it to convey a process of conflict between two powers:

> Each side may take certain positive steps either to bring the other to the bargaining table or to apply pressure during the negotiations. Sometimes these pressures tend to decrease with time or with a temporary solution to the problem at hand. At other times there is a tendency for each side to counter the other pressure with a somewhat stronger one of its own. This increasing pressure step by step is called 'escalation'.[76]

William Kauffmann, writing in *The McNamara Strategy* (1964), indicates that the phrase had become current usage in the strategic studies community, including at the RAND Corporation.[77] The highly influential military strategist Bernard Brodie had already analysed the concept of 'escalation' in a RAND Working Paper (September 1962), and went on to publish an important work, in 1966, with 'escalation' in its title, as Herman Kahn (also a RAND analyst) had done in 1965.[78] In the latter's *On Escalation*, Kahn proposed a careful graduation from rung one to rung 44, which had a 'powerful impact upon decision-makers and strategists alike'.[79] The artists' use of the 'ladder of escalation', in their three-fold demonstration, was a specific reference to the dangers of a change from a limited to a general war and one in which nuclear capabilities might eventually figure. They also saw that the phrase was being used to mean strategic escalation of warfighting by a technologically superior nation on a technologically inferior country. The United States would increase pressure by means of a strategic escalation of pain on a Third World country so that it would be forced to agree to the will of a major power, without the actuality of total war. The use of the symbol of the 'ladder of escalation' by the Artists' Protest Committee was to invert its meaning by the strategic escalation of the removal or denial of 'culture' from the wealthy and institutional elite.[80]

RAND: Artists Protest

This action was continued in 1965 in parallel to the statements by the Artists' Protest Committee in *The New York Times* with a demonstration at the RAND Corporation. The latter was one site of concern because of the contractual links between the State Department and the RAND Corporation and the latter's involvement in American foreign policy in Vietnam and the Dominican Republic. In an article in 1963 Saul Friedman described the RAND Corporation as

> the paramilitary academy of United States strategic thinking . . . [which] does the basic thinking behind the weapons systems, the procurement policies, and the global strategy of the United States. Unlike any strategic research organization anywhere else in the world, the Rand Corporation has become internationally famous, and controversial, for bringing a new mode of thought to problems of cold war strategy.[81]

Its origins, though, are rooted in the military and ideological concerns of the early Cold War. In late 1945, without Congressional approval and without taking bids, General H. H. 'Hap' Arnold, Commanding General of the Army Air Forces, signed a contract for the creation of an experimental institution linking the Douglas Aircraft Company and the Air Force. Known as 'Project RAND', it was set up as a department of Douglas under an initial $10 million contract with the Air Force, which was one of the most unusual and long-term contracts between the government and a private institution.[82] It allowed RAND extensive freedom to initiate research and eventually to extend its clients to various elements of the Penatgon, the Atomic Energy Commission and NASA. In 1948, RAND became a Corporation, independent of Douglas, with the help of various sources of funding including a grant of $1 million from the nascent Ford Foundation.

Two of the RAND Corporation's major objectives were to advance techniques of intercontinental warfare and to combat Communism, particularly in an atmosphere of Cold War partisanship. Although it was a research haven, all scholars within it had to relate their work to military applications and warfare with the knowledge that views and publications could end up in the White House or Penatgon. RAND's output was huge – thousands of books and reports as well as memoranda, briefings and communications, with about half of its annual work labelled secret. It maintained enormous security and secrecy, with all of its analysts required to have top-secret security clearances. Such an institution drew differing views. To those who viewed it positively RAND enabled the United States military to maintain a sophisticated, efficient and techno-logical superpower status. To sceptics, mostly in the early 1960s on the political left, RAND was regarded as 'a vital brain centre for the military-industrial complex, inspiring costly new weapons, mapping out counter-insurgency plans and computing kill rations and "megadeaths"'.[83] RAND strategists invented the words 'overkill' and 'megadeath' in their massive reliance on computer predictions in assessing ICBM (Inter Continental Ballistic Missile) programmes.

Through sources in the RAND Corporation, information on its theor-etical proposals for action in Vietnam were made known. For example: proposals for a programme of systematic uprooting of communities and of hamlet relocation; the diversion of rivers to dry up deltas; the drying up of the sea to locate fish in strategically enclosed and guarded villages; strategies of ethnic or population cleansing; the use of concentration camps. The overall RAND-derived policy was to make the country a 'freefire' zone to unleash the full effects of American technological war-fare on the 'Vietcong'. It was decided to picket the RAND Corporation to publicise its secret 'think tank' proposals. Its base, built in 1953 with assistance from the Ford Foundation, was a two-storey, two-million-dollar, palm-studded building overlooking the beach at the end of Santa Monica Pier. A five-storey building, providing more office space, was added in 1961. By 1962, RAND was earning about $3.5 million and its two subsidiaries Analytic Services (ANSER) and Systems Development Corporation (SDC) earning $1 million and $20 million a year respectively. All were non-profit organisations reinvesting resources for research and equipment. Staff in 1963 amounted to 1100, of whom about 730 were researchers, mostly post-doctoral, recruited through a scouting system from the science and university centres of the West Coast and Northeast. Members of the Corporation had established a community of intellectuals in the city, especially in Santa Monica, many of them young art collectors and patrons of galleries, with a public reputation for progressive research.

However, Petlin had an inside source who discussed with him less publicised activities and deliberations. He had met Roman Kolkowicz, a member of the RAND Social Science Department and specialist in Soviet politics, at a party. Kolkowicz, from a family shattered by the Holocaust, was a refugee from Eastern Europe and from totalitarian Communism, which he abhorred. However, when hired by RAND, he was greatly concerned not only by the escalation of the war in southeast Asia but also with the parallels between the Holocaust and the threat of genocide in Vietnam. He was prepared to share information with Petlin so as to aid the broader protest against United States foreign policy. They met secretly and never in the same place twice. Knowing this, Petlin and other members of the picket were aware of the necessity for their own secrecy and organised the event without the use of telephone contact. By this time the Artists' Protest Committee believed that it had been infiltrated or at least listened to. Postcards were handed to trusted people with details of time and instructions for each group from different areas of the city to meet at John Weber's apartment before going on to surround the RAND building. Weber was an important member of the initial group, and his apartment, near Santa Monica Pier, was a well-known place for artists to gather. However, at a meeting, Weber's door was smashed down by two Los Angeles policemen from the 'Red' squad: one hit Petlin in the chest and another photographed him and others illegally. Despite the picket's care, the police and the RAND Corporation knew they were coming. This knowledge may have been the reason for the Artists' Protest Committee to announce its demonstration, which appeared in the *Los Angeles Free Press* on the day before the protest, on 26 June, when leaflets entitled 'Why the RAND Corporation?' were handed out. The front-page story included the Committee's statement:

> The Rand Corporation is the site and target of this demonstration because it is for us here in Los Angeles a physical and visible symbol of the 'new' strategic thinking that dominates the Johnson administration. This area of function by the Rand Corporation supports administrative unilateral recourse in foreign lands and thereby violates our commitment to the United Nations as the proper peace-keeping agency for the world. Today, the United Nations celebrates its twentieth anniversary of founding on American soil. We respectively celebrate this U.N. anniversary. We DISHONOUR any national establishment which knowingly and indifferently eliminates this function of the United Nations.[84]

The artists and their friends were to meet by the well-known Merry-Go-Round on the Santa Monica Pier,[85] followed by an orderly march to the RAND Corporation with the possibility of a rally in front of the building, with Linus Pauling, Nobel laureate, as one of the speakers, if a loudspeaker permit could be obtained.[86] Alarmed and upset by the event, representatives of the Corporation invited a delegation from the picket into the building and offered them a future discussion, a closed debate. Petlin knew the possible strategy of the Corporation, which had been made aware of the potential protest, as had the Pentagon, by police activity. His source at RAND had given him a copy of a TWX (scrambling machine) communication from Robert McNamara, then Secretary of State for Defense, saying 'engage them', by all means find out what these people think. Get some sense of their criticism of the War, milk them for information. We need to plan ahead to nullify public opposition and to handle the public relations aspects of the war. Knowing of this communication, Petlin was confident that the RAND Corporation would respond positively to a proposal for an open meeting. Petlin recalls that when the artists at first refused the RAND's offer a further TWX communication between McNamara and the Corporation renewed the Defense Secretary's insistence that this opportunity should be used as a research exercise to assist the government's knowledge of the nature of dissent. The spring and summer of 1965 was a time when the Johnson administration was very nervous about and sensitive to protests, wishing both to pacify, by sending out speakers to university campuses and the like, and to secure more information about the opposition. RAND was also heavily involved in government-sponsored research in United States involvement in Southeast Asia and provided a large number of the elite group brought in by McNamara to run the Pentagon.[87] With the 'McNamara revolution' in the Pentagon, which began at the start of the Kennedy administration, it was claimed by J. R. Goldstein (RAND vice-president and with the corporation since its inception) that 'McNamara's techniques were RAND's techniques'.[88] Their extensive influence was felt in the Bureau of Budget, the Department of Health, Education and Welfare and elsewhere. RAND employees were also used on commissions, committees, task forces and planning groups: 'The 1966 RAND Annual Report, for example, stated that some ninety staff members were holding down 269 advisory posts, with groups serving such entities as the White House, Department of Defense, Commerce Department, and the National Science Foundation.'[89] In February 1967, Sol Stern published an incisive essay in *Ramparts* on the 'McNamara revolution', which he argued was born of 'changes in the technology and economics of modern warfare and by America's emergence as a self-appointed policeman for the world'. The revolution was brought about by 'those "professional defense intellectuals" – many of them RAND alumni . . . a revolution carried through by the most unlikely of revolutionaries: a business executive named Robert Strange McNamara'.[90] Stern, quoting the new president of the RAND Corporation, demonstrates that McNamara's 'hired intellectuals' regarded the war in Vietnam 'as merely a "problem" instead of recognizing it as a crisis in American ideology and values – a crisis which demands that some questions be asked *because* decent values demand them, and that some solutions be rejected not because they are invalid but because they are *wrong*'.[91]

For McNamara, the roles of intellectuals within, and as outside critics of, government were historically in transformation. RAND provided him with a great resource of 'defence intellectuals', one of the new intellectual elites in the United States. Many ideas and philosophies, for example, about nuclear weapons and their use, theories of deterrence and limited war were generated by civilians, by intellectuals, working independently from the military. Crucially, too, as Kolkowicz argues, these new intellectual elites became 'managers of the defence establishment, of vast budgetary resources, and of scientific-military establishments'.[92] Theodore H. White, the eminent historian of the American establishment, wrote in *Life* magazine, in 1967, that there is a 'new power system in American life, a new priesthood unique to this country and this time, of American action-intellectuals. In the past decade, this brotherhood of scholars has become the most provocative and propelling influence on all American government and politics, and their ideas are shaping our defense and guiding our foreign policy.' He went on to single out RAND as one of the 'best investments' made by the United States government and 'if Rand did not exist today there would be a most compelling reason for creating it'.[93]

Yet many intellectuals became leading critics of government, in particular over Vietnam. A report on the front page of *The Los Angeles Times*, on the morning of the gallery 'White-Out', 15 May 1965, stated that the President was greatly concerned that intellectuals were 'bitter and the gulf seems to be widening . . . At the bottom of the intellectual revolt is a fear that the Johnson course in Asia will lead to a nuclear holocaust.'[94] It is, therefore, no surprise that McNamara should have wanted to use his new action-intellectual elite at RAND to research the nature and character of the critique of government foreign policy as articulated by the intellectuals in the Artists' Protest Committee. A public relations agenda was becoming urgent for the government, not only because of the growing protests but also because June was a month when major decisions were taken to enlarge United States ground troops in South Vietnam, in the light of General Westmorland's recommendations. These decisions needed to be 'explained'. On 4 July 1965, *The New York Times Magazine* carried an extensive article by Henry F. Graff, a professor of history at Columbia University, on 'How Johnson Makes Foreign Policy', based on interviews with all the main decision-makers, starting with McNamara and ending with the President.[95] Fundamentally about 'Decision in Viet Nam', the article takes the reader through the public side of the escalation of the war. A month later, on 4 August, *The New York Times* carried a report on the start of a series of four one-hour television programmes, 'Vietnam Perspective', on CBS. 'United States diplomatic and military leaders will discuss this country's involvement in the Vietnam war . . . Secretary of Defense Robert S. McNamara and Secretary of State Dean Rusk will appear on the first programme' on 9 August.[96] Clearly, McNamara had a firm eye on public image and a need for research on the pulse of active protest.

It is, therefore, not surprising that a request for a closed and a public dialogue was agreed by the RAND representatives. Petlin knew that this would be so. He recalls that those present at the closed debate were himself and fellow artists Larry Bell, Leon Golub, Lloyd Hamrol, and Craig Kauffman; Michael McClure, the playwright; Robert Duncan, the poet; Max Kozloff, the critic; Annette Michelson, critic and soon to be contributing editor on *Artforum*; and Harold Dreyfus, a very effective and knowledgeable businessman.[97] A handwritten note in the Golub Papers lists Petlin, Golub, McClure and Bell; Harold Dreyfus, described as 'publicist'; Rolf Nelson, gallery owner; Annette Michelson; Jim Henderson, 'photographer'.[98] A typed list of 'Members of the RAND Staff Invited' lists nine and dates the event as 7 July.[99] The closed debate lasted for five and half hours. The participants sat around a large lozenge conference table with microphones, with a gallery above filled with at least a dozen RAND staff, one of whom could well have been Daniel Ellsberg. The debate was recorded by RAND on an old German AUER tape recorder, but when the Artists' Protest Committee asked for a transcript, which had been agreed, they were informed that the recording devices had malfunctioned and garbled the dialogue. Security was such that when artists visited the bathroom a guard accompanied them to, and stood by, the urinals.

The 'Dialogue on Vietnam' was held at 8.00 p.m. on 3 August, at the Warner Playhouse on North La Cienega Boulevard, 'featuring representatives of the Artists' Protest Committee and Southeast Asia specialists from the RAND Corporation'.[100] Representing the former were Dreyfus, Golub, Kozloff and Petlin; representing the latter were Bernard Brodie, military strategist and main organiser, Guy Pauker, a Southeast Asia (including Indonesian) specialist, and a 'China expert' named 'Dollard'.[101] The moderator for the evening was Dr Judd Marmor of UCLA, a well-known psychiatrist who was the first American psychiatrist to campaign for declassifying homosexuality as a mental disease. Admission to the around four-hundred-seat theatre was to be free. Twice the capacity turned up, necessitating an overflow audience in a parking lot outside with a loudspeaker relaying the dialogue inside. The general view of the artists was that they won both this and the earlier closed exchange. Albert Mall the reporter for the *Los Angeles Free Press* offered a different assessment, saying that the debate was 'doomed at the outset to be a recitation of hardened opinions rather than an attempt to find alternatives to the escalating violence in Asia'.[102] The opening statement by the RAND's Brodie that '"we are not here to defend government policy"' was followed by the scientists doing exactly that: 'in their evaluation of current policy the Rand representatives seemed to be as much the captives of expediency as their benefactor, the U.S. Government'. The Artists' Protest Committee was described as having a disturbing uniformity of opinion, and its 'failure to condemn all acts of violence on both sides was the basic flaw' in its position: 'The artists seemed more concerned with nailing the Rand men to the wall, rather than having a dialogue that would possibly provide an escape hatch from our present policy trap'. The audience was described as 'rude', using the occasion to 'express anger at the Rand men'.[103]

Golub, Kozloff and Petlin recall the debates very differently to the Albert Mall report in the *Los Angeles Free Press*. Petlin, for example, stresses one of the enormous differences between the two occasions.[104] The Warner Playhouse 'dialogue' he regards as having being character- ised, on both sides, by a more rhetorical approach to the subject largely conditioned by the highly public nature of the discussion. The inside debate was more thoughtful and circulatory, more historically minded, more informed by cultural values and what was possible in contem- porary American politics; much more give and take, as in a research seminar. None the less, on the substance of what the United States was doing in Vietnam, including the methods employed and their origins, and the RAND's defence of the military, there was no difference between the two debates. The artists attributed United States methods and their origins to historical Fascist methods of state terror, with technology being used as a new potential method of genocide either through indifference and inattention or through intent and focus: technology made either possible. The RAND representatives argued that different technologies and methods were essentially down to the nature of the difference between the two societies in the conflict; each one fought with what was 'best' for itself. For the artists the enormous differences between the relative effects of B-52 bombers and Third-World guerrilla warfare was ignored by RAND's ideological defence of the United States in Vietnam. A basic moral gulf that separated the two sides was the artists' disbelief that these intelligent RAND people could feel so positive about continuing such an unequal policy against a peasant society. A basic historical and political gulf centred on the role of the United States as an imperialist power since the late 1940s particularly in southeast Asia. Clearly, Petlin's source in RAND shows that there were dissenters in the Corporation.[105] The dissenters, and those at other 'think-tanks', expressed their views publicly only in 1969 when the Artists' Protest Committee's predictions about escalation, including the presence of 540,000 American service personnel in Vietnam, had been proved. The Hudson Institute, headed by former RAND theorist Herman Kahn, put forward radical reductions in United States presence in a strategy reported in *The New York Times* in June 1969.[106] But more sensational was a letter sent to *The New York Times* by six members of the RAND Corporation, including Ellsberg, urging 'the United States to make a unilateral withdrawal of its troops from Vietnam within a year'. All six had conducted research on Vietnam for the federal government and were convinced that 'an unconditional pullout was the only feasible alternative'. They identified four main reasons 'apart from persuasive moral argument', all of which undermined both the government's and RAND's own rationales for the war.[107]

'You can call it cultural diplomacy'

In the midst of the Artists' Protest Committee's activities with RAND, a report appeared in *The New York Times* drawing attention to the role of art and culture within the official apparatus of the state. The front-page article, continued inside and including five photographs, was on the use of American artists' work abroad: 'Pop, Op and Abstract Works Go Abroad as Cultural Envoys'.[108] Works were lent through the Art in Embassies programme, begun in 1963,

> a cooperative venture of the State Department, the Museum of Modern Art, and the Woodward Foundation of Washington that has made American art de rigueur in United states missions abroad. 'You can call it cultural diplomacy', says Mrs. Estes Kefauver, advisor on fine arts to the State Department who coordinates all Art in Embassies activities.[109]

An Andy Warhol and works by Josef Albers, Karl Zerbe, Larry Rivers and Alexander Calder adorned the walls of the American Embassy in Madrid. The programme had placed works by American artists in almost forty of the 110 United States embassies, with the number increasing rapidly. The report notes the 'Thousands of Soviet citizens calling at Spaso House, the Moscow residence of Ambassador Foy D. Kohler, to see works by such artists as George Bellows, Jasper Johns and Willem de Kooning', accompanied by a photograph of guests looking at Robert Rauschenberg's lithograph *Urban*. In New Delhi, visitors to the Ambassador's residence were drawn to see Grace Hartigan's *Essex Market* and other paintings by Ad Reinhardt, Stuart Davis, Ralston Crawford and Edward Hopper. The Museum of Modern Art and the Woodward Foundation had 'preceded the State Department in the venture. Since beginning its program in 1960 the Museum's International Council had sent more than 260 works to 19 embassy residences.' The Woodward Foundation, established in 1961 by Stanley Woodward, former United States Chief of Protocol and Ambassador to Canada, had spent between $100 and $50,000 for works and now circulated '248 works by such artists as Roy Lichtenstein, Robert Rauschenberg, Mark Rothko, Hans Hofmann and Robert Motherwell'.[110]

At the same time, the United States Information Agency (USIA) was, through the State Department, involved in its own 'cultural diplomacy' by planning the promotion of the United States at the VIII Bienal de São Paulo, Brazil, held from 4 September to 28 November.[111] In the 1960s these events involved big money. Walter Hopps, chosen to organise the exhibition in 1965, remembers that it was normally around half a million dollars; at least $400,000 for São Paulo.[112] Hopps recalls the highly charged political context of these exhibitions and places them in the light of the complexities of his own left-of-centre commitments, his history of avant-gardist activity at the Ferus Gallery and his involvement with a high-school classmate of Barbara Rose, Helen Goldberg, whom he describes as having an 'extreme political radicalism'.[113] According to Hopps, under Johnson's administration huge amounts of money were put at the dis-posal of the USIA to allow participation in the various biennials, includ-ing Venice in even years, and São Paulo in odd years.[114] Requests for participation in exhibitions would go to a cultural affairs officer at the State Department – 'usually they were political hacks' – and then to the USIA, 'a major propaganda arm, and it's an interesting cover for all sorts of CIA operatives . . . I have friends in the agency now and have had to deal with some. I've even used them for art errands.'[115] Whoever was chosen to be a State Department Commissioner to run an exhibition would be subject to the USIA's rules of the game, but a huge budget would be provided. Prior to this period, the State Department usually passed on such a job to MoMA or the Whitney.

Hopps recalls that Lois Bingham was 'the op inside the Washington USIA branch and there were USIS [United States Information Service] field offices all over, usually connected with embassies and consulates, and just full of CIA ops under cultural affairs cover with lots of money to help you get anything done'.[116] Significantly, Hopps states that there was no heavy interference with respect to the type of art, just an attitude by officials that '"Now is the time to have big, high visibility, American presence"'.[117] The way that Commissioners were chosen demonstrates how a particular intellectual patronage was perpetuated. The Commis-sioner from São Paulo in 1963, Martin Friedman, nominated around three people for the Venice job in 1964 and the USIA chose one of them. In 1964, Alan Solomon was selected to select contemporary art in New York, which was 'an extraordinary show of Rauschenberg, Johns, Dine, Oldenburg on the one hand; and Morris Louis, Ken Noland, Frank Stella . . . John Chamberlain, on the other. A blockbuster for Venice in '64.'[118] Hopps had helped out at Venice and was one of those nominated by Solomon. On his being chosen for São Paulo in 1965 'ops came out from USIA, [to] creep around the [Pasadena] museum, chat with trustees, and so on . . . They made a real production of it.'[119] Hopps worked on the exhibition in late 1964 and early 1965 at a time when he was back into the drug culture he had been into in the 1950s in Los Angeles. He recalls himself and his old friend Dennis Hopper being stoned out of their minds at one event and describes the contradictory aspects of 'almost everything going on then':

I have an absolutely extreme-leftist girlfriend, and I'm working with colleagues at the IPS [Institute for Policy Studies]. On the other hand I'm working
on this big show in Brazil where about every third person I have to deal with
is a CIA undercover . . . the whole operation is a cover for all kinds of miser-
able agency activity and operations. So it was a terrible strain . . . I was first
in Brazil just after the tanks had rolled and the generals put out . . . their
socialist president . . . I ended up on three kinds of shit lists for signing anti-
Franco petitions.[120]

Barnett Newman, the focal point of the exhibition selected by Hopps,
was interviewed at a 'heavy press conference' and Hopps recalls that
Newman spoke from his 'old-anarchist position' which made 'every
damned State Department person . . . fall off'.[121] Cultural image was clearly
important for the foreign policy of the state, whether in embassies or
in exhibitions. The State Department was tolerant of artists' radical
statements as long as they could be contextualised by well-packaged
'American' art. Hopps suggests that this art did not have to be connected
to the 'new American painting', though in the São Paulo in 1965 this
was a major thread. Paintings by Newman, an 'Abstract Expressionist',
were placed at the centre of an exhibition of largely abstract works that
provided anodyne symbols of American individualism: work by Bell,
Bengston and Irwin from Los Angeles along with Judd, Poons and Stella
from the East Coast. Concurrently with the USIA's activities and the Art
in Embassies programme abroad, the Johnson administration was concerned with its public image at home. The legacy of the 1950s and the
dissuasive processes of the CIA abroad and the agencies of the state at
home were at the forefront of the thoughts of the Artists' Protest Committee. Even with a Democratic administration, which had a relatively
progressive domestic reform programme, dissenters risked a great deal.
To ask Linus Pauling to address the RAND picket was to recall not only
the strength of previous protest but also an awareness of the potential
for reprisals against those who dissented from war. As Pauling stated in
1960, state organisations would use information about activists, including their names, 'for reprisals against those believers in the democratic
process; these enthusiastic, idealistic, high-minded workers for peace. I
am convinced of this because I myself have experienced the period of
McCarthyism and to some extent have suffered from it in ways I shall
not mention.'[122]

'Watts' as signifier

By the end of 1965, the Artists' Protest Committee realised that none of
the newspaper advertisements, debates, or demonstrations had made its
voice heard as effectively as it had hoped. How could it take the weakness

of its position – the lack of institutional support and the minimal media coverage of their previous activities – and turn it into a strength? How could it do this urgently to represent their abhorrence at the activities of their leaders? In looking back to the 'Dialogue on Vietnam' with the RAND Corporation on 3 August, artists from Los Angeles and southern California had much to be troubled about. Not only had the war in Vietnam greatly escalated but an internal war characterised by oppression, poverty and racism re-erupted. A week after the 'Dialogue on Vietnam', the Watts area of Los Angeles saw one of the largest uprisings that the nation had ever known. This 2.5-square-mile core of south-central Los Angeles housed around half a million African-Americans, a number swelled by migrants from the rural South, in an urban slum. On 11 August 1965, the residents of Watts believed that a routine arrest was marked by the police's use of unnecessary force and the beating of a woman. This event lit a fuse. Years of police oppression and forceful repression coupled with poverty and an inadequate urban infrastructure exploded into six days of riots, looting and burning: thirty-four people died, 1032 were wounded, 3952 were arrested and an estimated $40 million worth of damage was caused. The lead on the front page of the *Los Angeles Free Press* on 20 August, 'The Negroes Have Voted!', represented a widely held view in the community that normal democratic processes were ineffective for a large section of Los Angeles. For them, oppression, deprivation and the white power structure were root causes of the events.[123] The editor of the *Los Angeles Free Press*, Art Kunkin, observed that anyone who criticised the city administration or Chief of Police Parker for their role in the disturbances 'is called a Communist or a supporter of criminal elements. It is actually very dangerous in Los Angeles today to enter reasonable objections to the sensationalistic reporting and ridiculous charges of conspiracies.'[124] Protestors against the US war in Vietnam had similar experiences to this legacy of McCarthyite condemnation of opposition as Communist, or criminal or conspiratorial or all three.

The powerful relationship between 'Southeast Asia' and 'the South' in the United States had been a focus of an editorial in *Ramparts* in June 1965: 'Our "Niggers" in Asia'.[125] During the intensity of action and protest by the Artists Protest Committee over the summer, *Ramparts* had published consecutive issues devoted to two of the major domestic and foreign sites of protests and dissent: in June a large section 'The South at War'[126] and in July 'Southeast Asia: A Special Report'.[127] In the editorial to the June issue, the effects of 'white power' in the denial of justice and voting rights to 'millions of Negro Americans' for centuries is placed in the context of Selma, Alabama, and subsequent protest. But if justice was now on the agenda at home, the editorial asked how this could be reconciled with 'injustice for another people' with the United States obstruction of elections in Vietnam, agreed under the Geneva Accord of 1954.

The Editorial argued that the reason was basic. 'American neo-colonialist ambitions' could not entertain the possibility that free elections would lead, as Eisenhower thought they would in 1954, to possibly eighty per cent of the population voting for the Communist Ho Chi Minh as their leader. In 1965, there is a pressing moral question:

> If at last we seem capable of perceiving Negroes as human beings, thus to be honored with human rights, why are we so blind to the existence of the people of Vietnam? . . . Are they always to be fodder to our ambitions? Indeed these wretched people are the 'niggers' in our plans for Southeast Asia. They are destined to die as unrecorded and unlamented as died the thousands of Negro Americans who waged but one sort of war: that of trying to live as human beings.[128]

The Editorial concludes on the theme of conscience: the conscience of 'white America', which had begun to be awoken by the effects of the Civil Rights movement; the 'American conscience' in need of being awoken to the presence of silent victims dying in Vietnam. The people of Vietnam 'trying to live lives as human beings under a tyranny imposed by our fevered ambitions'.[129] Two months later, in Watts, Los Angeles, the conscience of 'white America' was given another reminder of domestic neo-colonialism.

One symbol of the Watts area remained untouched. The three Watts Towers (99, 97 and 55 feet high) had been built over a thirty-three-year period by Sabatino (called Simon or Sam) Rodia, an Italian immigrant who earned his living as a tilesetter, as a butcher, as a labourer. When they were completed in 1954, Rodia left the property to a neighbour never to return. Made out of broken plates and bottles, shells and tiles on an armature of iron and concrete the towers were variously valued as, for example, folk art; symbols of independence outside of institutional confines; a public site with an assemblage of everyday, ephemeral recycled materials. Rodia died on 16 July 1965, a month before the riots.[130] Within Watts, his Towers reminded inhabitants of the financial and social place of immigrant labour within the urban city geared to technology, entertainment and the car. The postwar Californian state master-plan, designed to build multi-million-dollar freeways within four miles of every metropolitan home, served only white car commuters and those able to afford airline tickets in the enormous expansion of the use of the city's airports. The once efficient interurban transit service of the early 1900s was replaced by car dependency and creation of an underclass reliant on an overburdened and inadequate bus system.[131] Arguably, Rodia's Towers were symbols of a Watts underclass. However, this did not prevent the works being appropriated differently within the 'art world'. For many of the artists of the region, the Towers signified the culturally resistant elements of assemblage, utilised as much in the subcultures of hotrod racing as in the Dadaist collages and tableaux of those in the centre and the periphery of Beat Culture. In many respects the emphases on collage and assemblage were characteristic of differences between West Coast artists and those in the East. However, the Towers also became appropriated within Museum high culture. In 1961, the Museum of Modern Art in New York held an exhibition, *The Art of Assemblage*, including the work of Bruce Conner, Ed Kienholz and Robert Rauschenberg, which served to legitimate 'assemblage' as an art form within the canon. The catalogue by William Seitz included a positive discussion of the Watts Towers, including a statement by Rodia.

In the October 1965 issue of *Artforum* there was a reference to Watts. As the journal was not published in July and August, October was the first month that any practical inclusion of a response to the events of August could have been made (the copy deadline for September's issue would have passed). But the reference did not include any mention of the causes, events or implications of the uprising. Instead *Artforum* published a four-page article, mostly photographs of the Watts Towers with a two-column text consisting of a letter by Alfred H. Barr Jnr, Director of Museum Collections at MoMA, to Kate Steinitz, the archivist of the Watts Towers Committee. Rodia's death, in July, prompted *Artforum* to use Barr's letter written after his five-day visit to Los Angeles in July 1965, accompanied by Dorothy Miller, also from MoMA: 'Homage to Sam: Alfred H. Barr Jnr Describes His Responses to the Towers at Watts'.[132] Barr recalls being driven 'through a flat, forlorn and endless cityscape', the area called Watts, and draws a parallel between Rodia 'and another idealistic immigrant Bartolomeo Vanzetti . . . Their agony was their triumph, the one in death, the other in his Towers, his marvellous evidence of things unseen.' This romanticised view of both Rodia and Vanzetti (executed in Boston in 1927, amidst protests that he and Nico Sacco had been tried more for their ethnic identity and anarchist beliefs than for any civil crime) is complemented by his reference to Seitz's discussion of Rodia in *The Art of Assemblage*. In its use of the Barr letter and photographs of Rodia's Towers, *Artforum* demonstrated that its representation of 'Watts', and its recent history, would not be within the realm of socio-cultural politics but be firmly indexed to a particular perspective on art and museum aesthetics.[133]

The October 1965 issue of *Artforum* was the first to be published out of Los Angeles, rather than San Francisco, though the advertising and editorial offices had been on La Cienega Boulevard for some time. Charles Cowles had become the publisher in September 1965 after he had invested money in the magazine in October 1964. It was broke, and had missed an issue. Cowles, whose family was in publishing, was in his last year at Stanford University studying journalism. When he finished in June 1965, he made a bid for the magazine. Taking over completely as publisher in the September, he moved the whole operation to the La Cienega, Los Angeles office. Significantly, the first full Los Angeles issue of *Artforum* represented a view of 'Watts', the heart of the city's current contradictions, with Alfred Barr, the embodiment of the Museum of Modern Art, New York, on the 'Towers at Watts'. Cowles's *Artforum* stated a particular stance.

For many members of the Artists' Protest Committee the escalation of both aggressive foreign policy, in Vietnam, and heightened Civil Rights tension, in the aftermath of Watts, were in contrast to the public face of the mainstream art world, even in its radical form at *Artforum*. In retrospect, there were palpable contradictions evidenced, for example, by Hopps talking about his experiences in mid-1965 or by Leider on the one hand writing about demonstrations in *Frontier* while on the other editing issues of *Artforum* that focus on the Watts Towers with no mention of the 'Watts riots'. It was in what is called the 'alternative' or 'underground' press, such as the *Los Angeles Free Press*, or in the activities of artists' 'situationist politics', to use Petlin's phrase, that signs of the contradictions erupt. With its letter of announcement, in November 1965, the Artists' Protest Committee attempted to repoliticise the meaning of the Tower, to signify a politics in the midst of a specific Los Angeles experience. Their Tower, evoking not only Rodia but also Tatlin, was produced in the practical and contingent space between utopia and dissent. By the time Hardy Hanson produced the poster, 'A Call From the Artists of Los Angeles', the Artists' Protest Committee had decided that this space had a particular rhetoric: 'Here we speak in a manner native to us as artists.'

Notes

1   Peter Plagens, 'Los Angeles: The Ecology of Evil', *Artforum*, 11:4 (December 1972), 67–76.

2   Mike Davis, *City of Quartz: Excavating the Future in Los Angeles* (London, Verso, 1990).

3   Peter Plagens, *Sunshine Muse: Contemporary Art on the West Coast* (New York, Praeger Publishers, 1974). In 1997, the Louisiana Museum of Modern Art, Denmark, organised an exhibition that suggested the schizophrenic image of the city's culture: *Sunshine & Noir: Art in L. A. 1960–1997* (Humlebaek, Denmark, Louisiana Museum of Modern Art, 1997).

4   On the latter see the exhibitions organised by the Centre for the Study of Political Graphics, Los Angeles. For example: *Los Angeles: At the Centre and on the Edge, Thirty Years of Protest Posters – The Issues*, Track 16 Gallery, Santa Monica (13 June to 16 August 1997) and *Los Angeles: At the Centre and on the Edge, Thirty Years of Protest Posters – The Collectives*, Laband Art Gallery, Los Angeles (22 August to 4 October 1997). See *Los Angeles: At the Centre and on the Edge* (Santa Monica, Smart Art Press, 1997).

5   '. . . A Collage of Indignation', *The Nation*, 20 February 1967, 248–51; *Renderings* (London, Studio Vista, 1970); Kozloff interview with the author (9 October 1992).

6   Generally, see Theodore Roszak, *The Making of a Counter Culture* (Berkeley, University of California Press, [1969] 1995).

7   In the advertisement placed by the organisers on the day of its opening it is called 'Peace Tower' (*New York Times*, 26 February 1966, 20). In the poster inviting artists to contribute, it is referred to as 'Artists Tower Against the War in Vietnam'. In photographs of its construction there are signs with 'Artist's Protest Tower' and in reports it is often described as 'The Artists Tower of Protest'. Participants viewed the issues of the Tower's 'title' and 'authorship' differently to the emphases in much contemporary art criticism. Partly this was because of the collective nature of the piece and partly because of the different investments and commitments of organisers and collaborators.

8   John Wilcock, 'Internationally Important Art Exhibit Played Down By LA's Press, Radio, TV', *Los Angeles Free Press*, 3:9 (4 March 1966), 1 (see, too, reports and photos of the Tower going up in previous issues: 4, 11, 18 February). Also: 'Anti-Viet Dedication Fight Brings 2 Arrests', *Los Angeles Herald Examiner*, Saturday 26 February 1966, Section A, 5; '700 See Dedication of Tower', *Los Angeles Times*, Sunday 27 February 1966, Section A, B; 'Boos, Coos At "Tower of Protest"', *Los Angeles Herald Examiner*, Sunday 27 February 1966, A-3; 'A Protasis', *UCLA Daily Bruin Spectra*, 15 March 1966, 5–7; John Wilcock, 'Artists Peace Tower', *The East Village Other*, 1:7 (1–15 March 1966), 1, 15; 'Potpourri of Protest', *Newsweek*, 14 March 1966, 101–2. The exact address of the site was 8477 Sunset Boulevard.

9   The various reports differ slightly on the hight of the Tower. Its official hight was 58 feet 4 inches as specified on the architect's drawing (sheet no. 2), 'Sculpture for Artist Tower Committee', approved by the Division of Building and Safety, Department of County Engineer, 24 February 1966. The architect was Kenneth H. Dillon with offices at 744 La Cienega Boulevard with the design credited on the drawing to Dillon and di Suvero. Many thanks to Irving Petlin for a copy of this drawing.

10 Letter, undated, 'Artist's Tower', written by Arnold Mesches, Chairman, Fund Raising Committee, inviting financial contributions (University of California, Department of Special Collections, Collection 50, 'A Collection of Underground, Alternative and Extremist Literature', Box 36, Folder 'Artist's Tower Los Angeles').

11 I am grateful to the following participants for allowing me to interview them: Rudolf Baranik, Charles and Barbara Brittin, Mark di Suvero, Leon Golub, Max Kozloff, Irving Petlin, Nancy Spero, May Stevens, John Weber.

12 The figure of Jackson Pollock was paradigmatic, as were the growing prices for his works especially in the context of the rapid growth in private and private galleries and museums. Generally on this see my 'The Politics of Representation' in Paul Wood, Francis Frascina, Jonathan Harris and Charles Harrison, *Modernism in Dispute: Art Since the Forties* (New Haven and London, Yale University Press, 1993) especially pp. 124–8. On the rise of prices for Pollock's paintings and other Abstract Expressionists see, for example: Clement Greenberg, 'The Jackson Pollock Market Soars', *The New York Times Magazine*, 16 April 1961, 42–3, 132 and 135; Diedre Robson, 'The Market for Abstract Expressionism: The Time-lag Between Critical and Commercial Acceptance', *Archives of American Art Journal*, 25:3 (1985), 19–23. Also Karl E. Meyer, *The Art Museum: Power, Money and Ethics* (New York, William Morrow and Company, 1979); Steven Naifeh, *Culture Making: Money, Success, and the New York Art World* (Princeton Undergraduate Studies in History: 2, History Department of Princeton University, 1976).

13 Hopps quoted in Therese Schwartz, 'The Politicization of the Avant-Garde' (Part I), *Art in America*, 59:6 (November/December 1971), 99.

14 See *Walter Hopps: Pasadena Art Museum*, Walter Hopps interviewed by Joanne L. Ratner (Department of Special Collections, Oral History Programme, University

Research Library, UCLA, 1990). See especially pp. 63ff. for interference by, particularly, Robert Rowan at Pasadena (including the latter's homophobic and anti-semitic attitudes) and pp. 80ff. for USIA activities.

15 Interview with the author (14 April 1997). Petlin recalls that Janss was connected both to Pasadena and to the Centre for the Study of Democratic Institutions. The latter pulled out partly because it feared losing its tax-exempt status by accepting such a blatantly political work.

16 Schwartz, 'The Politicization of the Avant-Garde' (Part I), and my interview with Irving Petlin (27 October 1992).

17 On the political posters produced by Los Angeles artists, art collectives, art centres and community organisations since the late 1960s, see *Los Angeles: At the Centre and on the Edge Thirty Years of Protest Posters*, 1997, organised by the Centre for the Study of Political Graphics, Los Angeles.

18 Charles Brittin, interview with the author (24 April 1997).

19 *Wallace Berman: Support the Revolution* (Amsterdam, Institute of Contemporary Art, 1992). Other important texts include: Richard Cándida-Smith, *Utopia and Dissent: Art Poetry and Politics in California* (Berkeley, University of California Press, 1995); Lisa Phillips (ed.), *Beat Culture and the New America: 1950–1965* (New York, Whitney Museum of American Art, 1995); Charles Desmarais, *Proof: Los Angeles Art and the Photograph 1960–1980* (Los Angeles, Laguna Art Museum, Fellows of Contemporary Art, 1992); Rebecca Solnit, *Secret Exhibition: Six California Artists of the Cold War Era* (San Francisco, City Lights Books, 1990); Anne Ayres (ed.), *Forty Years of California Assemblage* (Los Angeles, Wight Art Gallery, University of California, 1989); Anne Ayres (ed.), *LA Pop in the Sixties* (Newport Beach, Calif., Newport Harbor Art Museum, 1989); Anne Sandra Leonard Starr, *Lost and Found in California: Four Decades of Assemblage Art* (Santa Monica, James Corcoran Gallery, Shoshana Wayne Gallery, Pence Gallery, 1988); Maurice Tuchman (ed.), *Art in Los Angeles: Seventeen Artists in the Sixties* (Los Angeles, Los Angeles County Museum of Art, 1981); Betty Turnbull, *The Last Time I Saw Ferus 1957–1966*, with essay by Walter Hopps (Newport Beach, Calif., Newport Harbor Art Museum, 1979). For a useful photo-documentary source see Craig Krull, *Photographing the LA Art Scene 1955–1975* (Santa Monica, Smart Art Press, 1996).

20 Thomas Crow, *The Rise of the Sixties: American and European Art in the Era of Dissent 1955–69* (London, Weidenfeld and Nicolson, 1996). For example, in a book on 'dissent' in the 1960s it is extraordinary to find that artists such as Golub and Spero do not even appear in the index.

21 Kozloff, 'American Painting During the Cold War', *Artforum*, 11:9 (May 1973), 43–54 (a revised version of a catalogue introduction, *Twenty-five Years of American Painting 1948–1973*, Des Moines Art Centre, 6 March to 22 April 1973).

22 Kozloff, 'American Painting During the Cold War', 53. As for Rauschenberg, 'The artist is not aware of the Los Angeles Peace Tower, and certainly did not finance it' (letter from Rauschenberg's assistant, 28 September 1992).

23 Interview with the author (9 October 1992) and letter dated 16 September 1992. Kozloff continues: 'We are speaking of small, loose, shifting coteries, well intentioned sometimes, but always vague in effect . . . and of no great cultural moment.' This view needs to be compared with, for example, the 418 artists participating in the 'Tower' and the large numbers of artists in subsequent groups, such as the Art Workers' Coalition in 1969. The various 'effects' of the 'protests' and the 'works' are open to debate.

24 *Los Angeles Free Press*, 2:48 (26 November 1965), 5.

25 Grace Glueck, 'Art Notes', *The New York Times*, 30 January 1966, 24, 26. 'Tower Against the War', Editorials, *The Nation*, 7 February 1966, 143.

26   Hilton Kramer, 'Di Suvero: Sculpture of Whitmanesque Scale', *The New York Times*, 30 January 1966, 25, 26.

27   Glueck, 'Art Notes', 26.

28   Kramer, 'Di Suvero: Sculpture of Whitmanesque Scale', 25.

29   Thanks to Rudolf Baranik for a photocopy of the poster and other relevant information and to Irving Petlin for a photograph of the poster and information.

30   John Altoon; Rudolf Baranik; Larry Bell; Paul Brach; Helen Breger; Arnaldo Coen; Allen d'Arcangelo; Elaine de Kooning; Dijon Dillon; Ken Dillon; Mark di Suvero; Bella T. Feldman; Herbert Ferber; Llyn Foulkes; Sam Francis; Judy Gerowitz; Leon Golub; Leonel Gongora; Lloyd Hamrol; Hardy Hanson; Francisco Icaza; Donald Judd; Wolf Kahn; Howie Kanowitz; Richard Klix; Max Kozloff; Roy Lichtenstein; Phil Leider; Ivan Majdrakoff; Robert Mallory; Charles Mattox; Robert McChesney; Arnold Mesches; Robert Motherwell; Lee Mulligan; Rolf Nelson; Frank O'Hara; Miguel Hernandez Orban; Jacques Overhoff; Julia Pearl; Irving Petlin; Patrick Procktor; Byron Randall; Ad Reinhardt; Mario Orozco Rivera; Larry Rivers; Jim Rosenquist; Mark Rothko; Frank Stella; Hassel Smith; Arthur Secunda; George Segal; Artemio Sepulveda; George Sugarman; Maurice Tuchman; John Weber; Charles White; Jim Wines; Adja Yunkers; Jack Zajac.

31   I am indebted to Rudolf Baranik, including an interview (17 October 1992), for information on which the following is based.

32   'End Your Silence', *The New York Times*, 18 April 1965, Section 4, E 5. It said: 'We are grieved by American policies in Vietnam. We are opposed to American policies in Vietnam. We will not remain silent before the world. We call on all those who wish to speak in a crucial moment in our history, to demand an immediate turning of the American policy in Vietnam to the methods of peace.'

33   The activities of the CIA during this period have been documented, with its internal culture vividly represented, by H. Bradford Westerfield (ed.), *Inside CIA's Private World: Declassified Articles from the Agency's Internal Journal 1955–1992* (New Haven and London, Yale University Press, 1995). The relationship between the CIA and culture, particularly visual culture, is a contested issue.

34   *The New York Times*, 18 April 1965, Section 4, p. E 7.

35   *Ibid.*, 1, 3.

36   Copy of letter kindly supplied by Rudolf Baranik. Letter signed by Rudolf Baranik; Paul Blackburn; Kay Boyle; Ossie Davis; Ruby Dee; Elaine de Kooning; Lydia Edwards; Philip Evergood; Jules Feiffer; Jack Gelber; Allen Ginsberg; Mitchell Goodman; E. Y. Harburg; Nat Hentoff; Stanley Kunitz; Denise Levertov; Jack Levine; Norman Mailer; Lewis Mumford; Joseph Papp; Tony Randall; Ad Reinhardt; Muriel Rukeyser; Norman J. Seaman; May Stevens; Moses Soyer; Charles White.

37   NSAM 328 in George C. Herring (ed.), *The Pentagon Papers: Abridged Edition* (New York, McGraw-Hill, 1993), p. 121.

38   'End Your Silence!', *The New York Times*, 27 June 1965, Section 2, 18 X.

39   'British Artists' Protest', *The New York Times*, Sunday 1 August 1965, Section 2, 14 X. Signed by: John Arden; Kenneth Armitage; Benjamin Britten; Reg Butler; Elias Canetti; Kenneth Clark; Constance Cummings; William Empson; E. M. Forster; Elisabeth Frink; Alec Guinness; Jacquetta Hawkes; Doris Lessing; C. Day Lewis; Compton Mackenzie; Jonathan Miller; Iris Murdoch; Peter O'Toole; Eduardo Paolozzi; Peter Pears; Harold Pinter; William Plomer; Laurens Van Der Post; J. B. Priestley; Herbert Read; Vanessa Redgrave; Ceri Richards; I. A. Richards; Paul Schofield; William Scott; Alan Sillitoe; Graham Sutherland; Sybil Thorndike; Kenneth Tynan; Arnold Wesker; Leonard Woolf.

40   *The New York Times*, 25 July 1965, Section 4, E 5.

41   *Ibid.*, E 7.

42   *The New York Times*, 22 July 1965, 13.

43 For this and the following I draw upon interviews with Irving Petlin (27 October 1992 and 14 and 16 April 1997).

44 I draw upon my interview with Barbara and Charles Brittin (17 April 1997). See, too, Cándida-Smith, *Utopia and Dissent*; Phillips (ed.), *Beat Culture and the New America: 1950–1965*; Solnit, *Secret Exhibition*.

45 Davis, *City of Quartz*, p. 57.

46 Walter Hopps, *Kienholz: A Retrospective* (New York, Whitney Museum of American Art, 1996), p. 32. See, too, the following publications in the Department of Special Collections, Oral History Programme, University Research Library, UCLA: *Edward Kienholz: Los Angeles Art Community: Group Portrait*, interviewed by Lawrence Weschler (1977); *Irving Blum: At the Ferus Gallery*, interviewed by Joann Phillips and Lawrence Weschler (1984); *Craig Kauffman: Los Angeles Art Community: Group Portrait*, interviewed by Michael Auping (1984); *Walter Hopps: Pasadena Art Museum*, interviewed by Joanne L. Ratner (1990). Also: Turnbull, *The Last Time I Saw Ferus*.

47 Blum, who effectively dropped artists such as Berman as 'uncommercial', recalls the following as the Ferus stable under its more commercial phase from around 1962 to its closure in 1966: Altoon, Kauffman, Kienholz, Irwin, Bengston, Moses, Voulkos, Mason, Price, Bell. See *Irving Blum: At the Ferus Gallery*, pp. 205ff.

48 David Meltzer taped conversation with Rebecca Solnit in May 1988, in Solnit, 'Heretical Constellations: Notes on California, 1946–61', in Phillips (ed.), *Beat Culture and the New America: 1950–1965*, p. 75. In November 1964, the Ferus Gallery added to this male myth with an exhibition titled *The Studs: Moses, Irwin, Price, Bengston*.

49 *Irving Blum: At the Ferus Gallery*, pp. 114–15.

50 'Making Like Competition in LA', *The New York Times*, 11 July 1965, Section 2, p. 10 X. The earlier article, 'They Know What They Want', appeared on 4 July, Section 2, p. X 15.

51 Hopps, *Kienholz: A Retrospective*, p. 31. Whilst Kienholz declared himself a social critic, he thought of politics differently: 'Politics are a really murky area for me because politics are really our own abdication of our own responsibility. We hire someone to make decisions for us. We give up our own power to let someone else exercise power over us' (*Edward Kienholz, Los Angeles Art Community: Group Portrait*, I, p. 218).

52 *Irving Blum: At the Ferus Gallery*, p. 84.

53 *Ibid.*, p. 87.

54 *Edward Kienholz, Los Angeles Art Community: Group Portrait*, I, p. 217.

55 Art Kunkin, 'Teach-Ins, Teach-Outs, White-Outs: Protest Grows Over Vietnam', *Los Angeles Free Press*, 2:20 (14 May 1965), 4.

56 Irving Petlin, interview with the author (27 October 1992).

57 Philip Leider, 'Art: The Demonstration', *Frontier*, 16:9 (July 1965), 21–2. *Frontier*, in the mould of *The Nation*, was a Los-Angeles-based monthly journal whose publisher was Gifford Phillips, a collector of Ferus artists, among others (Phillips also became associate publisher of *The Nation*). An exhibition *The Gifford and Joann Phillips Collection* was shown at UCLA Art Galleries, November–December 1962.

58 Philip Leider, 'Art: The Demonstration', 21–2.

59 *Ibid.*, 22.

60 *Ibid.*

61 Interview with the author (27 October 1992).

62 Art Kunkin, 'Teach-Ins, Teach-Outs, White-Outs', 4.

63 *Los Angeles Free Press*, 2:20 (14 May 1965), 6–7. The signatories were: Peter Alexander; John Altoon; Sam Amato; Hans Ashauer; Ralph F. Ashauer; Ruth Baker; John Barbour; Molly Barnes; Wall Batterton; Larry Bell; Steven Belzman; Patricia

Berger; Charles Brittin; Barbara Brittin; John Bryson; Robert Borsodi; Dr Robert Bone; Sherry Brody; Edward Brooks; William H. Brown; Dorothy Ann Brown; Gilbert Brown; Barcaly Brown; Wm. Brun; Susan Brustman; F. W. Butts; John Caruthers; James Childs; Robert Cheuy; James Church; Jean Clark; Bernard Cohen; W. Pachaic Cooper; Ron Cooper; John Coplans; Emily W. Cordova; Ramon J. Cordova; Tamara Cotiauox; Barbie Cowling; Claire Deland; Annette del Zoppo; Jackson Dillard; Kenneth H. Dillon; Dejon Dillon; Morton Dimondstein; Paul Donin; Peter Douvos; Gilbert Draper; Harold Dreyfus; Maurice Ehrlich; Boyd Elder; Elliot Elgart; Herb Elsky; Evan Engber; Mark Feedman; Lola Feiner; Lilly R. Fenichel; Bruria Finkel; Max Finkelstein; Richard Frazier; Judy Friedman; Gene Frumkin; Frank O. Gehry; Milton Gershgoren; M. Gochenouer; Marvin Grayson; Edith & Lou Gross; Carol Hampton; Norman Hartweg; Clythe Hatch; Claude W. Hayward; Maryanne Heiman; Arleen Hendler; Maxwell Hendler; Ro Hineser; Robin Hirsch; Marvin Hughes; Charles A. Jaeger; Wallace Johnson; Pat Ishii; Ben Kalka; Craig Kauffman; Paul R. Kaufman; Debbie Kazor; Eugene Kazor; Julie Keeler; Carol Kerlan; Stanley Kiesel; Jane Klein; Peter L. Kleinert; Eugenie Klix; Richard Klix; Burt Kopelow; William Kosting; Art Kunkin; Ronald Kriss; Mary Kutila; Sandra Laemmle; Gladys Leider; Philip Leider; Arthur Levin; Joann Lopez; Lorraine Lubner; Marvin Lyons; John Maguire; Peter & Kat Marin; Lawrence Martin; Charles Mattox; Celia Mattox; Sharon McLaglen; Parke Meek; Arnold Mesches; Deena Metzger; C. McCome; Selma Moskowitz; Lee Mullican; Coliene Murphy; Tanya Neufeld; Anais Nin; James Olngy; Felicia Pappernow; Mallory Pearce; Edward M. Pearl; Sarah Petlin; Irving Petlin; Anna Purcell; Lavonne Regehr; Robert Regehr; Myrna Riseman; Paul Jay Robbins; Trina Robbins; Sandra Rocha; Allen Ruppersberg; Claire Russell; Marion Sampler; Anne Saville; Ruth Saturensky; Joyce Schiller; Thomas Sevel; Al Shean; Charlotte Sherman; Stanley Miles Shugarman; Bernice Silberman; Herbert Silberman; Jerry Simon; Rick Soltz; Joan Spevack; Mike Steiner; Deborah Sussman; Michael Zebulon Swartz; Galya Tarmu; Richard Taylor; Edmund Teske; Matthew Thomas; Carol Tolin; David Tolin; Frederick A. Usher; Al Villalotu; Cliff Vaughs; John Watson; Carole Westberg; Martial Westberg; John Weber; Richard Weston; Doug Wheeler; Nanci Wheeler; Sylvia Wolf; Ken Wynsma; Mary Yeomans; Colin Young; Curtis Zahn; Sid Zaro; Jill Zimmer.

64 Charles Brittin, 'Massive Climax to a Week of Civil Rights Protests in Los Angeles', *Los Angeles Free Press*, 2:12 (Friday 19 March 1965), 1–2.

65 Irving Petlin, interviews with the author (27 October 1992 and 14 April 1997).

66 *Irving Blum: At the Ferus Gallery*, p. 91.

67 'White-Out Blacked-Out: Protest by Art Community Gets Silent Treatment', *Los Angeles Free Press*, 2:21 (21 May 1965), 1–2, with three photos by Charles Brittin.

68 Leider, 'Art: The Demonstration', 22.

69 Charles Brittin, interview with the author (24 May 1997).

70 Petlin, interview with the author (14 April 1997).

71 Leider, 'Art: The Demonstration', 22.

72 *Ibid.*

73 'White-Out Blacked-Out: Protest by Art Community Gets Silent Treatment', 2.

74 *Ibid.*

75 Wayland Young, *Strategy for Survival: First Steps in Nuclear Survival* (London, Penguin Books, 1959), quoted in Lawrence Freedman, 'On the Tiger's Back: The Development of the Concept of Escalation', in Roman Kolkowicz (ed.), *The Logic of Nuclear Terror* (Boston, Allen and Unwin, 1987), p. 115.

76 Herman Kahn, *Thinking the Unthinkable* (New York, Horizon Press, 1962), p. 185, quoted in Freedman, 'On the Tiger's Back', pp. 127–8.

77 Kauffmann, *The McNamara Strategy* (New York, Harper and Row, 1964). McNamara in his *In Retrospect: The Tragedy and Lessons of Vietnam*, first published 1995, titles

his chapter 7 'The Decision to Escalate: January 28–July 28 1965' (New York, Vintage, 1996). Significantly, McNamara is very quiet about RAND and the 'Defense Intellectuals'.

78 Bernard Brodie, *Escalation and the Nuclear Option* (Princeton, Princeton University Press, 1966); Herman Kahn, *On Escalation* (London, Pall Mall Press, 1965).

79 Colin S. Gray, 'What RAND Hath Wrought', *Foreign Policy*, fall 1971, Part 4 118.

80 Petlin, interview with the author (14 April 1997).

81 Saul Friedman, 'The Rand Corporation and Our Policy Makers', *The Atlantic Monthly*, September 1963, 62. Friedman goes on to quote Roger Hagan, a Harvard historian, who argues that RAND had 'increased public acceptance of nuclear war as part of national policy. Rand thinking has always been negative in presupposing an eternal, ever spiralling conflict between the United States and the Soviet Union. Rand has done nothing to exert effort in thinking about reasons, alternatives and the way to end thermonuclear confrontation' (p. 67).

82 RAND's duties under the contract were enshrined in a single sentence: 'a program of study and research on the broad subject of intercontinental warfare, other than surface, with the object of recommending to the Army Air Forces preferred techniques and instrumentalities for this purpose'. Quoted in Paul Dickson, *Think Tanks* (New York, Atheneum, 1971), pp. 52–3 (also see chapters V and VI). See also: *The RAND Corporation: The First 15 Years* (Santa Monica, RAND, 1963); Saul Friedman, 'The Rand Corporation and Our Policy Makers', *The Atlantic Monthly*, September 1963, 61–8; Arthur Herzog, *The War-Peace Establishment* (New York, Harper and Row, 1965); Bruce L. Smith, *The RAND Corporation: Case Study of a Nonprofit Advisory Corporation* (Cambridge, Harvard University Press, 1966); Sol Stern, 'The Defense Intellectuals', *Ramparts*, 5:8 (February 1967), 31–7; Roger E. Levien, *Independent Public Policy Analysis Organisations – Major Social Intervention* (Santa Monica, RAND, 1969); Gray, 'What RAND Hath Wrought', 111–29; Stephen Kaplan, *The Wizards of Armageddon* (New York, Simon and Schuster, 1983).

83 Dickson, *Think Tanks*, p. 73.

84 In 'Artists Protest At Rand Corp.', *Los Angeles Free Press*, 2:26 (25 June 1965), 1.

85 See the advert 'MARCH ON RAND CORP . . . Saturday June 26 11 A.M.', *Los Angeles Free Press*, 2:26 (25 June 1965), 7, with the 'STOP' escalation ladder and an invitation to join in support of the UN on its twentieth birthday.

86 Dr Pauling had been an outspoken advocate of world peace and critic of nuclear testing and the arms race. In 1957, he originated a petition signed by 11,021 of the world's leading scientists urging an international agreement to stop the testing of nuclear bombs. In 1960, he was subpoenaed before the Internal Security Subcommittee to give testimony regarding 'Communist participation in, or support of, a propaganda campaign against nuclear testing'. The committee demanded that Dr Pauling should release the names of those scientists who had assisted in the circulation of the petition for signature. The names on the petition had been made public when forwarded to the United Nations but Pauling refused to name those who had aided him in its circulation. Pauling testified: 'I am convinced that these names would be used for reprisals against those believers in the democratic process; these enthusiastic, idealistic, high-minded workers for peace. I am convinced of this because I myself have experienced the period of McCarthyism and to some extent have suffered from it in ways I shall not mention. I am convinced of it because I have observed the workings of the Committee on Un-American Activities of the House of Representatives and of this Subcommittee on Internal Security of the Judiciary Committee of the Senate. I feel if these names were to be given to this Subcommittee the hope for peace in the world would be dealt a severe blow' ('Backgrounds on the Linus Pauling Case', Independent Student Union, No–1–6041,

in Folder 'Atomic Weapons and Disarmament', Collection 50, 'Extremist Literature' (Box 36, Department of Special Collections, University Research Library, UCLA)). Also see 'Statement by Linus Pauling, 12 July 1960' in the same Folder.

87 One of them was Dr Daniel Ellsberg, who was a national security expert and 'hawk' at RAND from 1959 to 1964. He was one of the RAND members drafted by McNamara to work in the Department of Defense where he worked until 1967 when he returned to RAND and worked on McNamara's 'History of U.S. Decision Making Process on Vietnam Policy' (later known as the 'Pentagon Papers'). The total number of RAND analysts working on this forty-seven-volume report was second only to the number of government employees in the team of thirty-five military and civilian analysts. Ellsberg's views on the war began to change after his visits to Vietnam (1964–7) and before leaving to join MIT in 1970 he smuggled out a copy of the 'Pentagon Papers' (of the four 'legitimate' copies of the report permitted outside of government, two were given to RAND for reference). One of his supporters was Anthony J. Russo, another ex-RAND analyst.

88 Quoted in Dickson, *Think Tanks*, p. 86. Among the many figures brought in from RAND, three of the most important were Charles J. Hitch, Pentagon Comptroller, Henry Rowen, Assistant Secretary of Defense, and Alan Enthoven, Deputy Assistant for Systems Analysis.

89 *Ibid.*

90 Stern, 'The Defense Intellectuals', 33.

91 *Ibid.*, 37.

92 Roman Kolkowicz, 'Intellectuals and the Nuclear Deterrence System', in Kolkowicz (ed.), *The Logic of Nuclear Terror*, p. 24.

93 White, 'Action Intellectuals', *Life*, 9, 16, 23 June 1967, quoted in Kolkowicz, 'Intellectuals and the Nuclear Deterrence System', pp. 22–4.

94 Robert J. Donovan, 'Intellectuals' Split with Johnson Over Vietnam to Be Debated Today', *The Los Angeles Times*, 15 May 1965, 1. See, too, the editorial in *The Los Angeles Times*, 18 May 1965, 'Vietnam and the "Teach-In"', which tried to analyse the nature of the protests by intellectuals. The conservativism of the newspaper was confirmed not least by its view that the public discussions on Vietnam 'do not alter the basic validity of U.S. policy there, to halt communism'.

95 *The New York Times Magazine*, 4 July 1965, 4–7, 16–20.

96 Val Adams, 'U.S. Aides Will Discuss Vietnam on C.B.S.-TV', *The New York Times*, 4 August 1965, 71.

97 Irving Petlin, interviews with the author (27 October 1992 and 14 April 1997).

98 Leon Golub Papers [Archives of American Art (AAA) Roll N69–22, Frame F317].

99 *Ibid.* The RAND Staff invited were: Bernard Brodie, Social Science Department, history and strategy; Edward C. De Land, Computer Sciences Department, mathematical models of blood chemistry, functions of organs etc.; Alton Frye, Social Science Department, politics of space, etc.; Brownlee Haydon, Assistant to the President, Communications; Amron Katz, Electronics Department, physicist, reconnaissance specialist, attendee of Pugwash Conferences, etc.; Roman Kolkowicz, Social Science Department, specialist in Soviet politics; Leon Lipson, Social Science Department (Consultant), Professor of Law, Yale University; Guy Pauker, Social Science Department, specialist in Southeast Asia; Robert Wolfson, Logistics Department, economist. Brodie, in particular, was 'a pioneer of modern strategic studies in the nuclear era whose work has powerfully influenced generations of strategists and decision makers' ('Introduction', in Kolkowicz (ed.), *The Logic of Nuclear Terror*, p. 3). Brodie was an intellectual, a civilian theorist, whose work on strategic deterrence policy from 1946 onwards led to the evolution of the doctrine of mutual assured destruction (MAD).

100 Copy of the invitation card in Leon Golub Papers [Archives of American Art (AAA) Roll N69–22, Frame F316]. Report of the forthcoming event on front page of the *Los Angeles Free Press*, 30 July 1965.

101 Leon Golub Papers [Archives of American Art (AAA) Roll N69–22, Frame F317]. Golub does not list Dreyfus, whose presence has been confirmed by Petlin in telephone conversation, 25 March 1997. 'Dollard', the 'China expert', appears without a forename. This may have been Charles Dollard, who was one of the first of RAND's trustees.

102 Albert Mall, 'Artist Versus RAND Debate Not a Fruitful Exchange', *Los Angeles Free Press*, 13 August 1965, 3. Mall erroneously dates the debate as Thursday 5 August.

103 All quotations from Albert Mall, 'Artist Versus RAND Debate Not a Fruitful Exchange'.

104 Interview with the author (14 April 1997).

105 Charles Brittin recalls that RAND was full of nice people who disliked what they had to do.

106 '"Think Tank" Offers Modified Policy for Vietnam', *The New York Times*, 27 June 1969, 3.

107 'Six Rand Experts Support Pullout', *The New York Times*, 9 October 1969, 9. The letter caused considerable upset at RAND and prompted an alternative view: 'Four at Rand Ask Gradual Troop Cuts', *The New York Times*, 18 October 1969, 11.

108 Grace Glueck, 'Home-Grown Art Blooms in U.S. Missions', *The New York Times*, 6 July 1965, 1, 40. See, too, 'Some Subjects Taboo in Art for Embassies', and 'Official Exposure of U.S. Art Abroad Is Recent', *The New York Times*, 6 July 1965, 40. Clearly, the latter article was written in ignorance of the use of art and culture abroad by American institutions (USIA, MoMA etc.) in the 1950s.

109 Glueck, 'Home-Grown Art Blooms in U.S. Missions', 1.

110 *Ibid.*, 40.

111 Museu de Arte Moderna, catalogue with text by Hopps. Travelled to Pasadena Art Museum; National Collection of Fine Arts, Washington, DC.

112 Hopps, *Walter Hopps: Pasadena Art Museum*, p. 88.

113 *Ibid.*, p. 80.

114 *Ibid.*, p. 84.

115 *Ibid.*, p. 81.

116 *Ibid.*, p. 85.

117 *Ibid.*, p. 86. Hopps comments that Max Kozloff's views from the early 1970s on the USIA's use of 'new American painting in Cold war propaganda' was not 'quite right. They didn't care what kind of art.'

118 *Ibid.*, p. 87.

119 *Ibid.*, p. 88.

120 *Ibid.*, p. 93.

121 *Ibid.*

122 'Backgrounds On the Linus Pauling Case'.

123 See the full-page advertisement 'Why We March on the Police Administration Building' and the call to 'Join Us' at the 'Congress of Unrepresented Peoples' picket line at the Police Administration Building, *Los Angeles Free Press*, 20 August 1965, 8.

124 Kunkin, 'The Negroes Have Voted! LA Times, Yorty & Parker Do Not Understand Events', *Los Angeles Free Press*, 2:34 (20 August 1965), 1.

125 'Editorial: Our "Niggers" in Asia', *Ramparts*, 4:2 (June 1965), 3–4.

126 'The South at War', *Ramparts*, 4:2 (June 1965), 17–52.

127 'Southeast Asia: A Special Report', *Ramparts*, 4:3 (July 1965), 15–44.

128 'Editorial: Our "Niggers" in Asia', 4.

129   *Ibid.*

130   See 'Homage to Simon Rodia', *Los Angeles Free Press*, 2:30 (23 July 1965), 1, 4, 5, together with Art Kunkin's 'One Year of the Free Press', 1, 3, 6.

131   See Peter Plagens, 'Los Angeles: The Ecology of Evil': 'the car . . . has created the worst, omnipotent oligarchy in the division of highways, chained us to the mercy of the oil/insurance/concrete/Detroit plutocracies, and exiled a peasant class of those who don't/can't own automobiles – the old, poor, and very young . . . To have a job in LA, or even to look for one, you must have a car; but to have a car you must have a job' (p. 73). Also Davis, *City of Quartz*. Under the editorship of John Coplans, from January 1972 to February 1977, *Artforum* published more articles, such as that by Plagens, with an explicit political and social edge: for example, Max Kozloff, 'American Painting During the Cold War', *Artforum*, 11:9 (May 1973), 43–54; William Hauptman, 'The Suppression of Art in the McCarthy Decade', *Artforum*, 12:2 (October 1973), 48–52; Eva Cockcroft, 'Abstract Expressionism: Weapon of the Cold War', *Artforum*, 12:10 (June 1974), 39–41.

132   *Artforum*, 4:2 (October 1965), 18–22.

133   Barr had visited collectors, the new Los Angeles County Museum and 'the disquieting moralities of Conner and Kienholz'. Barr may have thought of Vanzetti in relation to Kienholz's *The Psycho-Vendetta Case* (1960), which partly relies on a pun with the 'Sacco-Vanzetti Case', made famous by Ben Shahn's series of twenty-three works first exhibited in 1931.

2 '"There" and "Here"', '"Then" and "Now"': the Los Angeles Artists' Tower of Protest (1966) and its legacy[1]

Introduction

Plans for the Tower were partly a product of the blackout of previous activities by the media. How to avoid being marginalised, if not ignored? The front page of the new year issue of the *Los Angeles Free Press* reminded readers of the generally poor coverage of social and political problems and protests by large-circulation daily newspapers in the city. Eight photographs, including the 'Artists' March on Gallery Row, May 1965', summed up the important year's events for the 'underground press'.[2] They also brought home the limited effects of such protests to the participants themselves. On the one hand, a relatively large artists' community had been galvanised, politicised to a degree, and the consciousness of a broader community deepened by the actions of the Artists' Protest Committee. In Los Angeles such an achievement was remarkable. On the other hand, protest seemed ineffectual to many artists if it remained part of the personal or within a group which did not gain mass attention.

During this period in the United States there were two major paths of protest. One was individual action ranging from, for example, Norman Morrison's self-immolation to unpublicised non-participation in activities of the state as in the various ways of refusing the military draft, or in alternative community lifestyles. A second was to participate in organised events and demonstrations such as the several anti-war and Civil Rights mass protests in Washington, DC. In considering these choices, a central issue was the degree of priority placed on the role of publicity and mass appeal. By the autumn of 1965, the main members of the Artists' Protest Committee reflected on their earlier actions and decided that a high priority had to be given to more organised and long-lasting strategies. They believed that a collective event with a high public profile, lasting for months and in a conspicuous place, could not be easily ignored, marginalised or 'blacked-out'. In retrospect, Petlin regards the production and display of the Tower as an 'event', a version of 'situationist' street politics, even though none of the organisers was then aware of contemporary parallels in France. A public event, with the element of duration and created outdoors, cannot be avoided by the press and has reverberations within a wider constituency. Importantly, too, for the Artists' Protest Committee the planned event had elements that resisted being reduced to an 'art work', to be looked at in reproduction in a journal with the viewer turning the page, blanking out the issues and passing on to another glossy image. To break through both the blanket of press avoidance and the art journals' processes of aestheticisation were large but crucial struggles.[3]

Mobilising artists to political action in some form has a problematic history within the modern period. In the United States, after the Second World War, the effects of McCarthyism combined with a growing boom in the art market, and its cult of personalities, had transformed many of the aspirations of artists and intellectuals associated with the Old Left. The generation active or emerging in the 1930s, nurtured on Marxist debates and the actual struggles with Fascism, had to contend with the political and consumerist contradictions of the early Cold War. The writings of Greenberg, Schapiro and Rosenberg in the 1950s testify to some of the characteristics of those contradictions. For artists, the concept of the avant garde, with its politicised traditions of utopianism and dissent, was similarly renegotiated. A younger generation in their early to late thirties in 1965 and 1966 was severed from Old Left experiences and commitments but none the less had been concerned with avant-gardism, transformed into what has been described as a counter-cultural consciousness and lifestyle. In Los Angeles and southern California, artists within and around 'Beat Culture', such as Wallace Berman, Jess, Bruce Conner, Jay DeFeo, Wally Hendrick and George Herms, produced work in a context where the conventions of art market success and the cult of institutionalised personas were accorded a minor significance. Some of their major reference points were Dada, Surrealism and bohemianism. Whilst their work and lifestyles constituted a politics, including critical references to American imperialism and sexual norms, in terms of conventional institutions they were 'apolitical'. Two major conflicts, however, became pressing: Civil Rights and Vietnam. Both, but largely the anti-war movement, drew on supporters of the peace movement and the anti-nuclear campaigns.[4] Many artists became involved in the anti-war movement, through participation in protests and demonstrations as well as in actual work. Whilst all of these struggles were subjected to the overt and covert surveillance of the state, the Civil Rights struggle demanded a commitment which put physical safety at risk. It was directly on United States soil and evoked generations of state prejudice and violence. Physical danger was a part of the anti-war movement, but participation for many artists was relatively safe. The contribution of an art work to an anti-war event might lead to the inclusion of the artist's name on an FBI file but not to concussion as the result of a police baton.[5] In the early stages of the war, the physical distance of Vietnam was a factor in various perceptions of the conflict. Participation in an event such as the Tower, there/ appealed not only to activists but also to a range of more passive su_p porters who could express dissent, relatively safely, while getting on with their artistic careers.

'Building a Tower For Peace': November 1965 to February 1966

Between the letter announcing the project, from Irving Petlin in the *Los Angeles Free Press* in November 1965, and the opening in late February 1966 an enormous amount of organisational and practical work had to be completed. As many participants recall, Petlin's presence was crucial as a figurehead who commanded great respect both as an intellectual and creative force and as someone with European experience of organised dissent by artists and intellectuals.[6] The idea for a Tower, its structure and form, emerged from his conversations with Mark di Suvero, whose work was shown at the Dwan Gallery in late 1965. After one of the artists' meetings, they met and discussed the possibility of doing something beyond what had already happened, and agreed that the physicality of a public event, with a continuous and perilous life, was necessary to break through the press muffler. Many people, galvanised by the collective enterprise of the earlier artists' protests and the meetings at the Dwan Gallery, agreed to participate in this event. Planning meetings were characterised by the voices of organisational experience and inexperience. For instance, Mike Klonsky, who had been instrumental in setting up Students for a Democratic Society (SDS) in Los Angeles, tried to persuade the Committee to form various steering committees for such activities as fund-raising. Some artists, though, were suspicious of the hand of conspicuous political groups while recognising the need for planning. Three immediate issues had to be addressed: securing a site; obtaining building and safety approval for the Tower itself; and organising the appeal for artists' panels.

Securing a site

The site was a large vacant rental lot, in West Hollywood, on Sunset Boulevard at the T-junction with La Cienega Boulevard. The broad locale is rich in the symbols of postwar American culture and politics: ranging from the investigation of Hollywood radicals by the House on Un-American Activities Committee in 1947 and 1951, with the resultant blacklist and the resistance of the Hollywood Ten, to the Manson Murders at the Tate and at the La Bianca residences, within five miles of the site, in August 1969.[7] The owner of the site was a Greek American waiting for an offer to build a motel or the like. He was approached with a general inquiry to rent the lot for a short time without taking it off the real estate market. Believing that the rental was for a large outdoor art event, which was true, the owner was delighted that the presence of artists' work from all over the United States would bring a lot of attention to his real estate investment. Delicacy was necessary in the negotiations because of the political context. The owner was assured that a permit would be obtained to bring electricity to the site, that security would be organised, that the Tower would be not only well constructed but also easily disassembled after the three-month rental. The seemingly small details were vitally important. For example, to secure a permit for electricity via a line, post and box to plug into meant that the supply could not be taken away. To undertake the various tasks, the Committee developed a technical group, a planning group and a political group, all of whom acted quietly and with a degree of secrecy. They knew that if the owner learned that this would be an anti-war event he would most likely withdraw the property from the rental market. The Committee took the advice of a Civil Rights lawyer and sympathetic real estate lawyer. They explored basic issues of public liability, how to protect the event from being cancelled by the landlord once he realised the political dimension of the event. In the drafting of the agreement there was always a double coding; no lie was ever told about what was to happen on the site but minimum disclosure safeguarded the legal agreement. What was not legally necessary to be disclosed was omitted from conversations and the signed agreement, which had to stand up to any possible legal proceeding or injunction. Crucial was the advice and experience of people such as Harold Dreyfus, the astute Californian businessman involved in the RAND events, and Tyler (or Twila) Wilner, the leader of the group of women from the Old Left, from the Hollywood Ten days.[8] The contract was legally watertight, the rental $1000, and the product of much careful preparatory work to guarantee the legal security of the project. This was vital if the political impact of the event was to be maximised.

When the event opened as an anti-war protest, local television crews rushed to the site and interviewed the owner, who declared that he was horrified by the piece and had no foreknowledge of its political nature. He complained that this would ruin him and on local television vowed to tear the Tower down as soon as the lease expired.[9] One of the reasons was that he was being attacked by others in the business world as being 'soft on Commies'. The large attention of local television and radio stations meant that the full impact of the imposing site and its physical presence in the heart of Los Angeles high-cultural activity could be exploited by the Artists' Protest Committee. Physically, the area rises steeply from south to north up La Cienega to Sunset Boulevard and beyond. A large panoramic vista is, thus, afforded from the top of La Cienega, placing the location at a substantial geographical height which appealed to the organisers.[10] Open on one side to Sunset Boulevard, the site is a U-shape cutting into the steep landscape, providing shelter with grassed sides up to houses and telegraph poles. The base of the cutting is level, now a car park behind a single-storey strip mall with large advertising hoardings at either side.

In early 1966, the site was similarly edged by large hoardings, including one advertising whisky and another a mortuary, and had last been rented out to people selling Christmas trees. Billboard culture was a significant reference, not only with the erection of the continuous hundred-foot billboard wall for the individual two-foot-square panels but also with the critical conjunction of the signifiers of 'art' and of advertising, of specialised cultural forms and the demotic, within the site as a whole. The latter had a resonance specific to that period. As we have seen, to all interested viewers and readers North La Cienega Boulevard was regarded as 'art gallery row',[11] and at the 'height of the art boom in 1965–66 . . . twenty-five or thirty "serious" galleries operated, mostly on the short strip of La Cienega between Melrose and Santa Monica, and a few as far out as Westwood, near the UCLA campus'.[12] It also housed the editorial and advertising offices of *Artforum*, in an office above the Ferus Gallery, before the journal moved its base to New York in mid-1967. La Cienega was, therefore, one of the main focal points of contemporary high culture in Los Angeles. Forming the long straight tail to the T-junction with Sunset Boulevard, the junction[13] had a literal and a symbolic meaning in February and March of 1966. It was a place where, after a visit to the row of galleries, motorists waiting for the green light would have had their gaze filled by the Tower, its supporters and the billboards of images. On the weekly Monday night ritual of 'La Cienega art walk' hundreds browsed the galleries, open until 10 p.m., in the semi-tropical night air. Above, on the hill, the Tower was floodlit, reminding viewers of the critical relationship between the cultural, commercial and political significance of the art on display in galleries and that of the collective art of dissent. This literal effect was deepened by a complex and symbolic effect at the heart of the paradoxes and shifts in the art world, as they were represented by *Artforum*, in late 1965 and early 1966. This symbolic effect will be explored later in the chapter.

Obtaining building and safety approval for the Tower

The Artists' Protest Committee had since its inception attracted a wide range of supporters with diverse expertise. One was Kenneth H. Dillon, an architect with offices in the heart of La Cienega Boulevard.[14] He had been a signatory of the 'We Dissent' statement and now provided his professional services to obtain necessary approval for the design and safety of the structure. Dillon and di Suvero discussed the project, and the design was completed to satisfy a number of demands, some envisaged, some unexpected. Final approval was granted, on 24 February 1966, by the Division of Building and Safety, Department of County Engineer. Only two days before the official opening and dedication of the Tower, the approval was, as noted by the named county officer 'Parker', a 'revision and addition to existing permit'. Dillon's drawing notes that the drawing 'modifies structure under construction under permit 6104'.[15] The original proposal was unexpectedly denied approval because of two issues. One was that, as the structure was more than 5 feet high, a building permit was necessary; the second was the safety and stability of the structure. The Los Angeles Department agreed to issue a temporary permit in response to the argument that as a 'sculpture', a 'work of art', which could be moved and resited, the Tower was not in any sense a 'building'. Nevertheless, a safety test had to be undertaken: hence di Suvero's idea of suspending a wrecked car (photographed for the *Los Angeles Free Press*, 11 February 1966) from the underbelly of the Tower to prove its strength.

Kenneth Dillon's drawing details the polyhedrons and the materials used. The lower structure (referred to as the 'lower base') was an octahedron, 17 feet 6 inches high, with equilateral triangles at its base and top. A brace closed the plane of each of the six triangles forming the sides of the octahedron, thus producing its own hexagon. Concrete deadmen secured the corners of the base to the ground. The upper tetrahedron, forming the 'upper base', used the top triangle of the octahedron as its own base. Each leg was 20 feet long, made out of 2-inch pipe, as was the brace, again in the middle of the three triangles forming its sides (thus creating another triangle, which was echoed in the triangular brace for the top of the octahedron 'lower base'). Above, a double tetrahedron, each 18 feet 10 inches high with a base triangle of 9 feet sides, formed a 'diamond shape', 37 feet 8 inches high. Made out of 3-inch pipe, this double tetrahedron was held in tension by a hanging chain and brace cables. The taut half-inch chain connected the bottom point of the diamond to the top apex of the tetrahedron 'upper base' which was 14 feet above. The geometric volumes of these two polyhedra were thus intersected. The quarter-inch stainless steel cables were held in tension between the bottom of the 'diamond shape' and the three apexes of the upper triangle of the base octahedron (three in all); and each of the three apexes of the diamond's tetrahedron bases and the apexes of the top triangle of the base octahedron (six in all). Each of the cables had an adjusting turn buckle to maintain the tensional configuration. Apart from the diamond shape produced by stretched double tetrahedrons, the structures evoke direct references to polyhedra in the five Platonic solids. Dillon's drawing states that all of the shapes were 'to be fabricated in a certified shop'. Mark di Suvero recalls that this was in his New York studio with the bits shipped back to Los Angeles for final assembly and welding.[16]

Organising the appeal for artists' panels

Two initial issues had to be considered. The first was the format for the works to be invited from artists across the world. The second was how to organise and co-ordinate the logistics of shipping and receiving the works. The Committee settled on a uniform size of panel in a media and on a base that could withstand the elements: 'Any work of art, done on a panel, 2 feet square, weatherproof (for example, masonite, exterior plywood etc.), maximum 3/4 inch.' There would be hundreds of panels, from invited artists all over the world, 'each uniquely symbolizing the individual protest of artist'.[17] In the collective nature of the project it was important for all participants to submerge their egos. No one amongst the organisers wanted to use the normal art-world criteria of financial or aesthetic value. The stipulated identical size was one way of avoiding conventional aesthetic and commercial impulses and ensuring that there were conditions for egalitarian attempts to raise a collective voice. In this sense the organisers regarded the project as 'democratic'. The list of supporting artists on Hardy Hanson's poster 'A Call From the Artists of Los Angeles' indicates their ambition: it includes artists, gallery owners, curators, critics, architects.[18]

Although debates about 'democratic' practice have a long history in the modern period, there have rarely been successful attempts to evade either the ideological constraints of totalitarianism or the capitalist demands for commodity fetish, surplus value and the denial of what Marx called 'free conscious activity' in the pursuit of unproductive labour.[19] In the postwar years, especially in the United States, emphases on the 'democratic' were inimical to a boom in consumer products and specialist diversifications within both elite culture, as exemplified by the rapid growth in the art market, and mass entertainment, as exemplified by the monadic experiences of television. Notions of the 'democratic' or 'collective' were institutionally regarded in the Cold War atmosphere of the 1950s as socialist or, worse, as Communist. Often, too, emphases on humanism, existentialism or imagery in art were associated with European and, to a considerable extent, socialist debates and traditions. Many so-called 'imagists', especially those who emerged from the Chicago Art Institute (such as Golub, Petlin, Spero), found the United States so uncongenial that they moved to Paris to find a different attitude to their traditions of practice. Artists such as May Stevens and Rudolf Baranik also recall that such were the forces of omission in the United States that to pursue an 'art of content', which engaged with contemporary social and political issues, was largely to work 'underground'.[20] Institutionally, the highly critical reaction to the exhibition *New Images of Man*, organised by Peter Selz at MoMA, New York, from 30 September to 29 November 1959, set a negative agenda.

From early on, the Artists' Protest Committee wanted to ensure that there was no hierarchy of display. At first it was thought that the submitted works would be hung from the actual Tower. Although this proved impossible for a number of safety and organisational reasons, there remained a commitment to display works without regard to the status of the artist, to any formal criteria or to curatorial valuations. The system employed to elicit contributions combined using existing networks of supportive artists and open invitation. At first the invitation and the poster by Hardy Hanson were sent out to artists who were already on lists produced during Artists' Protest Committee activities during 1965. Some artists such as Petlin also had contacts in Europe. He personally knew many of the French Surrealists and had a supportive Parisian gallery, Galerie du Dragon, which offered to help organise from Paris. It also became the advertised Paris pick-up point.[21] The gallery gathered the signatures of French and European artists willing to participate as well as co-ordinating the positive interest of Sartre and other French intellectuals who sent telegrams of support. According to Petlin, the Tower enabled the idea of protesting against the war to break through the film, the 'scrim', that prevented the protest from being a worldwide effort. The collective effort facilitated a development of the New-York-based Artists and Writers Protest, which co-ordinated over a hundred participants in the Tower and further strengthened their network, making possible other protests such as 'Angry Arts Week' in February 1967. Leon Golub, participant in the RAND debates, used his address as the New York pick-up point, with inquiries for information in the city obtainable from Max Kozloff, Elaine de Kooning and George Sugarman.

Invitations were sent out and artists were asked to sign a deposition stating '[I] fully understand that the work I have contributed to the construction of the ARTISTS TOWER OF PROTEST AGAINST THE WAR IN VIETNAM may be destroyed in the course of the Tower's existence, and I hereby grant the use of my contribution for the life of the Tower.' An intention to contribute was requested by 1 February 1966, with the actual panel to be received in Los Angeles by 15 February. The address for receiving the works was c/o Cart and Crate, 530 North La Cienega, not only near to the final site but also in the heart of 'gallery row' and its surrounding art community. Whilst there were particular exceptions, a large section of the American art world replied and participated, irrespective of artistic allegiances to groups or styles. The project was largely devoid of factional interests. Whether this was a rare moment when such collective support across a range of interests could succeed is an open question. Petlin thinks that artists facing a growing realisation that the United States might be involved in genocide was a specific galvanising factor amidst other conducive conditions for agreement – agreement, that is, for providing more protest and greater information about the realities of the war that was domestically perceived as the exploitation of the poor and the working class for an overseas colonial conflict.

The 418 works arrived at the site to be incorporated within the whole project. A list of all those who participated has to be provisional, not least because most of the elements no longer exist. As we saw in Chapter 1, the panels were scattered through the process of being sold anonymously in a lottery organised by the Los Angeles Peace Centre. Irving Petlin has an incomplete typed list which incorporates the names of European artists included in the Galerie du Dragon's shipments.[22] This includes 319 names (though a couple seem to be repeated). A second published list of 166 New York artists is in the advertisement in *The New York Times* published on 26 February, the day of the opening.[23] A further source is the letter inviting financial contributions written by Arnold Mesches, Chairman of the Fund Raising Committee, which names twenty-two artists, some not on the other two lists.[24] Selecting names from these lists retrospectively is highly problematic. The letter written by Mesches, in 1966, selects artists tactically both to represent the range of participants but also to appeal to those with potential funds for whom cultural legitimation was important. Europeans would, for example, be aware of César, Karel Appel and Jean Helion, who were well-known artists, with Helion enjoying different reputations as an abstract artist in the 1930s and as a figurative one after the war. Leon Golub and Sam Francis had both worked as artists in Paris. Philip Evergood was a well-known social realist painter active since the Works Progress Administration in the 1930s; Robert Motherwell, Ad Reinhardt, Mark Rothko, Herbert Ferber and Elaine de Kooning were deeply associated with the generation of Abstract Expressionists; Roy Lichtenstein, Jim Rosenquist, Larry Rivers, George Segal, and Claes Oldenburg had been critically received, in the 1960s, as Pop artists of various kinds (with Oldenburg also producing 'Happenings'), and Frank Stella was championed by Modernist critics; Lee Mullican, George Sugarman, and Jack Zajac had established careers; and both Judy Gerowitz (Judy Chicago) and Lloyd Hamrol were beginning theirs.

Mesches's selection of new and established artists was understandable given the nature of the project and the need for financial support. His selection *could* be replicated from the other lists too: from Raphael and Moses Soyer to Tom Wesselmann, Eva Hesse and Louise Nevelson. However, such a process may not only be partial but may also replicate canonical judgements and *misrepresent* the collective project that was the Tower. What, for instance, do we make of the presence of Jean Dewasne, an abstract painter who, paradoxically, was a member of the French Communist Party during the early 1950s when it was dominated by the doctrine of Socialist Realism? What, too, is the significance of the participation of Wallace Berman, Jess (Collins), Charles Brittin and Jay De Feo, all significant members of what has been described as 'Beat Culture' on the West Coast? Women were also much better represented than in the conventional gallery system. Symbolically, one participant was Hedda Sterne, the sole woman in the famous photograph, by Nina Leen, of the so-called 'Irascibles' published in *Life* 15 January 1951. Many others, such as Nancy Spero, May Stevens, Betye Saar and Judy Chicago, were to become major figures in a variety of critiques of power, patriarchy and racial oppression.

Importantly, too, the construction of the 'Tower' itself was a collective enterprise, with sculptors such as Mel Edwards assisting di Suvero. Lists are valuable sources but the selections of names can be no more than an attractive convention based on assumptions about the status of authenticity, authorship and individualism. The largest type in the advertisement in *The New York Times* is for the words 'Peace Tower'. The type for the names of artists is the smallest and produces an amalgam of words which makes selection of individuals hard work; as it should.

Installation

The project encountered opposition from the start. Early on the weekend of 28–9 January 1966, the artists erected a large billboard with 3-foot-high letters, 'STOP WAR in VIETNAM' and two hexagonal signs, one with 'ARTISTS' PROTEST TOWER' and the other with 'TO BE ERECTED HERE'. Some time before midnight on the same day it was knocked down by unknown vandals. Reconstructed, it was again knocked down late in the evening with attempts made to burn the sign material. With three photographs by Charles Brittin charting the events, the *Los Angeles Free Press* notes that the sign was again erected 'bearing mute testimony to the senseless violence'.[25] At first the artists were content to rebuild the sign in order to extract maximum publicity. However, after a lesson in non-violent action from the local CNVA chapter, they implemented a plan to counter attacks. It was decided to mount an around-the-clock guard of the project. A furnished apartment with its bathroom overlooking the site was rented as committee headquarters and to co-ordinate security. A truck was parked next to the Tower and its occupants in touch with headquarters via citizens' band radio. A phone call could bring a police squad to the site in six minutes while non-violent reasoning could be employed.[26] But, as we have seen, another complication was a stop order issued by the Los Angeles County forbidding construction of anything over 5 feet in height without a building permit. Arguing that the tower was a piece of sculpture, designed to be moveable, the artists persuaded the County to issue a safety permit allowing work on the tower to continue. Two weeks later, the *Free Press* included a photograph of Mark di Suvero at work on the Tower, and news of an impending city stress inspection when an old wrecked car was hung from the centre of the structure.[27] An extraordinary photograph of the latter was shown on the front page of the next issue with news that the 'well designed tower easily passed' the stress test. A second photograph, from several days later, shows a further section added by di Suvero and the sculptor Eric Orr. As the paper went to press, a large crane was being used to hoist a prefabricated 20-foot section to its apex. A third photograph shows some of the panels in the warehouse of the committee, with an inset of Petlin examining submissions.[28]

The day before the opening, the *Free Press* announced that, after two months in construction, the 'Artists Tower of Protest Against the War in Vietnam' would be formally dedicated, and thereafter the works of art would be on display, free, to the public: 'the tower soars over Sunset and La Cienega Boulevards in a dramatic configuration of steel girders, chains and cables, held together in a tensegrity construction'.[29] The principles of 'tensegrity' had been developed over the previous twenty years by Buckminster Fuller in a utopian, ecological design ethos. In his sculptures, Mark di Suvero had made variations of 'tensegrity constructions'. Chains and cables are held in tension between metal and/or wood whereby the solid materials are held in space without touching one another. In his review of the Tower, Kurt von Meier drew a direct association with Fuller and suggested that perhaps 'the anti-authoritarian, anti-militarist, anti-war people, both citizens and artists, are discovering that their position does not necessitate sardonic passivity or utter cynicism'.[30] The inscription 'Create, not destroy' in the concrete base anchoring one foot of the tower acted as the producers' own dedication. A number of professional sculptors, apart from di Suvero and Orr, worked on the construction – welding and rigging – including Ed Burrell, Melvin Edwards, Judy Gerowitz and Lloyd Hamrol. But so, too, did practioners from the margins of official demarcations such as Anthony Safiello, described by Meier as a 'modern primitive sculptor-artist-engineer' who soon came to be virtually di Suvero's assistant: 'he could be seen daily perched atop one of the beams, identified by a large red dot on his sweatshirt'.[31]

Such was the impact of the Tower and of physical work involved in its construction that Arnold Mesches, one of the major participants and Chairman of the Fund Raising Committee, completed a series of paintings depicting work on it and exhibited at the Santa Barbara Museum of Art from 20 March 1966. One of them, described as typical of Mesches's 'socially oriented point of view', was reproduced in the *Los Angeles Free Press* as part of a major policy statement on the war in Vietnam by the American Civil Liberties Union.[32] Clearly, too, reports on the Tower were regarded as landmarks for the *Los Angeles Free Press*, as can be gleaned from the cover of the issue marking its two-year anniversary, 15 July 1966. Art Kunkin, the editor, included the front pages from 18 February and 4 March, with photographs of the Tower, in the selection of twenty-four of its previous 103 covers.[33]

Specific panels made up the plethora of images on the billboard walls, a striking aspect of the photographs which dominated the front page of the *Los Angeles Free Press* on 4 March. Of these John Wilcock writes:

> There were some standouts: Roy Lichtenstein's mushroom cloud – white on a blue dotted background – was prominently displayed; and a naive, officer-type blindly saluting while his eyes were blindfolded with an American flag (this by Patrick Blackwell) drew attention. One picture showed a red octopus, that symbol that obsesses the rightwingers; a giant dollar bill had replaced Washington's face with that of Ho Chi Minh. A plain red STOP sign; a highway marker reading 'U.S.'; the nuclear disarmament SANE symbol roughly painted in white on a blue background were all simple and effective. James Rosenquist's panel merely said 'Body Count' spelled out in plain, stencilled lettering. 'All Wars are Boyish and Fought by Boys' read one panel; another collaged part of the LA Times' front page – 'LBJ War Trip' was the head – with paintings of dark, brooding Rand corporation-type men. There was a painting of a baby impaled on a spike.[34]

Reception: conflict, contradiction, and paradox

There are two main aspects of the culture of reception. One is the conventional printed forms of expression found in newspapers and journals. There is, however, little evidence of such printed response to the Tower, locally or nationally, in 1966.[35] Only in 1971 did a colour photograph of the work, by Charles Brittin, appear in the art press, on the cover of the issue of *Art in America* that contained the first of Therese Schwartz's articles on the 'Politicization of the Avant-Garde' (Plate 12).[36] A second aspect of the culture of reception is the immediate and ephemeral response in, for instance, daily local television and radio and the dramatic events of the streets, the normally unrecorded voices of the everyday. As there was much of this second form of reception, the crowds came. Some saw it as a freak event, others as an inspiration, and others again who were interested only in the possibilities for wrecking the whole thing. Many people hated it, both wanting and attempting to tear it down. On all levels situationist doctrines were fulfilled in one event. There were daily occurrences including media interviews, attacks and various visits, such as those by the singer Judy Collins, and by Ken Kesey and the Merry Pranksters in their Day-Glo bus travelling around the West Coast. The latter's first public 'acid-test', accompanied by amplified rock music, strobe lights and free-form dance had taken place in 1965. The visit by Kesey and the Merry Pranksters had mixed significance. For

12 'Artists Protest Vietnam War', cover of *Art in America*, November/December 1971, with photograph of 'Artists' Tower of Protest' in construction by Charles Brittin.

many, they represented an oppositional drug culture, as did Dr Timothy Leary, who promised that the kids who had taken LSD would not fight any war or join any corporation. For others, Kesey, in converting thousands of young people to acid (by one estimate ten thousand during his twenty-four presentations),[37] began to undermine, if not destroy the organised political culture of the West Coast. The proselytising of both Kesey and Leary was aimed at what they regarded as the traps of the old 'political games'. To the consternation of many, the influence of the drug culture, advocated by Kesey and Leary, began to deflect radicals from campaigns for Civil Rights, workers' rights and the withdrawal of the United States from Vietnam.

The Tower and Ken Kesey and the Merry Pranksters may have appeared compatible in some perceptions of counter-cultural dissent. But there were also fundamental contradictions, particularly centred on the differences between the proactive Artists Protest Committee and the more passive non-participation politics of Kesey and the Merry Pranksters. In the eyes of some theorists, the activities and the recommendations of the latter were of potential assistance to the state in its regulatory dissuasion of active and organised dissent. This view had been considered by the brainstormers at the RAND Corporation in one of their research papers. A technocratic society, epitomised by the United States, may well be tempted to incorporate into its range of social controls methods of emotional release, safety valves, as sophisticated as the psychedelics. Private 'trips', drug and sexually induced, become a threat to the established order only if associated with disruptive forms of dissent. RAND had already considered the effect of introducing tranquillisers and sedatives as a means of releasing the pressure of desperation in the post-attack fall-out shelter. The author of the research memorandum was Herman Kahn, who, as we have seen, also promoted the theory of 'escalation'.[38]

The problems and paradoxes of dissent were considered in Meier's short review of the Tower:

> Admittedly any mass of officially-indoctrinated citizens are fundamentally frightened by dissent itself, however genteel, yet the Peace Tower draws upon itself that further disapprobation traditionally reserved by society for lavishing upon its artists. That is, whenever artists stop their safe production (as it is seen) of beguiling bagatelles or amusing anodynes, whenever artists have the audacity to participate in the 'real' world, whenever artists step up to the great shooting gallery in the carnival of life, they are likely to discover the bull's eye painted on their own backs.[39]

Meier argues that such a discovery, together with the vulnerability to destruction of art taken out of the 'anaesthetic atmosphere of the academy, or the marble museum's hallowed halls of death' and set down in 'the middle of life', adds an element of martyrdom to the Tower: underscoring 'the paradox of violence-threatened, seemingly integral with all non-violent protests'.[40]

Paradox is important to Meier's discussion of dissent. He suggests, for example, that within the United States, represented by its agencies as the symbol of freedom, democracy and the open society, there is a 'mass of officially-indoctrinated citizens'. This observation can be indexed historically to the legacies of early Cold War rhetoric and to McCarthyism. For commentators and activists such as Linus Pauling and Bertrand Russell, indoctrination was both administered and surveyed by agencies such as the Committee on Un-American Activities of the House of Representatives, the Subcommittee on Internal Security of the Judiciary Committee of the Senate and the CIA. The FBI can be added in the light of what has been revealed about files held by the Bureau on a broad range of people regarded as 'dissenters'. As we have seen, in 1965 and 1966 the Johnson administration was very anxious not only about the protests against its foreign policy but also about its public image. Depending on points of view, the latter could be variously described as 'public relations', 'informing citizens', 'official indoctrination'. Apart from the historical context, Meier's observation can be indexed, theoretically, to the work of the Frankfurt School on capitalist societies and specifically to Adorno and Horkheimer. To some extent the analyses made by Arendt and Marcuse are also in that tradition. For example, these authors variously analysed how within a capitalist society dissent is both produced within and contained by demarcated sites for a variety of art forms and activities. Capitalism, they argued, thrives on those instances of novelty and radicalism that are commodified and/or used as safety valves for the maintenance of control and discipline within the system. Such instances have been described as the product of a paradox or a dialectic. The latter has roots in a famous letter from Adorno to Benjamin (March 1936), where Adorno is concerned with 'kitsch film' and 'autonomous art': 'Both bear the stigmata of capitalism, both contain elements of change . . . Both are torn halves of an integral freedom, to which, however, they do not add up.'[41] Meier observes that one of the consequences of artists moving from 'safe production', autonomous art, to participation in the 'real' world, is their work becoming vulnerable to destruction and potentially to martyrdom. Traditionally, the latter implies death or suffering for a great cause.

A belief that they were suffering for a great cause also characterised the involvement of French intellectuals, since the late 1940s, in anti-colonialist protests against the presence of France in Indochina and in Algeria. On the day of the opening and dedication of the Tower, Irving Petlin received a Western Union Telegram of support from a dozen intellectuals in Paris. The message, 'SOLIDARITE TOTALE AVEC ENTERPRISE ARTISTES PROTEST COMMITTEE', came from Colette Audry, Michel Butor, Maurice Nadeau, Oliver Demagny, Simone de Beauvoir, Jean-Paul Sartre, André Breton, Michel Leiris, André Masson, René Leibowitz, Matta and Max Clarac.[42] The substance of the telegram was published in the *Los Angeles Free Press* in the middle of a page with a continuation of Donald Duncan's speech, from the opening, and Art Kunkin's report on violence against one of the volunteer guards of the Tower.[43] This conjunction, together with Charles Brittin's three photographs accompanying Kunkin's report, represents some of the forces and issues that underpin Meier's discussion of dissent in the United States. Duncan drew upon direct experience in Vietnam and attempted to dispel some of the propaganda myths about the Vietnamese people. Heckled about the example of the invasion of Hungary by the Russians, Duncan discussed the implications of United States military violence and the escalation in the context of 'a war about which we only have half-information. You cannot have an effective electorate within this country if those [American] people are operating on half-information. Get the truth out to the people.'[44] In 1960, the 'Manifesto of 121' signed by French intellectuals advocated 'insubordination' to France's colonial war in Algeria. That war was also characterised by incomplete information and by violence against dissenters within France. In 1966, Kunkin, the editor of the *Los Angeles Free Press*, reported on the 'horrendous . . . beating of Tower guard Jim Gallagher and his subsequent arrest by Sheriff's Deputies for "disturbing the peace and resisting arrest"'.[45]

Gallagher and some 'fifteen or twenty' other guards were attempting, in the early hours of the morning, to control the more boisterous spectators in a crowd of some three hundred. Amongst them were servicemen, including a nineteen-year-old sailor, one Jerry Lee Barr, who was dressed in civilian clothes, from the USS Galveston. Objecting to one of the signs on the Tower tableau, he threatened to tear it down. After being calmed by Gallagher and other guards, Barr walked away only to return a few minutes later. Agitated, he was shouting again and this time punched Gallagher in the face. Calling to the nearby Sheriff's Deputies to arrest Barr, Gallagher dropped to his knees in the classic non-violent position, as all guards had been instructed to do in the event of a physical assault. Barr hit and kicked Gallagher several times, and he thought that one of these kicks shattered his eardrum. When Gallagher asked the Deputies to record his request to prefer charges against the assailant he was refused and, in the words of Charles Brittin's affidavit, given the 'brushoff'. On repeating his request he was 'grabbed rudely by at least three deputies and shoved against the side of the police car'. Handcuffed, he was roughly put into another police car and struck in the back by a deputy. Gallagher stated that he was shoved on his face and crawled on by a deputy who said that 'if I didn't keep my face down, he would "blow my head off"'. His repeated requests to prefer charges against his assailant were refused. Barr was, in fact, released to the Shore Patrol without being booked or a crime report having been written on him. The American Civil Liberties Union (ACLU) Attorney called Gallagher's arrest 'an outrage' and a violation of his First Amendment rights.[46]

Petlin recalls that this was only one of several problems with the local police force. A twenty-four-hour guard had to be organised. The apartment overlooking the rented lot became the organisational centre, with walkie-talkies used in the co-ordination of security. Early volunteers were African-Americans from Watts, who had heard about attacks on the 'Tower'. They formed a tough, well organised group, and worked in rotating shifts to help enormously in securing the safety of the site. The waist-high wooden fence across the front of the lot joining the sidewalk was closed at night, as a perimeter, and open during the day for people to circulate around the Tower and art works. Not a single work was destroyed despite the several attacks, initially by 'the belligerent motor-cycle Hells Angels' Type, who hang around at an outdoor cafe a few blocks down the strip'.[47] One of the attacks is recalled by Petlin. 'Two cars quickly drove up and out poured all kinds of people. Most of them were Marines or army recruits from one of the bases near San Diego. Many of them were Asians. They came flying over the fence, knives in hand.' With too few people to respond, Petlin grabbed a light stanchion from one of the lights and broke it off. He swung it around and because it had a live wire at the end, with sparks spitting, he kept the attackers at bay. Petlin recalls that a report of this attack on the Tower appeared in 'the *New York Times*, which Frank Stella read . . . In a letter he said, "any artist who would risk his life defending a work of art deserves my support" and he sent $1000 to the fund-raising committee created by women who were wives of the Hollywood Ten.'[48] Funds to pay ongoing expenses and to pay accumulated debts were raised by the committee, which used the rented apartment overlooking the lot as a base and office. This co-ordinated everything from fund-raising to twenty-four-hour security, from publicity to making soup for the guards and participants.

The Artists' Protest Committee also had to contend with a generally unsympathetic police force. The *Los Angeles Free Press* had already reported on Michael Hannon, a Los Angeles police officer who had been in conflict with the police department over his right to engage in political and Civil Rights activities in his off-duty hours. The *Free Press* had also included articles on police malpractice and on how to avoid a violent response in contacts with the police.[49] The head of the ACLU in California, A. L. Wirein, realised that the Artists' Protest Committee was increasingly coming under attack from the Sheriff's Deputies, who were looking for an opportunity either to wreck the whole event or to allow people to do so. Petlin recalls that they had already beaten up one of their people. It was not the sailor who had damaged Gallagher's eardrum but in fact the Sheriff's Deputies. That was not the only time that they had hit people. It was evident that the Sheriff's Deputies were co-ordinating with the people who were attacking the Tower. They appeared only after an attack, not during it, and it was the defenders who were arrested, as was Gallagher. The attackers were rarely chased by the patrol cars, and the defenders were handled roughly by the Sheriff's Deputies. They were not interested in recording or pursuing complaints against assailants, and many of them, identifying with the Marines, were unsympathetic to the politics of the Artists Protest Committee, which they would have regarded as unpatriotic and quasi-Communist.

Petlin recalls that the Sheriff at the time was a Greek American known as a good-natured but intensely corrupted human being. He ran a fiefdom including the La Cienega neighbourhood which was under the jurisdiction of Los Angeles County as distinct from the City Police.[50] His Sheriff's Deputies were known as a particularly fascistic bunch who drove around in Porsches with Dobermann pinschers when off duty. Wirein was aware of and greatly concerned at the increasingly vicious attacks, and knew that something had to be done. He came to see Petlin and said that the head of the Greek Cypriot court was currently visiting southern California and speaking at UCLA as an honoured visitor. He came from the same village as the Sheriff of Los Angeles County. Wirein had invited this eminent jurist to meet the Sheriff and asked Petlin to come along as well. He arranged to pick Petlin up, and together with the Greek Cypriot Supreme Court Justice they drove down to the Sheriff's office. They were ushered in, and the Sheriff was clearly honoured, not least because of southern European traditions of loyalty and respect to a fellow villager. The Greek Cypriot Supreme Court Justice said how pleased he was to be visiting the United States with its history of freedom of speech and liberty. He then said, Petlin remembers: 'I want you to meet someone who is a great example of that freedom of speech. An artist who has put up a tower, exercising his First Amendment Rights and it is under so much pressure. I am sure that you could do something about it.' From that moment all harassment stopped, basically for the last month of the Tower's existence. Protected by the result of clever manoeuvring by the head of the ACLU in California, the Artists' Protest Committee realised that the system could be turned to secure constitutional rights.

Issue 1: intellectuals and action

In her speech at the dedication of the Tower, on 26 February 1966, Susan Sontag drew attention to 'one of the most fundamental problems we have': the need 'to invent and sustain an appropriate response . . . [an] intelligent, creative action' against the role of America in Vietnam. She continued:

> What is this tower doing here, and what are we doing here? We're here to bear witness to our sorrow and anxiety and revulsion at the American war on Vietnam. Many of us have already signed the petitions and statements that have appeared in newspapers, written our Senator or Congressmen, gone on peace marches, proselytized among friends. Today we're doing something else – establishing a big thing to stand here, to remind other people and ourselves that we feel the way that we do.

That the tower is an act addressed to other people, our fellow citizens who don't feel as we do – and some of them are here today – is obvious . . . So far as I can determine, we are here on the simplest basis – because we are choking with shame and anger, because we are afraid for ourselves and for our children, and because we are profoundly discouraged.[51]

In 1966, Sontag regarded effective collective action, including that by artists and intellectuals, as manifest in the Tower. She concluded: 'Let's be angry, truly angry. Let's be horrified. And let's be afraid.'[52] Such a mixture of feelings and appeals to her audience was made in the belief that there could be a successful mobilisation of protest at and resistance to the 'American war on Vietnam'. Thirty years later, in the midst of another bloody conflict, Sontag observed a contemporary failure to develop the legacy of protest, which in the 1960s was exemplified by the Tower. In November 1995, returning from her ninth stay in Sarajevo (her first was in April 1993), Sontag wrote of what she regarded as a very different response to current anger, horror and fear: a failure amongst intellectuals to invent and sustain an intelligent creative action in response to the war in Bosnia.[53] In the Christmas Day 1995 issue of *The Nation*, she observed:

If the intellectuals of the 1930s and the 1960s often showed themselves too gullible, too prone to appeals to idealism to take in what was really happening in certain beleaguered, newly radicalized societies that they may or may not have visited (briefly), the morosely depoliticised intellectuals of today, with their cynicism always at the ready, their addiction to entertainment, their reluctance to inconvenience themselves for any cause, their devotion to personal safety, seem at least equally deplorable . . . All that makes sense is private life. Individualism, and the cultivation of the self and private well-being – featuring, above all the ideal of 'health' – are the values to which intellectuals are most likely to subscribe.[54]

Published just two months before the thirtieth anniversary of the dedication of the Tower in Los Angeles, Sontag's article identifies not only major shifts and changes in the moral and political role of 'all those who could be called intellectuals'[55] but also, by implication, transformations in capacities to imagine and to enact what has often been called 'activist art'.[56] Sontag's characterisation of many intellectuals of the 1930s and the 1960s is open to debate, as is clear from studies of the role of intellectuals in that period. As for the intellectuals of the 1990s, her view has numerous echoes in those analyses of the academic world which argue that the production of radical theoretical texts, with an indeterminate political project, has replaced a capacity for organisation and planning necessary in examples ranging from the Tower to the African National Congress.[57]

The Christmas 1995 issue of *The Nation* raises other parallels, apart from the role of intellectuals, to Sontag's speech in February 1966. One is

United States support for what Chomsky and Herman refer to as 'constructive terror': the maintenance of bloodbaths and terror to protect and enlarge a favourable investment climate.[58] Directly after Sontag's article, *The Nation* published one by John Pilger, which includes an interview with the imprisoned commander of the forces of the East Timorese National Liberation Front.[59] Twenty years earlier, to the month, the Indonesian military dictatorship invaded East Timor; as a result of the occupation a third of the population, two hundred thousand East Timorese, have died. Thirty years earlier, in February 1966, Sontag reminded those attending the dedication of the Tower of the slaughter of a hundred thousand Indonesian Communists following an alleged Communist 'coup' in October 1965.[60] The military establishment used the events to begin to destroy the Indonesian Communist Party (PKI), the only serious large institutional opposition with a broad base and good organisation. The PKI was opposed to the Indonesian military's growing dependence on the United States in terms of both its ideological ties and its reliance on arms supplies and training. The PKI was also highly critical of what Chomsky and Herman describe as the 'corruption and mismanagement of the military-dominated bureaucratic capitalism of the early 1960s, which was breaking new ground in looting and shakedowns even before the post-1965 consolidation of military power'.[61]

Sontag would have been unaware in 1966 of the detailed activities of the CIA and Pentagon in Indonesia,[62] though there were informative articles. One was that by Bertrand Russell, on the CIA as a 'vast international agency of subversion', published in the February 1966 issue of *Frontier*.[63] However, two paragraphs earlier in Sontag's speech she makes clear her views about the implications of the then public evidence of United States global activities: 'America has become a criminal, sinister country, swollen with priggishness, numbed by affluence, bemused by the monstrous conceit that she has the mandate to dispose of the destiny of the rest of the world and of life itself, in terms of her own interest and jargon.'[64] Such a view had developed rapidly amongst radicals in the previous year. Since 13 February 1965, when President Johnson ordered Operation Rolling Thunder, the programme of sustained air strikes over North Vietnam, effects of the escalation of the war led to a substantial increase in organised protests.[65] Although the bombing was halted on 24 December 1965, it was resumed on 31 January 1966. In her speech, on 26 February, Sontag reminded the audience of the horrific effects of that bombing 'in the name of freedom by the richest, most grotesquely overarmed, most powerful country in the world':

> At this very moment, fertile land is being drenched with poison, an honorable world culture is being steam rollered with asphalt and strung with barbed wire. At this moment, as we stand here, babies are being charred by napalm

bombs, young men – Vietnamese and American – are falling like trees to lie
forever with their faces in the mud, and we who are here – not there – alive,
not poisoned or burned, are being injured morally in a way that is very
profound.[66]

While readers of the *Los Angeles Free Press* were looking at the photographs of the Tower and speeches made at its dedication, they could also
read disturbing statistics and details on 'The War in Vietnam' in mainstream news magazines such as *Newsweek* and *Time*. In the same issue
of *Newsweek* that included a short report on the 'Tower', Arnaud de
Borchgrave's article, 'Then and Now – the Difference', compared the
French and American methods of waging war in Indochina.[67] Twelve
years earlier, de Borchgrave had been a *Newsweek* senior editor when he
landed with the first French paratroops at Dienbienphu, which in March
1954 was at the start of an epic fifty-seven-day seige by Viet Minh
troops. In 1966, he had recently returned to Vietnam and in his article
makes several observations, many of which inadvertently reinforce the
content of Sontag's speech. Two of them relate to the link between
capitalism and colonial terror. An informant tells de Borchgrave about
'the scandals that wrack the United States commercial-import programme,
the licensing arrangements that benefit a chosen few, the illegal traffic in
piasters . . . the names of the wives of Vietnamese generals and colonels
who act as fronts for their husbands' business ventures, and the fortunes
being amassed by American civilian contractors'. Twelve years earlier,
the same informant had provided similar details about the fortunes
amassed by French businessmen and 'about *le trafic des piastres* which
turned many French civil servants into gentlemen of leisure by the
war's end'.[68]

If the 'scandals' were similar, within a few paragraphs de Borchgrave
details 'the difference' between the French and American way of war:
mostly centred on the massive increase in United States firepower. He
provides statistics publicly available to the general citizen. United States
air sorties had averaged 13,000 per month, now doubled to 26,000.
Ammunition alone cost the United States $210 million a month. According
to de Borchgrave, in 1965 United States forces in Vietnam fired 1 billion
rounds of small arms ammunition, 89 million airborne machine-gun rounds,
5 million rockets, 7 million air-launched grenades, 10 million mortar and
artillery shells and 2 million air-dropped bombs. Guam-based B-52s had
been modified to carry 108 bombs of 500 to 700 pounds each, and had
flown two hundred raids so far. These statistics signify a range of
meanings: colossal United States power; multiple Vietnamese deaths and
destruction of habitat; United States investment in its domestic armaments
industry; expansion and profit for manufacturers and shareholders; and
to students a reminder of the products of corporations who were also

endowing universities and fostering research and the arts.[69] In the world of escalating numbers and consumer commodification, de Borchgrave's sentence at the end of his paragraph of statistics is macabre: 'Amateur statisticians have computed the killing of one VC at $375,000.'[70]

In the parallel issue of *Time*, its 'The Nation' overview of 'The War' comments on the numbers of casualties and the nationally televised Fulbright hearings on the war, which ran from 28 January to 18 February 1966. Arkansas Democrat J. William Fulbright was chair of the Senate Foreign Relations Committee. In evidence to it, viewers heard challenges to the Johnson administration's defence of the war. Significantly, these included Lieutenant-General James Gavin and Ambassador George Kennan. The latter's criticism was even more telling as he was the author of Policy Planning Study 23 (24 February 1948) advocating the doctrine of Cold War 'containment' which had been a main element in United States foreign policy. Viewers also witnessed a callous disregard for civilian victims by General Maxwell Taylor, who regarded the horrific effects of America's napalm bombing on Vietnamese babies as an 'unhappy concomitant' of the air war.[71]

Much to the Johnson administration's irritation, Fulbright proposed a United States withdrawal from Asia. Consistent with the administration's views that sheer numbers of troops and firepower were bound to overcome Vietnamese resistance, *Time*'s report offers a negative response to Fulbright's recommendation. Both *Time* and de Borchgrave in *Newsweek* make the claim that the 'VC' or the 'Communists' are low in morale or cannot endure the 'punishment' they are receiving. Proved to be erroneous, the claims were consistent with the administration's ideological 'messages' designed to convey optimism and encourage support for United States actions. *Time* reported that Defense Secretary McNamara had announced an increase of thirty thousand troops to become 235,000; that the 'heaviest raids over the North to date' had been made in the previous week; and that during the last four months '16,000 Communist troops have been killed in battle (*v.* 4,000 South Vietnamese and 1,500 U.S. dead)'.[72] In the rhetoric of statistics a supposedly favourable balance in the death count was often used, explicitly or implicitly, to erase doubts about the massive American war of attrition. Sontag's speech on 26 February drew very different conclusions, as did those by Irving Petlin and ex-Green-Beret Master-Sergeant Donald Duncan,[73] who in March 1966 became a contributing editor (Military) of *Ramparts* magazine.[74]

Duncan's detailed critique of American military action in Vietnam and the machinery of incompetence and misrepresentation, '"The whole thing was a lie!": Memoirs of a Special Forces Hero', appeared in the February 1966 issue of *Ramparts*.[75] This essay was a first-hand analysis by an honoured veteran who had left the United States Army in September 1965 with an honourable discharge after ten years' service, including six years in Special Forces and eighteen months' active service in Vietnam. Duncan outlines his early experience in relation to the prevalence of anti-Communism in the news media during the 1950s. His military training was also characterised by a strong anti-Communist theme: 'The enemy was THE ENEMY. There was no doubt that THE ENEMY was communism and Communist countries. There never was a suggestion that Special Forces would be used to set up guerrilla warfare against the government in a Fascist-controlled country.'[76] Apart from rampant anti-Communism, Duncan discovered that the military hierarchy in Special Forces was massively racist, beginning with the attitudes to African–American GIs. When in Vietnam he saw colour prejudice replicated in military references to Vietnamese as 'slopes' or 'gooks', two words derived from the Korean War. He continues: 'Other fine examples of American Democracy in action are the segregated bars. Although there are some exceptions . . . Negroes do not go into white bars except at the risk of being ejected.'[77]

Military propaganda also meant that preconceived notions of the Vietnamese were hard to correct because neither the daily civilian or the military contacts were 'representative of the Vietnamese people'. The Vietnamese military (Army Republic of Vietnam, ARVN) was full of officers who had gained their status through family position, political reward or wealth. In this sense they were deeply embedded in the corruption of French colonialist rule. Paradoxically, members of the ARVN were denigrated by the Americans – as lazy, undisciplined, ineffective – while being used as 'allies' in the defence of United States presence and to do the dirty business of war, such as torture and executions, so as to preserve the United States military's reputation as honourable defenders of the Geneva Accord of 1954.[78] Civilians, 'taxi drivers, labourers, secretaries, contractors, bar girls', all depended on Americans for a living and had a vested interest in telling 'Americans anything they want to hear as long as the money rolls in'. This corrupt compliance was mixed with resentment. As Duncan observes, the Americans were making the same mistakes as the French, and worse: 'Arrogance, disrespect, rudeness, prejudice, and our own brand of ignorance . . . It is so common that if a Vietnamese working with or for Americans is found to be sincerely cooperative, energetic, conscientious, and honest, it automatically makes him suspect as a Viet Cong agent.'[79] Despite the propaganda, it was well known that the 'Viet Cong' were highly disciplined and committed to their cause in contrast to the AVRN, who were largely forced into pro-United-States activities. Duncan stresses that the rhetoric of anti-Communism was so strong that Americans were dissuaded from considering its alternative and from understanding indigenous support for 'the enemy'. Although the 'Viet Cong' would pass through villages stopping to sleep or to help plant and harvest crops, invariably government troops ransacked and burnt: 'Rape is severely punished among the Viet Cong. It is so common among the AVRN that it is seldom reported for fear of even worse atrocities.'[80]

Duncan details the ways in which Americans lied about involvement in military actions, such as in Laos, so as not to embarrass the government during elections; inflated, mistaken, body counts; military incompetence placing United States ground troops in vulnerable situations; terrorising civilians through mass bombing; implicating the AVRN in United States atrocities corrupting their values; hypocrisy and double standards. He writes:

> The whole thing was a lie. We weren't preserving freedom in South Vietnam. There was no freedom to preserve. To voice opposition to the government meant jail or death . . . It's not democracy we brought to Vietnam – it's anti-communism . . . When anti-Communist napalm burns their children it matters little that an anti-Communist Special Forces medic comes later to apply bandages.[81]

Duncan's speech at the opening of the Tower was a powerful précis of the arguments and details in his article. It drew conclusions, reiterated by the speeches by Sontag and Petlin, but ones that were highly unpopular to many Americans.[82]

Their conclusions were made in the midst of one of the paradoxes of the Johnson administration: an escalation in the casualties of America's foreign war of terror in Vietnam and at the same time a radical reformist domestic policy that addressed central issues of civil rights, poverty, health, education and cultural provision. One element of the latter had direct potential benefits to many of the participants in the 'Artists Tower of Protest'. In March 1965, President Johnson asked Congress to pass legislation to establish a National Foundation on the Arts and Humanities. By the end of September legislation was passed creating the National Endowment for the Arts and National Endowment for the Humanities. On 31 October $2.4 million in federal funds was appropriated for the NEA to cover the eight months of fiscal year 1966 (on 1 July 1966 the sum for fiscal year 1967 was budgeted at $7.96 million). At the same time, Congress had either passed or was prepared to vote on bills establishing Johnson's 'Great Society' which characterised his domestic policy from 1964 onwards. For example, the Civil Rights Act of 1964 was followed in 1965 by Medicare and Medicaid, Voting Rights Act, War on Poverty, major egalitarian education legislation (the Elementary and Secondary Education Act and the Higher Education Act) and the Housing and Urban Development Act. Much of this legislation was subsequently attacked by Republican administrations, first by Nixon and then by Reagan and Bush.

Even in 1965 and 1966 it was apparent that there would be difficulties in Johnson's commitment to *both* domestic welfare and reform, his Great

Society as a development of Roosevelt's New Deal,[83] *and* the military's demands for their needs in Vietnam. Robert Buzzanco argues that the effects of Johnson's budgetary strategy, trying to have it both ways, had serious implications for the war and the economy. Not only did this strategy

> make it more difficult to discover the true cost of the war, but it also increased the military's tendency to focus on domestic political battles [including protests] rather than seek alternatives in Vietnam, while at home it led to exorbitant defence spending – real funding for Vietnam outpaced budget estimates by $1.5 billion in FY 66, over $9 billion in FY 68 – and ultimately caused greater inflation, higher interest rates and tax increases.
>
> By autumn 1965, as McNamara and [General] Westmorland were debating the meaning of [the battle of] Ia Drang, the dollar-gold crisis added more problems to the policy-making mix.[84]

Issue 2: art and politics, 'autonomy' and 'commitment'

Within these circumstances artists and intellectuals planned and produced work designed to represent creative dissent to 'America in Vietnam'. They often did so with ambiguous, sometimes ambivalent, attitudes to the institutions and processes of official culture. It is perhaps these attitudes that rendered creative dissent problematic. Was the Tower the product of intellectuals who were, in terms of Sontag's retrospective view, 'too gullible, too prone to appeals to idealism to take in what was really happening' in Vietnam? Was the Tower merely an act of anti-war publicity, an act of protest, that at best was confused about the boundaries between 'art', 'morality' and 'politics' and at worst a well-meaning 'aesthetic' embarrassment?

Such questions were posed at the time in various ways. One negative attitude to such questions and activities was to ignore them: this was particularly evident in the paucity of reviews or comments on the Tower in the established art journals. Another was artists' reluctance, or unease, about mixing 'art' and 'politics'. This was sometimes manifest by rapid shifts from participation to hostility. An example of the latter was Ad Reinhardt, who participated in the Tower with a painting consisting of the words 'NO WAR' on a blue background. Yet, just over a year later, in a radio interview broadcast on 13 June 1967, he had become extremely negative about such activity:

> I think an artist should participate in any protests against war – as a human being. There's no way they can participate as an artist without being almost fraudulent or self-mocking about what they're doing. There are no good images or good ideas that one can make. There are no effective paintings or objects that one can make against the war. There's been a complete exhaustion of images. A broken doll with red paint poured over it or a piece of

barbed wire may seem to be a symbol or something like that, but that's not the realm of the fine artist anyway.[85]

Two months later he was even more forthright in a panel discussion, 'How Effective is Social Protest Art?', with Leon Golub, Allan D'Arcangelo, and Marc Morrel:

> I'm not so sure just from a social and political point of view what protest images do and I would raise a question. I suppose this is an advertising or communications problem. In no case in recent decades has the statement of protest art had anything to do with the statement in the fine arts.[86]

Clearly, specific notions of 'fine arts' and of 'protest art' were important to Reinhardt in 1967; and equally the notion that a 'statement' in each area should be kept *separate*. In the later broadcast he was also negative about both the growing power of the mass media (from television to advertising) and the legacy of Social Realists from the 1930s. With the former, for Reinhardt, television coverage of 'protest art' rendered the work a spectacle of publicity, and advertising established criteria of measurable effectiveness that could be dangerous to the critical integrity of an 'art' work as sign or symbol. With reference to the latter, Reinhardt suggests that not only were there very few Social Realists remaining but also that many of them had become compromised in the 1940s by becoming artist war correspondents for *Life* magazine. He also raises the example of a 'fine artist' such as Ben Shahn producing visual images that had to have a popular appeal and relevance to the Congress of Industrial Organisations and Union recruitment drives.[87] For Reinhardt, Shahn's 'fine art' experience rendered his posters statements of 'culture' which were inappropriate as statements of protest or of working-class solidarity and encouragement. Some of his observations are the legacy of debates about modernism and socialism rooted in the 'Old Left', where distinctions and defences were inseparable from the cultural, social and political transformations of the late 1940s and 1950s. What then the role, function and effect of the Tower for a participating artist such as Ad Reinhardt?

The specific site, format and collective nature of the Tower and its organisational planning reveal some of the contradictions and paradoxes of 'creative action' and protest in the middle of the 1960s.

Issue 3: site, place and difference: *Artforum* and representation

The literal effect of the Tower on the hill, at a busy T-junction, was rendered more complex by a symbolic effect produced by the paradoxes and shifts of the art world. A focal point of the latter in Los Angeles was *Artforum*, with its editorial offices in the heart of gallery row and its editor in the social world of political dissenters. Founded in 1962, *Artforum* was, under the editorship of Philip Leider, ambitious to secure the high ground of contemporary art criticism. Though there was a variety of articles on a number of themes and artists and reviews of exhibitions in the art triangle of Los Angeles, San Francisco and New York, Leider's commitments became more strongly consistent with a Greenbergian cultural elitism. This is clear from his correspondence with Greenberg from 1966 onwards, which demonstrates his belief in the pre-eminence of Greenberg as a critic and of his followers, such as Michael Fried, who became a contributing editor of *Artforum* in March 1966.[88] By 1970, his commitment to the Modernist aesthetic had become so firmly entrenched that Leider could write in the September issue of *Artforum*: 'I argued for Michael Fried's idea that the conventional nature of art was its very essence, that the great danger was the delusion that one was making art when in fact you were doing something else, something of certain value but not the value of art.'[89] This is not to say that Leider was clear and consistent, as a critical analysis of his and other articles in the issue of *Artforum* in September 1970 reveals.[90] Earlier, at the time of the planning and construction of the 'Peace Tower', Leider was entwined in the social and political debates of artists in and around Los Angeles as well as in the specialist nuances of those authors he commissioned to write in the journal. Most of the people writing for *Artforum* were young, mostly in their twenties and thirties. This was the journal where they began to make their reputations: for example, Max Kozloff (who was then the New York Associate Editor), John Coplans, Barbara Rose, Sidney Tillim (Contributing Editors), Michael Fried, Rosalind Krauss, Lucy Lippard and Linda Nochlin. It was also a journal where extracts from catalogues by curators were given wider circulation. John Coplans, a Los-Angeles-based contributing editor, recalls visiting New York at the time of the Larry Bell and Bob Irwin exhibition at the Sidney Janis Gallery (May 1964), with the intention of contacting younger writers, particularly those associated with *Art International*. He asked Barbara Rose, Michael Fried, Max Kozloff and Robert Rosenblum to write for *Artforum*, promising them that they could write whatever they wanted to write, that they could agenda their own articles and, unlike *Art International*, *Artforum* would actually pay.[91] To be in *Artforum*, therefore, as a critic or as an artist under review was a significant career step. Securing advertising space was also a priority, not least for galleries and organisations in Los Angeles.

In late 1965 and early 1966, three of the most active participants in the Tower had exhibitions in galleries on La Cienega Boulevard. Mark di Suvero had a show of large-scale sculpture in the Dwan Gallery in late 1965. John Weber, then running the gallery, recalls that di Suvero was regarded as one of the 'hottest' artists around.[92] Images of his work had already appeared in *Artforum* in May 1965 and both a full-page installation view of his Dwan Gallery exhibition and a short review appeared in December 1965.[93] Judy Gerowitz had a two-part exhibition of sculpture at the Rolf Nelson Gallery in January–February 1966 and Irving Petlin an exhibition of paintings at the same gallery in February. Both were reviewed in *Artforum*, as they had been advertised.[94] These three artists were major organisers of the group constructing the Tower. Larry Bell, an active supporter of the Artists' Protest Committee, was also in a group exhibition which was covered in a major article by John Coplans in *Artforum*, February 1966, '5 Los Angeles Sculptors at Irvine: the New U.C. Campus exhibits Bell, DeLap, Gray, McCracken and Price'.[95] Other collaborators included John Weber and Philip Leider. Although, as Petlin recalls, Leider had remained on the sidelines of previous activities, along with other 'observers',[96] it was a reasonable expectation that Leider would include a piece on the Tower, or a review, or at least an advertisement. On being asked, he declined such requests, saying that 'art and politics do not mix'.[97] This statement is at the centre of an unease, if not a contradiction, within *Artforum* as a representation of the broader art world. Leider was not wholly against advertisements with a social or political agenda. For example, in the February 1965 edition there appeared a full-page advertisement for the 'Artists Civil Rights Assistance Fund, Inc.' (ACRAF), which was established in 1964 'out of concern for a significant part of the population of the United States whose constitutionally protected Civil Rights are being denied on a daily and continuing basis'.[98] In contrast to this inclusion, the politics of the Tower were not acceptable within the confines of *Artforum*. The art works of artists, and associated reviews and commentaries, who were active in the Tower's production were acceptable as long as these works were within the gallery system. Leider clearly wished to keep the journal 'pure', uncontaminated by something *other*. Other, that is, than the 'conventional nature of art', which Leider later claimed 'was its very essence',[99] and the legitimated world of galleries and critics. Leider, an ex-social-worker from New York, regarded reductive, formalist art and criticism as a type of radicalism. He loved the work of Frank Stella, who was married to Barbara Rose, and Richard Serra and the emphasis on autonomous art characteristic of the criticism of Clement Greenberg, Michael Fried and Rosalind Krauss. The journal he edited would be a site for cultural radicalism as defined by the politics of autonomous art.

In November 1965, Leider wrote a review of the São Paulo Bienal which has all the hallmarks of Greenberg's 'Modernist Painting' (1961, reprinted in *Art and Literature* in spring 1965), and Fried's *Three American Painters: Kenneth Noland, Jules Olitski, Frank Stella* (1965), an exhibition that came to Pasedena.[100] Leider singles out Noland and Stella (the chosen New York artists were Judd, Poons and Stella) and evokes Greenberg's highly selective notion of the logic of an immanent self-critical development of Modernist art from Impressionism to the so-called reductive emphases of the Abstract Expressionists:

Hopps's grand design at São Paulo, therefore, turned on three points: first, to present a clear, unsoftened and uncompromising view of a direction the most talented younger artists [Noland, Stella, Irwin, Judd, Bell and others] have been taking since the late fifties; second, to present the large scale, severely reductive art of Barnett Newman as one of the sources of the logic of this direction, and third, in doing so, to suggest not a rebellious reaction to the accomplishments of the Abstract Expressionist generation, but a rich continuity based on that unending, dialectic of self-examination which has been the major characteristic of all modern art since Impressionism.[101]

Over the summer, the Los Angeles County Museum held a major exhibition (*The New York School: the First Generation – Paintings of the 1940s and 1950s*), at the same time as Fried's *Three American Painters* was at nearby Pasadena.[102] A special issue of *Artforum* was devoted to 'The New York School', with the first article by Leider on 'The New York School in Los Angeles', followed by Michael Fried on 'Jackson Pollock'.[103]

Yet it is evident that Leider in 1965, 1966 and 1967 had a political view outside of this mixture of Greenbergian formalism, becoming more associated with a political conservatism, and Adornoesque emphasis on the political effects of autonomous art. He wrote, as we have seen, for *Frontier* on, for example, the Artists' Protest Committee and provided financial and other practical assistance to political protests. Petlin also recalls that Leider helped the Artists' Protest Committee with printing and other logistical needs.[104] In 1967, he was a co-chair of the 'Assembly of Men and Women in the Arts Concerned with Vietnam', which had the same address as *Artforum,* and held a major convention in Los Angeles in June with Noam Chomsky as one of the key speakers.[105] When *Artforum* moved to New York, he was one of six signatories, on behalf of Angry Arts and Artists and Writers Protest, appealing for art works to be sold to fund artists of New York supporting the peace movement on the March on Washington, 21 October 1967.[106] In 1966, he also seemed intent on including an article on the Tower. Charles Brittin provided *Artforum* with a series of colour transparencies which were never used. *Life* magazine also sent a team of photographers to cover the construction, though nothing materialised.[107] Reports on Vietnam were a significant part of *Life*'s coverage in February. The issue dated 11 February 1966 includes 'On With the War and "Operation Masher"', with several photographs of military action by Henri Huet,[108] and the issue dated 25 February included a 'Special Section on Vietnam' with several articles including a long pro-government editorial, 'Vietnam: The War is Worth Winning', by Headley Donovan, Editor-in-Chief, and an unsympathetic consideration of 'The Dissent'.[109] The question to be asked, in general, is why did the seemingly planned coverage in various journals and magazines never appear? Specifically, why not in *Artforum* when its editor was clearly supportive of the Artists' Protest Committee?

In April 1966, *Artnews* published a short anonymous article with four photographs, on the 'Los Angeles: Tower for Peace', in which Leider is quoted:

> From the meetings and activities which produced the event, West Coast critic Philip Leider (who was also active in the groups which collaborated on the scheme) properly deduces that a watershed has been reached between the apolitical art worlds of the 1950s and the energetic social consciousness of today. This would seem to be a regional rather than a national inference. Many of the East Coast contributors to the Tower (each artist was asked to donate a work 2 feet by 2 feet) long have been actively associated with liberal causes – Civil Rights, Ban-the-Bomb, anti-Capital Punishment etc.: Elaine de Kooning, Ad Reinhardt, Esteban Vicente, Jack Levine, Robert Motherwell, et al. Indeed, the New York scene never was quite as disengaged from politics as might be surmised from rereading its exhibition catalogues and reports on round-tables. But on the whole, Leider's point is well taken, especially as the Tower and the manifestations that led up to its construction seem to signal a new stage in the awakening of West Coast artists to a sense of community and to their roles as intellectuals.[110]

This piece may have been written by the editor Thomas B. Hess, or by John Coplans, based in Los Angeles, who was a Contributing Editor of both *Artnews* and *Artforum* (though the article makes an error in stating that funding was partly advanced by Robert Rauschenberg). Or it might have been a version of a piece by Leider to appear in *Artforum* but for unknown reasons dropped. Whoever was the author, what are we to make of Leider's reported distinction between 'the apolitical art worlds of the 1950s and the energetic social consciousness of today' and his view about a 'watershed'? His notion of 'apolitical art worlds' has a cleansed McCarthyite ring to it, and 'social consciousness' redolent of sidestepping the 'political'. Such processes were, however, not uncommon even amongst those who were to be radically politicised in the next couple of years. For example, in the December 1965 issue of *Artforum*, Lucy Lippard claims that Rosenquist's *F-111*, first exhibited in April 1965, was 'entirely devoted to a social theme', and that 'The idealism of today is irony. Satire and social protest are not major elements in Rosenquist's art. In fact, the only painting which is conspicuously "political" is a large triptych entitled *Homage to the American Negro* [1964].'[111]

Although *F-111* was in part devoted to a social theme, it was also highly charged politically, as is made evident in the range and type of references discussed by Rosenquist in an interview published in *Partisan Review* in the autumn of 1965.[112] The work was made up of fifty-one panels not much larger than the 2-foot-square contributions to the Tower. These were intended to be sold separately as a critique of commodification both in everyday life and in the world of art collecting.[113] The political meaning of *F-111* was side stepped by many critics for whom emphases on consumer culture and irony were manageable ways of interpreting 'Pop Art'. Lippard's article in *Artforum*, as with the majority of others in the journal, was based on the assumption that the 'idealism of today is irony'. As the *Artnews* article suggests, rereading 'exhibition catalogues and reports on round-tables' can lead to the view that artists were 'disengaged from politics'. Clearly, there was a difference between New York and the West Coast, though the activities during 1965 and 1966 had changed this with a new emphasis on community and the active role of intellectuals. However, the evidence of *Artforum* through the rest of the 1960s is that Leider's 'watershed' came down on the side of the 'irony', 'autonomy' and a specialising 'apolitical' community of artists and critics.

Issue 4: 'social protest' in 1966, Kienholz at the Los Angeles County Museum of Art

Work by Kienholz from the early 1960s also attracted critical emphases consistent with Lippard's 'irony' and Leider's 'the energetic social consciousness of today'. At the time that the Tower was dedicated and on public display, Kienholz had installed *Barney's Beanery* (1965) in the recently opened New York quarters of the Dwan Gallery and was preparing for his major exhibition at the Los Angeles County Museum of Art (LACMA). The latter, organised by Maurice Tuchman, ran from 30 March to 15 May 1966,[114] and was accompanied by two articles in the April issue of *Artforum*: 'The Underground Pre-Raphaelitism of Edward Kienholz' (on *Barney's Beanery*), by Sidney Tillim, and 'A Decade of Edward Kienholz', by Tuchman (a slightly altered version of the catalogue essay for the exhibition).[115] Apart from the attention of the art journals and magazines, the exhibition received massive reaction in the local and national press; much more than the work of the Artists' Protest Committee. The nature of the critical reaction to the Kienholz show reveals a great deal about the cultural and political conditions in which the Tower was produced and received.

As we have seen, Kienholz was unsympathetic to the Artists' Protest Committee. He was hostile to the Tower and had turned up at the site in his pick-up with a gun, threatening Petlin with violence because he thought the Tower un- or anti-American.[116] Kienholz's work did, though, deal with critical issues in contemporary America. In 1966, according to Tuchman, Kienholz's assemblages 'were explicitly conceived as interpretations of topical issues and gave rise to Kienholz's reputation as a "social critic"'.[117] Tuchman, curator of the exhibition, was keen to qualify 'social' as concerned with generalised 'topical issues' rather than with more specific 'political' struggles. After discussing the nuances of *The Psycho-Vendetta Case*, 1960 (a critique of capital punishment with references to the recent execution of Caryl Chessman and, by a pun, to the

Sacco and Vanzetti case), and *History as a Planter*, 1961 (a memorialisation of the Holocaust), Tuchman makes a sweeping claim: 'As "social protest" this is remote from the simplistic espousals and condemnations of 1930s art, or from other conscience-stricken art implying a recognizable dichotomy of good and evil.'[118]

Such a partisan view was characteristic of blanket condemnations of '1930s art' or that with a 'realist' tag. Tuchman, clearly sympathetic to Kienholz's work, emphasised issues of time, experience and multiple perspectives to characterise the 'social' inasmuch as it could be hitched to the aesthetic. His emphases were consistent with Modernist critical attitudes such as those articulated by Barbara Rose, a New-York-based contributing editor of *Artforum*, who had written in 1963 of Kienholz's work being too focused on themes and social commentary. In line with the distinctions made in Greenberg's influential 'Modernist Painting' (1961), she saw Kienholz's need to say something as perhaps better suited to the verbal rather than the visual.[119] Tuchman had been lured from the social and critical world of New York, with its powerful Modernist allegiances in the early 1960s, to become curator of modern art at the LACMA.[120] To theorise Kienholz's work involved Tuchman and Tillim, who was more of a Greenbergian, in locating the 'social' within a disciplined formal context.

Kienholz's works and characterisations of them signify a particular paradox. His literary or verbal or cultural references were, for some, inconsistent with a particular notion of Modernism propounded by influential critics later referred to as 'Greenberg and the Group'.[121] Yet, when asked to participate with artists wishing to make a 'social protest' against America in Vietnam, he militantly refused. He and others did not wish to associate his work with the interrelationships between the political as well as the social and sexual aspects of American values. Even in *Barney's Beanery*, the reference to Vietnam is incorporated in a way that deflects its potentially political significance. The newspaper in the rack, outside of the door to the bar, is the *Los Angeles Herald Examiner* of 28 August 1964, with the headline 'Children Kill Children in Viet Nam Riots'.[122] The story detailed 'savage religious rioting which spread through Saigon as government authority came to an end'. A group of Buddhist teenagers had captured a Catholic boy and 'executed him with a butcher knife in the central market place. A 10-year-old boy was the first to stab him.'[123] An accompanying photograph shows a Buddhist official being mobbed by Catholic youths just before police intervened. Although the report continues with a spokesman commenting that 'the conflict "appears to be between various elements for political power"',[124] it does not consider the conditions producing the violence, including the role of the United States in its support of the three generals who now led the country.

Kienholz came from straight-down-the-line staunch Republican parents. Whilst aware of the failures and mistakes made by Americans, he had strong feelings about America, basically a love of his country, which resulted from being raised in a farming community.[125] He regarded himself as apolitical because, he claimed, politics 'stink'. In the late 1950s and early 1960s he and his friends in the actual Barney's Bar, Los Angeles, did not talk much about politics. Personally, he listened to radio KFAC continuously, mostly to classical music, rather than to the news.[126] One night he saw the newspaper headline 'Children Kill Children in Viet Nam Riots', bought that edition of the *Herald Examiner*, went back to sit in his car in front of Barney's and read the article. He recalled that this was a catalyst in his decision to make the work in which inside all the heads of figures are clocks with the same time of 10.10: 'The whole thing symbolizes going from real time – the August 28 headline – to Surrealist time inside the bar where people waste time, lose time, escape time, ignore time.'[127] For Kienholz, the main emphasis was to re-create a metaphor about strangers in a bar killing time. Its specific Los Angeles references were reinforced when the work was exhibited for three days, in 1965, outside the original artists' bar-and-grill on Santa Monica Boulevard, on which it was modelled. When asked how people reacted to the Vietnam reference at the entrance to the tableau, Kienholz said that it was the same as when the newspaper was on Barney's actual bar: they walked straight past it and went inside. Kienholz's view was that people did not really care about the Vietnam War until television brought it into their living rooms and they had to cope with the realities.[128] For him this dated from the autumn of 1968, the time of his *Eleventh Hour Final*.[129] Clearly not everyone agreed with this view. The autumn of 1968 may have been a moment of Kienholz's politicisation with respect to the war in Vietnam. In 1965 and early 1966, however, he did not share the deep and informed politicised consciousness of participants in the Tower.

Although Kienholz's work became manifestly politicised in 1968, in 1966 the forty-six pieces in his exhibition produced strong reaction copiously reported in the press.[130] The nature of the controversy reveals how issues of sex, obscenity and pornography, particularly when centred on an institution – the legitimated world of a major art gallery – were more manageable public obsessions than the politics of the Tower. The latter was censored, it can be argued, through omission. The Kienholz exhibition, in contrast, became a *cause célèbre* comparable to Mapplethorpe's *The Perfect Moment* in the 1980s and in a more modest way Berman's first exhibition at the Ferus Gallery in 1957. About a week before the opening of the show, the elected Board of Supervisors of the Los Angeles County became aware of some of the exhibits and were particularly exercised by *Back Seat Dodge – '38* (1964) and *Roxy's* (1961). On 23 March the front pages of both the *Los Angeles Times* and the *Los Angeles Herald*

Examiner carried stories on the Supervisors' wish to close the exhibition on the grounds that it was 'repugnant, degrading and pornographic'.[131] The two supervisors who were particularly exercised were Warren M. Dorn and Kenneth Hahn, both of whom had political aspirations and careers. For example, on the day that the story broke, the *Los Angeles Times* reported that Dorn had entered the Republican primary race for governor, pitting himself against three others including Ronald Reagan on 'a program to "save our two-party system and the state from moral and fiscal bankruptcy"'.[132] On the day before, 22 March, the *Los Angeles Times* reported on a Supreme Court ruling setting new criteria in 'obscene publications'.[133] The ruling, adding impetus to the rhetoric of Republican campaigns, was significant in the history and nature of dissent in the United States. Although it overturned a Massachusetts ban on the novel *Fanny Hill*, the Supreme Court affirmed two convictions: a Philadelphia federal court's conviction of Ralph Ginzburg, publisher of *Eros* magazine and other periodicals, for distributing obscene publications through the mails, and a New York state court's conviction of bookseller Edward Mishkin for publishing and intending to sell fifty books, including *Screaming Flesh* and *Cult of the Spankers*, dealing with sadism and masochism. Both had been heavily fined, with Ginzburg sentenced to five years' and Mishkin to three years' imprisonment. According to the report, the Ginzburg ruling was the most far-reaching:

> The court said obscenity may be determined if a 'purveyor's' sole emphasis is on the sexually provocative aspects of his material . . . The net effect of Monday's rulings is a move toward a harder line on obscenity. But the court fell short of producing what some legal experts had hoped for – a clearer standard for determination of obscenity.[134]

Ginzburg was quoted as saying that he was 'confident that history will vindicate him and adding: "America is not only no longer a peace-loving country . . . but it is no longer a liberty-loving country"'.[135] A major protest ensued, with an advertisement, 'What did Ralph Ginzburg do?', appearing in *The New York Times* on Sunday 3 April 1966, from the Committee to Protest Absurd Censorship. It was reprinted in the *Los Angeles Free Press* on 13 May in an issue which also included a report on the formation of the Los Angeles Committee Against Censorship.[136] There had been major controversies about censorship and pornography in the Los Angeles area in the previous two years. For example, taking reports in the *Los Angeles Free Press* as an indication, its first 'sample copy' issue (25 May 1964) led with Seymour Stern's 'Puritanism Scores Victory All-Woman Jury Finds Ken Anger's Anti-Fascist Film "Obscene"'.[137] The manager of the Cinema Theatre, Hollywood, was convicted of having exhibited a lewd film, *Scorpio Rising*, by Kenneth Anger, winner of a $10,000 Ford Foundation Grant in film-making. Soon after, an exhibition of approximately forty works, *Studies in Desperation,* by the artist Conner Everts at the Zora Gallery, La Cienega Boulevard, in June 1964, attracted the attention of the Sheriff's office and the District Attorney. Everts was accused of and tried on charges of obscenity and outraging public decency. Reports and interviews appeared, with a final not-guilty decision in May 1965.[138] This did not prevent the Chinouard Institute of Art, where Everts had taught for five years, from deciding not to renew his contract for the coming year. In asking why this might have occurred, Al Saxton in the *Los Angeles Free Press* suggested that Everts's new notoriety did not fit in with the present 'revolution in reverse' in the Chouinard Institute, which was being transformed into a 'huge monolithic degree and certificate-granting factory to turn out artists with interchangeable parts who can go into the art "industry" and produce'. Saxton went on to consider who might be behind this transformation:

> It is an interesting but little known fact that Walt Disney, the Great Mouseketeer (and a man of reactionary political and aesthetic views) is the major contributor to Chouinard. It is rumoured that he donates possibly $4 million annually to the school, a sum adequate to allow him a major voice in Chouinard policy setting, if not the actual title of owner. Is it possible that the influence of Disney is involved in the decision to remove Everts?[139]

A year later, after a student rebellion in 1966, the Chinouard Institute of Art was moved by Disney endowers to a 'safe' and isolated suburb of Los Angeles and renamed the California Institute of the Arts. Disciplining cultural organisations and transgressive visual products was carried out by both corporate and elected agencies. The Everts example was a precursor of the Supervisors' attempts in 1966, represented by Dorn and Hahn, to discipline both Kienholz and the LACMA.

Dorn had sent a letter to Edward W. Carter, president of the Board of Trustees of the LACMA, attacking the Kienholz exhibition as 'pornographic' and 'beyond the limits of public decency'. On receiving his letter, the Board of Supervisors promptly and unanimously voted their opposition to the exhibition, which County Counsel Harold W. Kennedy said was tantamount to a ban. In response, an executive committee of Carter and five of the trustees unanimously supported the exhibition. The full Board of Trustees backed the executive committee, again unanimously.[140] Dorn and Hahn continued their objections. Hahn and other Supervisors threatened both the supplementary salaries of staff and the operating agreement under which the county and private individuals among the Trustees operate the museum. The Los Angeles County had paid a substantial amount of the $12.5 million cost of the museum and had seen its investment in raising the cultural status of Los Angeles rewarded by 2.5 million visitors to the museum in less than a year.[141] Now, in an attempt to control the selection of exhibitions, they threatened to withdraw future financial support which in the current fiscal year amounted to a budget of some $1 million. In the escalating exchanges, Supervisor Bonelli declared that there must be a clear distinction between a public and private art gallery and demanded that either *Back Seat Dodge − '38* and *Roxy's* be removed or the whole show be banned completely.[142] Some of the objections were articulated by Dorn in an interview with the *Los Angeles Times*:

> In the back seat of the *Dodge − '38* are figures of a man and woman in an erotic embrace. In *Roxy's*, Dorn specifically objected to a portrait of Gen. Douglas A. MacArthur, an Army Eisenhower jacket hanging on a clothes pole and a sewing machine table on which rested a nude torso of a woman. 'Look at that,' said Dorn pointing to the portrait. 'Gen. MacArthur standing guard at a house of prostitution [Las Vegas, during the Second World War]. And that jacket has a "good conduct" ribbon on it.' This he maintained was 'unpatriotic.' The figure on the sewing machine was 'obscene,' he said. Regarding the automobile display, Dorn said he had no objection to showing the outside of the car. It was what was inside that bothered him, he said.[143]

In the same report, Kienholz is recorded as saying that the car display 'represents juvenile immorality in the automobile age'. Evidently posed, Dorn was photographed closing shut the door of *Back Seat Dodge − '38*. His views, however, were regarded by many in the press as an opportunist attempt to boost his election prospects linking his politics to the Mothers Union for a Clean Society. He especially weakened his position when at a televised press conference he replied to reporters' challenges to his competence as an art critic: 'My wife knows art, I know pornography.'[144] His unfortunate claim to knowledge led many drivers to include stickers in their cars: 'Dorn is a Four Letter Word.'

The press continued to report the daily events up to the opening. Splashed across the top of the *Los Angeles Herald Examiner* on 29 March was the headline 'ART WAR "TRUCE" It will Open with Curbs' and a separate story '"Inside Story" of Art Pact'.[145] The *Los Angeles Times* also placed the story on the first page, though not as a headline.[146] The compromises included allowing under eighteen-year-olds into the show if accompanied by an adult or with parental permission; opening the door of *Back Seat Dodge − '38* only at certain times; protective platforms in front of the two disputed works; and 'all agreed that a motor would not be turned on that would have swayed the exhibited torso of a prostitute, and that two obscene four-letter words on the exhibit would not be in view [part of *Five Dollar Billy* (1961), which forms part of *Roxy's*]'.[147] The exhibition opened with further dispute by the Supervisors. Bonelli attempted to separate them from the actions of the Museum by proposing that a contract be investigated whereby the county would lease the land on which the Museum was built to the Museum Associates − the private, non-profit corporation that built the facility − for $1 a year.

The subsidy, reported as being for 'this year . . . more than $1.3 million', would no longer be provided. Bonelli argued that such an action would remove the Supervisors from repetitive horns of a dilemma: '"If we can divorce ourselves of museum operations and let the trustees call the shots of what is pornographic and what is not we will end this situation of 'be damned if you do, be damned if you don't'"'[148] After a bitter argument the motion was defeated (while Bonelli and Hahn voted in favour, three others, including Dorn, voted against) and followed by a vote of confidence in the Board of Trustees and acting Director. Despite this controversy, the 'invitational reception and preview', on the previous evening, was attended by a reported two thousand.[149]

The *Los Angeles Times* covered the actual opening with a photograph of some two hundred people waiting in line for the doors to open. The consensus of the fifteen hundred visitors on the first day was that 'the exhibition is not pornographic' and there was little public objection expressed by those who saw the four letter words (including 'fuck') on *Five Dollar Billy* or by 'about 85%' of the visitors who viewed the scene when the door of *Back Seat Dodge – '38* was opened '32 times during the day'.[150] Dorn's objections continued, claiming that the compromised agreement in the 'art world truce' had been breached and threatening arrests and closures.[151] By the time the exhibition had been on for a week, with substantial numbers of visitors, Dorn's campaign attracted criticism from a fellow Supervisor in a meeting. Ernest E. Debs accused him of 'milking' the controversy and forgetting 'that there are people who are willing to defend unto death the right of an artist to do what he wants and to show it. All we've done is give this man [Kienholz] $5 million worth of publicity, and he'll now be able to sell anything he makes.'[152] Whilst supporting Dorn, Hahn was also concerned at the effect of their actions: 'People stand in line for hours in the smog and heat to see this trash. I really think we should have given him the silent treatment.' Bonelli added that he 'still objected to the whole exhibition, "especially during Holy Week as a condemnation of both Christianity and Judaism"'.[153]

The *Los Angeles Free Press* noted that the two major downtown daily newspapers offered conflicting editorial viewpoints. The *Los Angeles Times* and its cartoonist came strongly 'to the side of the art lovers and those opposed to art censorship' while the *Los Angeles Herald Examiner* 'took a dim view of the reported contents of the Kienholz exhibit'.[154] In fact, many of the editorials and the cartoonists in both papers were suspicious of Dorn's motives. Just prior to the opening, the *Free Press* devoted the whole of its front page to the controversy and included a centrefold 'This is What the Fuss is About' with five photographs of Kienholz's work.[155] The main story starts with: 'Politics invaded the field of art in Los Angeles . . . and, as is usually the case, art came out second best.' Dorn's descriptions of the work as 'pornographic', 'depressing', 'nauseating', 'repugnant' and 'revolting' were repeated, as was his claim that the show was '"a filthy exhibit"'. Censorship was identified as a major threat. However, the exhibition continued with large numbers of visitors and bags of mail. The Museum's Educational Services reported that '"the attendance has been astronomical compared with the usual shows"' and that eighty-five per cent of the mail was positive; one member of the public with an old Dodge contributed a new bumper sticker, STAMP OUT DORNOGRAPHY.[156]

While the exhibition was on show the media continued with daily news reports about, opinion polls on and protests against the war in Vietnam. Two extracts from the *Los Angeles Free Press* reveal some of the tensions. One was an appeal for contributions to re-establish the head-quarters of the Vietnam Day Committee, an active part of the anti-war movement, after its headquarters in Berkeley was bombed. The attack, described by the police as attempted murder, destroyed the headquar-ters and injured three of the eleven people present.[157] A second was the report on a study of the opinions of a random sample of 101 students attending Cal State College at Los Angeles. The conclusion was that 'students are very ambivalent about the Johnson administration's con-duct of the Vietnam war and that they have a high level of distrust about whether the U.S. is doing everything it can to end the war'.[158] For example, whilst sixty per cent of students thought that complete and accurate information from the government about the war was not given, seventy per cent disagreed that the United States should begin military withdrawal immediately.

On the Sunday after the opening, the *New York Times* carried an article by Philip Leider: 'Los Angeles and the Kienholz Affair'.[159] Full of indignation at the interference of politicians, Leider's agenda was domin-ated by issues of culture as they are defined by institutions, the status of the individual artist and the dominance of formal criteria in contempor-ary art. Although it was a major parallel event, he did not mention the Tower. Leider was concerned with paradox and irony but largely within the delimited framework of cultural autonomy and a preoccupation with the limitations of non-experts such as the County Board of Supervisors when interfering in questions of art. He started by stating that the events preceding the Kienholz exhibition were 'remarkable' even 'for a city that has as great an appetite for disgracing itself culturally as Los Angeles'. While applauding the dignity of the Board of Trustees in defending the exhibition, Leider is ironic about the Supervisors. Their repudiation of the exhibition is quoted: it is '"not only in bad taste, but inconsistent with the repeatedly expressed views of this board [of Supervisors] in its efforts to halt the moral decline of the community"'.[160] Leider suggests that there was irony in their efforts by claiming that '"the moral decline of the community" is what Kienholz's work is all about'. He continued:

Kienholz himself is a man of an oddly conservative temperament who hunts his own venison, and is rather desperately concerned with trying to raise two children in an age without moral fiber . . . Kienholz, a malcontent in the Elizabethan sense, like Shakespeare's Jacques [*sic*] transposed into a more hellish age, catalogues the stages of modern man's violent play.[161]

Leider's characterisation of Kienholz joined a variety of a verbal and visual rhetorics. One of them was the front cover of the exhibition catalogue, which was completed well before the opening and the controversy. Showing Kienholz photographed with his two young children, Jenny and Noah, the image of this single-parent family was laid out like an old picture album, with the little cut-outs that pictures are placed behind. This image was in stark contrast to Dorn's claim about the nature of the work in the exhibition and by implication the person who was the producer. Kienholz recalled this period resisting the way in which the notion of the artist as a specialised and limited entity was used. He identified a broader range of activities, interests and skills – being a carpenter, a mechanic, a mother, a dad, a dealer in real estate, a pool player – that constitute a broad, ordinary, life as distinct from those claimed by ideologically defined notions of the specialised 'artist'.[162] The catalogue not only represented Kienholz in such a familial way but also included a number of reproductions of his work, revealing his activities, interests and skills. The only colour illustration, ironically, was *Back Seat Dodge – '38*.

Leider's text contrasts the themes of the work, such as perverted love (*Back Seat Dodge – '38* and *Roxy's*), empty forms of religion (*The Nativity*, 1961), desolation of birth and abortion (*The Birthday*, 1964, and *Illegal Operation*), with what he regards as the current demands on practice:

These are themes out of which it as been difficult to make serious art in recent times. Without considerable sophistication of contemporary formal means, the themes simply cannot be handled. That Kienholz has been able to achieve his standing in a formalist-orientated art world is evidence of the originality and intelligence of his attack.[163]

Leider, however, fell between a desire to write favourably about the social, if not political, themes which accorded with his own politicised allegiances and his professional preferences for Modernist paradigms of aesthetic value. He could not resist drawing upon Modernist discriminations of value which were largely dependent on judgements of taste and an adherence to a formalist-orientated art world: 'A temperament – evangelical, exhortative, violent – like Kienholz's, and a medium as permissive as assemblage are bound, in combination, to produce a good many indifferent or bad pieces, and too many of these, by far, have been included in the exhibition.'[164] Leider does not say which of the forty-six works are 'indifferent or bad'.

By the time the exhibition opened, Kienholz was probably *the* Los Angeles artist in the minds of those governed by the effect of publicity. One consequence was that judgements about the quality and status of his work also became more desirable currency in the contemporary art world's insistence on the cult of the artist. Leider's judgements, in the *New York Times*, are part of a particular community's interests: a community in which characterisations and judgements are part of exercising a power and belief system marked out by journals, critics, dealers, solo exhibitions, and career makers. There were paradoxes. For many, one of the attractions of Los Angeles, including Kienholz, was its anonymity.[165] The city was perceived as an anonymous place, without a community interest in actions or alliances. However, becoming very famous was also part of the city's image of careerist success and instant celebrity status. Both of these contradictory aspects were important to Kienholz, and he promptly set out to work to become very famous.[166] For others, the manifest lack of community was one of the frustrations of the city. It is not surprising, therefore, that the production of an organised and committed community around the ant-war movement was one of the remarkable achievements of the Artists' Protest Committee. Leider was himself caught in the contradictions and paradoxes of the art, culture and politics of Los Angeles.

The Kienholz exhibition became notorious a week before it opened: the notoriety was the product of a mixture of Dorn's political opportunism, prevalent assumptions about obscenity and pornography, attitudes to the role and function of art within an institutional display, and the effects of a bureaucratic structure where accountability and freedom of expression became confused by both moralistic (guardianship of public morals) and financial (the use of local resources) responsibilities. In contrast to the heat of this controversy about a single artist's work in a symbol of a 1960s art boom, the LACMA, there was evident ambivalence about the Tower, with its collective production and political effect. The Tower was an event subjected to physical attack and intimidation necessitating a twenty-four-hour guard. It, too, attracted much local television and radio coverage but little by mainstream newspapers or specialist journals. In that sense its politics were transgressive.

Notes

1 This title refers to two texts that provide vivid landmarks in the terrain of this discussion: Susan Sontag, '"There" and "Here": A Lament for Bosnia', *The Nation*, 25 December 1995, 818–20; Arnaud de Borchgrave, 'Then and Now – the Difference', *Newsweek*, 14 March 1966, 40–2.
2 *Los Angeles Free Press*, 3:1 (7 January 1966).
3 Petlin, interviews with the author (27 October 1992 and 14 April 1997).

4 See, for example, the 186 names of the plaintiffs, ranging from Linus Pauling to Joan Baez, on the legal injunction attempting to restrain the United States from detonating nuclear weapons (21 June 1962). The defendants were McNamara, Glenn Seaborg, Chair of the Atomic Energy Commission of the United States and four other members of the Commission. In Folder 'Atomic Weapons and Disarmament', Collection 50, 'Extremist Literature', Box 36 (Department of Special Collections, University Research Library, UCLA).

5 Charles and Barbara Brittin, for example, became active in Civil Rights. Basically this meant Charles Brittin giving up his artistic commitments; he was on constant call as a photographer of events in the struggle.

6 For example, Charles and Barbara Brittin, interview with the author (24 April 1997), emphasise the difference Petlin made to the commitments of Los Angeles based artists. Many people, such as the Brittins, were active in Civil Rights and peace movements which had an organisational structure traditionally absent in artists' groups.

7 On the former see Larry Ceplair and Steven Englund, *The Inquisition in Hollywood: Politics in the Film Community 1930–1960* (Berkeley, University of California Press, 1983), and Paul Buhle, 'The Hollywood Left: Aesthetics and Politics', *New Left Review*, 212 (July/August 1995), 101–19; on the latter see Vincent Bugliosi with Curt Gentry, *Helter Skelter: The Manson Murders* (London, Bodley Head, [1974] 1975). On Los Angeles, generally, see Mike Davis, *City of Quartz* (London, Verso, 1990) and Peter Plagens, 'Los Angeles: Ecology of Evil', *Artforum*, 11:4 (December 1972), 67–76; for a contemporary account of the art of the 1960s see Plagens, *Sunshine Muse: Contemporary Art on the West Coast* (New York, Praeger Publishers, 1974).

8 Author's interviews with Irving Petlin (14 April 1997) and Charles and Barbara Brittin (24 April 1997). The surname Wilner is recalled by all but there is some minor uncertainty about her exact forename.

9 John Wilcock, 'Artists Peace Tower', *The East Village Other*, 1:7 (1–15 March 1966), 1. Wilcox was a founder of *The Village Voice*, and had recently been involved in establishing *The East Village Other*, in New York.

10 I draw upon my interviews with the following: Max Kozloff (9 October 1992); Leon Golub (13 October 1992); Rudolf Baranik (17 October 1992); May Stevens (17 October 1992); Irving Petlin (27 October 1992 and 7 June 1993); John Weber (20 May 1993); Mark di Suvero (3 June 1993).

11 As pointed out by Kurt von Meier in one of the few reviews of the Tower: 'Los Angeles Letter', *Art International*, 10:4 (20 April 1966), 68. La Cienega is described as 'Los Angeles street of art galleries' in 'Los Angeles: Tower for Peace', *Art News*, 65:2 (April 1966), 25, 71.

12 Plagens, *Sunshine Muse*, p. 28.

13 The *Los Angeles Free Press*, one of the several 'underground' or 'counter-culture' newspapers of the period, was based at 8226 Sunset Boulevard, adding to the significant contrast at the T-junction with the Tower site, at 8477.

14 At 744 North La Cienega Boulevard.

15 Kenneth H. Dillon, 'SCULPTURE FOR ARTIST TOWER COMMITTEE', sheet no. 2, in possession of Irving Petlin.

16 Interview with the author (3 June 1993).

17 'A CALL FROM THE ARTISTS OF LOS ANGELES', poster by Hardy Hanson.

18 John Altoon; Rudolf Baranik; Larry Bell; Paul Brach; Helen Breger; Arnaldo Coen; Allen D'Arcangelo; Elaine de Kooning; Dijon Dillon; Ken Dillon; Mark Di Suvero; Bella T. Feldman; Herbert Ferber; Llyn Foulkes; Sam Francis; Judy Gerowitz; Leon Golub; Leonel Gongora; Lloyd Hamrol; Hardy Hanson; Francisco Icaza; Donald Judd; Wolf Kahn; Howie Kanowitz; Richard Klix; Max Kozloff; Roy Lichtenstein; Phil

Leider; Ivan Majdrakoff; Robert Mallory; Charles Mattox; Robert McChesney; Arnold Mesches; Robert Motherwell; Lee Mulligan; Rolf Nelson; Frank O'Hara; Miquel Hernandez Orban; Jacques Overhoff; Julia Pearl; Irving Petlin; Patrick Procktor; Byron Randall; Ad Reinhardt; Mario Orozco Rivera; Larry Rivers; Jim Rosenquist; Mark Rothko; Frank Stella; Hassel Smith; Arthur Secunda; George Segal; Artemio Sepulveda; George Sugarman; Maurice Tuchman; John Weber; Charles White; Jim Wines; Adja Yunkers; Jack Zajac.

19 See my 'Picasso's Art: a Biographic Fact?', *Art History*, 10:3 (September 1987), 401–15, especially 402–4.

20 Interviews with the author: May Stevens (17 October 1992); Rudolf Baranik (17 October 1992).

21 19 rue du Dragon, Paris 6e. Max Clarac-Sérou, Directeur. All the names appear on Petlin's incomplete typed list of participants.

22 Petlin's typed list is as follows (as typed and uncorrected): Ailland, Gilles; Aitkin, S.; Allen, Tom; Appel, Karl; Arcilisi, Vincent; Armoto, Sam; Arnal, Francois; Aronson, Sardo; Arroyo; Asher, Elsie; Avalon, Helen; Baker, Walter; Baranik, Rudolf; Barnet, Will; Baruchello, Gianfranco; Beberman, Edward; Belzono; Bleek, Margit; Bubalo, Vladamire; Bayer, Walter; Boutin, Allen; Blaire, Camille; Brill, J.; Butts, Freeman; Blackwell, Patrick; Berlant, Anthony; Brown, Ray; Brooks, James; Blaine, Nell, Brach, Paul; Bolles, Bob; Brittin, Charles; Benjamin, Karl; Brown, M.; Bird, Annette; Bromfomel, I.; Botts, Edward; Bowin, Milton; Bleckman; James Brooks; Berman; Biras; Busse, Jacques; Benoit, Jean; Collins, Jess; Contino, E.; Crampton, Rollin; Cannon, J.; Cajori, Jim; Cruz, Emilo; Clayberger, Sam; Clutie; Colbern, Jan; Camacho; Cardenas; César; Chemay; Cremonini; Cueco; Candell, Victor; Copley, William; Cohen, G.; Coleman, John; Chavez, Roberto; Celmins, Vija; Curtis, Ron; Canin, Martin; Dougherty, Frazer; De Hirsch, Storm; Donley, Robert; d'Archangelo, Allen; Di Meo, Dominich; Dimondstein, Morton; Dovvos, Peter; de Kooning, Elaine; Dash, Robert; Diebenkorn, Richard; Dillon, Dejon; De Feo, Jay; Dimetrakas; Dmitrienko; de Noailles, Marie; Dewasne, Jean; Erythrope, Ilse; Eunese, Mariano; Evans, D.; Evergood, Philip; Elgard, Elliot; Etherton, Tom; Fuller, Mary; Francis, Sally; Feldman, Bella; Flomelbalch, Sidro; Fine, Perle; Finch, Kieth; Ferrer, Joaquin; Freedensohn, Elias; Filmus, Tully; Finkelstein, Max; Formica, Rachel; Frasconi, Antonio; Golpinopoulas, P.; Gikow, Ruth; Golden, Leon; Girona, Julio; Goodman, Sidney; Golub, Leon; Greene, S; Gordon; Greene, Cynthia; Gershgoren, M.; Gutman, Walter; Garcia, Jose; Gwathmey; Gilchriest, Loreno; Greene, Balcomb; Grayson, Marvin; Gillson, George; Guston, Philip; Gill, James; Gelber, Anne; Gebhardt, Al; Goswell, Stephen; Greenough, Lowell; Gilbert, Hugo; Gerardo, Chaves; Hunt, Richard; Hanson, Bert; Hui, H; Hielihia; Hirsh, Joseph; Hopkins, Budd; Halkin, Theodore; Holbrook, Peter; Hubbard, W; Honig, Etheleym; Hornisher, Anna; Hanson, Hardy; Hesse, Eva; Hatch, David; Hardin, Marvin; Hairer, Carol; Hulpberg, J.; Harris, Kay; Helion, Jean; Ippolito, Angelo; Johnson, Ives; Jakoson, Ward; Junkers, Adja; Joffey, W.; Jaffee, Nora; Juke, Richard; Kramer, Harry; Kahn, W.; Kaufman, Jane; Kippelman, Chaim; Kadish; King, Raymond; Kapsalio, Theodore; Kosta, Angela; Kraicke, Jane; Kantowitz, Howard; Katzman, Herbert; Kaplan, S.; Kishing, William; Koppelman, Dorothy; Kassay; Kline, Jane; Klix, Richard; Kadell, Katherine; Koster, Sue; Krof, N.; Kozloff, Max; Lysowski, J. S.; Little, John; Lyons, Marvin; Liebowitz, Diane; Lawrence, Michael; Lublin, Lee; Leroy, Phillipe; Leap, June; Levin, Kim; Levin, Jack; Lunk, David; Lewen, Si; Lindaberg, Linda; Lubner, Lorraine; Laderman, Gabriel; Lichtenstein, Roy; Lawless, David; Matter, Herbert; Matter, Mercedes; Mattox, Charles; Miller; Maurice, Henry; Melliken, Margaret; McKnight, Eine; Motherwell, Robert; McNee, Joan; Main, D.; Martiner, Joseph; Monoru; McChesney, Robert; Merz, R.; Majdrakoff, Ivan; Maggi, Anthony; Moesle, Robert; Matta; Mercado;

Mellon, James; Marcus, Mardin; Mesches, Arnold; Mugnaimie, Joe; Neufeld, Tanya; Nevelson, Louise; Nesbitt, Lowell; Oster, Gerald; Ohlson, Douglas; Petlin, Irving; Pearl, Judith; Presonello, Harold; Pedreguera, R.; Parker, Ray; Padron, Abilio; Picard, Lil; Pittenger, Robert; Passirntino, Peter; Pazzi, L.; Pessillo, Christina; Paris, Freda; Paris, Harold; Pinsler, Jorry; Pollack, Sam; Palestino, Dominick; Pearlstein, Philip; Pfriem, Bernard; Parker, Keith; Piqueras; Pellon, Gina; Parre, Michel; Rosenbein, Sylvia; Rosenquist, Jim; Rosenhouse, Irwin; Reisman, Philip; Rieti, Falio; Robert, Niki; Rockless, Robert; Rooney, Pauline; Rapoport, Sonya; Roff, Richard; Richenheimerk, Alice; Rubens, Richard; Reinhardt, Ad; Raffaele, Joe; Rosofasky, Seymore; Russ, Charlotte; Rich, Marsha; Rivkin, Jay; Rancillac, Bernard; Ramon; Secunda, Arthur; Sterne, Hedda; Saar, Betye; Sherman, C.; Serisawa; Spaventa, George; Stefanelli, Joe; Schapiro, Meyer; Schwartz, Ellen; Schnackenberg, Roy; Sotz, Rick; Szapocznikow, Alina; Stewart, Michelle; Sanders, Joop; Sonberg, A. H.; Stevens, May; Simon, Ellen; Soyer, Moses; Speyer, Nora; Swartz, Shol; Spero; Sonenberg, Josh; Soyer, Rudolf; Sugarman; Seley, Jason; Sugarman, George; Sherman, S.; Talachnik, Acne; Teschout, David; Tytell, Lois; Toney, Anthony; Tauger, Susanna; Todd, Mike; Tavoularis, Constantine; Tunberg, Wm; Thek, Paul; Telemaque, Nerve; Tabuchi, Yasse; Uraban, Reva; Vicente, Esteban; Vlack, Don; Valentin, Helene; Vincent, Richard; Voss, Jan; Van Veer, S.; Walters, Charles; Wines, James; Weal, Alica; Weber, Ellen; Wesselmann, Tom; Wolf, Sara; Witherspoon; White, Charles; Watlin, Larry; Wiegand, Robert; Yamii, Alice; Yeargans, H.; Zajac, Jack; Zaro, Sid; Zaslove, Allen.

23   *The New York Times*, 26 February 1966, 20. The advertisement names the following 'New York artists': Susie Aitkin; Elise Asher; Helen Daphnis Avlon; Tony Balzano; Rudolf Baranik; Walter Barker; Will Barnet; Baruchello; Margit Beck; Milton Berwin; Edward Betts; Nell Blaine; R. O. Blechman; Bob Bolles; Paul Brach; L. Bronfman; James Brooks; Charles Cajori; Victor Candel; Martin Canin; Herman Cherry; George Cohen; Cply; Emilio Cruz; Robert Corless; Ron Curtis; Allan D'Arcangelo; Robert Dash; Storm De Hirsch; Elaine de Kooning; Fraser Dougherty; Georfe Dworzan; Isle Erythropel; D. Evans; Philip Evergood; Tully Filmus; Perle Fine; Rachel Formica; Elias Friedensohn; Sideo Fromboluti; Ruth Gikow; Lorenzo Gilchrist; George Gillson; Julio Girona; Leon Goldin; Peter Golfinopoul; Leon Golub; Ron Gorchov; Balcomb Greene; Cynthia Greene; Stephen Greene; Philip Guston; Walter Gutman; Robert Gwathmey; Carol Haerer; Kay Harris; Burt Hasen; John Heliker; Eva Hesse; Joseph Hirsch; Budd Hopkins; Helene Hui; John Hultberg; Robert Huot; Angelo Ippolito; Donald Judd; Ward Jackson; Nora Jaffee; William Jeffrey; Reuben Kadish; Wolf Kahn; Howard Kanowitz; Bernard Kassoy; Herbert Katzman; Jane Kaufman; Chaim Koppelman; Dorothy Koppelman; Max Kozloff; Harry Kramer; Gabriel Laderman; Jacob Landau; David Lawless; June Leaf; Kim Levin; Jack Levine; Si Lewen; Roy Lichtenstein; Linda Lindeberg; John Little; David Lund; Manuel Manga; Ernest Marciano; Marcia Marcus; Emily Mason; Herbert Matter; Mercedes Matter; Eline McKnight; James Mellon; Jack Mercado; Margaret Milliken; Robert Motherwell; Bob Natkin; Alice Neel; Lowell Nesbitt; Louise Nevelson; Doug Ohlson; Gerald Oster; Ray Parker; Peter Passantino; Philip Pearlstein; R. Pedreguera; Christina Pesirillo; Harold Pesirillo; Bernard Pfriem; Lil Picard; Bob Pittinger; Lucio Pozzi; Andre Racz; Joe Raffaele; Ad Reinhardt; Philip Reisman; Pauline Roony; Irwin Rosenhouse; James Rosenquist; Richard Rubens; Joop Sanders; Jason Seeley; Meyer Schapiro; Sarai Sherman; Burt Silverman; Ellen Simon; Jack Sonenberg; Phoebe Sonenberg; Moses Soyer; Raphael Soyer; George Spaventa; Nancy Spero; Nora Speyer; Joe Stefanelli; Hedda Sterne; May Stevens; Sahl Swarz; Michelle Stuart; George Sugarman; Susanne Tanger; Paul Thek; Mike Todd; Anthony Toney; Louis Tytell; Reva Urban; Helene Valentin; Stuyvesant Van Veen; Esteban Vicente; Richard Vincent; Don Vlack; Ellen Weber; Tom Wesselman; Robert Wiegand; John Willenbacher; James

Wines; Sara Wolf; Alice Yamin; Heartwell Yeargens; Adja Yunkers; Sidney Goodman; Eddie Johnson.

24 Elaine de Kooning, Herbert Ferber, Sam Francis, Judy Gerowitz [Judy Chicago], Lloyd Hamrol, Roy Lichtenstein, Robert Motherwell, Lee Mullican, Ad Reinhardt, Larry Rivers, Jim Rosenquist, Mark Rothko, Frank Stella, George Segal, Jack Zajac, Philip Evergood, George Sugarman, Claes Oldenburg, César, Karel Appel, Jean Helion, Leon Golub. Letter, undated, 'Artist's Tower', written by Arnold Mesches, Chairman, Fund Raising Committee, inviting financial contributions (University of California, Department of Special Collections, Collection 50, 'A Collection of Underground, Alternative and Extremist Literature', Box 36, Folder 'Artist's Tower Los Angeles').

25 'Protest Tower Going Up', *Los Angeles Free Press*, 3:5 (4 February 1966), 4.

26 John Wilcock, 'Artists Peace Tower', 1.

27 *Los Angeles Free Press*, 3:6 (11 February 1966), 4.

28 'Artists' Tower to be Dedicated Feb. 26', *Los Angeles Free Press*, 3:7 (18 February 1966), 1.

29 'Peace Landmark to be Dedicated on February 26', *Los Angeles Free Press*, 3:8 (25 February, 1966), 3. This issue contained 'VIET NAM – FIVE POSITIONS' (p. 11) reprinted from the *UCLA Daily Bruin*.

30 Kurt von Meier, 'Los Angeles Letter', *Art International*, 10:4 (April 1966), 68.

31 *Ibid.*

32 'Out of the Crucible of War', *Los Angeles Free Press*, 3:12 (18 March 1966), 8–9, with the Mesches painting on p. 8.

33 *Los Angeles Free Press*, 3:28 (15 July 1966), 1.

34 *Los Angeles Free Press*, 3:9 (4 March 1966), 1, 5.

35 The main sources are: John Wilcock, 'Internationally Important Art Exhibit Played Down By LA's Press, Radio, TV', *Los Angeles Free Press*, 3:9 (4 March 1966), 1, 5 and in the same issue: speech by Donald Duncan pp. 4, 5, 7; speech by Susan Sontag, pp. 4–5; Art Kunkin, 'When a Victim is Arrested', p. 7; photos p. 8; 'Protest Tower Going Up', p. 9 (see, too, reports and photos of the Tower going up in previous issues: 4, 11, 18 February). Also: 'Anti-Viet Dedication Fight Brings 2 Arrests', *Los Angeles Herald Examiner*, Saturday 26 February 1966, Section A, 5; '700 See Dedication of Tower', *Los Angeles Times*, Sunday 27 February 1966, Section A, B; 'Boos, Coos At "Tower of Protest"', *Los Angeles Herald Examiner*, Sunday 27 February 1966, A-3; 'A Protasis', *UCLA Daily Bruin Spectra*, 15 March 1966, 5–7; John Wilcock, 'Artists Peace Tower', *The East Village Other*, 1:7 (1–15 March 1966), 1, 15; 'Potpourri of Protest', *Newsweek*, 14 March 1966, 101–2. The art journals included only brief responses: Kurt von Meier, 'Los Angeles Letter', *Art International*, 10:4 (April 1966), 68–70; Dore Ashton, 'Art', *Arts and Architecture*, 83:3 (April 1966), 6–8; 'Los Angeles Tower for Peace', *Artnews*, 65:2 (April 1966), 25, 71. In October 1966, a short piece, 'The Tower' by Rudolf Baranik, was published in *El Corno Emplumado*, Mexico City. This radical journal, edited by Margaret Randall, was vociferously opposed to United States intervention in Vietnam. In April 1966, it published an edition (no. 18) 'Stop the War in Vietnam Now', with a Baranik image taken from Picasso's *Guernica*.

36 Therese Schwartz 'The Politicization of the Avant-Garde', Part I, *Art in America*, 59:6 (1971), 97–105; Part II, *Art in America*, 60:2 (1972), 70–9; Part III, *Art in America*, 61:2 (1973), 69–71; Part IV, *Art in America*, 62:1 (1974), 80–4.

37 Tom Wolfe, *The Electric Kool-Aid Acid Test* (New York, Bantam Books, 1969) as quoted in David Caute, *Sixty-Eight: The Year of the Barricades* (London, Hamish Hamilton, 1988), p. 41.

38 Herman Kahn, 'Some Specific Suggestions for Achieving Early Non-military Defense Capabilities', RAND Corporation Research Memo (RM-2206-RC, 1959), 48. See

Theodore Roszak, *The Making of a Counter Culture, Reflections on the Technocratic Society and Its Youthful Opposition* (Berkeley, University of California Press, [1969] 1995), p. 176.

39 Kurt von Meier, 'Los Angeles Letter,' 68.

40 *Ibid.*

41 In comparing 'kitsch film' and 'autonomous art', Adorno claimed that 'Both bear the stigmata of capitalism, both contain elements of change (but never, of course, the middle-term between Schönberg and the American film). Both are torn halves of an integral freedom, to which however they do not add up. It would be romantic to sacrifice one to the other, either as the bourgeois romanticism of the conservation of personality and all that stuff, or as the anarchistic romanticism of blind confidence in the spontaneous power of the proletariat in the historical process – a proletariat which is itself a product of bourgeois society.' Letter, translated by Harry Zohn, in *Aesthetics and Politics* (London, New Left Books, 1977), p. 123.

42 Telegram, 12.03 p.m. Pacific Standard Time (26 February 1966) to Petlin, 520 Strand, Santa Monica. Copy of the telegram kindly provided by Charles Brittin.

43 Kunkin, 'When a Victim is Arrested', *Los Angeles Free Press*, 3:9 (4 March 1966), 7.

44 *Ibid.*

45 *Ibid.* All following quotations from this report.

46 See the conflicting letters in *Los Angeles Free Press*, 3:11 (18 March 1966), 4; *Los Angeles Free Press*, 3:12 (25 March 1966), 4.

47 Wilcock, 'Artists Peace Tower', 1.

48 Petlin, interview with the author (14 April 1997).

49 'Hannon on his Trial', *Los Angeles Free Press*, 2:31 (30 July 1965), 1, 4; 'Hannon Describes Police Indifference to Poverty', *Los Angeles Free Press*, 2:34 (20 August 1965), 9; 'Hannon Runs for Congress; Seeks Primary Victory', *Los Angeles Free Press*, 3:5 (4 February 1966), 1, 3; 'Documented Case-Studies of Police Malpractice', *Los Angeles Free Press*, 2:35 (20 August 1965), 6, 10; 'Policemanship: a Guide', *Los Angeles Free Press*, 3:7 (18 February 1966), 7.

50 Interview with the author (14 April 1997) which also informs the following paragraph.

51 Susan Sontag, 'Inventing and Sustaining an Appropriate Response' (Speech at the Artists' Tower Dedication), *Los Angeles Free Press*, 3:9 (4 March 1966), 4.

52 *Ibid.*, 5.

53 For a comprehensive account see Laura Silber and Allan Little, *The Death of Yugoslavia* (London, Penguin Books and BBC Books, 1995).

54 Susan Sontag, '"There" and "Here": A Lament for Bosnia', 820. Thanks to Amy Schlegel for drawing this article to my attention.

55 *Ibid.*

56 Lucy Lippard has been a central figure in both the manifestations of 'activist art' and its documentation. See, for example, the following texts by Lippard: *Get the Message? A Decade of Art for Social Change* (New York, E. P. Dutton, 1984); 'Trojan Horses: Activist Art and Power', in Brian Wallis (ed.), *Art After Modernism: Rethinking Representation* (New York, New Museum of Contemporary Art New York and Godine, 1984); *A Different War: Vietnam in Art* (Seattle, Whatcome Museum of History and Art and the Real Comet Press, 1990). Generally, too, see publications and activities of Political Art Documentation/Distribution (PAD/D) and the journal *Heresies* (Lippard was a central participant in both).

57 For a short telling example of a political critique of deconstruction's contradictions, see Terry Eagleton, 'Marxism without Marxism' (a review of Derrida's *Spectres of Marx*), *Radical Philosophy*, 73 (September/October 1995), 35–7: 'If Derrida thinks, as he appears to do, that there can be any effective socialism without organization, apparatuses and reasonably well formulated doctrines and programmes, then he

is merely the victim of some academicist fantasy which he has mistaken for an enlightened anti-Stalinism' (p. 37).

58 See Noam Chomsky and Edward S. Herman, *The Washington Connection and Third World Fascism* (Boston, South End Press, 1979) especially chapter 4, sub-section 4.1, pp. 205–17.

59 'East Timor's Comandante "X": Messages from a Jakarta Prison', *The Nation*, 25 December 1995, 820–4.

60 Guy Pauker, a RAND Indonesian specialist, representing the Corporation in the debates with the Artists Protest Committee in 1965, was the author of revealing memoranda. In 1964, he feared that the Indonesian anti-Communist forces 'would probably lack the ruthlessness that made it possible for the Nazis to suppress the Communist Party of Germany' in 1933, since they 'are weaker than the Nazis, not only in numbers and in mass support, but also in unity, discipline, and leadership'. But, as he explained four years later, 'The assassination of the six army generals by the September 30 Movement elicited the ruthlessness that I had not anticipated a year earlier and resulted in the death of large numbers of Communist cadres'. Cited by Peter Dale Scott, 'Exporting Military-Economic Development: America and the Overthrow of Sukarno, 1965–67', in Malcolm Caldwell (ed.), *Ten Years' Military Terror in Indonesia* (Nottingham, Spokesman Books, 1975): see Chomsky and Herman, *The Washington Connection*, p. 403, n. 8.

61 Chomsky and Herman, *The Washington Connection*, p. 206. The number killed in the Indonesian bloodbath has always been uncertain but ranges from 'more than 500,000' to 'many more than one million'; see pp. 208ff. and notes. See frontispiece for a diagram of total United States military aid (1946–75) to, and number of United States trained military personnel (1950–75) in, countries using torture on an administrative basis in the 1970s.

62 *Ibid.*

63 'A Communication', *Frontier*, 17:4 (February 1966), 26–7.

64 Sontag, 'Inventing and Sustaining an Appropriate Response' (Speech at the Artists' Tower Dedication), 4. At the end of her speech, Sontag makes an understandable but erroneous prediction which is paradoxically revealing about the pattern of subsequent United States global involvement (and a haunting premonition of the failure of US/UN/NATO action to prevent escalation of the war in Yugoslavia followed by various 'aid programmes'): 'even if the Administration decides to negotiate instead of pressing for the unconditional surrender of the Vietnamese, it's not at all likely that Americans will be let off the hook, that we'll be able to expiate our crimes or cover over our folies with aid programs for those who survive our bombs' (p. 5).

65 Hundreds of protests, small and large, across the country. For example: three hundred Women Strike for Peace (WSP) and Women's International League for Peace and Freedom (WILPF) picketed the White House on 11 February 1965, just before the public announcement of Rolling Thunder; on 20 February four hundred Students for a Democratic Society (SDS) and others demonstrated in Washington, as well as other marches in at least nine other cities; the Artists Protest Committee in Los Angeles demonstrated in front of museums and galleries and picketed the RAND Corporation, a government-backed 'think-tank', on 26 June; on 15–16 October the first International Days of Protest were organised in which a hundred thousand people (including twenty-five thousand in New York) marched and protested in dozens of cities in the United States; the Committee for a SANE Nuclear Policy organised an anti-war march on Washington with thirty thousand participants on 27 November; on 2 November Norman Morrison, a thirty-two-year-old Quaker anti-war protestor, burned himself to death with gasoline on the steps of the Pentagon,

near to the office window of Robert McNamara; the following week Roger LaPorte, a Catholic pacifist, repeated Morrison's self-immolation outside the UN building in New York. Both of the latter had strong effects, and were referred to in Sontag's speech in 1966. On these protests see: Fred Halstead, *Out Now! A Participant's Account of the Movement in the U.S. Against the Vietnam War* (New York, Pathfinder Press, 1978) especially chapters 4–6; and Tom Wells, *The War Within: America's Battle Over Vietnam* (Berkeley, Los Angeles and London, University of California Press, 1994), chapters 1 and 2. Significantly, 1965 saw the beginnings of an escalation of FBI (local 'Red Squads') and CIA anti-Left intervention and surveillance.

66 Sontag, 'Inventing and Sustaining an Appropriate Response'.

67 Arnaud de Borchgrave, 'Then and Now – the Difference', *Newsweek*, 14 March 1966, 40–2.

68 *Ibid.*, 40.

69 Later in the same issue of *Newsweek* (14 March 1966), under its 'Education' heading, appears an article on the role of foundations titled 'The American Way of Giving', 87–92, dwelling on some of the paradoxes and contradictions of their activities: 'Today certain foundations are under attack from liberals who decry the right-wing pamphleteering that masks itself as educational activity. Some critics claim that large foundations are a benevolent-aid society for the Eastern Establishment [Washington and the White House] . . . "We still suffer from the old John D. Rockefeller kerosene trust," [Wright Patman] the 72-year old Congressman said last week. "Foundations are perpetuating themselves in office. It's like feudal Europe."'

70 'Then and Now – the Difference', 41.

71 Quoted in Wells, *The War Within*, p. 68.

72 *Time*, 11 March 1966, 27.

73 See, too, report of Duncan's subsequent speech to two thousand UCLA students in Philip Fradkin, 'S. Vietnam Civilians Betray U.S. Troops, Ex-GI Declares', *Los Angeles Times*, 1 March 1966, Part 1, 3.

74 The journal carried two critical essays on Vietnam in the December 1965 issue: Robert Scheer, 'The Winner's War' and Bernard B. Fall 'Vietnam Album', *Ramparts*, 4:8 (December 1965), 19–22, 23–9. The editorial in the January 1966 issue discussed the need for protest against the war and the government: *Ramparts*, 4:9 (January 1966), 3–4.

75 Donald Duncan, '"The whole thing was a lie!"', *Ramparts*, 4:10 (February 1966), 12–24.

76 *Ibid.*, 14.

77 *Ibid.*, 16.

78 *Ibid.*: getting ARVN to torture and kill prisoners, 21; acceptance of commonplace rape by ARVN, 23; Special Forces and CIA involvement in illicit operations, 24.

79 *Ibid.*, 16.

80 *Ibid.*, 23.

81 *Ibid.*, 23–4.

82 See the range of letters in response to Duncan's article in *Ramparts*, 5:1 (June 1966), 9.

83 On the relationship between art, culture and the New Deal see Jonathan Harris, *Federal Art and National Culture: The Politics of Identity in New Deal America* (New York, Cambridge University Press, 1995).

84 Robert Buzzanco, *Masters of War: Military Dissent and Politics in the Vietnam Era* (New York, Cambridge University Press, 1996), pp. 238–9. Budget deficits rose from $3.8 billion in fiscal year 1966 to over $25 billion in fiscal year 1968, the largest in postwar history and 3 per cent of GNP. Generally see Gabriel Kolko, *Anatomy of War: Vietnam, The United States, and the Modern Historical Experience* (New York,

Pantheon, 1985); and Anthony J. Campagna, *The Economic Consequences of the Vietnam War* (Westport, Praeger, 1991).

85 'Ad Reinhardt: Art as Art', Reinhardt interviewed by Jeanne Seigel, broadcast on radio station WBAI, Manhattan, New York (13 June 1967) in the series 'Great Artists in America Today', reprinted in Seigel, *Artwords: Discourse on the 60s and 70s* (Ann Arbor, UMI Research Press, 1985), p. 28.

86 Reinhardt in a panel discussion, 'How Effective is Social Protest Art? (Vietnam)', moderated by Jeanne Seigel, broadcast on radio station WBAI, Manhattan, New York (10 August 1967), reprinted in Seigel, *Artwords: Discourse on the 60s and 70s*, p. 105.

87 *Ibid.*, p. 119.

88 See correspondence in the Greenberg Papers (Archives of American Art, Smithsonian Institution, Washington, DC).

89 Philip Leider, 'How I Spent My Summer Vacation or, Art and Politics in Nevada, Berkeley, San Francisco and Utah', *Artforum*, 9:1 (September 1970), 40–1.

90 See Frascina, 'The Politics of Representation', chapter 2 of Paul Wood, Francis Frascina, Jonathan Harris and Charles Harrison, *Modernism in Dispute: Art Since the Forties* (New Haven and London, Yale University Press, 1993), particularly pp. 90–114.

91 John Coplans, *Pasadena Art Museum: John Coplans*, interviewed by Joanne L. Ratner (Department of Special Collections, Oral History Programme, University Research Library, UCLA, 1989), p. 9.

92 John Weber, interview with, the author (20 May 1993).

93 'Mark di Suvero: Three New Works', *Artforum*, 3:9 (May 1965), 36–8; *Artforum*, 4:4 (December 1965), photograph 12, review by Nancy Marmer 13–14 under 'Los Angeles' gallery review section.

94 Reviews, including photographs, of the first and second half of Judith Gerowitz's exhibition by Peter Plagens in *Artforum*, 4:7 (March 1966), 14, and *Artforum*, 4:8 (April 1966), 14, 15; Review, with photograph, by Fidel A. Danieli, of Irving Petlin's exhibition in *Artforum*, 4:8 (April 1966), 15. An advertisement for both exhibitions appeared in the January edition, *Artforum*, 4:5, 11.

95 *Artforum*, 4:6, 33–7. The essay was a version of the catalogue essay for the exhibition catalogue, by Coplans, at the Art Gallery of the University of California, Irvine (7 January to 6 February 1966).

96 Petlin, interviews with the author (27 October 1992 and 7 June 1993).

97 John Weber, interview with the author (20 May 1993).

98 *Artforum*, 4:6 (February 1966), 13.

99 Leider, 'How I Spent My Summer Vacation', 40–1.

100 Greenberg, 'Modernist Painting' (1961), Radio Broadcast Lecture 14 of *The Voice of America Forum Lectures: The Visual Arts*, reprinted, as spoken, in the paperback edition of all eighteen lectures (Washington, DC, United States Information Agency, 1965), pp. 105–11. After its broadcast, 'Modernist Painting' was published in *Arts Yearbook*, 4 (1961), 101–8. It appeared in revised form in *Art and Literature*, 4 (spring 1965), 193–201, and then in Gregory Battcock (ed.), *The New Art: A Critical Anthology* (New York, E. P. Dutton, 1966), pp. 100–10. Fried, *Three American Painters: Kenneth Noland, Jules Olitski, Frank Stella* (Fogg Art Museum, Harvard University, 21 April to 30 May, 1965) and thence to the Pasadena Art Museum (6 July to 3 August 1965).

101 Leider, 'Art: São Paulo', *Frontier*, 17:1 (November 1965), 23.

102 18 June to 1 August, 1965.

103 *Artforum*, 4:1 (September 1965), 3–13, 14–17.

104 Interview with the author (14 April 1997).

105 See contents of Folder, 'Assembly of Men and Women in the Arts Concerned with Vietnam' (University of California, Deptartment of Special Collections, Collection 50, 'A Collection of Underground, Alternative and Extremist Literature', Box 36).

106 Letter from John Ashberry, Thomas B. Hess, Max Kozloff, Phil Leider, Barbara Rose, Meyer Schapiro in Ashton and Baranik files (PAD/D Archive, Museum of Modern Art, New York).

107 Charles Brittin, interview with the author (24 April 1997). The *Life* photographers were mentioned, along with other potential coverage, in Mesches's letter appealing for funds for the Tower: Letter, undated, 'Artist's Tower', written by Arnold Mesches, Chairman, Fund Raising Committee, inviting financial contributions (University of California, Department of Special Collections, Collection 50, 'A Collection of Under-ground, Alternative and Extremist Literature', Box 36, Folder 'Artist's Tower Los Angeles').

108 *Life*, 60:6 (11 February 1966), 20–5.

109 *Life*, 60:8 (25 February 1966). The former 27–31; the latter 56Bff. *Life* was interested in contemporary art, with its radical agenda exemplified by an article on Kienholz 'Beanery Built for Art', 60:2 (14 January 1966), 78–80 including five photographs. *Life* was consistent with other contemporary publications in that it could include coverage of the controversies represented by Kienholz's work but not engage with the issues raised by the collective dissent of the 'Artists Tower of Protest'.

110 'Los Angeles: Tower for Peace', *Artnews*, 65:2 (April 1966), 25, 71.

111 Lucy R. Lippard, 'James Rosenquist: Aspects of a Multiple Art', *Artforum*, 4:4 (December 1965), 42.

112 G. R. Swenson, 'F-111: An Interview with James Rosenquist', *Partisan Review*, 32:4 (fall 1965), 589–601.

113 *Ibid.*, 597. Rosenquist goes on to say: 'Even though this picture was sold in one chunk [to Robert Scull, for a reported $60,000], I think that the original intention is still clear. The picture is in parts.'

114 With a catalogue, including an essay by Maurice Tuchman, *Edward Kienholz: An Exhibition Organized by the Los Angeles County Museum of Art in Cooperation with the Museum's Contemporary Art Council* (Los Angeles, Los Angeles County Museum of Art, Lytton Gallery, 1966).

115 *Artforum*, 4:8 (April 1996); Tillim, 38–40; Tuchman, 41–4.

116 Irving Petlin, interview with the author (27 October 1992). In April 1968 Kienholz used an axe to chop a desk in TWA offices, Los Angeles airport, after the airline had destroyed, in shipping, a cherished glass lamp that he wanted to carry as hand luggage on a flight from the East Coast. His revenge was in the biblical tradition of an 'eye for an eye'.

117 Tuchman, 'A Decade of Edward Kienholz', 41.

118 *Ibid.*

119 Barbara Rose, 'New York Letter', *Art International*, 7 (25 March 1963), 65–8. Rose was married to Frank Stella, who became an important artist for Fried, one of Greenberg's most ardent followers. Greenberg's notions of modern specialisation and the exclusion of all references to the literary or social from the demands of media-specific immanent qualities were developed in his *Post Painterly Abstraction*, an exhibition at the Los Angeles County Museum of Art (23 April to 7 June 1964) and published as an article in *Art International*, (summer 1964).

120 Tuchman had been recruited from the Guggenheim Museum in New York. On Tuchman's intellectual energy, obsession with his job and social world defined by collectors, dealers, artists and trustees see Kienholz, *Edward Kienholz, Los Angeles Art Community: Group Portrait*, II, pp. 366ff.

121 See Barbara M. Reise, 'Greenberg and the Group: A Retrospective View', *Studio International*, 175:901 (May 1968), 254–7 (Part 1); 175:902 (June 1968), 314–16 (Part 2). Reise singles out Jane Harrison Cone, Michael Fried, Rosalind Krauss and Sidney Tillim. Even though Tillim wrote at length on *Barney's Beanery*, in the April 1966 issue of *Artforum*, his conclusions were generally negative.

122 *Los Angeles Herald Examiner*, 28 August 1964, 1, 6.

123 *Ibid.*, 1.

124 *Ibid.*, 6.

125 *Edward Kienholz, Los Angeles Art Community: Group Portrait*, I, pp. 47–8.

126 *Ibid.*, pp. 217–19.

127 Kienholz quoted in Tuchman, 'A Decade of Edward Kienholz', 44.

128 *Edward Kienholz, Los Angeles Art Community: Group Portrait*, II, p. 374.

129 *Ibid.*, I, p. 222.

130 Kienholz's account of the events can be found in *Edward Kienholz, Los Angeles Art Community: Group Portrait*, II, pp. 376–407. See, too, Richard Cándida-Smith, *Utopia and Dissent: Art, Poetry and Politics in California* (Berkeley, University of California Press, 1995), chapter 11, pp. 318ff.

131 *Los Angeles Times*, 23 March 1966: 'Supervisors Urge Removal of Modern Exhibit at Museum', 1, 31; and *Los Angeles Herald Examiner*, 23 March 1966: 'Dorn Lashes "Raw" LA Museum Art', 1, 4, 'Exhibit Draws Fiery Protest' and 'Museum Salaries Under Fire', 2. The Board of Supervisors were Burton W. Chance (Chair), Frank G. Bonelli, Ernest E. Debbs, Warren M. Dorn, Kenneth Hahn and Lindon S. Hollinger (Chief Administrative Officer).

132 'Dorn Will Enter GOP Race Today', *Los Angeles Times*, 23 March 1966, 3.

133 'High Court Sets New Criterion in Obscenity Cases', *Los Angeles Times*, 22 March 1966, 1, 7.

134 *Ibid.*, 1.

135 *Ibid.* On 27 March the *Los Angeles Herald Examiner* carried a report on the Los Angeles County district Attorney's office which included two deputy district attorneys who had been working in the area of obscene literature for several years. They welcomed the rulings not least in their campaigns against 'material that appeals to the homosexual community' and had already established a rating system of 1 to 10 for assessing the 'prurient' and 'sexual deviation' content of publications.

136 *Los Angeles Free Press*, 3:19 (13 May 1966), 4. 'Anti-Censorship Meeting Plans Permanent Group', 1–3, 6. Amongst telegrams and letters of support was one from Maurice Tuchman, Curator of the Kienholz exhibition at LACMA.

137 *Los Angeles Free Press*, 25 May 1964, 1, 4.

138 See Norman Hartweg, 'The D.A. vs. Obscenity', *Los Angeles Free Press*, 1:5 (20 August 1964), 3; Norman Hartweg, 'Interview with Connor Everts', *Los Angeles Free Press*, 1:6 (27 August 1964), 3, 4; Norman Hartweg, 'The D.A. vs. "Obscenity", Part Three', *Los Angeles Free Press*, 1:9 (17 September 1964), 3, 5; Claude Hayward and Art Kunkin, 'On Three Trials: Venice West Poetry; Connor Everts Art; Marijuana Poster', *Los Angeles Free Press*, 2:2 (8 January 1965), 1, 4; Al Saxton, 'Judge's Memo On "Obscenity" Clarifies Everts' Acquittal', *Los Angeles Free Press*, 2:22 (28 May 1965), 1, 3.

139 Al Saxton, 'Judge's Memo On "Obscenity" Clarifies Everts' Acquittal', 3.

140 As reported in *Los Angeles Times*, 23 March 1966, 3, 24. See, too, report in *Los Angeles Herald Examiner*, 23 March 1966, 3.

141 A figure claimed by Stephen F. Brody, a vice-president of the trustees, quoted in *Los Angeles Times*, 25 March 1966, 24.

142 See 'Hahn Will Try to Block Extra Pay for Art Museum Officials', *Los Angeles Times*, 24 March 1966, 1, 3; 'Dual Pay Threat in LA "Art War"', *Los Angeles Herald*

Examiner, 24 March 1966, 1, 16; 'Museum Threatened with Loss of Funds,' *Los Angeles Times*, 26 March 1966, 2; 'Showdown Near in LA Art "War"' and 'Clergy Differs on Controversial Art', *Los Angeles Herald Examiner*, 26 March 1966, 3.

143 'Background of Art Exhibit Controversy Told By Dorn', *Los Angeles Times*, 25 March 1966, 24. See, too, 'Dorn Lashes "Raw" LA Museum Art', *Los Angeles Herald Examiner*, 23 March 1966, 1, 4.

144 See *Edward Kienholz, Los Angeles Art Community: Group Portrait*, II, p. 384; Richard Cándida-Smith, *Utopia and Dissent*, pp. 325–6.

145 'ART WAR "TRUCE" It will Open with Curbs' and '"Inside Story" of Art Pact', *Los Angeles Herald Examiner*, 29 March 1966, 1. Both stories continued on 14 with a photograph on 3.

146 'Kienholz Exhibit to Be Shown Intact at County Art Museum', *Los Angeles Times*, 29 March 1966, 1, 26, with another report, 'Social Part of Show Set for Kienholz', Part 4, 2.

147 '"Inside Story" of Art Pact', 14.

148 Bonelli quoted in 'Storm's Over; Art Exhibit Open', *Los Angeles Herald Examiner*, 30 March 1966, 3 (evening edition). See, too, 'Art Show to Open With Heavy Guard', *Los Angeles Times*, 30 March 1966, 3, 31.

149 'Storm's Over; Art Exhibit Open', *Los Angeles Herald Examiner*, 30 March 1966, A-3.

150 'Public Sees Art Exhibition; Consensus: Not Pornographic', *Los Angeles Times*, 31 March 1966, 3, 35.

151 See 'Museum Row Flares Again', *Los Angeles Herald Examiner*, 1 April 1966, 1, 5; 'Museum Row On Again', *Los Angeles Herald Examiner*, 2 April 1966, 3; 'Dorn Issues Ultimatum in Art Row', *Los Angeles Times*, 3 April 1966, 1, 8; 'Dorn Warns of Arrest Over Art Works' 4-Letter Words', *Los Angeles Times*, 5 April 1966, 3, 18.

152 'Debs Claims Dorn "Milks" Art Dispute', *Los Angeles Times*, 6 April 1966, 3.

153 *Ibid.*, 23.

154 Ridgeley Cummings, 'Kienholz Exhibit Opens on Schedule; Move to End Museum Subsidy Blocked', *Los Angeles Free Press*, 3:13 (1 April 1966), 3.

155 Two stories: Ridgely Cummings, 'Supervisors Say Kienholz Offends Public Decency; Art Museum Stands Firm', 1, 3, with two photographs of *Roxy's*; 'Kienholz Assemblage Show to Open March 30', 1 and centrefold, 8–9, *Los Angeles Free Press*, 3:12 (25 March 1966).

156 Jeanne Morgan, 'Last Chance at the Savage Truth', *Los Angeles Free Press*, 3:19 (13 May 1966), 9. The 'New Bumpersnicker' advertised as available from the *Los Angeles Free Press*, 3:19 (13 May 1966), 4. The high attendance figures basically put the LACMA on the local and national map with many visitors visiting the Museum for the first time.

157 *Los Angeles Free Press*, 3:15 (15 April 1966), 13.

158 *Los Angeles Free Press*, 3:19 (13 May 1966), 4, 6.

159 Leider, 'Los Angeles and the Kienholz Affair', *New York Times*, 3 April 1966, Section 2, 23, 25.

160 *Ibid.*, 23.

161 *Ibid.*, 23–5.

162 See *Edward Kienholz, Los Angeles Art Community: Group Portrait*, II, p. 397.

163 Leider, 'Los Angeles and the Kienholz Affair', 25.

164 *Ibid.*

165 See Kienholz in *Edward Kienholz, Los Angeles Art Community: Group Portrait*, II, pp. 398–9.

166 *Ibid.*

3 Angry Arts, the Art Workers' Coalition and the politics of 'otherness'

Introduction: 'the politics of "otherness"'

By 1967, many of the contradictions and differences in the art world's responses to Vietnam, to Civil Rights and to the early stages of the women's movement became marked.[1] For example, in New York Angry Arts Week (29 January to 8 February 1967) was a collective programme of cultural events and protest with roots in a variety of precedents including Dada, performance and happenings, and radical politicised theatre. *The Collage of Indignation*, one product of Angry Arts Week, resulted partly from the example of the 'Artists' Tower of Protest', in Los Angeles in early 1966. Participating artists such as Leon Golub, and critics such as Max Kozloff (also on the organising committee), published texts on the significance of *The Collage of Indignation*.[2] These raise several issues about the role of 'art' and of 'art criticism' in relation to 'protest'. The Kozloff text, from *The Nation*, in particular, reveals the problems of addressing various constituencies within the world of 'art and culture'.

Such problems were in stark contrast to Michael Fried's 'Art and Objecthood', published a few months later, which is firmly entrenched in the preoccupations of a radically elite cultural community.[3] His article appeared in *Artforum*, which, as we have seen, was a major player in the powerful world of art journals and during the summer of 1967 moved its base from Los Angeles to New York.[4] The editor, Philip Leider, was both a participant in anti-war activities and a cultural elitist. From an Old Left perspective, cultural elitism was inconsistent with social and political protest or dissent, the struggle for equality. However, transformations in the 1940s and 1950s led many members of the political left to value the specialist products of high culture as a separable sphere of human activity. For such intellectuals no inconsistency was identified in being a cultural elitist while supporting the rights of workers and the marginalised and oppressed in society.[5]

Correspondence between Leider and Greenberg at the time reveals Leider's desire to locate *Artforum* in the forefront of debates about the efficacy of Modernism and its high-art alternatives such as Minimalism, Land Art and early Conceptualism. Leider, under various pressures, rarely published articles which explicitly raised political issues or controversies.[6]

This is not to say that articles such as Fried's 'Art and Objecthood' were not politicised, *implicitly*. The point is that Leider was an editor of a journal that in part represented his own contradictory responses to contemporary socio-political demands and pressures. These can be traced back to one aspect of the transformations of intellectuals in the 'Old Left' and their ambivalence toward the ideas, values and beliefs of the 'New Left'.[7] Many of the former emphasised, in the late 1950s and early 1960s, the 'achievements' of modernism within bourgeois culture as qualitative landmarks and signs of human liberation in contrast to capitalist 'kitsch' and the barbarism of Fascism and Stalinist Socialist Realism. Two texts that exemplify such transformations in various ways are Meyer Schapiro, 'The Liberating Quality of Avant-garde Art' (1957), and Clement Greenberg's 'Modernist Painting' (1961).[8] Importantly, these texts and intellectuals were the product of a deep engagement with the cultural status and political life of New York and its leftist history.[9]

The 1960s in the United States are a decade often described in terms of the divisions between, or the transformations in, the 'Old Left' and the 'New Left'. The 'Old Left' is characterised as having roots in the debates and struggles of the 1930s, centred on Trotskyism and Stalinism and the fight against Fascism. Central issues were the role of the Communist Party; debates about 'modernism' and 'realism'; the role of 'culture' as populist or avant-gardist; the effects of mass culture and capitalism; the relationship between socialism and comprehensibility. In contrast, the 1950s were marked by McCarthyism and the attacks on Communists, Marxists and socialists. It was also characterised by an aggressive economic, ideological and military involvement by the United States globally. For many members of the 'Old Left', the possibility of sustaining their beliefs and projects from the 1930s not only became practically difficult but also several shifted their views on 'culture and politics'. The latter meant privileging high culture and autonomous art as the last defensible enclaves of political activity and dissent – revolutionary aspirations having been bracketed by McCarthyism, a consumer boom and Cold War imperialism. The 'New Left', on the other hand, was associated with the Students for a Democratic Society (SDS) and the Port Huron Statement (written by student activist Tom Hayden) which was not allied to the political party traditions of the 'Old Left'. The 'New Left' was wedded less to Marxist analyses and more to a mix of notions and optimistic aspirations with a greater emphasis on the 'personal' or 'individualist'. Because of its broad-based appeal, politicians, the military, the press, industrial corporations were all hostile to the 'New Left', with the FBI mounting a campaign to undermine its effectiveness.[10]

Was the adherence to the certainties of Modernist values an ideological product of McCarthyism and a bid for cultural power? Evidence in support of such a view may be gleaned from critics' persistent adherence to art/cultural emphases on the canon, reliance on the hegemonic market and institutional attention, replication of male white supremacy in visual high culture and celebration of individual oeuvres over collaborative achievements. Such emphases were acknowledged by Benjamin Buchloh in a three-way discussion with Michael Fried and Rosalind Krauss, in a section entitled '1967/1987, Genealogies of Art and Theory', in which Fried's essay 'Art and Objecthood' was singled out as a crucial landmark.[11] Fried and Krauss, as is well known, were deeply affected by the cultural values and social world of Clement Greenberg, to whom they became allied in the early 1960s. For this social formation the worlds of the Beats and of 'counter-culture' were deeply unsettling. For Greenbergian Modernists, both were associated with a lack of clarity, unverifiable values and an existentialist psychology. In 1972 Rosalind Krauss recalled adopting 'that curiously dissociated [Modernist] tone' a decade earlier:

> For I was being carried by an idea of historical logic, buoyed like the others by the possibility of clarity.
>
> In the '50s we had been alternately tyrannized and depressed by the psychologizing whine of 'Existentialist' criticism. It had seemed evasive to us – the impenetrable hedge of subjectivity whose prerogatives we could not assent to. The remedy had to have, for us, the clear provability of 'if x then y'.[12]

Such a remedy had a powerful influence, as is well known. However, to many artists and critics who reached their twenties and thirties in the mid- to late 1960s the social and cultural developments of the decade produced an alternative agenda – for example, to those who look on '1968' as a radical turning point in their practice, such as those indebted to the women's movement whose politicisation, partly activated by anti-Vietnam-War protest and Civil Rights struggles, transformed their work and relationships to cultural institutions. The four years from 1967 to 1970 were characterised by rapid transformations in individual and collective responses to contemporary political struggles. In the aftermath of United States bombing of Cambodia in Indochina and the killings of student protestors at home, most notoriously at Jackson State College and Kent State University, artists renewed their critical interventions. One manifestation was the New York Artists' Strike Against Racism, Sexism, Repression and War on 22 May 1970 and subsequent actions.[13] This included mass picketing of museums and the participation of hundreds of artists. Another site, paradoxically, was in the heart of the Museum of Modern Art, New York, where in summer 1970 the *Information* exhibition was held.[14] This was one of the most radical exhibitions held in the citadel of Modernism, largely because of the political context of 1970. However, it is often conventionally contained in art-world terms as an exhibition of 'Conceptual art', as it still was in the 1995 catalogue to the major exhibition *Reconsidering the Art Object: 1965–1975*.[15] In contrast, the catalogue to *Information*, edited by Kynaston L. McShine, was in his words 'essentially an anthology' of contributions by exhibiting artists and included photographs of demonstrations and protests and reprints of newspaper articles about the Vietnam War:

> which is not very surprising, considering the general social, political, and economic crises that are almost universal phenomena in 1970. If you are an artist in Brazil, you know of at least one friend who is being tortured; if you are one in Argentina, you probably have had a neighbor who has been in jail for having long hair, or for not being 'dressed' properly; and if you are living the United States, you may fear that you will be shot at, either in the universities, in your bed, or more formally in Indochina.[16]

The last three references are to the killing and wounding of students at Kent State University and Jackson State College, an African-American campus, in May 1970; to the recent killing of Black Panthers in police set-ups; and to deaths in Vietnam and Cambodia. McShine, an Associate Curator at MoMA, born in Trinidad, may well have been drawing attention to ethnic oppression in all of his references. As he continues: 'It may seem inappropriate, if not absurd, to get up in the morning, walk into a room, and apply dabs of paint from a little tube to a square of canvas. What can you as a young artist do that seems relevant and meaningful?'[17]

Many artists produced a variety of work in response to contemporary events. Two of the best-known exhibited works were produced by members of the Art Workers Coalition, a heterogeneous group of artists formed in 1969. One was Hans Haacke's *MoMA-Poll* 'installation for audience participation', which explicitly politicised his previous information/ systems work. Visitors were given colour-coded ballot papers and asked to cast them into one of two boxes with photoelectric counting devices in response to the question: 'Would the fact that Governor Rockefeller has not denounced President Nixon's Indochina policy be a reason for you not to vote for him in November?'[18] The question referred to Nixon's bombing of Cambodia and to Nelson Rockefeller, Republican Governor of New York who was running for re-election in 1970. The Rockefeller family helped to found and financially support MoMA, with Nelson a member of the Board of Trustees since 1932. In November 1969 the Guerrilla Art Action Group, affiliated to the Art Workers Coalition, called for the resignation of the Rockefellers from the Board of Trustees because of their financial interests in companies such as Standard Oil and Chase Manhattan Bank. These and other Rockefeller companies were documented as connected to the production of napalm, chemical and biological weapons research and to armaments, some of which were linked to the Pentagon.

The other work was the Art Workers Coalition's *Q. 'And babies?'; A. 'And babies'*, a lithographic poster based on a photograph of the My

Lai massacre of Vietnamese civilians by United States Military in 1968. The massacre was first reported in the press and television in late 1969 with Sergeant Ron Haeberle's photograph appearing in colour in *Life* magazine in December 1969. The complex story of the production and publication of this poster will be discussed in the next chapter.

The *Information* exhibition was produced at a time when the relationship between 'the artist and politics' was intensified. It was intensified by, on the one hand, reactions to more details emerging from the trial of Lieutenant Calley for the massacre of Vietnamese civilians by the United States military at My Lai and to the killing of students protesting against further escalation of the war in Indochina and, on the other hand, artists' and writers' collective action under organisations such as the Art Workers' Coalition, Women Artists and Revolution, Ad Hoc Women Artists' Committee, Women Students and Artists for Black Art Liberation and Puerto Rican Art Workers' Coalition. MoMA was very concerned about the mixture of pressures by these groups. In June 1970, James Soby wrote to David Rockefeller and Bill Rubin (with a copy to Alfred Barr) worried about protests by what he called 'ethnic and biological groups' and claimed that the Museum could not 'show or buy more works by Negro or female artists without letting down our standards'.[19] Barr replied saying that he thought Soby's letter was 'excellent'. He wished that 'we had talked more about the Blacks' and that the Museum 'should do something – perhaps a careful show or even a small exhibition of what we have in our collection'.[20] A Trustees Executive Committee Meeting was held on 25 June to discuss the 'subject of Museum involvement in minority concerns' which Paley thought too important to bring to a head at a recent Trustees meeting. It was resolved to set up a Committee of the Trustees: a 'Black, Puerto Rican and Other Ethnic Studies Program' to recommend any changes in the operations of the Museum. The whole investigation and proposals were largely to be kept in house and relatively private.[21] None of these comments or decisions would have encouraged any of the protestors. Rather they would have confirmed their view about the assumptions held within the institution – assumptions that positioned the interests, identities, art practices and critiques of the protestors as 'other' but in need of ameliorating through the processes of public relations.

Similarly, although the Director John Hightower thought that the *Information* show was 'a bench mark for the Museum',[22] he had to respond to a number of internal and external pressures. Hilton Kramer in *The New York Times* attacked the exhibition:

> what we are offered here is, if anything, a development even worse to contemplate than the politicization of art – it is the estheticizing of political clichés. Having trivialized the very concept of art, the exhibition takes perhaps the next logical step by ingesting a large diet of serious social and political issues

and transforming them into a waste product of esthetic trifles . . . it is the sheer weight of its boredom that is most repellent.[23]

Kramer opens his review with a jaundiced discussion of Haacke's *MoMA-Poll*. It was this work that led Hightower to write to David Rockefeller, whose reply locates the trustees' major defence mechanism when confronted by fundamental questions. Rockefeller agreed that the material should not have been removed from the show nor Haacke's question changed, for artists 'have every right to express their political viewpoints in their works' which should be displayed if 'the art is up to MoMA standards . . . The Museum should continue to be in the vanguard of what is happening in art.' But Rockefeller states that he cannot see 'how many of these works can be considered art. I simply do not understand how a poll, a collection of newspaper articles placed side by side, a blown-up page from a magazine, or a quotation from Andy Warhol have any artistic content whatsoever.'[24]

In this chapter my aim is to introduce aspects of 'the politics of "otherness"' in some of the activities of artists and critics based in New York in the period from early 1967 onwards. This means that my concerns are historical; and my interests are less with specific objects and more with the social conditions within which *some* visual objects and their meanings were produced.

1967

In February 1967 Max Kozloff addressed the readers of *The Nation*:

> To write of art and politics in the United States in 1967 is surely to court futility in a context of provocation . . . It is the predicament of trying to resolve divergent obligations – intellectual and moral – which public life in this country is always prying further apart, with stupefying results . . . We are in a time when the public that is aware of art assimilates all *avant-garde* hypotheses into an apparatus of mild titilation. It is the obverse of our insensitivity to the war images, the photos of burnt children, which daily flood it. How can a people that does not choke with revulsion and guilt at this visual evidence of its government actions be in the least responsive to art's involuted censure? And how can artists who have all this time been hyper-defensive about their autonomy as creators, strive consciously to reach this population, and still view themselves as artists?[25]

In stark contrast Michael Fried addressed the readers of *Artforum* in June 1967:

> This essay will be read as an attack on certain artists (and critics) and as a defense of others. And of course it is true that the desire to distinguish between what is to me the authentic art of our time and other work which,

whatever the dedication, passion, and intelligence of its creators, seems to me to share certain characteristics associated here with the concepts of literalism and theater, has largely motivated what I have written. More generally, however, I have wanted to call attention to the utter pervasiveness – the virtual universality – of the sensibility or mode of being which I have characterized as corrupted or perverted by theater. We are all literalists most or all of our lives. Presentness is grace.[26]

Kozloff's review of aspects of Angry Arts Week in February 1967 and the publication of Michael Fried's 'Art and Objecthood' *Artforum* in June 1967 represent distinct and paradoxical positions and attitudes. The works referred to in their texts also represent dilemmas. For many artists the long-term historical developments in legitimated art practices provided the context for their work. Modernist painters and sculptors and Minimalist artists could, for example, trace the roots of their practice within general and specific traditions of art in the twentieth century. Such processes of historical context and retrospect were crucial factors in preserving what they regarded as the self-critical autonomy of their art. This was one of the central aspects of both artistic production and critical judgement advocated in Fried's pursuit of 'grace': instantaneous and involuntary recognition of aesthetic quality, immediately and totally *other* to the world of what characterises 'most of our lives'. The latter include the actual dilemmas of morality and politics; the experience of the body in space, time and gender relations; the position of the viewer as critical participant in cultural representation.

In contrast to Fried's belief in the authentic 'grace' of the imaginative life of art, a place where the mind can escape corruption and perversion, the Artists and Writers Protest opted for intervention, collectivity and the 'theatrical'. In late 1966, its New York base joined in plans for Angry Arts, a week of protest against the war in Vietnam to run from 29 January to 5 February 1967. Many of the participants, organisers and sympathisers of the Tower in Los Angeles were central to this project. In December 1966, the art critics and historians Max Kozloff and Dore Ashton, both based in New York City, sent out a letter of invitation on behalf of the Artists and Writers Protest. Kozloff had participated in the RAND debate in Los Angeles in 1965 and in the 'Tower of Protest' in 1966. Ashton reviewed the latter and had been highly active in anti-nuclear and peace movements since the late 1950s.[27] They wrote:

We, the ARTISTS AND WRITERS PROTEST, call upon you to participate in a Collage of Indignation, to be mounted in the cause of peace, from January 29 to February 4, 1967, at Loeb Student Centre, New York University. Titled *The Angry Arts*, it will feature, in a context of happenings, poetry readings, films, music and theater, panoramic sized canvases, upon which you the artists of New York, are asked to paint, draw, or attach whatever images or objects that will express or stand for your anger against the war . . . We are also interested in whatever manner of visual invective, political caricature, or related savage materials you would care to contribute. Join in a spirit of cooperation with other artistic communities of this city in a desperate plea for sanity.[28]

The letter opens with vivid reference to the 'flesh lacerating effects of American fragmentation bombing in North Vietnam' and to 'the black-mail of pointless escalation'. This was to be a collective protest against 'a U.S. policy perpetrated in our name'. The Artists and Writers Protest were co-sponsors of the week with the Greenwich Village Peace Centre, New York University (NYU) Students for a Democratic Society and Committee of the Professions. Organisation was vital. Committees with heads were formed, a chairman (Robert Reitz) elected and a co-ordinator appointed, Carol Grosberg, who became the only full-time paid member of Angry Arts. The main committees were under the headings of Theater; Films and Photography; Painters and Sculptors; Poets and Writers; Folk Rock; Music; Dance. A specific committee for *The Collage of Indignation* was set up.[29] An initial list contains seventy-three names of participating artists, Rudolf Baranik's report cites 150, a draft of an advertisement in the *New York Times* lists 143,[30] Kozloff's review says 'more than a hundred' and an official 'Supporters and Participants – Partial List' from February 1967 lists thirty under 'Painters and Sculptors'.[31] The large advertisement in *The Village Voice* and *The New York Times* included seven headings under 'Angry Arts Sponsors and Participants (Partial List)' with fifty-one names under 'Painters and Sculptors'.[32]

Angry Arts

The Collage of Indignation, exhibited at the Loeb Students Centre gallery, New York University, was a linked sequence of twenty 10-feet by 6-feet many-imaged canvases. Much of it was made in a loft in Prince Street over five days by the artists painting, fixing on objects, images, and slogans. Baranik, one of the participants, stated that the '150 artists' who contributed to the collage were as diverse as the New York art world, and especially so as many of the 'artists went out of their vein to say what they wanted to say':

Thus Allan D'Arcangelo's Highway-culture-hard-edge made way for 10th Street-Protest-spattered-doll-expressionism. Many artists simply wrote, or combined writing with their images. Dorothy Koppelman painted a falling dove, and then wrote 'I am ashamed of what my country is doing in Vietnam' – honest and simple. Most voices were more accusing. Verbal branding of Johnson as a child-murderer were repeated again and again, as were savage caricatures. Such were the works of Herb Leopold, Jay Midler, Irving Petlin, Bud Hopkins, Eddie Johnson, Anton Refregier, Antonio Frasconi. Mark di Suvero planked down a slab of rusty metal on which he cut with a torch a curse to Johnson and a remembrance of the killed children of Vietnam. He placed sheets of paper next to his sculpture-testimonial, and the people, including the students of NYU, instinctively knew what to do: they signed their names, voting with Mark against Johnson. There were pleas and there were slogans. May Stevens wrote 'Morrison Shall never Die,' reminding us about the Quaker who died at the steps of the Pentagon, and whom the Peace movement should at least remember. Raphael Soyer simply said 'Stop bombing women and children.' The Black Mask group wrote: REVOLUTION.[33]

Alongside such works, Baranik identified works by artists whom he described as using a 'broadly defined expressionist language' such as Leon Golub's *Burnt Man*, a scorched image by Si Lewen and Baranik's own black print cancelled out by a white band across. In contrast was 'the statement' by James Rosenquist in 'true Pop language':

> Here a coil of shiny silvery barbed wire told the whole story. The rusty wire of the thirties gave way to the silvery shine, because this is the language of today. But more important was the other level of understanding this statement: the war waged by the richest country on earth against the aspirations of the poor was described here with great laconic precision.[34]

Some of the other artists represented were Roy Lichtenstein, Ad Reinhardt, Jack Youngerman, Nancy Spero, Balcomb Greene, Jack Levine, Matta, Karel Appel, Richard Serra, Jon Hendricks, Nancy Graves, Alice Neel and Pheobe Sonenberg. Nancy Spero depicted a helicopter as a monstrous people-eater, an image related to her bombs and helicopter series; Nancy Graves produced a piece with 'Hump War'; Alice Neel's subject was McNamara and Vietnamese victims; Si Lewin stuck matches to a burnt head signifying the issue of napalm, which was also echoed by Golub's photostats from his 'Burnt Man' series. As Baranik discusses, a central target was President Johnson, with many critical portraits and slogans including Chaim Koppleman with his flame-thrower President.[35] Drawing parallels with 'a collective "large character poster" as it is called in today's China', Baranik regarded the strengths of *The Collage of Indignation* as its 'immediacy and strident insistence . . . drawn in cliches and deliberate vulgarity . . . [hitting] out in every possible direction with fury and channeless force. And so the cluttered and spattered white canvas became, if not the most eloquent, surely the most angry voice of the Angry Arts.'[36] Described as an extraordinary spectacle, the gallery containing the *Collage* was jammed at all times by 'hordes of visitors': while a tape of Pope John's arrival in New York and his message to the UN was played, spectators closely and attentively "read" the *Collage*.'[37]

The schedule of events for the week of Angry Arts consistently stressed the word 'Dissent': 'Broadway Dissents'; 'Off-Broadway Dissents'; 'Dancers Dissent'; 'Folk Rock Dissent'; 'Avant Garde Musicians Dissent'; 'Musicians Dissent'; 'Artists Dissent'; 'Poets and Writers Dissent'; 'Photographers

Dissent'.[38] All these were headings to events and performances by leading artists and practioners. Carol Grosberg, co-ordinating plans for the
week at the Greenwich Peace Centre, made an important distinction: 'It
will be a real artistic protest rather than a political protest of artists.'[39]
She emphasised the spontaneity of the plans and the co-operation among
the artists, film-makers, dancers, actors and musicians: a week which
'will be a collage of expressions'.[40] One of these started as an advertised
part of 'Poets and Writers Dissent', with fifty participants co-ordinated
by the playwright Robert Nichols, at the Washington Square Methodist
Church, entitled 'An Act of respect for the Vietnamese People':[41]

> Musicians will play – not interpret – Vietnamese music. Susan Sontag will
> read from Buddhist texts. Some people will talk about the rivers, others
> about the villages, the food, the families of the country. 'Each scene,' Nichols
> said, 'will be dedicated to an individually named Vietnamese, a real person,
> alive or dead, burned or whole.'[42]

The event included Peter Schumann's Bread and Puppet Theatre presentation. This radical political production group was founded by the
pacificist Schumann, sculptor and choreographer, who came to the United
States from Germany in 1961. He thought that theatre should be as basic
as bread, and the group, using enormous puppets and masks, became a
focal point of dissent at rallies, demonstrations and in the streets. In this
particular event, a physician lectured in dispassionate medical language
five medical students in white masks. As the physician's voice described
the variety of napalm burns, the treatment of burns and dosages of
morphine, he paced in front of a table with a motionless puppet representing a Vietnamese citizen. Slowly the puppet moved, extended a giant
hand to the audience to try to bind up its wounded fingers with sliding
sheets of newspaper in a fumbling gesture of the helplessness of the
victims of war. The day continued with folk tales, facts about the rape
of eleven-year-olds, slides of napalmed faces, scenes from a Vietnamese
wedding, segments of the lives of six Vietnamese women, and piercing
tapes of bombings and bodies. The event moved late in the evening with
the cast and many of the audience descending on

> the black-tie culture seekers at Lincoln Center. As the first sequined toe
> emerged from the opera at 10.50, bird calls – presumably dove – were
> sounded . . . the angry artists, dressed for their night at the opera, wore
> bracelets of oriental bells, pendants of engraved gongs, cardboard peasant
> hats – inscribed with the words 'Peace' and 'Vietnam'. A high-fashion lady
> stopped and stared incredulously at the group through four pairs of false
> eyelashes.[43]

Alongside such events, there was a 'Special Angry Arts Film Programme'
during the week, a 'Children's Programme' and a 'Caravan of the Angry

Arts'. The latter was an ancient 24-foot flat-bed former garbage truck that visited some fifteen street corners in Manhattan (Greenwich Village, Metropolitan Museum of Art, Harlem etc.), Brooklyn and the Bronx on the Tuesday, Thursday and Saturday between 12 noon and 9 p.m.[44] It carried fifteen to twenty poets and actors (the 'Pageant Players'),[45] 'folk singers and rock-rollers', artists and films. Twelve thousand leaflets, prepared by Joel Sloman, were distributed. With a cover of a napalmed child and the caption 'FOR THIS YOU'VE BEEN BORN?', the leaflet contained eight pages of poems and a last page asking whether readers were 'alarmed because we have burned alive a quarter of a million Vietnamese children'. It appealed for help in stopping the mutilation and killing of Vietnamese children and their families – 'America is Obliterating Vietnam, both Land and People: Can You Ignore It?' – and said how to get in touch with the peace movement. At first, the truck had an enormous float sign prepared by Allan D'Arcangelo of a huge painting of LBJ as a dragon with Lady Bird Johnson riding him.[46] After the painting had been half destroyed 'by accident' while the truck was being moved in its storage garage, D'Arcangelo's float sign was replaced by six enormous blow-ups of photographs of napalm victims by William F. Pepper.[47] Napalm had a vivid contemporary resonance referenced by the distributed leaflet: 'read the December issue of *Ramparts* magazine and look at the 16 pages of our fire-carving'. The leaflet was actually referring to the January issue, which published 'The Children of Vietnam', containing a 'Preface' by Dr Benjamin Spock' and 'Photographs and Text' by Pepper.[48] The twenty black and white and three colour photographs of disfigured Vietnamese children and mothers burned by napalm had deeply affected many Americans, including Martin Luther King, who became radically opposed to the war on seeing them in January 1967.[49] *Ramparts* had already explored the role of napalm, drawing readers' attention, in August 1966, to the application by United Technology Centre (UTC), a subsidiary of United Aircraft, to 'produce 100 million pounds of napalm under a contract with the department of Defense' in the port area of Redwood City, California. Standard Oil Company wished to sublease the 2.18 acres to UTC that they already leased.[50] The article describes both the horrific effects of napalm in Vietnam and the protests in Redwood City against the approval of the sublease. Earlier in the December 1965 issue, Bernard F. Fall produced photographs and text in his 'Vietnam Album' on his return from the war which he found 'depersonalized' and 'dehumanized'.[51]

Mixing the conventions of carnival, caravan, agit-prop, the 'Caravan of the Angry Arts' drew large crowds, some hostile with shouts of 'Commie', during the week. The performances were finally ended on the last day by the police in Harlem. On 124th Street and Lenox Avenue all of the performers received massive support. Then the police arrived: 'After

45 minutes of an hour program they show, examine permits. "Where's your American flag?" We hadn't had one all week and had never been asked for one. "The law says you gotta have one."' After a hunt by supporters, a small paper flag mounted on a tooth pick is found: 'Huge cheer. Man from crowd leaps on truck and holds flag aloft. Cop, "Sorry, it has to be three feet by four." . . . David Henderson takes the mike and tells the crowd that the cops are making us go, but that this didn't happen in any other neighbourhood . . . A Super Finale, thanks to the police.'[52] Why had the police turned up in Harlem on the last day? One possible reason was anxiety about the potential powerful links between Civil Rights activities and the peace movement. Another was the growing awareness of the relationship between higher instances of poverty amongst African-Americans at home and the higher percentage of African-American United States soldiers dying in the war in Vietnam.

Only a month later, on 4 April 1967, in the pulpit of the Riverside Church, a few blocks away at Riverside Drive and 122nd Street, Martin Luther King condemned the United States' role in the war to an overflowing audience of three thousand. Identifying the United States government as 'the greatest purveyor of violence in the world today', he called attention to the vicious destruction of the hopes of the poor in the United States and in Vietnam:

> it became clear to me that the war was doing far more than devastating the hopes of the poor at home. It was sending their sons and their brothers and their husbands to fight and to die in extraordinarily high proportions relative to the rest of the population. We were taking the young black men who had been crippled by our society and sending them 8000 miles away to guarantee liberties in Southeast Asia which they had not found in Southwest Georgia and East Harlem.[53]

King also asked Americans to consider the destructive connections between racism, militarism, materialism and anti-Communism. He argued that, in the previous decade, such connections placed the United States on the wrong side of a world revolution, particularly the non-white poor throughout the developing world.[54] The choices he proposed, for peace in Vietnam, for justice, for a 'true revolution in values', was addressed to a packed audience in this huge church on the edge of Morningside Heights and Harlem.

A few weeks earlier, the performers in the Caravan of the Angry Arts were addressing a similar constituency but admitted to having 'ambiguous feelings' about being a group that was '80% white' in the midst of Harlem; the reception was, however, one of 'incredible friendliness'.[55] Some of these 'feelings' were the product of domestic social and economic relations that also produced a 'cruel irony', identified by King a few weeks later: 'we have been repeatedly faced with the cruel irony of watching Negro and white boys on TV screens as they kill and die together for a nation that has been unable to seat them together in the same schools. So we watch them in brutal solidarity burning the huts of a poor village, but we realize that they would never live on the same block in Detroit.'[56] Nor would they live on the same block in Harlem – a block where the police asked the Caravan of the Angry Arts a question that presupposed a notion of a unified nation and its symbols: ' "Where's your American flag?" '[57]

The American flag

Nationhood and its ironic symbol of the American flag had another specific resonance for *The Collage of Indignation*. On Monday 30 January a construction by Marc Morrel was removed from the *Collage* on the orders of C. D. Spiegel, director of the student centre, on the advice of John Blazys, University co-ordinator of protection. The construction incorporated a facsimile of the American flag, as had previous sculptures by the artist. The University authorities regarded Morrel's work as showing 'disrespect' to the American flag and, therefore, open to the prosecution under federal legislation. Within nationalist ideology, the American flag was a symbol of particular values and beliefs that remained unquestioned and which must not be 'desecrated'. Perhaps the most public symbolic embodiment was, and is, the Iwo Jima statue, in Arlington National Cemetery, with five sculpted Marines, 32 feet high, raising a bronze flag pole 62 feet long. This public art work, celebrating a particular patriotic event in the war with the Japanese in 1945, includes a massive bronze flag pole from which permanently flies an actual Stars and Stripes. In 1968 the statue became a major element in Kienholz's *The Portable War Memorial*.[58]

In the United States the flag had become a secular symbol endowed with religious majesty and religious reverence, not least after the Second World War, enshrined in an act of the early Cold War when Flag Day had been instituted in 1949. Not surprisingly, then, during the 1960s the American flag, the official flag code enacted by Congress in 1942, and its various official presentations became focal points of anti-government protests. The flag or its official code of display were frequently altered by flag burning, flying it inverted or wearing it on clothes such as on the seat of your pants. Consequently, during 1967 federal legislation was going through, passed by Congress in 1968, to deter such acts and to punish anyone who knowingly cast contempt upon any flag of the United States by publicly mutilating, defacing, defiling, burning or trampling upon it. With a possible five-year prison sentence if found guilty, such legislation was a serious dissuasion to any protester. Morrel's art work entered into this space of official patriotism, nationalism and the state's reinvestment in its symbol of censorial power. Ironically, there were other works in the *Collage* that also made reference to the American flag. Ellen and Johan Stellenrad collaged on a United States flag made of paper dolls cut from Chinese newspapers. Above it was Rosenquist's barbed wire evoking the fences in internment camps. On the same panel was Matta's war personage and Petlin's 'L. B. J. Infant People Burner, Long May You Roast in History's Hell.' Cply placed a Stars and Stripes girdle on a painted eagle. None of these was removed. Paradoxically, though, the censorship of Morrel's piece drew attention away from many more defamatory works.[59]

In a press release, the Artists and Writers Protest committee viewed the removal of Morrel's construction as 'an act of unwarranted censorship on the part of New York University'. The press release continues: 'the act was directed against the artist's freedom of expression, and is equally a threat to the autonomy and dignity of the university. It was further viewed as a frightened reaction to the free expression of opinions against the United States' position in the Vietnam conflict.'[60] Morrel's construction was relocated on display at the American Civil Liberties Union, Fifth Avenue, 'in order to make evident the free nature of all works of art. The Artists and Writers Protest committee considers that both Mr. Morrel's work *and* the university are both in essence casualties of the antagonistic climate generated by anti-war actions.'[61] *The Village Voice* reported that, after the police had received complaints from local residents, 'The curtains of the ground floor exhibition hall were ordered closed to shield the protest from passers-by. Morrel's sculpture, which incorporated the likeness of what appeared to be a stuffed American flag, was locked in a closet.'[62]

Another Morrel work, in which he incorporated an American flag, had been hung in the window of his dealer Stephen Radich, on Madison Avenue, in December 1966. Radich was charged with violation of the section of the state Penal Law.[63] It states that no person shall publicly mutilate, deface, defile or defy, trample upon or cast contempt upon the American flag. Morrel exhibited thirteen constructions, one of which was a flag stuffed to suggest a symbolic figure hanging from a yellow noose, another in which the flag was draped in chains, and a third with the flag shaped into a phallus on a cross. In the background to the show were taped anti-war songs. The New York branch of the American Civil Liberties Union which defended Radich called 'the prosecution "a form of cultural suppression" by the police'.[64] In May, Radich, who maintained that the works were 'a kind of "protest" art', was found guilty on a judges' majority decision of 2–1 of '"contemptuous" use and exhibition of the flag' with the alternatives of sixty days in jail or a $500 fine.[65] In a panel discussion, in August 1967, Morrel talked about his use of American flags in his works:

Already it's been proved in court that these are desecrated flags. Therefore I'm illegal, my ideas and my art are illegal, and I'm a walking felon. I may have to flee. If all of a sudden they busted down my door while I am working on one of my sculptures, I'm committing a crime . . . the patriarchs are very upset. I felt that this was the one symbol that could reach people other than a burnt or bloody doll or a draft card. This is a very sacred image to some people – the very people we're fighting, intellectually, not physically, yet.[66]

Gender: politics and performance

Attempts to 'reach people' were rendered problematic by a number of institutional as well as ideological closures. Artists working outside of the mainstream were, in particular, marginalised by the exercise of power in its various forms. Many attempts at critique used radical methods and procedures such as transgression of conventional boundaries of the art object. An example is the work of Carolee Schneemann. Her *Snows*, a 'Kinetic Theatre' performance in the Martinique Theatre on Broadway, was produced to support and be one of the events of Angry Arts Week.[67] *Snows* marked a shift from her earlier emphases on the body in performance to a mixed media event in which both audience and performers were involved in a politicised intervention, which brought home a representation of 'Vietnam' to a winter in New York. Schneemann states:

> *Snows* was built out of my anger, outrage, fury and sorrow for the Vietnamese. The performance contained five films whose related content triggered juxtaposition of a winter environment and Vietnam atrocity images. Of all the films 'Viet-Flakes' was the heart and core of the piece: a source of confirmation and insistence from which movement and related imagery spilled onto the 'snow-bound' audience.[68]

It is important to understand the politicised character of Schneemann's *Snows* in the critical context of 'happenings', performance and other related acts in the United States and Europe. For example, the Fluxus group, from around 1961, attempted both to subvert the conventional notions of 'museum', 'production' and 'commodification', through a diverse set of practices, including performances, events and transgressive critical productions, and to establish an alternative constituency to that normally associated with elite museum-based culture. Viewed by many as a radical, subversive art movement, Fluxus none the less exhibited gender bias. Mariellen Sandford observes in her assessment of the literature on happenings and Fluxus, in particular the special issue of *The Drama Review* (*TDR*) edited by Michael Kirby and Richard Schechner in 1965, that there is an 'underrepresentation of women artists and the back issues of *TDR* are no exception . . . readers of the 1965 issue may have been left with the impression that most of the women participants were those ubiquitous "naked girls" . . . The most obvious omission [in the

1965 issue] was Carolee Schneemann.'[69] By the time of Angry Arts, Schneemann was at the 'forefront of the 1967/68 movement that led to the "politicization of the Happenings genre" as Berghaus puts it'.[70] Sandford also draws attention to the gender exclusive language of these early texts and to Schneemann's critical importance in critiques of the contemporary male-dominated art world. Further, Rebecca Schneider discusses at length how Schneemann's work of the 1960s was paradoxically essentialist and constructivist at once: using her own female body in performances, regarded by many males as 'messy', which were the product of her own agency, 'her status as constructor, artist, active creator'.[71] In performances such as *Meat Joy* (1964) and films such as *Fuses* (1964/5), Schneider argues that Schneemann

> wanted her body to remain erotic, sexual, both 'desired and desiring,' while underscoring it as clearly volitional as well: 'marked, written over in a text of stroke and gesture discovered by my creative female will' . . . Schneemann was making it hard as possible to attribute her active creation to a 'stray male principle.' The male/female binarism was thus confused. Was the artist making or finding the object or was the object making the artist?[72]

This 'double gesture', or 'double agency', was deeply unsettling to many contemporary viewers, for whom it undermined conventional power boundaries of gender and sexuality.[73] In *Fuses*, Schneemann made a film of her long-time lover and herself lovemaking, stressing its material status as *film* and her role as producer. Whilst the film is of her body in intimacy, it is also altered by Schneemann materially: 'baked, stamped, stained, painted, chopped, and reassembled . . . I wanted to put into that *materiality* of film the energies of the body.'[74] Her active creation was to make the film different from sexually explicit pornography because there was 'no objectification or fetishization of the woman'.[75] In this sense it had a particular implicit politics.

In *Snows*, Schneemann's 'double agency' was characterised by a more explicit politicisation of these boundaries by references to Vietnam. As far back as 1960, Schneemann and her partner, musician James Tenney, had become conscious of the relationships between United States military action in Vietnam and the legacy of McCarthyism. While both on graduate fellowships at the University of Illinois they meet a young woman Vietnamese poet who told Schneemann about

> the deep and pervasive traditions of poetry among all the Vietnamese; that reverence for nature and for ancestors was shared by rural and urban settlements, that the French had long been a disruptive presence there controlling oil, tin, rubber and opium; that American military forces were subverting the economy and were destroying farming villages, building barbed wire encampments for farmers, radical professors, intellectuals. We had heard nothing of this before.[76]

At the same time there were numerous unofficial and official reports that confirmed 'an uncanny paranoia we felt to be the unravelling fabric of the cold-war and McCarthy pursuits'.[77] In 1966, Schneemann returned to these concerns with a renewed awareness of both 'mass murder' in Vietnam[78] and the 'helpless apathy over, what is now, our Dirty War; there is almost no motion towards political engagement, statement, by the advanced artists here'.[79] One reaction was 'Peace Parade Committee Commitment',[80] which was largely an urban product and part of experiences in that part of her life which was centred on the culture and society of New York. Another was to give expressive potential to experiences in the rural settlement, in upstate New York, that formed an alternative place from the early 1960s onwards:

> In the Summer of '66 Jim [James Tenney] was witness to hallucinations I suffered in the country, of Vietnamese bodies hanging in the trees; the kitchen stove became a miniature village, smouldering – seen from above – and I was afraid to bake in it. I was editing 'Fuses' (16mm) and began to make super 8 film from Viet-nam atrocity photographs; gradually drawings and notes formed a sinister reverie building towards a theatre piece.[81]

During 1966 Schneemann completed the super-8 film, entitled *Viet-Flakes*, using Vietnam atrocity photographs cut from papers and magazines during the years 1958–64. She used a close-up lens and a magnifying glass to travel across and within the photographs laid on the floor in arcs. The effect was a rough animation of in and out of focus images of Vietnamese 'people burning, dragged, drowning' with a soundtrack by Tenney of fragments of Bach, Mozart, the Beatles, Jackie de Shannon, and Vietnamese, Laotian and south Chinese songs.[82] *Viet-Flakes*, 11 minutes long, ended the whole performance, which began with a silent newsreel from 1947 of a series of catastrophes. While the latter is projected a performer sweeps snow debris along the stage and a sound collage of trains is overlaid and juxtaposed with sounds of orgasm. Within the performance the bodies of performers become 'victims', 'pursuers' and 'interference' in a structured score. Towards the end a dragged body is hung from a looped rope as in photographs of Vietnamese bodies hanging in the trees. This powerful image of the body hung by its feet was also used in George Segal's *The Execution*, a tableau exhibited in *Protest and Hope*, an exhibition in the New School Art Centre in autumn 1967.

Schneemann's *Snows* and Morrel's United States flag construction, removed by the New York Police Department and New York University from *The Collage of Indignation*, represent two distinct interventions within the dominant structures of the contemporary art world. Both engage with a range of intellectual, moral and public issues that were excluded from the art world as defined by the critical paradigms of Michael Fried, *Artforum* and the Museum of Modern Art. The context of their interventions raises fundamental issues about audience and cultural values. Angry Arts estimated that in the week 62,000 people saw 40 performances in theatres and churches, comprising 10 plays, 17 concerts, 9 film showings, a napalm poetry reading, 3 panel discussions and one seven-hour Vietnamese life project. These numbers were apart from those who visited the Caravan or the members of the concert audience who became surprised parts of the Vietnam Life Happening at Lincoln Centre. The Loeb Student Centre estimated that ten thousand visited *The Collage of Indignation* and the Werner Bischoff exhibition of photographs, *Life in Vietnam*. There was also a 'Contemplation Room' event in which 220 colour slides of Vietnamese life were combined with tapes from Dale Minor's WBAI reports,[83] and a War Toy Exhibit. In all, these programmes and projects engaged some five hundred artists, painters, sculptors, writers, poets, film-makers, musicians, playwrights, dancers, actors and stage technicians.[84] *The Collage of Indignation* itself was again on show at Columbia University in May 1967. It came, eventually, to a specific end. An un-named central member of the enterprise is reported to have burnt the whole thing in order to ensure the critical aspects of its production and reception. It was designed to be an intervention, a specific act of dissent against the government and the war, an angry critique of the autonomous art object. It was not to be enshrined in a museum or art gallery nor turned into the marketable commodities of particular artists.

Angry Arts as an organisation continued to engage in activities, obtaining a Certificate of Incorporation in June 1967 'to sponsor programs and activities by artists related to their media and to social issues, and to raise funds through these and other programs to affectuate [*sic*] such purposes'.[85] Following Angry Arts Week several activities were pursued, with committee heads meeting regularly to co-ordinate events in New York and to liaise with groups planning similar weeks in Chicago, Washington, DC and Philadelphia. Several universities, including Colorado, Pittsburg, MIT and Oregon, had requested film programmes, folk-song programmes, concerts and napalm poetry readings. Particularly popular was the film collage, which was a parallel, by several film-makers, to *The Collage of Indignation*. Angry Arts also contributed to the Spring Mobilization to End the War in Vietnam that was held in New York (and San Francisco) on 15 April. The rally and parade were the largest then recorded in the United States. Protesters gathered in Central Park's Sheep Meadow where Angry Arts had six decorated performing platforms along the periphery and another six floats in the parade itself. One of them by Morrel was a float bearing a 20-foot mound of yellow cloth, representing Vietnam, topped by a coffin covered by an American flag. The expenditure for the day ($2500) threw Angry Arts into serious financial crisis, and several plans, appeals and pledges of support were implemented.[86] The strength of commitment and organisation was unparalleled amongst artists. Just prior to the Spring Mobilization plans were made to take Angry Arts to Washington, DC from 6 to 9 April as a forerunner to the events on 15 April and to ensure that the momentum for Angry Arts did not simply fade. James Rosenquist designed a float for the poets for an event on 11 March which was planned to go to Washington where poets would read in conjunction with the Pageant Players. Plans included Robert Bly to set up a napalm poetry reading and Peter Schumann's Bread and Puppet Theatre.[87]

The Collage of Indignation: 'gross, vulgar, clumsy, ugly'; 'nasty, degraded Expressionism'

Central participants and supporters of Angry Arts and of *The Collage of Indignation* characterised the events in unusual terms. For Leon Golub the *Collage* was 'gross, vulgar, clumsy, ugly! – exaggeration to the point of bombast'.[88] For Max Kozloff 'this aesthetic wailing wall, this convocation of clichés and cretinisms, which was the "Collage of Indignation," was alienated and homeless in style, as well as embattled in content . . . it might charitably be described as a nasty, degraded Expressionism, long ago discredited as an atavism in the history of American art'.[89] Significantly, for both writers the type of evaluations and interpretations to be found in the specialist currency of critical rhetoric was inappropriate to the activities and events of Angry Arts which were designed to be outside of established gallery, museum and art journal conventions. But this inappropriateness was also the basis for paradox.

How to characterise Angry Arts when, as Golub states, 'Today art is largely autonomous and concerned with perfectibility'?[90] How to avoid criticisms of special pleading? How to invert the specialist rhetoric of contemporary art? Kozloff's long review reveals the difficulties and discomforts of such ambitions, not only in his actual text but also in the light of his position as one of the originators of the project itself.

Kozloff was the resident art critic of *The Nation*, as well as a regular contributor to *Artforum*. In the opening paragraphs of his text on the *Collage*, he struggles with a number of dilemmas. His specialist vocabulary and distinctions as a critic for *Artforum* were not those expected by readers of *The Nation*, with its politically left-wing and culturally broad allegiances, wishing to learn more about 'Angry Arts'. He puts the *Artforum* specialisms to one side but, in doing so, a series of fissures open up in the specialist assumptions and definitions of 'art', 'artist' and 'public life'. Almost immediately Kozloff raises the problem of the relationship between art and politics in the United States in terms of the world of 'print' – the public domain – and the world of the troubled mind: the private concerns with permissible and legitimated pronouncements. This becomes a metaphor for his subsequent struggle over the pressing social and political character of public protest as distinct from the insulated world of art. For example, Kozloff writes of the 'predicament of trying to resolve divergent obligations – intellectual and moral' particularly when 'artists' had 'been hyper-defensive about their autonomy as creators'.[91] Art critics, too, had repeatedly created the conditions in which such a hyper-defensive attitude was accepted as normal. Kozloff writes in his first paragraph about the 'misgivings of an art critic' and, within a short time, argues that artists are at fault socially and politically because of 'their piety about art's boundaries'.[92] One problem for Kozloff is that the category 'artist' is not explored, thereby presupposing a particular model of behaviour, interests and values. Perhaps he did not wish to examine the dominant persona of the 'artist' which sustained his own career as a contemporary art critic. Alternatively, he may have been making ironic and critical reference to a specialist art world about which he was ambivalent. His career and cultural commitment to such a specialism, a significant 'other' to the world of *The Nation*, could not be denied as a core of his own identity. Yet he thinks that present social and political circumstances render claims for autonomy as 'excessively delicate' and make a mockery of current art's 'presumption to operate within the "gap" between art and life'.[93] Similarly, when he writes about 'the public', a generalisation is used: 'The failure of imagination on the part of the public is its blindness to the truths behind socio-political protests or documentary images (let alone art).'[94]

Kozloff develops his discussion by examining what makes 'this condition so paradoxical' and in so doing enters into further paradoxes of his own. He characterises both 'artists' and 'the public' as too uncritical, too lacking in imagination, too afraid of 'informing passion'. There is, he argues, a contemporary 'insulation from disturbance' and, with an acknowledgement of his own predicament, he states that a 'refusal to work to minimize one's own complicity in it, may become signs of an anxious rigidity'.[95] 'Complicity' and 'anxious rigidity' are revealing characterisations given the powerful paradigms of the dominant contemporary art world which in its critical endorsement of the autonomy of art encouraged apathy with respect to a range of current social and political struggles and a rigid condemnation and exclusion of art with signs of political engagement. Yet Kozloff is caught in a dilemma: as a successful art critic he is complicit in the defence of the autonomy of art, while as a citizen participant he is active in political engagement. In an attempt to infuse the former with some texture of the latter, Kozloff claims that the diversity of current pictorial and sculptural American art is 'charged with a proper disquietude'. Realising the risks of such a claim, he immediately adds a qualification: 'Or rather, a latency that can be read as such.' And in another claim and qualification, Kozloff characterises contemporary art as more 'caught up with the confounding issues and pressures of its society' than any other serious avant garde in the previous hundred years 'which is not to say at all that ours is a "protest" art'.[96]

With *The Collage of Indignation* Kozloff sees an attempt by artists 'to enfranchise their protest'. Not with an 'actual anti-war iconography' but with a series of individual attempts to overcome the 'mute and immobile' character of painting and sculpture. In a conventional bifurcation he identifies a tradition of art concerned with 'political activism', singling out the WPA and Ben Shahn in American art, the Surrealists, Picasso's *Guernica*, the Mexican Muralists, Grosz, and Kollwitz. In the *Collage*, which Kozloff describes as a 'frenzy of Expressionism', he perceives a series of negatives. The artists responded with 'borrowed rags', a 'vocabulary of the past', a 'failure of quality of mind, or artistic imagination'. The art was characterised by 'tawdriness and slovenliness' and became a 'self-sacrificing target' attracting the arrows of criticism that should have been aimed at the country's industrial military complex.[97] Two-thirds through the review Kozloff begins to open up some of the central paradoxes. Should he impose 'aesthetic criteria' on an exhibition were artists were clearly indifferent to such judgements? Perhaps in such circumstances, he suggests, a critic can forgo professional scruples. But in the *Collage* he only sees a 'visual expletive', an hysteria on which no one will act. For him those examples of 'ambitious art' within the piece (such as Rosenquist's) are too sophisticated for the 'body politic'. Many other practioners of 'ambitious art' did not participate because they were confounded by the conflicts between 'ethics and métier' and so convinced of their powerlessness that they *become* powerless. Others – the affluent, abstract, better-known practiners – were absent 'almost out of a sense of self-preservation' for their art world status.[98]

In his final paragraphs Kozloff returns to the positive effects of Angry Arts in general – the poetry, film, performance, posters – while critical of that work with which he had a professional interest: 'to find the crystallization of metaphor and language which would kindle an audience to an antiwar purpose (and avoid the pitfalls of the "Collage" artists) is still beyond the imagination, if not the talents and energies of current painters'.[99] Kozloff's heavy criticism and unease about the issues of art and politics, on the one hand, and the relationship between large career and cultural investment in the autonomy of art, on the other hand, produced a review full of the paradoxes both of his own position and of the contemporary art world. These paradoxes are compounded by Kozloff's participation in Angry Arts as an organiser and in *The Collage of Indignation* itself, in which he exhibited a landscape spattered with red paint.

Leon Golub in his article in *Arts Magazine* is not worried about the paradoxes identifiable in Kozloff's review. He regards many of the same characteristics of *The Collage of Indignation* differently, locating them in the specific context of 1967. He is less troubled by the general concerns of 'aesthetic criteria' that preoccupied Kozloff. Whilst Golub acknowledges that the success of the *Collage* as art is problematic, its public success was 'remarkable'. Much of the basis of this judgement rests on a view of 'art' which is the product of Golub having been marginalised by the critical mainstream. This marginalisation had been since, at least, the art establishment's critical reaction to *New Images of Man*, an exhibition, in which Golub participated, held at the Museum of Modern Art, New York, in autumn 1959. This exhibition, organised by Peter Selz, included work that did not subscribe to modernist abstraction and to the claimed apartness of art from life. Golub was aware in 1967 that an artist angry at United States involvement in Vietnam and the specific use of napalm could not easily burst through the channels that sustained beliefs and institutional investments in autonomous art. For Kozloff it was important that *alternative* practices should be established where the particularity of reference could replace what he called the melancholy fatalism or a willed powerlessness of much contemporary art. Such an ambition is predicated on positive assumptions about the value of individual art objects and the institutional paradigms of legitimation and control. For Golub, alternatives were no replacement for *oppositional* practices which included inverting existing evaluative criteria and establishing venues that 'spill over into the street':

> Disaffection explodes as caricature, ugliness or insult and defamation – the strong disavowal of intellectuals and artists (comparable to French protests about Indochina and Algeria). Such anger today can only be made up of pieces of art, guises of art, gestures using art habits, caricature, calumny, etc. This is not political art but rather a popular revulsion. Artists came to demonstrate their fury and shame. There is refined and subtle protest on the Collage. But essentially the work is angry – against the war, against the bombing, against President Johnson etc. The Collage is gross, vulgar, clumsy, ugly! – exaggeration to the point of bombast. The artist breaks the contained limits of his art. His actions spill over into the street.[100]

Golub emphasises aspects which are the inversion of the contemporary discourse of critical evaluation. He does so with reference to 'the street', a symbol of otherness to the enculturation experience of middle-class America, designed to keep people off the streets and in their living rooms. 'The street' is an actual site of protest and dissent but in the 1960s it was also a symbolic place being transformed by the growing effects of television. In 1967 was published Marshall McLuhan's and Quentin Fiore's *The Medium is the Message*, in which they argued that a politics of participation via the television – in freedom marches, in war, in revolution, pollution and other events – would change everything.[101] But, despite McLuhan's and Fiore's optimism, some things were still rooted in unquestioned assumptions. For example, the radicalism of Golub's views, as with most other texts of the period, still presupposes a male artist despite the numerous women who participated in the *Collage* and in Angry Arts generally. Even radical texts and practices that sought active critique of the structures of power, permissibility and control lacked a consciousness about gender. Artists such as Schneemann testify to this lack, in for example Fluxus, as does Poppy Johnson, a core member of the Guerrilla Art Action Group which included Jon Hendricks and Jean Toche.[102]

'The street'

'The street', though, was an important signifier in the political transformations of the late 1960s, with Civil Rights marches, mass anti-war demonstrations, the Yippies' 'Museum of the Streets' and Peter Schumann's Bread and Puppet Theatre, whose huge political puppets and masks were at most rallies and demonstrations from 1964 to the autumn of 1967.[103] Golub indexes the *Collage* to traditions of current oppositional practices by claiming that the artists strove to 'rough-up' their attitudes 'to spit, to let go' so that the whole work became a 'carrier of indignation harking back to street art, graffiti, burlesque, the carnival, the dance of death'.[104] It was these aspects of practice that informed work shown at the Judson Gallery when run by Jon Hendricks, such as the '12 Evenings of Manipulations' in October 1967, followed by the 'Judson Publications Manifesto' signed by Al Hansen, Jon Hendricks, Ralph Ortiz, Lil Picard and Jean Toche. The latter declared that they were 'concerned with the corruption of culture by profit. We believe the function of the artist is to subvert culture, since our culture is trivial.'[105] In his 'Some Notes, 11 December, 1967', Hendricks locates the 'Manipulations' events of 'destructionist art' in a series of oppositions to contemporary American life such as the preoccupation with media rhetoric and image, news coverage of 'body counts' as distinct from the realities in Vietnam, the hypocrisies of law, order and justice in the 'American way' dominated by racism, poverty and self-protection. The events were characterised as an opposition both to apathy and to 'a condition of art that says pure/ considered/constructed/classic. The destructionists are in opposition; they are a romantic movement. They are messy and aren't very polite. It would be kind of hard to show them at Castelli's this year. Not much to buy either. Maybe they are anti-American.'[106]

Leo Castelli's Gallery was a main commercial venue establishing artistic careers and guaranteeing a trading provenance for collectors' investments. As we have seen, a boom in American domestic consumer durables was matched by one in high art at time when struggles for Civil Rights, crises of poverty and violence in Vietnam were at the forefront of many

Americans' experiences. Structures of government and media denial, dissuasion and evasion made it hard to place basic questions of realism and statements of truth on a broad public agenda. It was a major aim of the Judson Publications Manifesto to give voice to artists who wished to 'shout fire when there is a fire; robbery when there is a robbery; murder when there is a murder; rape when there is a rape'. Further, the 'Judson Publications will attempt to serve the public for as long as the trivial culture of the establishment distracts us from the screams of crises'.[107]

The first of the twelve evenings[108] was Ralph Ortiz's 'Destruction Room' and 'Brainwash', which was an attempt to produce a happening whereby participants became aware of their most destructive and aggressive urges. These were, Ortiz argued, turned into depersonalised war psychologies in an American civilisation dominated by a machine aesthetic. Participants were encouraged to realise their urges in the destruction of the contents of the room – furniture, china, bric-à-brac, clothing, pictures of loved and hated ones, magazines such as *Reader's Digest, Life, Time* and *Playboy*. For Ortiz, in the process 'we educate ourselves to these awesome forces and their awesome possibilities and personalize an aspect of ourselves long depersonalized'.[109] This aim and the two parts of the event evoke Georges Bataille's analyses, in the 1930s, of the way that similar depersonalised processes underpinned Fascism. Accompanying Ortiz's text and images in the *Manipulations* publication was an 'explode this war in Vietnam bag' – reminiscent of sick bags – covered in media images and newspaper text of military action in Vietnam. Bici Hendricks used ice, and in the Judson publication included a small paper flag mounted on a tooth pick in a plastic bag with the instruction 'Defrost the American Flag'. In the same publication Al Hansen addressed newspaper obsessions with bizarre murders and disasters. In Malcolm Goldstein's *State of the Nation*, President Johnson's speech, a statement on Vietnam, was excerpted, spliced and looped on several tape machines around the room with the audience invited to participate and to transform by new editing, splicing new relations together, changing the speeds and volumes of machines.

In a development of her *Snows*, Carolee Schneemann produced an environmental work, entitled *Ordeals*, on the theme of Vietnam at the Judson Church on 29 August 1967. Two months later, on 19 October, her *Divisions and Rubble*, 'a destruction event', was the ninth in the evenings of *Manipulations*. This, too, was directly indexed to Vietnam and included photos from her film *Viet-Flakes*: 'An environment which people will have to destroy to enter it, to move in it: means of action altering action/means of perception altering perception. An exposed process.'[110] The room was a place where materials from previous manipulations could be incorporated: 'A discomforting labyrinth, cubicles, closures all through it of paper or fabric which participants would have to first cut and tear their way through. Grim, dark and dirty.'[111] In stepping forward, spectator-participants activated a switch under the foot which started fans blowing on a suspended wire cage full of Vietnam atrocity photographs. As Schneemann notes, the space was very small, no money was available, found materials had to be used from the local Thompson and West 4th Street vicinity and there were few days to construct the environment. She used a rotten mattress, plastic garbage bags filled with leaves, old clothes, food containers, discarded toys and dirty papers, and collaged one wall with a huge torn image of LBJ and photos from *Viet-Flakes*. Every such event has what Schneemann calls its 'Star Stars', activists with energy, presence, response and reaction:

> Star of Divisions and Rubble happened to be Carol Grosberg (director of Angry Arts) . . . self-involved she moved rags around, kicked open doors, knocked piles of leaves open, napped on the rotten mattress, rhythmically attacked ripped montage of LBJ with red paint, became immersed in a hacking structure of red and black stroked over walls, molding, windows, around into photo images. Her activity setting off impulses in others; rich confusion of actions.[112]

Such practices were the antithesis of those valued by Michael Fried as represented by his 'Art and Objecthood' published in *Artforum* in June 1967. Significantly, though Schneemann's work and the events of Angry Arts would appear to characterise the sensibility or mode of being that for him was corrupted or perverted by 'theatre', his text did not even register their existence. Within his Modernist aesthetic, they did not register as 'art' at all, not least because of their associations with the broader cultural values and activities of the New Left. As we have seen, a critic such as Kozloff also had major problems with work that undermined the traditions, conventions and evaluations of modernism in its various theoretical forms. In this he was in a similar position to radical critics and historians associated with the Old Left such as Meyer Schapiro and Harold Rosenberg.

In *The New Yorker* in 1968, Harold Rosenberg, rooted in the traditions of the Old Left, told a revealing story about a five-day conference of artists and intellectuals in Caracas in the autumn of 1967 under the auspices of the Inter-American Foundation for the Arts. The exchange of views centred on 'the definition of "living artistic problems"':

> For some speakers from the New York art world, the issue for painting today is universal recognition of the revolutionary heights scaled by artists to whom the essential significance of painting lies in the shape (square, vertical or horizontal) of the canvas. For the Latin Americans, the issue was 'Yankee imperialism' – an artist, they felt, was obliged to indicate his resistance to existing conditions as a matter of professional honor. The aesthetics of this

resistance ranged from art forms involving audience participation (designed to awaken the masses) to the Dada-related belief that in 'post-modern' art the artist's 'manifestation' counted for more than the art object – a circumspect way of saying that art could go to the devil. In response, a New York painter asseverated that for him painting was bounded by the piece of material he was working on, and his companions, an art critic and a curator, nodded in assent and murmured the word 'quality' . . . The Latin Americans got the point that in New York artists feel themselves exempt from human history – a state of mind which confirmed their feelings about the 'Yankees' and which several confessed to envying. Perhaps the mistake of the New York aesthetes lay in going to a conference, since in the world of 'quality' there are no problems, 'living' or otherwise, to be debated.[113]

Rosenberg was critical of New York aesthetes obsessed with 'the world of "quality"', but he was by no means an uncritical advocate of artists being concerned with 'human history'. In the same article he was negative about 'Angry Arts' while more positive about *Protest and Hope*, an exhibition by forty-three artists at the New School Art Centre in autumn 1967.[114] The latter he saw as an example of artists who 'braved the issue of aesthetic quality versus politics'.[115] Here resides one of the fundamental dilemmas for practioners and critics steeped in particular conventions of high art and its validations, where notions of 'aesthetic quality' and the creative imaginative life had an ineffable value. These were partly rooted in both a commitment to particular modernist pursuits, including institutional manifestations, and a dislike of the implications of leftist attacks, particularly in the 1930s, on the uselessness of abstraction. For Rosenberg, '"Angry Arts" . . . expressed the hopelessness of artists in regard to political art and their contempt for politics or their fear of it in that almost all the works were dashed off without regard for style or standards, as if in a rush to return to the serious business of making paintings and sculptures'.[116] Despite his later reservations, Rosenberg had been named as one of the 'Supporters and Participants' of Angry Arts (under 'Painters and Sculptors') and had participated in the second of the two panel discussions on 'The War, The Artist, His Work' during the week-long events.[117]

In contrast to Angry Arts, Rosenberg regarded *Protest and Hope* as 'an adventure of the artistic intelligence analogous, in a way, to the opposite movement by abstract artists of the 1940's in cutting loose from politics after their discovery that what they had been trying to do under the goading of the left was in conflict with basic processes of the creative imagination'.[118] The latter phrase signals Rosenberg's, and other intellectuals', association in the 1930s with Trotskyism in the face of many leftist emphases on social realism. Many moves towards abstract art (Rosenberg has in mind the generation later labelled Abstract Expressionists) were implicitly or explicitly political. 'Politics' here is associated with parties, groups and factions. For Rosenberg's generation, such associations had been traumatised by the Popular Front, Stalinism and the dissuasive and punitive effects of McCarthyism. Deeply suspicious of organisations and the persuasive possibilities of uncritical doctrine, many artists and critics of Rosenberg's generation appealed to concepts of the individual as a source of 'creative imagination' *other* to capitalist production, mass communications, and commodity fetish. Such acts of dissent did not prevent emphases on 'the aesthetic' with dangers of authoritarian pronouncements, disputes about critical doctrines and aspect blindness about questions of power and politics. Rosenberg ends his article by observing that artists who try to renew art by its own means end up in a 'blind alley'. For him, 'Art today needs political consciousness in order to free itself from the frivolity of continual insurrections confined to art galleries and museums. The actions of society present a resistance against which modes of art can test their powers and reinstate the creation of images as a vocation of adult minds.'[119] The work that Rosenberg regarded as the 'showpiece' of *Protest and Hope* was George Segal's *The Execution*, one of the fourteen works done expressly for the show.[120] One of his series of 'dramatic tableaus' using white life-size plaster casts, it comprised a male figure hanging head down with a rope around both ankles from a bullet-scarred wall. Three other figures lay on grassed ground, apparently victims of 'the execution'. Rosenberg refers to the figures' 'eerie effect' produced by their whiteness and to 'a sense of quiet and timelessness, as if each work surrounded itself with a museum of its own'. These qualities, he believed, 'induced a mood of reflection – precisely the mood belonging to art and dissipated by the mass media. In this sense, the work was a contribution to political consciousness, despite the conventionality of the concept of people stood against the wall.'[121]

Rosenberg, like Kozloff, believed that art could produce a critical distance, an opportunity for thinking spectators to develop an awareness of experience and consciousness other to the world of mass media. He was, like many of his social group, committed to the conventional means and sites of art, the traditions of the Old Left's belief in radical politicised modernism. He was also hostile to an avant garde predicated on insulated concerns where debates about realism and contemporary history were positioned as bad others. However, unlike a younger generation of artists, which paralleled New Left politics, he could not entertain a destruction of conventional forms of art, or rather the established intellectual and institutional criteria for assessing their value. This itself may be regarded as a failure of political imagination or of consciousness, for the values and assumptions beginning to be scrutinised by the burgeoning art practices of dissent in 1967 were those central to power and permissibility in a broader-based politics, not least those of collectivity and gender critique.

Reading 1968: the Art Workers' Coalition and the critique of museums

Rosenberg was and has not been alone. Influential readings of art and theory since the 1960s have continued not only to single out a conventional canon and traditional critical categories but also to minimise a dialectical relationship between culture and politics. For example, Hal Foster opens his essay 'The Return of the Real' thus:

> In my reading of critical models in art and theory since 1960 I have stressed the minimalist genealogy of the neo-avant-garde. For the most part, artists and critics in this genealogy remained sceptical of realism and illusionism. In this way they continued the war of abstraction against representation by other means . . . Even if realism and illusionism meant additional things in the 1970s and 1980s – the problematic pleasures of Hollywood cinema, for example, or the ideological blandishments of mass culture – they remained *bad* things.[122]

A moral negativity towards notions of realism, variously defined, permeates many of the accounts of the 1960s and 1970s, although Pop Art, particularly Warhol and his legacy, is traced and referenced. Yet during the period there were significant instances and developments related to and outside of Pop Art that continue to be marginalised. Such instances, especially those that emphasised a dialectical relationship between culture and politics, were actively discussed. For example, in 1971 *Art in America* published the first of a four-part series of articles by Therese Schwartz on 'The Politicization of the Avant-Garde'.[123] Schwartz was an artist and an editor of the radical bimonthly newspaper, *The New York Element*. She had been active in many of the groups and manifestations discussed in her pioneering overview, including in the Art Workers' Coalition (AWC).

The AWC was formed in 1969 as a result of a number of factors.[124] Some of the artists had been participants in earlier anti-war activities such as the Artists' Tower of Protest and *The Collage of Indignation*. Others became involved because of a growing concern with the rights of artists. These rights related both to the exhibition as an institutionalised system and to the definitions of ownership of an art work. In an early documentation of the first few months of the AWC, a specific moment of artists' intervention at MoMA was identified as inaugurating the group. On 3 January 1969, the Greek sculptor Takis (Takis Vassilakis), based mostly in Paris and with French nationality, entered the Museum to remove his *Tele-Sculpture* (1960) from the exhibition *The Machine as Seen at the End of the Mechanical Age*. Although this particular work was in the Museum's collection, it was exhibited without the artist's wishes and despite his protestations. John Perreault describes the event in *The Village Voice*:[125]

> In a crowded gallery, in front of stunned guards, Takis moved in on his own work, cut the wires, unplugged it, and protected by Farman and Willoughby, gently carried it out into the museum garden . . . After an hour-and-a-half 'sit-in' and then finally a two hour talk with Bates Lowry, the new director of the museum, he at least got a verbal agreement. The piece is no longer in the show.[126]

Handbills, signed by Takis, were distributed. One raised the hope that this act 'will be just the first in a series of acts against the stagnant policies of art museums all over the world. Let us unite, artists with scientists, students with workers, to change these anachronistic situations into information centres for all artistic activities.'[127] The AWC was in many ways a version of several of the 'counter-culture' groups dominated by students (such as SDS) and its eventual demise, in 1971, was not unlike the self-destructive in-fighting of these larger groups. Within it there were various factions including those advocating direct intervention such as the Guerrilla Art Action Group (GAAG), which saw itself indebted to Dada and Fluxus.[128] Others wished to organise and establish a cohesive organisation through a variety of means from intellectual debate to leaflets and artistic projects. And within the AWC there were representatives of other groups struggling to achieve representation within society, let alone within the art world. Analysis of the AWC also says much about the social world of artists who tried to address both their political beliefs (anti-war and hostile to the repressive forces of the state) and their artistic aspirations and careers. Bringing the two together produced massive problems for individuals and the larger group. Again, these problems paralleled aspects of broader groups and movements at the time. Many of the splits produced other groups which pressed for: the rights of women and women artists such as Women Artists and Revolution (WAR) and Ad Hoc Women Artists' Committee (leading in 1975 to the formation of 'Heresies' in 1975); and those for Black rights such as Women Students and Artists for Black Art Liberation (WSABAL).

One reason for the early unity of purpose was a powerful realisation of the East and West Coast centres as fundamental to international constructions and perceptions of avant-gardism. The statistics of culture-making show that both in the growth of galleries and in attendance figures New York was a major centre in the growth of the status of the United States.[129] Naifeh, for instance, estimates that there were seventy-three serious galleries in New York in 1945; 123 in 1955; 246 in 1965; and 287 in 1970. And 'Across the nation, the number of galleries had risen at least five-fold since the end of World War II'.[130] Crane provides similar statistics charting the rapid growth in museums, art centres and corporate collections: for example, of the ninety-nine corporate collections existing in 1979, seventy-six had been established since 1960.[131] Questions began to be raised about who were the actual constituencies for these museums and galleries; who owned and ran them? in whose interests? why were there so few women artists represented? why so few artists from the many cultures and races that made up the United States?; what relationship was their between specialist art, the careers of particular artists, dominant critical institutions (including the institution of the critic) and the political and social realities of contemporary America? Many of these questions were asked by the AWC.

The 'artist' and the politics of autonomous art

Don Judd was a member of the Art Workers' Coalition, though to the annoyance of several fellow members he was not active in the AWC's protests against institutions and the war in Vietnam. Judd's views were representative of many others in the 1960s who argued that art should be based on artists following their own specialist interests. Fundamentally, this was a commitment to 'autonomy' which in effect ruled out political readings of work other than in the most oblique terms or only through 'implication'. For example, in 1970 Judd claimed that his work did possess 'attitudes', had 'implications': 'I've always thought that my work had political implications, had attitudes that would permit, limit or prohibit some kinds of political behavior and some institutions.'[132] Such implications fundamentally reside in two areas. One is the readings produced by the viewing subject; a viewing subject aware of and open to the politics of 'autonomous art'. The second is more banal in that the work of Judd, and others such as Serra and Morris, provided museum curators and the collectors with practical problems of display and storage that act as implicit critiques of the conventions of the modern museum and collection. These two elements, a pursuit of the specialist character of particular art works and a concern with a critique of the mechanisms of display and reading, including who has power over these elements, were part of Minimalism's agenda.[133]

As a citizen, Judd had been active politically. He was in the pacifist War Resisters' League, founded in 1923, as can be seen from his and Julie Judd's names at the base of an advertisement for the League in *The Aspen Times* of 29 August 1968. The War Resisters' League (WRL), a pacifist organisation, was founded in 1923. It staged anti-war parades and conducted a mass pledge drive asking for signatures to the following statement: 'War is a crime against humanity. We therefore are determined not to support any kind of war and to strive for the removal of all causes of war.' During the 1960s and 1970s it gained an intensely pacifist following for its magazine *WIN* which stood for 'Workshop in Non-Violence'. WRL also helped found other magazines such as *Liberation* in 1956 to represent a 'third-camp' position on the Cold War as an alternative to the United States and Soviet Union. The magazine continued to publish until 1977, involving most of the major national writers around the New Left (Paul Goodman, Barbara Deming, Staughton Lynd, David Bellinger): '*Liberation* found wide acceptance among a proto-New Left, in part by linking the old notions of anti-monopoly and anti-imperialist republicanism with the decentralist and non-hierarchical themes of the new generation.'[134] The WRL led the first draft-card burnings and attempted direct action to close army induction centres.

For Judd it was important that his political activity was kept parallel to his artistic activity. In his reply to 'The Artist and Politics: a Symposium', published in *Artforum*, Judd sought to locate his decision historically. He discusses his pursuit of art within the politics of isolation and a parallel refusal to engage with contemporary events, which had begun to change during the 1960s:

> Also, I've thought that the situation was pretty bad and that my work was all I could do. My attitude of opposition and isolation, which has slowly changed in regard to isolation in the last five years or so, was in reaction to the events of the fifties: the continued state of war, the destruction of the UN by the Americans and Russians, the rigid useless political parties, the general exploitation and both the Army and McCarthy.
>
> Part of the reason for my isolation was the incapacity to deal with it all, in any way, and also work. Part was that recent art had occurred outside of most of the society. Unlike now, very few people were opposed to anything, none my age that I knew . . . So my work didn't have anything to do with the society, the institutions and the grand theories. It was one person's work and interests; its main political conclusion, negative but basic, was that it, myself, anyone, shouldn't serve any of these things, that they should be considered very sceptically and practically.[135]

Judd goes on to explain that his interest in 'doing something' grew partly because his work had developed to the point 'that I didn't feel I would be swamped by other interests' and partly because of the example of the Civil Rights movement and the Vietnam War. The former demonstrated that things 'could change a little'; the latter presented a 'situation of either/or', a choice that led him to join protest marches. He also felt that there was a difference between art and politics. For the latter 'the organization of society . . . had its own nature and could only be changed in its own way'. Art for him was something else, but with its own paradoxical politics: 'Art may change things a little, but not much; I suspect one reason for the popularity of American art is that museums and collectors didn't understand it enough to realize that it was against much in the society.'[136]

For Judd, in 1970, politics was an 'other' area of experience, distinct from the experience and the making of art, with its own demands on activity. His claim suggests that politics has an 'autonomy' and an immanent critical process of change not dissimilar to the claims made by Greenberg for the autonomy of art in 'Modernist Painting'. Such a view about politics did not sit well with the aims and activities of participants in the AWC. However, that is not to say that members of the AWC were consistent in their views about the relationship between art and politics. Several shared the contradictory tension evident in Judd's response: his claim, for instance, that the pursuit of his own interests and work which 'didn't have anything to do with society' resulted in a 'political conclusion, negative but basic'. He was also in the midst of a real paradox in which an 'attitude of opposition and isolation' coexisted with a specialised popularity among museums and collectors. They owned objects which Judd suggests were produced partly for reasons 'against much in the society', the society in which museums and collectors had a privileged status.

Judd's views evoke two related claims to be found in earlier critical texts.[137] The first is that art produced with little or no reference to the events and moral values of actual life can act as a resistant 'other', as an exemplar of alternative liberating production. Such a view underpinned Schapiro's 'The Liberating Quality of Avant-garde Art' of 1957. It is also a major element in Theodor Adorno's 'Commitment' of 1962, which is a classic statement of his postwar views on the politics of 'autonomous art'. Adorno argued that the emphasis on 'art for art's sake' or on 'autonomous' works is itself 'sociopolitical in nature'. It presupposes a particular notion of the value and critical complexity of high culture, a moral integrity in the preservation of art as insulated from kitsch and consumer culture on the one hand, and from political commitment or tendency on the other. In 1962 Adorno asserted: 'This is not a time for political art, but politics has migrated into autonomous art, and nowhere more so than where it seems to be politically dead.'[138] Adorno, as with Judd in 1970, had a pessimistic view of the public politics of the early Cold War, which in Adorno's terms 'oblige the mind to go where it need not degrade itself'.

Here we see the second related claim which stresses the retreat to autonomy as a liberating isolation and resistance. Such an emphasis can, Adorno argued, produce works of literature, music and art that in their rejection of 'empirical reality' arouse a 'fear', a 'shudder', an 'indignation' in the audience for 'avant-garde' culture. Here is the active critical potential for such works. Their austerity, internal complexity and intellectual difficulty are, it is claimed, a lingering moral counter to the supposed quick fix of populist art such as pulp fiction, Hollywood movies, jazz and pop music, on which the market and developing mass communication thrives. Adorno, as with many of the Old Left in the United States during the 1950s and 1960s, distrusted those cultural forms that could produce a manipulative effect on viewers and readers: he feared that references to 'empirical reality' have the potential for messages to be turned into propaganda. He thought that this was as possible in totalitarian and Fascist regimes, such as Nazi Germany and the Stalinist Soviet Union, as it was in democratic societies governed by capitalism, such as the United States. Mass audiences in the latter in particular, he argued, could become reliant on instant gratification, such as the 'kitsch' products of the mass media or the promise of consumer-driven utopias. He feared that a technologically dependent populace could become uncritical consumers of any totalitarian ideology. Clearly, there were and are vivid instances of such effects, but should these fears and terms be applied to all works of art, all forms of visual culture, that have a political tendency or engage with 'mass culture'? Adorno was aware of such problems as he was of the dangers of the politics of autonomous art: '[art that] concludes that it can be a law unto itself, and exist only for itself, degenerates into ideology no less. Art which even in its opposition to society remains a part of it, must close its eyes and ears against it: it cannot escape the shadow of irrationality.'[139]

Judd's work of the mid- and late 1960s has a high reliance on industrial materials and fabrication; on relationships between the space, mass, texture and colour of his specific objects; on the effects and demands of particular installations and locations. For instance, his exhibition at the Dwan Gallery, New York, in 1967 included his untitled installed work, of 1966, consisting of six galvanised steel cubes, with regular dimensions of 40 inches, hung on a wall for a total length of 25 feet 4 inches. From one perspective such works demanded new notions of artistic enterprise, of historical precedents, and of private and institutional display. Their critical radicalism was established partly by not having signifiers that promoted Modernist readings and validations; partly by departing from existing conventions of the manufacture and display of 'sculpture'. From another perspective, Judd's works signified, metaphorically at least, aspects of postwar experience in an ever-technologised United States characterised by blandness, the meaningless repetition of manufacture, industrialised geometry and the rhetoric of male power.[140]

In his response to *Artforum*, Judd is aware of the precarious political and social significance of his work. He is rooted in a tradition which had minimised the possibilities for a productive relationship between art practice and political tendency. One indication of this is his belief that art and politics are different, each having its 'own nature and could only be changed in its own way'. This legacy of the transformations in the Old Left resulted in an insistence on separate activities. Artists should politicise themselves as citizens, demonstrating and protesting when necessary, but their art should be free of political responsibilities and used only 'when the purpose is extremely important and when nothing else can be done'.[141] Judd's participation in the Tower in Los Angeles in February 1966 is an instance. However, a major dilemma for politically conscious citizens who made art that 'didn't have anything to do with society' was that their art work could be read, in the words of Carl Andre, a fellow member of the AWC and respondent to the *Artforum* symposium question, as 'Silence is assent'.[142]

The difference between what artists produced and what they claimed was their politics, in words and action, was at a volatile pitch in 1970 and the couple of years following. For example, in November 1970 Lucy Lippard took Judd to task for being silent in public about his private 'disgust' at the meetings and activities of the Art Workers' Coalition. In her 'The Art Workers' Coalition: Not a History', published in November 1970, she asked: '[Judd] says that those museums "who refuse [to talk with artists] can be struck"; by whom? Judd and the rest of the art community's silent majority?'[143]

Lippard's use of the words 'silent majority' is a negative reference to President Nixon's famous appeal in November 1969 to the 'silent majority' in the United States. Nixon claimed that, unlike the huge student and anti-war protests, a 'silent majority' of United States citizens supported the government's intervention in Vietnam.

Lippard continued:

> as long as the AWC's notorious sightseers, now perennial ([Robert] Smithson, [Richard] Serra and editor Philip Leider come to mind) many of whom are respected members of the art community and good talkers and would be able to convince a lot of people; as long as they play with themselves in the bar, telling everyone how absurd or mismanaged the AWC is, instead of saying the same things in the public arena (arena it often is, unfortunately), they will be the bane and to some extent the downfall of the Coalition.[144]

Two years later, in the *Feminist Art Journal*, the critic Cindy Nemser was even more direct: 'Judd, Morris, and [Carl] Andre know how to play the radical chic game very nicely. They rant and rave and make a little excitement for the bored bourgeoisie and no one gets hurt.'[145]

It is the contradictory tension between a professed and active participation in political activity and a commitment to a seemingly apolitical visual rhetoric that makes Judd a revealing case study of the paradoxes and contradictions of contemporary practice and criticism. For example, in *A Different War: Vietnam in Art* (1990), Lucy Lippard recalled organising, with Ron Wolin, peace activist, and Robert Huot, Minimal painter, a 'striking show of major Minimal art whose content had nothing to do with the war' as a benefit for the Student Mobilization Against the War.[146] The exhibition, in the autumn of 1968, inaugurated the new Paula Cooper Gallery in SoHo, New York. Amongst the fourteen 'non-objective artists' were Robert Ryman, Robert Morris, Jo Baer, Don Judd, Carl Andre and Sol Le Witt, and 'some $30,000' was raised for the cause.[147] The organisers stated that the selected artists were against the war in Vietnam and *middle ground*

supporting their commitment in 'the strongest manner open to them' by contributing examples of their current work presenting a 'particular esthetic attitude, in the conviction that a cohesive group of important works makes the most forceful statement for peace'.[148]

Sometimes the state of being other, of having a separate identity, was explicitly mentioned, at other times implied. In the latter sense, 'otherness' was an important part of how artists and critics carved out a position, an identity, by some thing or existence that was *not* the thing mentioned or was *not* the thinking or speaking subject. To consider this, historically, entails an awareness of politics, variously defined. Here I do not mean politics as a binary opposition of left wing and right wing. There are too many contradictions within the period for such an opposition to hold without problems. But I do mean that to understand the production of art and its meanings requires awareness of artists and critics as agents, explicitly or implicitly, within political affairs or life.

A case of 'otherness': *Artforum*

Artforum is a significant case of this textual embedding of such processes. As we have seen, when based on La Cienega Boulevard, Los Angeles, *Artforum* was at the heart of the gallery community of contemporary West Coast art. At the end of that period, just prior to the move to New York, it became a focal point of the well-known dispute between Modernists and Minimalists. This centred on its publication of 'Art and Objecthood' by Michael Fried in an issue (June 1967) devoted to 'American Sculpture' which included essays by Robert Morris, Sol Le Witt and Robert Smithson. All three were sympathetic to ideas and practices which centred on Minimalism, Land Art and Conceptual Art. 'Art and Objecthood', on the other hand, was explicitly hostile to Minimalism and implicitly to Land Art and Conceptual Art. Fried's essay produced hostile reactions in return from, amongst others, Robert Smithson and Dan Flavin. These were published in *Artforum* in subsequent months.

Although not yet thirty, Fried had already established a major reputation as a representative of that social formation often referred to as 'Greenberg and the Group'.[149] This formation, which also included Rosalind Krauss, Jane Harrison Cone and Sidney Tillim, was indebted to the views and judgements propounded by the older critic Clement Greenberg, particularly his influential essay 'Modernist Painting' and the selected collection of earlier publications in his book *Art and Culture*, both of which appeared in the United States in 1961.[150] As we saw in previous sections, in terms of critical opportunities the editor of *Artforum*, Philip Leider, was committed to the specialist interests of the Greenbergian social formation. By social formation I mean a group which sustains or promotes work within a particular medium or branch or style of visual art.[151] This is *not* to say that Leider excluded work from outside of this formation but that his agenda was predicated on an acceptance of the main tenets of Modernism.

As editor in Los Angeles, Leider's aim for *Artforum* was for it to become *the* journal for the review and discussion of a range of highly specialised art and art criticism, not solely in the United States but internationally. The move to New York was a major development in this strategy which was matched by the inclusion of art and criticism which demanded attention because of the Modernist agenda of the dominant social formation. 'Otherness' or the production of dissent, within particular traditions and conventions, is necessary for the paradigmatic concerns of a social formation to be strengthened and elaborated by critical engagement with and rebuttal of variations or alternatives. In *Artforum*'s case this meant the inclusion of, for example, articles on Minimalism, Land Art and Conceptual Art. Major areas neglected because of adherence to main items on the agenda were art and criticism recognisably political or realist, other than, for example, Pop Art, which was characterised as social and consumerist rather than political critique.[152]

Specifically, for Greenbergians it was thought that questions of political or realist art had been seen off by the power of Modernist critical judgements. Generally, the effect of anti-Communism in the 1950s, politically, was to make many journals, critics and institutions wary of art with political purpose. Pop, for instance, could be accommodated within a non-Marxist social critique. Hence its relevance to accounts which emphasised consumerist and mass cultural aspects of American life. This is not to say that Pop was without political impact: Rosenquist's installation *F-111* from 1965 is an example. Evidence of Leider's commitment, apart from the publications he promoted in *Artforum* and his appointment of contributing editors,[153] can be found in his correspondence, between 1966 and 1970, with Greenberg, whom he had met at Frank Stella's in 1964 or 1965. For example on 21 April 1967, just prior to the publication of Fried's 'Art and Objecthood', Leider wrote to Greenberg: 'you are *cher maitre* to all of the staff' at *Artforum*. In the same letter Leider reported, approvingly, Michael Fried's view, expressed to him in conversation, that Greenberg was the *only* living person to have 'produced a body of reputable criticism'.[154]

In September 1967 Leider again used the term 'master' and pleaded with Greenberg 'to consider publishing on a regular basis' in *Artforum*. A particular sign of his commitment to 'Greenberg and the Group' was Leider's negative comments on Harold Rosenberg's collection of essays *The Anxious Object*, published in 1962, which he had only recently read: 'I never suspected how bad he [Rosenberg] really was. And how dishonest. And how *thick*.'[155] Rosenberg, from the same generation as Greenberg, had since the 1950s been as influential a critic but with a different political constituency. In an important sense they represented distinct traditions of leftist thought and activity. Rosenberg still believed that intellectuals had a responsibility to articulate social and political dissent within their work and in their judgements about art and literature. Greenberg, on the other hand, believed that a close attention to the autonomy of art and of aesthetic judgements was the only guarantee of ethical and political integrity. To be explicit about politics was, for him, vulgar, naive and to confuse the world of art and the world of everyday life.

What of Leider's commitments when it came to critics who were contemporaries of Michael Fried and Rosalind Krauss? We can glean something of this from a note Leider sent to Greenberg after Greenberg had given a talk at the Museum of Modern Art in New York in May 1968. In it he makes disparaging reference to the young Lucy Lippard. Leider writes to Greenberg: 'That was me cringing in embarrassment next to dogface Lucy Lippard: she came in and sat beside me (nasty spider beside mild Mr. Muffett) mumbling garbage beneath her breath, working herself up into the despicable scene which she enacted during the question period.'[156]

This is more than tittle-tattle. Leider, with the power to publicise particular views and voices, was establishing his position in relation to a specific social formation. In part this was achieved, privately, by articulating his otherness to critics, such as Harold Rosenberg and Lucy Lippard, who were despised by that formation. One further example from this correspondence informs us not only of the position Leider wished to establish for *Artforum* in the art world but also of the tensions and contradictions in that ambition. On 24 October 1966, Leider wrote to Greenberg attempting to get an already promised major piece on Manet out of him by the end of November. He ends his letter: 'Thank you, of course, for the nice comments about the magazine; as I think I wrote to you before, the only thing that stands between the magazine and an absolute identification with quality in art is quality in writing, but that is turning out to be more of a stumbling block.'[157] What is meant by 'quality' is not defined. Leider's *use* of the term implies that whilst it is some sort of criterion shared with Greenberg, its meaning is ineffable. What *we can say* is that in his attempt to secure more articles by Greenberg, Fried, Krauss and other Modernist critics Leider clearly equated that group with whatever he meant by 'quality in writing'. To publish them would, he believed, link *Artforum* to 'an absolute identification with quality in art'.

There is more to this letter. Leider sent it care of the Cultural Affairs Office of the United States Embassy in Tokyo, Japan, for Greenberg was on a State Department tour talking about art and the central role of the United States in its development since 1945. Greenberg's trip rankled with Leider, who, as we have seen, in 1966 lent his name to anti-Vietnam-War protests, particularly in Los Angeles where *Artforum* was then based. Leider had chided Greenberg about the trip in an earlier letter only to receive a sideswipe back about the supposed insulting and meaningless *display* of intellectuals' political opinions. In his letter of 24 October 1966, Leider recalls Greenberg's admonition with measured irony. Leider writes:

> The attitude of the French Intellectuals (and Robert Lowell, here) is 'square', like mine, because they feel, as Socialists, or whatever, that their differences with the government are serious enough, and deep enough so that any attempt to display them or parade them is regarded not only as deeply insulting but another proof that their opinions are really meaningless. OK, I'm clear now.[158]

And just prior to this a raw edginess spits out from Leider:

> I understand your position exactly. You are a Socialist, but it is OK for the State Department to make a show of you because they tell you that you can say what you please (seein' as how this is such a democracy and the proof is that the American Government can parade out American intellectuals at will just for the price of a ticket to Tokyo.) Besides, all the State Department has to do with is Vietnam, Cuba, Franco, South Africa, hydrogen bombs and the Dominican Republic. Its [*sic*] not as if they had anything to do with how we treat *Negroes* and its a lucky thing the *Justice Department* didn't buy that ticket or you'd tell them to do you-know-what with it. I see.[159]

Leider is in quandary here. Greenberg's writings, his influence and status, his supporters are special to his art-world ambition for *Artforum*. However, there are aspects of everyday life which will not leave his consciousness. How does all this assist in the case study of art practice and art criticism in and around 1967 and Fried's 'Art and Objecthood' in particular?

Fried opened his manifesto piece with the following assertion:

> The enterprise known variously as Minimal Art, ABC Art, Primary Structures and Specific Objects is largely ideological. It seeks to declare and occupy a position – one which can be formulated in words, and in fact has been formulated by some of its leading practioners. If this distinguishes it from modernist painting and sculpture on the one hand, it also marks an important difference between Minimal Art – or as I prefer to call it, *literalist* art – and Pop or Op Art on the other.[160]

'*Literalist* art' was Fried's own term for what was more commonly described as Minimal Art, which he associated primarily with the sculpture of Donald Judd and Robert Morris. And, whilst Fried did distinguish between Minimal Art and Pop Art, for him both entailed the beholder, the viewer, in a 'duration of experience', similar to that prompted by the 'theatre'. This 'duration of experience' inevitably for Fried included associations, from everyday life, that threatened the established boundaries of self-referential, or autonomous, 'art'. Hence he regarded Minimalism and Pop Art as 'largely ideological', 'theatrical', 'literary, 'historically specific' and the 'negation of art'.

Fried concluded 'Art and Objecthood' by condemning Minimal or 'literalist' sculpture as 'corrupted' and 'perverted'; as consistent with what characterises 'most or all of our lives'. Fried's desired otherness to this tainted state, the positive other to the 'negation of art', is 'presentness' which, he says, 'is grace'.[161] The notion of 'presence' is taken directly from Greenberg's contemporary essay 'Recentness of Sculpture'.[162] Presentness, instantaneousness, essence are, for Fried, characteristics of the work of Modernist sculptors and painters such as Jules Olitski, Kenneth Noland, David Smith and Anthony Caro. In arguing that such works 'compel conviction' and instantaneous transubstantiation from object to 'grace', Fried reveals both the disciplinary and religious basis for his aesthetic. For those unfamiliar with Fried's terminology and the vehemence of his distinctions, 'Art and Objecthood' may seem either compelling in itself or arcane and ideological.

'Art and politics': Minimalism and utopia

One of the few texts which attempts to dig deep into the minutiae of Fried's essay with informed critical purpose is Hal Foster's 'The Crux of Minimalism' from 1986.[163] In it Foster argues that for Fried the real threat of Minimalism is 'not only that it disrupts the autonomy of art but that it corrodes belief in art'. Foster goes on to suggest that here we have 'art for art's sake' in its authoritative or authoritarian guise: 'a guise which reveals that, far from separate from power and religion . . . bourgeois art is a displaced will to power and a secret substitute for religion – and ultimately *is* a religion'.[164]

In arguing against Fried's view, Hal Foster celebrates Minimalism as an avant-gardist critique of the conventionality of art. Therein lies, for Foster, Minimalism's oppositional politics. However, in conclusion he poses a question:

> is it too conjectural to suggest that however critical minimalism and pop [art] are, they still in one way or another carry forth the American order: pop (ironically but brazenly) with its consumer culture icons, minimalism (connotatively) with its 'universal' forms that conjure up the architectural monoliths and corporate logos of American business?[165]

This is an important question taken up by Anna Chave in her 'Minimalism and the Rhetoric of Power', published in 1990.[166] Significantly, though, Foster's concluding question was posed both in practice and criticism in the late 1960s. This lack of historical awareness in an otherwise incisive essay says something about the capacity for amnesia within American life. One example of Foster's question comes from within the covers of *Artforum* itself in March 1969.

In January 1969 one of the contributing editors of *Artforum*, Barbara Rose, published the second of her articles on 'The Politics of Art',[167] the first having appeared in the previous year. In March 1969 *Artforum* published a critical letter from Leon Golub in response to Barbara Rose's articles.[168] This letter is an acerbic interruption in a whole special issue devoted to Fried's 'Manet's Sources'. At the time the AWC was in its formative months and Golub's own work was centred on the theme of napalm. He takes issue with the utopian claims made by Barbara Rose for Minimalism and argues that she ignores contemporary politics and history as they occur. Golub writes:

> The work of Judd, Morris, etc., is [in Rose's article] related to 19th- and 20th-century predecessors whose 'cleanliness, integrity, efficiency and simplicity' is correlated with a democratic and utopian America. Standard units, the 'natural, the uncontrived, the immediate,' relate to an 'ideally levelled, non-stratified democratic society.'[169]

Golub argues that such precedents are erroneous, particularly ones which relate to Constructivism in Russia after the 1917 Revolution: 'America in the 1960s doesn't correspond to a Constructivist utopia. Nor does Minimal art, etc., correspond to a Constructivist vision.' In the context of Americans in Asia or Guatemala, of street rioting and the military-industrial complex that is the United States, Golub asks: 'Is it possible to export destruction, to burn and drive peasants from their homes, and maintain the dream of the perfectibility of art? Well, it is possible if art concerns itself with itself and does not dare to presume political meanings.'[170] And, with echoes of Bertold Brecht's writings on art, culture and politics from the 1930s, Golub argues:

> The abstract sculptures etc., in our cities become grimacing monsters if viewed in political or utopian contexts . . . Those arts that began with the modernist dream of human freedom may find they serve technological masters and the American empire. Art then will service the consumption habits of a triumphant managerial class, a cyberneticized elite civilization protected from the outside by the fantastic weapons and control agents of the future.[171]

We are back here with Hal Foster's question about 'American order' and Minimalism. In Foster's words, do its 'universal' forms 'conjure up the architectural monoliths and corporate logos of American business'?[172] We are also back with Leider's correspondence from 1966 with Greenberg who, as you will recall, was on a State Department trip to Japan bemoaning the naive, vulgar and meaningless display of intellectuals' political protest. The State Department on the other hand was busy with Vietnam, Cuba, Franco, South Africa, hydrogen bombs and the Dominican Republic.

In the wake of My Lai and the trial of Lieutenant Calley, Altamont, the Weathermen, the Black Panthers, Kent State and the art world's

'Strike' in summer 1970 *Artforum* asked about politics. Selected artists were asked to respond to a 'symposium question' about their view on the role of 'the artist and politics' in the light of what it called the 'deepening political crisis in America'. Responses published in the September 1970 issue were, not surprisingly, mixed. The responses included a long one from Donald Judd arguing essentially for the world of art and the world of politics to be kept separate. For Leider the relationship between art, politics and lived experience kept coming up like a toothache. Over that summer he had been out with Richard Serra and Joan Jonas to visit Michael Heizer's *Double Negative*, completed in 1970. He then met up with Robert and Nancy Smithson to see Smithson's *Spiral Jetty*, also recently completed.[173] *Spiral Jetty* impressed Leider as a project but worried him that it was no more than an artist's 'fantasy in the middle of Utah'. Leider writes: 'Art is nature, re-arranged. Like everyone else, Smithson learned it in high school. In a free society, artists get to re-arrange nature just like everyone else, lumber kings, mining czars, oil barons; nature, a kind of huge, placid Schmoo, just lays there aching with pleasure.'[174]

Leider's report of the trip, also published in the September issue of *Artforum*, is characterised by a similar unease and managed irony evident in his letters to Greenberg four years earlier. Perhaps he had seen newspaper photographs, in the *New York Times* of 5 April 1970, of the United States forces' rearrangement of 'nature' in Vietnam with defoliants. One such military earthwork was an emblem, a mile and a half long, of the First Infantry division; a pentagon with a '1' in the centre bulldozed in the jungle, northwest of Saigon. This was juxtaposed with *Spiral Jetty* by Luis Camnitzer in his colour photo-etching, *April 1970*, from the 'Agent Orange' series of 1984. Camnitzer was comparing the military's earthwork north of Saigon and Smithson's earthwork in Utah, both completed in April 1970.

Comparisons made and questions asked by artists within the AWC and later by critics and historians such as Hal Foster and Anna Chave echo those made and asked since at least the Second World War in the United States. How they are answered, in letters, conversations, essays and specific visual objects, is for us to learn from, historically. And it is the contradictions which tell us most. Although Don Judd continued to be active in the War Resisters' League, his experience of the same period left his work relatively unchanged. How would he have answered Hal Foster's question, posed in 1986, about the possible relationship between Minimalism and the monoliths and corporate logos of American business? No doubt as he did in *Artforum* in 1970, and again in 1975 in a piece called 'Imperialism, Nationalism and Regionalism' in which he makes reference to his colleague, Dan Flavin. Judd wrote in 1975: 'Dan Flavin was scolded by the Art Workers Coalition a few years back because the fluorescent tubes he used were made by a company that made something for the Vietnam War. It all gets silly. Flavin pointed out that the most common toilet was made by a company that also supplied something for the War.'[175]

Notes

1   See retrospective sources: Lucy Lippard, *A Different War: Vietnam in Art* (Seattle, Whatcome Museum of History and Art and the Real Comet Press, 1990); Deborah Wye, *Committed to Print: Social and Political Themes in Recent American Printed Art* (New York, Museum of Modern Art, 1988); Michele Wallace, 'Reading 1968: The Great American Whitewash', in *Invisibility Blues: From Pop to Theory* (London, Verso, 1990), pp. 187–98; Mary Schmidt Campbell (ed.), *Tradition and Conflict: Images of a Turbulent Decade, 1963–73* (New York, Studio Museum in Harlem, 1985); Alice Echoles, *Daring to Be Bad: Radical Feminism in America 1967–1975* (Minneapolis and London, University of Minnesota Press, 1989); Shiela Rowbotham, *The Past Before Us: Feminism in Action since the 1960s* (London, Pandora, 1989); Monica Threlfall (ed.), *Mapping the Women's Movement: Feminist Politics and Social Transformation in the North* (London, Verso, 1996).

2   Max Kozloff, '. . . A Collage of Indignation', *The Nation*, 20 February 1967, 248–51; Leon Golub, 'The Artist as an Angry Artist: the Obsession with Napalm', *Arts Magazine*, April 1967, 48–9.

3   Michael Fried, 'Art and Objecthood', *Artforum*, 5:10 (June 1967), 12–23; also slightly revised in Gregory Battcock, *Minimal Art: A Critical Anthology* (New York, Dutton, 1968) reprinted with an introduction by Anne Wagner (University of California Press, Berkeley and Los Angeles, 1995).

4   See Barbara Reise, 'Greenberg and The Group: A Retrospective View', *Studio International*, 175:901 (May 1968), 254–7 (Part 1) and 175:902 (June 1968), 314–16 (Part 2). Reprinted in Francis Frascina and Jonathan Harris (eds), *Art in Modern Culture* (London, Phaidon, 1992), pp. 252–63; Anna Chave, 'Minimalism and the Rhetoric of Power', *Arts Magazine*, 64:5 (1990), 44–63 edited version in Frascina and Harris (eds), *Art in Modern Culture*, pp. 264–81; Lucy Lippard, *Six-Years: The Dematerialisation of the Art Object from 1966–1972* (London, Studio Vista, 1973); Ann Goldstein and Anne Rorimer, *Reconsidering the Object of Art: 1965–1975* (Los Angeles, The Museum of Contemporary Art, Los Angeles, and MIT Press, 1995).

5   In an interview (December 1990) conducted by the author, for an Open University programme on MoMA, the art historian Linda Nochlin argues this point. For her, MoMA in the 1940s and 1950s was a cultural resource of radical art and film; enjoying and learning from the products on display had a value which was different from intellectual and social commitment to egalitarianism. No inconsistency was perceived until '1968' when major questions about institutions and the links between political, economic and cultural interests were made.

6   Articles such as: Barbara Rose's three-part article 'The Politics of Criticism IV: The Politics of Art, Part I', *Artforum*, 6:6 (February 1968), 31–2; 'The Politics of Criticism V: The Politics of Art, Part II', *Artforum*, 7:5 (January 1969), 44–9; 'The Politics of Criticism VI: The Politics of Art, Part III', *Artforum*, 7:9 (May 1969), 46–51. Also 'The Artist and Politics: A Symposium', *Artforum*, 9:1 (September 1970), 35–9. For a critique of Rose's Modernist assumptions see the two letters in reply, *Artforum*, 7:7 (March 1969) by Leon Golub, 3–4, and by Cindy Nemser, 4.

7   On the one hand, there were attempts to consolidate a moral and ethical defence of cultural taste as separable from issues of social class and economic wealth. Greenberg

took up the cultural distinctions between 'highbrow', 'middlebrow' and 'lowbrow' to reaffirm his earlier defence of a particular notion of the 'avant garde' in postwar terms. For him, 'highbrow' became a repository of values and judgements insulated from the pernicious dilutions of 'middlebrow' consumer culture and of 'lowbrow' popular culture. See Greenberg, 'The Plight of Our Culture': Part I ('Industrialism and Class Mobility'), *Commentary*, 15 (June 1953), 558–66; and Greenberg, 'The Plight of Our Culture': Part II ('Work and Leisure under Industrialism'), *Comment-ary*, 15 (August 1953), 54–62. Significant, too, were attitudes to Beat Culture. For many adherents to the Old Left the anxious and persistent search for 'values' was a characteristic of the 'best' of modern artists and novelists. 'Beat generation' litera-ture represented for Irving Howe a threatening destruction of such a search. See, for example, his 'Mass Society and Post-modern Fiction', *Partisan Review* 26:3 (summer 1959), 420–36, especially 434–6 where he criticises 'the young men in San Francisco' in terms that he would reuse in the late 1960s when attacking New Left politics. In contrast, James Rosenquist, when interviewed about his *F-111*, regarded the Beats differently. For him, they were conscious of the shocking and threatening potential of atomic war in sharp contrast to the post-Beat generation who 'are blasé and don't think it can happen'. So for Rosenquist this, *F-111* 'is a restatement of that Beat idea, but in full color'. See G. R. Swenson '*F-111*: An Interview with James Rosenquist', *Partisan Review*, 32:4 (fall 1965), 589–601.

8   Schapiro, 'The Liberating Quality of Avant-Garde Art', *Art News*, 56:4 (1957), 36–42. Reprinted in Meyer Schapiro, *Modern Art 19th and 20th Centuries: Selected Papers Volume Two* (London, Chatto and Windus, 1978). Clement Greenberg, 'Mod-ernist Painting', 1961, Radio Broadcast Lecture 14 of *The Voice of America Forum Lectures*, as reprinted in Frascina and Harris, *Art in Modern Culture*, pp. 308–14. Was the Schapiro article an appeal for individual artistic resistance and dissent amidst contemporary values of consumerism, technocracy and manipulated mass communications? Was his text a coded address to those critical of McCarthyist effects but mindful of its disciplinary legacy on the permissable utterance? What do these texts reveal about a defensive desire to consolidate the 'achievements' of radical modernist art in the face of Cold War rhetoric, McCarthyite attacks on the left, capitalist consumerism and a so-called debased 'mass culture' geared towards the market place? For example, was Greenberg's 'Modernist Painting', 1961, com-missioned by the 'Voice of America', a metaphor for reaction and an implicit collu-sion with the forces of the state or an authoritative defense of 'quality' in a world dominated by capitalist and imperialist priorities?

9   See Alan M. Wald, *The New York Intellectuals: The Rise and Decline of the Anti-Stalinist Left from the 1930s to the 1980s* (Chapel Hill and London, University of North Carolina Press, 1987).

10 See for instance documents in chapter 10 of Robert Griffith (ed.), *Major Problems in American History Since 1945* (Lexington, D. C. Heath and Company, 1992).

11 Michael Fried, Rosalind Krauss, Benjamin Buchloh, 'Theories of Art After Minimalism and Pop', sub-section in '1967/1987, Genealogies of Art and Theory', in Hal Foster (ed.), *Discussions in Contemporary Culture* (Seattle, Bay Press, 1987), pp. 55–87. For Buchloh's acknowledgement, see pp. 65–70. A circular defence of Modernist theory and art as pre-eminent in the period also characterises Charles Harrison's and Paul Wood's 'Modernity and Modernism Reconsidered', chapter 3 of Paul Wood, Francis Frascina, Jonathan Harris and Charles Harrison, *Modernism in Dispute: Art Since the Forties* (New Haven and London, Yale University Press, 1993), pp. 170–260.

12 Krauss, 'A View of Modernism', *Artforum*, 11:1 (September 1972), 49.

13 See Therese Schwartz, 'On the Steps of the Met', *New York Element*, 1:4 (June–July 1970), 3–4, 19–20; Elizabeth C. Baker, 'Pickets on Parnassus', *Art News*, 69:5

(September 1970), 30–3, 64; Corinne Robbins, 'The N.Y. Art Strike', *Arts Magazine*, 45:1 (September–October 1970), 27–8. Also: Sean H. Elwood, *The New York Art Strike of 1970: A History, Assessment, and Speculation* (MA Thesis, Hunter College, City University of New York, 1982).

14   2 July to 20 September 1970.

15   See Susan L. Jenkins, 'Information, Communication, Documentation: An Introduction to the Chronology of Group Exhibitions and Bibliographies', in Goldstein and Rorimer (eds), *Reconsidering the Art Object of Art: 1965–1975*, p. 271.

16   Kynaston L. McShine, *Information* (New York, MoMA, 1970), p. 138.

17   *Ibid.*

18   For full details, see Haacke's own text in the 'Catalogue of Works: 1969–1986', in Brian Wallis (ed.), *Hans Haacke: Unfinished Business* (New York, New Museum of Contemporary Art New York, and MIT Press, 1986), pp. 86–7.

19   Copy of letter (19 June 1970), Museum of Modern Art Archives, Alfred H. Barr Jnr, Papers [Archives of American Art (AAA) Roll 2196, Frame 326].

20   Copy of letter (4 July 1970), Museum of Modern Art Archives, Alfred H. Barr Jnr, Papers [Archives of American Art (AAA) Roll 2196, Frame 325].

21   See memo (dated 29 June 1970) and minutes of the Trustees Executive Committee Meeting in the Museum of Modern Art Archives, Alfred H. Barr Jnr, Papers [Archives of American Art (AAA) Roll 2196, Frames 328 to 331].

22   In a memo to David Rockefeller (7 July 1970) in the Museum of Modern Art Archives, Alfred H. Barr Jnr, Papers [Archives of American Art (AAA) Roll 2196, Frame 387].

23   'Show at the Modern Raises Questions', *The New York Times*, 2 July 1970, 26.

24   Letter from Rockefeller to Hightower (10 July 1970) in the Museum of Modern Art Archives, Alfred H. Barr Jnr, Papers [Archives of American Art (AAA) Roll 2196, Frame 390].

25   Kozloff, '. . . A Collage of Indignation', 248.

26   Fried, 'Art and Objecthood', 23.

27   Ashton's extensive political activity can be gleaned from the records in the PAD/D Archive, Museum of Modern Art Library, Dore Ashton File. She was an art critic on *The New York Times* from 1955 to 1960 and in extraordinary circumstances was 'sacked', ostensibly because of a public dispute with John Canaday who was appointed editor of the art page in 1959. Canaday disagreed with her view of modern and contemporary art; Canaday's views were subjected to strong criticism by a collective letter by artists, academics, critics and collectors published in *The New York Times*, 26 February 1961, Section II, 19, producing a flurry of reactions in subsequent editions. Some of the events are retold in Sophy Burnham, 'The Ashton Affair', *The Art Crowd* (New York, David McKay Company, Inc., 1973). Ashton is convinced that she was 'sacked' not only because of her critical defence of contemporary art but also because her leftist politics did not conform to the right-wing values of *The New York Times* (interview with the author, 2 June 1993).

28   Copy of letter in Dore Ashton File, PAD/D Archive (Museum of Modern Art Library).

29   A typewritten list, in Rudolf Baranik File, PAD/D Archive (Museum of Modern Art Library) cites as members of the Committee, in order on the list: Leon Golub, Jack Soneneberg, Cyply, Irving Petlin, Max Kozloff, Dore Ashton, Frazier Dougherty, Nancy Spero, Burt Hasen, Les Packer, Gene Tulchin, Bernard Aptekar, Rudolf Baranik, May Stevens, Pheobe Hellman Soneneberg, Irwin Rosenhouse, George Sugarman.

30   Draft of an advertisement in the *New York Times*, Rudolf Baranik File, PAD/D Archive (Museum of Modern Art Library). List as typed: Admiral; Aitkin; Appel; Aptekar; Ariella; Asher; Ashton; Aylon; Baranik; Bishop; Black Mask (group); Blackburn; Blauston; Boardman; Boyd; Brach; Beer; Burlin; Calcagno; Cherry; Cibula;

Cply; D'Arcangelo; Daugherty; Dean; Di Suvero; Dobkin; Dvorzon; Dunbar; Fine; Forst; Framboluti; Frasconi; Geller; Georgakis; Gikow; Gillson; Goldin; Goldstein; Golub; Gorchov; Graves; S. Greene; B. Greene; Halpern; Hare; Harris; Hasen; Helmen; Hendler; Hendricks; Herscowitz; Hill; Hinman; Hopkins; Humphrey; Hui; Huot; Jennings; Johnson; Kadish; Kamen; Kimmelman; Knight; Konzal; C. Koppelman; D. Koppelman; Kozloff; Kriesberg; Kullaway; Landau; Lane; Lawrence; Leaf; Lippold; J. Levine; Lichtenstein; Lurie; Martin; Matta; Meiselman; Mellon; Milder; Millet; Michel; Morrel; J. Natkin; R. Natkin; Neel; Ohlson; Packer; Passuntino; Petlin; Philips; Picard; Pinkerson; Poleskie; Preston; Raffaele; Refregier; Reinhardt; Reisman; Reisman; Reubens; Rosenhouse; Rosenquist; Rubington; Schlanger; Sesley; Sellenrad; Serra; Shapiro; M. Shapiro; Sherman; Silverman; Simon; Sloan; Snider; Sonenberg; R. Soyer; Spero; Nora Speyer; M. Stevens; Stuart; Sugarman; Swarz; Tecla; Todd; Toney; Tulchin; Tuten; Tytell; Van Veen; Weber; Weisman; Werner; I. Wiegand; R. Wiegand; Yamin; M. Yeargens; P. Yeargens; Youngerman; Zver.

31 For the list containing seventy-three names of participating artists see Rudolf Baranik File, PAD/D Archive (Museum of Modern Art Library). See the same file and that of Dore Ashton's for Rudolf Baranik's report, 'The Angriest Voice', in an overall review, 'The Week of Angry Arts Against the War in Vietnam'; a draft of an advertisement in the *New York Times*; 'Supporters and Participants – Partial List' accompanying the announcement of a meeting to discuss future projects after a decision to continue the Angry Arts organisation. The large advertisement included seven headings under 'Angry Arts Sponsors and Participants (Partial List)' with fifty-one names under 'Painters and Sculptors', *The New York Times*, 29 January 1967, Section II, p. 17. Kozloff's review, '. . . A Collage of Indignation'.

32 *The New York Times*, 29 January 1967, Section II, 17; *The Village Voice*, 26 January 1967, 17: Bernard Aptekar; Elise Asher; Dore Ashton; Rudolf Baranik; Paul Brach; Paul Burlin; Allen D'Arcangelo; CPLY; Mark Di Suvero; Fraser Dougherty; Elaine de Kooning; Friedel Dzubas; Peter Forakis; Antonio Frasconi; Leon Golub; Robert Gwathmey; David Hare; Burt Hasen; Pheobe Hellmen; Thomas B. Hess; Charles Hinman; Bud Hopkins; Ruben Kadish; Allan Kaprow; Max Kozloff; Gerald Laing; Jacob Landau; Jack Levine; Roy Lichtenstein; Richard Linder; Knox Martin; Matta; Claes Oldenburg; Les Packer; Irving Petlin; Joe Raffaelli; Shai Rieger; Ad Reinhardt; Harold Rosenberg; James Rosenquist; Robert Scull; Jason Seeley; Jack Sonenberg; Raphael Soyer; May Stevens; George Sugarman; Mike Todd; Gene Tulchin; David Weinrib; James Wines; Adja Yunkers.

33 Baranik, 'The Angriest Voice', 10–11.

34 *Ibid*.

35 See also Golub, 'The Artist as an Angry Artist', 49.

36 Baranik, 'The Angriest Voice', 11.

37 Golub, 'The Artist as an Angry Artist', 48.

38 Full-page advertisements in *The New York Times*, 29 January 1967, Section II, 17; *The Village Voice*, 26 January 1967, 17. Also 'Angry Arts, The Week Continues', *The Village Voice*, 2 February 1967, 15. See, too, brief discussion of the week, 'Viet "No" Vote', by Grace Glueck under 'Art Notes', *The New York Times*, 29 January 1967, Section II, 26.

39 Quoted in Don McNeill, 'Week of the Angry Arts: Protest of the Artists', *The Village Voice*, 26 January 1967, 13.

40 *Ibid*.

41 Saturday 4 February starting at 2 p.m. to include: Paul Blackburn, Bread and Puppet Theatre, Irene Forbes, Denise Levertov, Jackson Maclow, Meredith Monk, Robin Morgan, Joel Oppenheimer, Pageant Players, Grace Paley, Susan Sontag.

42 McNeill, 'Week of the Angry Arts: Protest of the Artists', 19.

43 Marlene Nadle, 'Angry Arts: Aiming Through the Barrier', *The Village Voice*, 9 February 1967, 1 (and 15).

44 On 13 January the 'Poets Caravan' had already carried their literary protest to the streets stopping at seven street corners from Greenwich Village to Harlem. See press release (10 January 1967), Rudolf Baranik and Dore Ashton Files, PAD/D Archive (Museum of Modern Art Library).

45 The Pageant Players of New York performed on street corners, in parks, in lofts, inside laundromats and sometimes in theatres throughout the New Left period. One of their hallmarks was the inclusion of live rock-and-roll music.

46 See photograph in *The Village Voice*, 26 January 1967, 13.

47 Sam Abrams, 'The Poets Caravan', 'The Week of Angry Arts Against the War in Vietnam', 9.

48 *Ramparts*, 5:7 (January 1967), 44–68.

49 The authorised text of his ensuing speech, 'Declaration of Independence from the War in Vietnam' (4 April 1967), connecting domestic racist oppression, poverty and United States intervention in Vietnam, was published in *Ramparts*, 5:11 (May 1967), 32–7. The speech was sponsored by Clergy and Laymen Concerned about Vietnam.

50 James F. Colaianni, 'Napalm: Made in the USA A Small Town Diary', *Ramparts*, 5:3 (August 1966), 46–50.

51 *Ramparts*, 4:8 (December 1965), 23–9. See, too, Robert Scheer, 'The Winner's War', 19–22.

52 Abrams, 'The Poets Caravan', 9.

53 King, 'Declaration of Independence from the War in Vietnam', 33.

54 *Ibid.*, pp. 36–7. Generally see Tom Wells, *The War Within*, 129ff., including the contrasting memos to President Johnson from John Roche and from J. Edgar Hoover after King's speech; and Vincent Harding, 'A Long Time Coming, Reflections on the Black Freedom Movement', in Schmidt Campbell (ed.), *Tradition and Conflict*, especially pp. 35ff.

55 Abrams, 'The Poets Caravan', 9.

56 King, 'Declaration of Independence from the War in Vietnam', 33.

57 Abrams, 'The Poets Caravan', 9.

58 For an example of how this work irritated particular political rather than acceptable social sensibilities see letter from Robert Witz, *Artforum*, 7:7 (March 1969), 4: 'Kienholz is insulting our country.'

59 A point made by Golub in his 'The Artist as an Angry Artist', 49.

60 Press Release by 'The Angry Arts', dated 1 February 1967, with Leon Golub as contact for Artists and Writers Protest in Rudolf Baranik and Dore Ashton Files, PAD/D Archive (Museum of Modern Art Library).

61 *Ibid.*

62 *The Village Voice*, 2 February 1967, 3.

63 See 'Hanging the American Flag', *The New York Times*, 8 January, 1967, Section II, 26D. Also John Perreault's 'Art' column, *The Village Voice*, 12 January 1967, 11–12.

64 'New Police Board Finds Complaints Drop Sharply', *The New York Times*, 9 January 1967, 22.

65 'Gallery Head Guilty of Mutilating Flag', *The New York Times*, 6 May 1967, 36. Also, Grace Glueck's 'Oh, Say, Can You See . . .', *The New York Times*, 21 May 1967, Section II, 33, 35.

66 Morrel in a panel discussion, moderated by Jean Siegel, with Leon Golub, Allan D'Arcangelo and Ad Reinhardt broadcast 10 August 1967 on WBAI in Jean Siegel (ed.), *Artwords: Discourse on the 60s and 70s* (Ann Arbor, UMI Research Press, (1985), pp. 116–17. Radich was convicted for 'casting contempt upon the flag' but

this was overturned after a series of court appeals several years later. By then Morrel had fled to Europe.

67 21, 22, 27, 28, 29 January 1967; 3, 4, 5 February 1967. Advertised separately, *The Village Voice*, 19 January 1967, 25, in the same issue as a half-page advertisement for the January edition of *Ramparts*, which included the Pepper article and photos of napalm victims, and an extraordinary cover combining the crucifixion and Americans in Vietnam. On 'Snows' see Schneemann, *More Than Meat Joy: Performance Works and Selected Writings* (Kingston, New York, Documentext, McPherson and Company, [1979] 1997) pp. 128–49. Also *Carolee Schneemann: Up to and Including Her Limits* (New York, The New Museum of Contemporary Art, New York, 1996).

68 Schneemann, 'Snows', *More Than Meat Joy*, p. 129. Heavy snow fell on New York at the time, with blizzard warnings on the final night, 5 February 1967, of the eight performances watched by capacity audiences.

69 Mariellen R. Sandford (ed.), *Happenings and Other Acts* (London and New York, Routledge, 1995), p. xxi.

70 *Ibid.*, p. xxii.

71 Rebecca Schneider, *The Explicit Body In Performance* (London and New York, Routledge, 1997), p. 37. On a historical review of the issues of essentialism and social construction see Amelia Jones, 'Power and Feminist Art (History)', *Art History*, 17:4 (September 1995), 435–43, and Amelia Jones (ed.), *Sexual Politics: Judy Chicago's* Dinner Party *in Feminist Art History* (Berkeley, UCLA/Hammer/California University Press, 1996), especially 'The "Sexual politics" of *The Dinner Party*: A Critical Context', pp. 82–118.

72 Schneider, *The Explicit Body In Performance*, p. 37.

73 Schneemann, active in the early years of Fluxus, was excommunicated from the 'Art Stud Club' by George Maciunus, the founder of Fluxus, for 'expressionist tendencies' which he found too messy. See Schneider, *The Explicit Body In Performance*, pp. 34ff.

74 Schneemann, interviewed by Andrea Juno, *Angry Women, RE/Search* 13 (1991), 70, quoted by David Levi Strauss, 'Love Rides Aristotle through the Audience: Body Image and Idea in the Work of Carolee Schneemann', in *Carolee Schneemann: Up to and Including her Limits*, p. 31.

75 *Ibid.*

76 Schneemann, 'On the Making of *Snows*', *More Than Meat Joy*, p. 146.

77 *Ibid.*

78 See her 'Notes on and around *Snows*', *More Than Meat Joy*, p. 121.

79 Letter (7 February 1966), *More Than Meat Joy*, p. 119.

80 See her 'Notes on and around *Snows*', *More Than Meat Joy*, p. 121.

81 Schneemann, 'On the Making of *Snows*', *More Than Meat Joy*, p. 146.

82 See Schneemann, 'Snows', *More Than Meat Joy*, p. 131.

83 WBAI, founded in 1960, was a non-profit, non-commercial, listener-subscribed radio station located in midtown Manhattan. In the mid 1960s, it was regarded as one of the few voices of the free press.

84 See 'Report of Angry Arts Week', dated May 1967, in Rudolf Baranik and Dore Ashton Files, PAD/D Archive (Museum of Modern Art Library).

85 Copy of 'Certificate of Incorporation' (13 June 1967) signed by the 'Directors of said Incorporation' who were: Karl Bissinger, Leon Golub, Irving Petlin, Wolfgang Zuckermann, Jules Rabin. Rudolf Baranik and Dore Ashton Files, PAD/D Archive (Museum of Modern Art Library).

86 Including a portfolio of sixteen original, signed and numbered lithographs and serigraphs accompanied by a suite of poems in April. Artists were: Baranik, Burlin,

Cajori, Cply, D'Arcangelo, di Suvero, Golub, Hinman, Nevelson, Petlin, Reinhardt, Sonenberg, Sugarman, Summers, Weinrib, Yunkers. Poets were: Antin, Blackburn, Bly, Creely, Duncan, Eshelman, Hecht, Kunitz, Levertov, Lowenfels, Oppenheimer, Planz, Rothenberg, Samperi, Sorrentino, Stein, Towle, Wright. Max Kozloff provided an introduction. This portfolio included a rare Reinhardt political or 'propaganda' work, entitled *No War*, a double-airmail postcard addressed to 'War Chief, Washington, D.C., USA'. There were also 'Art Sales for Peace' to which many of the artists associated with Angry Arts donated works to raise money. See various advertisements and lists in Rudolf Baranik and Dore Ashton Files, PAD/D Archive (Museum of Modern Art Library).

87   See plans 'Angry Arts in Washington' outlined in a typed and handwritten page by Pheobe Sonenberg, Rudolf Baranik and Dore Ashton Files, PAD/D Archive (Museum of Modern Art Library).

88   Golub, 'The Artist as an Angry Artist', 48.

89   Kozloff, '. . . A Collage of Indignation', 249.

90   Golub, 'The Artist as an Angry Artist', 48.

91   Kozloff, '. . . A Collage of Indignation', 248.

92   *Ibid.*

93   *Ibid.*

94   *Ibid.*

95   *Ibid.*, 248–9.

96   *Ibid.*, 249.

97   *Ibid.*

98   *Ibid.*, 250.

99   *Ibid.*, 251.

100   Golub, 'The Artist as an Angry Artist', 48.

101   New York and Toronto, Bantam Books, 1967. See for example p. 22.

102   Poppy Johnson writes of Hendricks's and Toche's own criticism of their 'many years of feminist consciousness' in 'Statement of Poppy Johnson, June 16, 1966', in John Hendricks and Jean Toche, *GAAG: The Guerrilla Art Action Group 1969–1976, A Selection* (New York, Printed Matter, 1978), unpaginated.

103   On the latter two, see Hoffman, *Soon to be a Major Motion Picture* (New York, Perigree, 1980); Stefen Brecht, *The Bread and Puppet Theatre*, I (London, Methuen, 1988). On Schumann's removal of the theatre from the public rallies after autumn 1967 to 1971, see Alexis Greene, 'The Arts and the Vietnam Antiwar Movement', in Barbara Tischler (ed.), *Sights on the Sixties* (New Brunswick, Rutgers University Press, 1992), pp. 149–61.

104   Golub, 'The Artist as an Angry Artist', 49. Marlene Nadle said of the *Collage*: 'it was a giant eschatological mess, which is exactly what it should have been, given the subject matter' in 'Angry Arts: Aiming Through the Barrier', *The Village Voice*, 9 February 1967, 12.

105   In John Hendricks (ed.), *Manipulations* (New York, A Judson Publication, 1967), a series of texts and images without pagination contained within an envelope (thanks to John Hendricks for sight of a copy). The links to Fluxus are clear both in the format and in the participation of Nam June Paik and Yoko Ono in the twelfth, and last, of the events.

106   'Some Notes, 11 December, 1967', in Hendricks (ed.), *Manipulations*.

107   'Judson Publications Manifesto', in Hendricks (ed.), *Manipulations*.

108   Ortiz was the first (5 October 1967), followed by Bici Hendricks, Jean Toche, Allan Kaprow, Al Hansen, Geoffrey Hendricks, Malcolm Goldstein, Steve Rose, Carolee Schneemann, Lil Picard, Kate Millet. The final evening (22 October) was Nam June

Paik's *Soft Transformations* with Philip Corner, Fred Lieberman, Charlotee Moorman, Yoko Ono, Thomas Schmit and Ken Warner.

109 'Destruction Theater Manifesto: Destruction Realizations', in Hendricks (ed.), *Manipulations*.

110 Schneemann, 'Divisions and Rubble at Judson, 1967', in Hendricks (ed.), *Manipulations*.

111 *Ibid.*

112 *Ibid.*

113 Harold Rosenberg, 'Art of Bad Conscience', reprinted in *Artworks and Packages* (Chicago, University of Chicago Press, 1982), pp. 162–4.

114 At the New School Art Centre (24 October to 2 December 1967). In the accompanying catalogue, Paul Mocsanyi, Director of the Centre, described the exhibition as 'a commentary on Civil Rights and Vietnam', 'Foreward', *Protest and Hope: An Exhibition of Contemporary American Art* (New York, New School Art Centre, 1967), p. 2. The exhibition comprised forty-three contemporary artists, forty-eight works, with fourteen of the exhibited works produced expressly for the show. George Segal's *The Execution*, which Rosenberg regarded as the highlight of the show, was used on publicity, including for the New School's symposium, 'The Artist as a Social Critic', in conjunction with the exhibition.

115 Rosenberg, 'Art of Bad Conscience', p. 164.

116 *Ibid.*

117 The panel also included Robert Bly, Leon Golub, Maxwell Geismar and George Tabori. The discussion was held in Washington Square Methodist Church, near to the NYU Loeb student centre where *The Collage of Indignation* was on display.

118 Rosenberg, 'Art of Bad Conscience', pp. 164–5.

119 *Ibid.*, p. 170.

120 Others were Leonard Baskin, *Our General*; Charles Cajori, *Pax Americana*; Elaine de Kooning, *Countdown*; Rosalyn Drexler, *Oh Say Can You See . . . ?*; Red Grooms, *Patriot's Parade #1* and *#2*; Luise Kaish, *Equation*; Robert Mallary, *Viet Variation #2*; Robert Rauschenberg, *Caller*; Ray Sanders, *Smile*; Ben Shahn, *Goyaesca #2*; Van Loen, *The Victim*; James Wine, *Untitled Poster*.

121 Rosenberg, 'Art of Bad Conscience', p. 165.

122 Hal Foster, *The Return of the Real: The Avant-garde at the End of the Century* (Cambridge, Mass., and London, MIT Press, 1996), p. 127.

123 Therese Schwartz 'The Politicization of the Avant-garde', Part I, *Art in America*, 59:6 (1971), 97–105; Part II, *Art in America*, 60:2 (1972), 70–9; Part III, *Art in America*, 61:2 (1973), 69–71; Part IV, *Art in America*, 62:1 (1974), 80–4.

124 See: Lucy Lippard, 'The Art Workers' Coalition: Not a History', *Studio International*, 180:927 (November 1970), 171–4, reprinted in Lippard, *Get the Message: A Decade of Art for Social Change* (New York, E. P. Dutton, 1974); Art Workers Coalition, *Documents 1* (New York, AWC, 1969); Art Workers Coalition, *Open Hearing* (New York, AWC, 1969). Generally see Schwartz 'The Politicization of the Avant-garde', Parts I to IV.

125 See John Perreault's regular art column, 'Whose Art?', *The Village Voice*, 9 January 1969, 16–17.

126 *Ibid.*

127 Handbill in Art Workers Coalition, *Documents 1*, p. 1. See also 'Statement of January 5, 1969', p. 5.

128 See Hendricks and Toche, *GAAG: The Guerrilla Art Action Group*. Hendricks was an active anti-Vietnam-War protester with Quaker roots. In the late 1960s, he was closely connected with the Judson Gallery and has been curator of The Gilbert and Lila Silverman Fluxus Collection, for example see: Hendricks, *Fluxus Codex* (New

York, The Gilbert and Lila Silverman Fluxus Collection, in association with Abrams, 1988); Clive Phillpot and Jon Hendricks, *Fluxus: Selections from the Gilbert and Lila Silverman Fluxus Collection* (New York, Museum of Modern Art, New York, 1988).

129 See for example the statistics and tables in Diane Crane, *The Transformation of the Avant-Garde: The New York Art World, 1940–1985* (Chicago and London, University of Chicago Press, 1987). Also K. E. Meyer, *The Art Museum: Power, Money, Ethics* (New York, William Morrow and Company, 1979); Steven Naifeh, *Culture Making: Money, Success, and the New York Art World* (Princeton, Princeton Undergraduate Studies in History: 2, History Department of Princeton University, 1976).

130 Naifeh, *Culture Making*, pp. 81–2.

131 Crane, *The Transformation of the Avant-garde*, p. 6.

132 Judd in 'The Artist and Politics: A Symposium', *Artforum*, 9:1 (September 1970), 36.

133 They were both brought nearer to Judd's control when he eventually located himself and much of his work in Marfa, Texas.

134 David McReynolds and Paul Buhle, in Mari Jo Buhle, Paul Buhle and Dan Greorgakas (eds), *Encyclopedia of the American Left* (Urbana and Chicago, University of Illinois Press, 1992), p. 552.

135 Judd in 'The Artist and Politics: A Symposium', 36–7.

136 *Ibid.*, 37.

137 An earlier version of some of the arguments here can be found in my 'The Politics of Representation', chapter 2 of Wood, Frascina, Harris and Harrison, *Modernism in Dispute*, especially pp. 95–102.

138 Theodor Adorno, 'Commitment', in A. Arato and E. Gebhardt (eds), *The Essential Frankfurt School Reader* (New York, Continuum, 1985), p. 318.

139 *Ibid.*, p. 317.

140 See, for example Hal Foster, 'The Crux of Minimalism', in Howard Singerman (ed.), *Individuals: A Selected History of Contemporary Art* (New York, Abrams, 1986), pp. 162–83; Anna Chave, 'Minimalism and the Rhetoric of Power'.

141 Judd in 'The Artist and Politics: A Symposium', 37.

142 Andre in 'The Artist and Politics: A Symposium', 35.

143 Lippard, 'The Art Workers' Coalition: Not a History', 172.

144 *Ibid.*

145 'Hans Haacke and the Guggenheim', *Feminist Art Journal*, 1:1 (April 1972), 24.

146 Lippard, *A Different War: Vietnam in Art*, p. 18.

147 *Ibid.*

148 Quoted by Lippard, *A Different War*, p. 20.

149 See Reise, 'Greenberg and the Group: A Retrospective View'.

150 'Modernist Painting', first as radio broadcast no. 14 for *The Voice of America Forum Lectures: The Visual Arts* printed in *Arts Yearbook*, 4 (New York, 1961), pp. 101–8; *Art and Culture* (Boston, Beacon Books, 1961).

151 This notion is indebted to Raymond Williams's distinction between Specializing, Alternative and Oppositional Social Formations in *Culture* (London, Fontana, 1981).

152 Leider ran a series of articles on the subject 'Problems of Criticism', which included Greenberg's notorious 'Complaints of an Art Critic', *Artforum*, 6:2 (October 1967), 38–9. Three of the series were devoted to 'politics' in strange articles by Barbara Rose, 'The Politics of Criticism IV: The Politics of Art, Part I', *Artforum*, 6:6 (February 1968), 31–2; 'The Politics of Criticism V: The Politics of Art, Part II', *Artforum*, 7:5 (January 1969), 44–9; 'The Politics of Criticism VI: The Politics of Art, Part III', *Artforum*, 7:9 (May 1969), 46–51. I say strange for a number of reasons. For example,

in Part I, Rose claimed that Fried's criticism was characterised by the tone and vocabulary of Marxist polemics. This was a serious error on Rose's part. Leider's commitment to Fried's view about the separation of art and politics can be found even in 1970 at the hight of *Artforum*'s flirtation with issues of art and the anti-Vietnam-War protests: 'I argued for Michael Fried's idea that the conventional nature of art was its very essence, that the great danger was the delusion that one was making art when in fact you were doing something else, something of certain value but not the value of art' (in Leider, 'How I Spent My Summer Vacation or Art and Politics in Nevada, Berkeley, San Francisco and Utah', *Artforum*, 9:1 (September 1970), 40–1). Rose's attack on Greenberg's and Fried's criticism as examples of 'the disenchanted left' finding a 'rapprochement with the society it once rejected' mixes defensible observations with a view of politics circumscribed by the narrow perspectives of *Artforum*'s community.

153 At various points including Michael Fried, Rosalind Krauss, Jane Harrison Cone and Sidney Tillim.

154 Letter (21 April 1967) from Leider to Greenberg in Greenberg Papers (Archives of American Art, Smithsonian Institution, Washington, DC).

155 Letter (9 October 1967) from Leider to Greenberg in Greenberg Papers (Archives of American Art, Smithsonian Institution, Washington, DC).

156 Letter (9 May 1968) from Leider to Greenberg in Greenberg Papers (Archives of American Art, Smithsonian Institution, Washington, DC).

157 Letter (24 October 1966) from Leider to Greenberg in Greenberg Papers (Archives of American Art, Smithsonian Institution, Washington, DC).

158 *Ibid.*

159 *Ibid.* Greenberg and Leider fell out in 1970 over something which always drew Greenberg's uncomfortable anger. On 15 October 1970, Greenberg's lawyers wrote to the publisher of *Artforum* seeking an apology. In that month's issue of *Artforum*, 9:2 (October 1970), 38, appeared 'An Ad Reinhardt Monologue'. Greenberg's lawyers suggested that *Artforum* apologise for its implications thus: 'We are aware of no basis in fact which would sustain the late Mr. Reinhardt's implication that Mr Greenberg "became" an "agent and dealer" as well as critic'. In a letter to Leider (dated 9 November) Greenberg refers to Reinhardt as a 'cur' and to Leider as 'some undetermined kind of *rodent*' and 'scum'. In 1961 Greenberg had a letter and an apology printed in *The Sunday Star* for an article by Frank Getlein (31 December 1961, C-6) which suggested that Greenberg had been a 'picture dealer' and that 'his judgement of the qualities of these artists [Morris Louis and Kenneth Noland] had an interested motive behind it'. All letters and press cutting in Greenberg Papers (Archives of American Art, Smithsonian Institution, Washington, DC).

160 Fried, 'Art and Objecthood', 12.

161 *Ibid.*, 23.

162 See Fried, 'Art and Objecthood', 15, and 23 n 3.

163 Foster, 'The Crux of Minimalism', in Howard Singerman (ed.), *Individuals: A Selected History of Contemporary Art*, pp. 162–83.

164 Foster, 'The Crux of Minimalism', p. 174.

165 *Ibid.*, p. 180. In a footnote to his question, Foster refers the reader to a discussion 'on these mediations' from 1975: Karl Beveridge and Ian Burn, 'Don Judd', *The Fox* 2 (1975).

166 *Arts Magazine*, 64:5 (January 1990), 44–63.

167 Rose, 'The Politics of Criticism V: The Politics of Art, Part II'.

168 Golub, *Artforum*, 7:7 (March 1969), 3–4 (see, too, letter from Cindy Nemser, 4).

169 Golub, *ibid.*, 3.

170 *Ibid.*, 4.

171 *Ibid.*
172 Foster, 'The Crux of Minimalism', p. 180.
173 Heizer, 1969–70, 240,000 ton displacement, Mormon Mesa, Overton, Nevada; Smithson, 1970, 10 acre site, coil of 457 metres, Rozel Point, Great Salt Lake, Utah.
174 Leider, 'How I Spent My Summer Vacation or Art and Politics in Nevada, Berkeley, San Francisco and Utah', 48–9.
175 Judd, 'Imperialism, Nationalism and Regionalism', *Donald Judd Complete Writings 1959–1975* (Halifax Nova Scotia and New York, Press of the Nova Scotia College of Art and Design, 1975), pp. 221–2.

4 My Lai, *Guernica*, MoMA and the art left, New York 1969–70[1]

Introduction

This chapter considers a specific moment in the history of the contradictions within the political left in the United States. My starting point, a way of beginning, is a particular letter of 'refusal', dated February 1970, from Meyer Schapiro, an eminent art historian, critic and theorist who had deep associations with the 'Old Left' since the 1930s. His letter was a response to an invitation from a younger generation of artists and writers who were seeking to act collectively in a protest against the My Lai massacre in Vietnam.[2]

I wish to explore how Schapiro's 'I will not' was not simply a personal statement but also a social utterance: an utterance that signified a resistance to *both* the political actions and the socio-cultural beliefs of those who made the invitation *and* any risk to Schapiro's perceptions of the achievements and institutional status of modernism. In his act of resistance was Schapiro caught, like many others, in a historically repetitive collusion with the forces and agencies of an economic and political system which he abhorred? This paradox was common to those of the Old Left who perceived the New Left of the 1960s as a threat to those elements of progressive modern liberal democratic culture in the United States regarded by the older generation as the products of struggle.

What are the effects of loss and denial, of collusion and conformity, in attempts to preserve the claimed achievements of modernism and modernity? My intention here is to explore a specific instance of the ways in which unconscious desires and denials interact with social agency in the production of meanings and conditions for action.

Why Schapiro? His roots and activities establish him as one of that group of New York intellectuals, with Jewish backgrounds and steeped in the traditions of revolutionary politics, often characterised as the heart of the Old Left.[3] He was born in Lithuania in 1904, moved with his family to the United States in 1907 and became a naturalised citizen in 1914. A brilliant student, he enrolled at Columbia at the age of sixteen, completed a pioneering doctoral dissertation on a Romanesque topic and spent the rest of his professional life as an academic at Columbia and the New School for Social Research. Although never a member of the

Communist Party, he retained strong ties with it and assisted the Party in various ways during the 1930s. He helped found, and in 1936 addressed, the First American Artists Congress, established as part of the Popular Front. His 'The Social Bases of Art' became an important statement on the need for artists to ally themselves to the revolutionary working class. Whilst allied to Trotskyism he had a major editorial role on the short-lived *Marxist Quarterly*, for which he wrote a long and important essay on the 'Nature of Abstract Art' (1937). Schapiro contributed to several leftist journals including *Partisan Review*, where in 1943 his 'sensational' debate with Sydney Hook was published. Schapiro knew Theodor Adorno well, while the latter was in New York, and he visited Paris in the summer of 1939, at Max Horkheimer's request, on a mission to persuade Walter Benjamin to emigrate to the United States. After 1945 Schapiro continued to develop his original Marxist analyses, publishing major articles, including a defence of Abstract Expressionism in 'The Liberating Quality of Avant-garde Art' (1957), and remained politically engaged in the traditions of leftist intellectuals of the 1930s such as Irving Howe and Sydney Hook.[4]

The letters

In February 1970 the Art Workers' Coalition (AWC) and Artists and Writers Protest (AWP) sent out invitations asking members and supporters to sign an open letter to Pablo Picasso. The letter included this appeal: ·

> Tell the directors and trustees of the Museum of Modern Art in New York that *Guernica* cannot remain on public view there as long as American troops are committing genocide in Vietnam. Renew the outcry of *Guernica* by telling those who remain silent in the face of Mylai [*sic*] that you remove from them the moral trust as guardians of your painting.[5]

By 11 March 265 signed letters were ready to be sent to Picasso. Although the AWC/AWP press release of 13 March states that a package containing the letters was mailed to Picasso's home in the south of France, it was actually taken to Paris by the artist and activist Irving Petlin. He was to seek the assistance of Michel Leiris to ensure that the letters reached Picasso directly.[6] That they never did despite Petlin's every effort is a story I will come to.

A major absentee from the 265 signed letters was Meyer Schapiro. On 27 February he replied to the AWC/AWP invitation from Sarasota, Florida:

> To ask Picasso to withdraw his painting from the Museum because of the massacre at Mylai is to charge the Museum with moral complicity in the crimes of the military. This I cannot do. Though I share your feelings about the government's whole action in Vietnam, I will not sign your letter to Picasso.[7]

When back in New York, Schapiro sent a copy of this refusal, with a covering letter dated 16 March, to Alfred H. Barr Jnr at MoMA. Barr, still the symbolic embodiment of MoMA's institutionalised modernism,[8] sent an approving reply on 7 April. In contrast Schapiro's refusal prompted a critical letter, dated 3 March, from Rudolf Baranik for the AWC.[9] I will return to all these letters in due course.

Schapiro's support was clearly expected by the AWC/AWP for, as Petlin recalls, to keep the whole project discreet, envisaged supporters were contacted directly. This procedure was designed to minimise outside pressure on Picasso so that he could make a decision based on the package of signed letters from fellow artists and writers. The AWC/AWP hoped that Picasso would be swayed by the parallel between the atrocity at Guernica and the massacre by the United States military at My Lai. However, their strategy was complicated by one of Lawrence Alloway's regular 'Art' columns in *The Nation*, on 23 February 1970.[10] Here he talked of the AWC's project to embarrass the Museum of Modern Art with 'an open letter to Picasso suggesting that he remove "Guernica" which hangs in the museum but is still owned by the artist'.[11] Alloway went on to invoke Picasso's political allegiances: 'the question is whether or not his communism is the sort to force him to protest My Lai by initiating an artistic scandal'.[12]

Schapiro was contacted by the AWC/AWP not only because of his eminent status on the non-Stalinist left since the 1930s but also because of his contributions to anti-Vietnam-War activities. As we have seen, he is listed in the advertisement for the Los Angeles Tower in 1966, among over a hundred New York artists who exhibited one of the 'hundreds of Panels for Peace by artists from the US and abroad'.[13] His name appears also on an AWP appeal on behalf of Angry Arts for artists' support to help finance the march on Washington 21 October 1967, which became the famous seige of the Pentagon by ninety thousand anti-war protesters.[14] And, apparently, he signed an Angry Arts petition organised in April 1967: '1000 AMERICAN ARTISTS PETITION TO PICASSO URGING HIM TO WITHDRAW GUERNICA AS AN ACT OF PROTEST AGAINST UNITED STATES BOMBING IN VIETNAM.'[15] These examples counter suggestions that Schapiro's refusal to sign the 1970 letter to Picasso indicates a process of 'de-Marxification' or that he had become one of the New York intellectuals who had moved from the left rightward in the period since the 1950s. This was the case with many, Clement Greenberg being the most prominent in art criticism, but the evidence of Schapiro's writings and activities demonstrates a continued development of ideas, methods and analyses rooted in his radicalism of the 1930s. Schapiro had always been committed to a type of democratic socialism but overall his development had more in common with the move to a relatively pluralistic liberal socialism exemplified by Irving Howe, who founded and edited *Dissent,* than with the New Left of the 1960s. Schapiro was on the editorial board of *Dissent* when it started in 1954, though he rarely contributed. Unlike Howe, Schapiro did not explicitly repudiate Marxism and while he did not approve of many of the New Left's actions he did not attack them as Howe did in print in *The New York Times Magazine*, in 1968 and 1970.[16]

I am less concerned with trying to explain why Schapiro said no to the AWC/AWP, though some reasons will emerge from examining the texts of relevant letters. My major aim is to consider Schapiro's choice in the specific context of what '*Guernica*', 'My Lai' and 'the Museum of Modern Art' signified in late 1969 and early 1970. In doing so, I wish to consider the contradictions in that constituency of the United States left which was preoccupied with the relationship between art and politics. These months, politically and emotionally intense, were the turning point in anti-war protests, gaining more broad-based support.[17] Not only was the Nixon administration struggling to regain the tacit collusion of the media but also news and images of United States atrocities in Vietnam were brought home to greater effect on the television news and in establishment publications such as *The New York Times*, still a standard read, and *Life* and *Time* magazines. Atrocities, once safely far away, returned with a vengeance to the United States in several forms, firstly to its homes via television – and most violently on United States soil on 4 April 1970 at Kent State University when the National Guard opened fire on students, who were demonstrating against Nixon's announcement of military intervention into Cambodia, killing four of them. Within two weeks police forces killed six blacks in Civil Rights disturbances at Augusta, Georgia, and on 14 May a black student and a delivery boy were killed by police during anti-war actions at Jackson State College. To understand the context of Schapiro's choice necessitates recovery of this intensity and its particular detail.

Guernica as sign

I'll start by examining the AWC/AWP open letter to Picasso, which begins by reminding him of the Franco government's recent invitation to 'you to return and bring *Guernica* to Madrid'. This 'invitation' was first reported in *Le Monde* on 24 October 1969.[18] Picasso's refusal made through his lawyer was contained in a public reply in the same newspaper on 14 November, with the headline '"Guernica" ne reiendra en Espagne qu'avec la République'.[19] In the words of the AWC/AWP letter, 'only when Spain is again a democratic republic will *Guernica* hang in the Prado'. On 29 October 1969, *The New York Times* carried the story 'Franco Favors the Return of Picasso and "Guernica"', noting that the 'Spanish Government has already begun construction of a $28.8 million *museum of modern art* [my italics] on the campus of the Madrid university, which it hopes will be centred on the Civil War masterpiece'.[20] Florentino Perez Embid, the Spanish director-general of fine arts, is reported as saying that although it would not be easy to bring *Guernica* back to Spain there would be no conditions placed on Picasso if he accepted the invitation to return to his native land.

It was not 'easy' for the Franco regime to bring *Guernica* to Spain for several reasons. One was the question of the legal 'ownership' of the work, which the director-general wanted to avoid. The issue of artists' rights over 'ownership' of their work had been one of the stimuli for the formation of the AWC and its running disputes with MoMA. As we have seen, in January 1969 Takis and a group of supporters had entered MoMA and removed a work of his from the exhibition *The Machine as Seen at the End of the Mechanical Age* because it was on show against his wishes: he felt that the piece from 1960 was unrepresentative of his work and that its selection without consultation was an insensitive example of the unwarranted power of museums. Now in November MoMA was faced with another instance of rights and ownership. With *Guernica* the issue was more manageable because, as a Museum official is reported to have told a representative of the Spanish government, 'It is in deposit for the artist'.[21] An unspoken difficulty, though, was Picasso's politics, which since he joined the French Communist Party (PCF) in 1944 had continually embarrassed the art establishment's attempt to aestheticise the artist and to minimise his connections to what the anti-Communist Cold War press had continually condemned as 'the Reds'.[22] In Vietnam, United States capitalist interests were still cloaked by their anti-Communist rhetoric.

Another difficulty was *Guernica*'s political significance in Spain. As was well known, the painting had been commissioned by the Republican government in 1937 and its title refers to the ancient Basque capital which the German Condor Legion bombed in April 1937 to assist Franco's Fascist cause and to assess the effects of mass aerial bombing. *Guernica* thus signified a particular act: the bombing, by foreign forces, of civilians, including children and babies, who were also an ethnic minority supporting the Republican coalition which included socialists, anarchists and Communists. During the Second World War and subsequently in its disciplinary wars, primarily against Communism, the United States military developed the strategy of 'mass' into 'saturation' bombing to staggering proportions, its technological apotheosis being the Gulf War of 1991. By the time the United States withdrew its troops from Vietnam, seven million tons of bombs had been dropped. This was twice the total used on Europe and Asia in the Second World War. It has been estimated that there were twenty million bomb craters in Vietnam. But the United States didn't just drop bombs. During operation Ranch Hand, four million gallons of herbicide and defoliant were dropped over the countryside. This one instance

> was said to be more than four times the annual capacity of all American chemical companies put together. 'We seem to be proceeding', wrote one unimpressed critic in the Pentagon, 'on the assumption that the way to eradicate the Viet Cong is to destroy all the village structures, defoliate all the jungles, and cover the entire surface of Vietnam with asphalt.[23]

The United States war strategy, reiterated by Secretary of State McNamara and Commander-in-Chief General Westmorland, was designed, along the Guernica model, to expend shells not United States men. Hence, overt and covert plans were set in motion early in the 1960s to exploit saturation bombing and the use of defoliants and napalm. The horrific effects of the latter were well known and became an 'obsession' amongst many artists such as Leon Golub and Rudolf Baranik. One of Baranik's posters for Angry Arts week in early 1967 became a haunting signifier of the left's protest at the war and the indiscriminate strategies of the United States military.[24] In 1976 General Fred C. Weyand, whose troops had defended Saigon during the Tet offensive of 1968, recalled:

> The American way of war is particularly violent, deadly and dreadful. We believe in using 'things' – artillery, bombs, massive firepower – in order to conserve our soldiers' lives. The enemy, on the other hand, made up for his lack of 'things' by expending men instead of machines, and he suffered enormous casualties.[25]

In areas designated by the United States as 'free fire zones' every Vietnamese was assumed to have made a choice about staying there – rather than moving to refugee camps or to shanty towns on the edge of cities. The deaths of civilians were regarded by the United States government as a 'tragedy of war' in this strategy of mass bombing. Areas were to be cleared with the destruction of people, houses, livestock, water supply and all that would sustain life. Largely illiterate peasants were informed of their choice – stay and be killed – by leaflets dropped over Vietnam: fifty billion from 1965 to 1972, fifteen hundred for every member of the population.

My Lai and Nixon's 'silent majority'

The anti-war movement had grown stronger especially after the Tet offensive launched by Ho Chi Minh's forces on 31 January 1968 during the Tet (New Year) holiday. Ho's forces captured provincial capitals, including the ancient capital of Hue, and, for a time, controlled parts of Saigon. These events were a massive shock in the United States because the official propaganda message asserted that such an offensive was impossible. Only saturation bombing and intense bloody battles with large

Vietnamese deaths repulsed Ho's forces. More of the characteristics of both official propaganda and the realities of the United States' 'way of war' became exposed despite the manipulation of news by the Pentagon and other state agencies. Not even the negative effects of Tet on the credibility of the government could deflect President Nixon's covert plans in 1969: to escalate bombing in an attempt to force the Vietnamese to the conference table on United States terms and at the same time to build up a self-sufficient South Vietnamese army, already hated by the majority of indigenous peasants. On 3 November 1969, Nixon appealed to the so-called 'silent majority' in a television address to the nation. His Cold War rhetoric did not acknowledge the facts of Vietnamese deaths nor the realities of United States bombing. On 20 November 1969, *The New York Times* carried a story on its front page: 'A "Silent Majority" Backs Nixon In USIA [United States Information Agency] Film Sent Abroad'. This fifteen-minute film, including footage of the previous week's anti-war demonstrations in Washington, sought to cast the protesters as a rowdy minority within the country, with the 'silent majority' in support of the Nixon administration. Of this film, supposedly made as an immediate patriotic response to Nixon's speech on 3 November, the USIA had since 17 November already shipped out two hundred prints to 104 foreign countries, including 'versions dubbed in nine languages . . . USIA officials said that additional versions were being dubbed in 13 other languages and that more prints were being sent out daily'. This film and Nixon's television appeal to the 'silent majority' were propaganda strategies of containment and deflection. Nixon's speech was made in full knowledge of news of the atrocity by United States troops at My Lai – murder, rape and mutilation – that was about to break publicly.

News of My Lai became crucial in changing public attitudes to the war and was central to the AWC/AWP letter to Picasso:

> What the U.S. government is doing in Vietnam far exceeds Oradour and Lidice [Nazi SS atrocities in France, 1944, and Czechoslovakia, 1942]. The continuous housing of *Guernica* in the Museum of Modern Art, New York, implies that our establishment has the moral right to be indignant about the crimes of others – and ignore our own crimes.
>
> American artists want to raise their voices against the hundreds of Guernicas and Oradours which are taking place in Vietnam. We cannot remain silent in the face of My Lai.[26]

On 13 November 1969, Seymour Hersh's article which broke the news of My Lai to a major audience appeared. The exact number of unarmed women, old men, children and babies massacred on 16 March 1968 has never been agreed and ranges from 'at least 175' to 'around 500'.[27] Hersh's first article basically details the murder of 'at least 109 Vietnamese civilians' with which Lieutenant Calley was charged. He notes not only that the area was a 'free fire zone . . . common throughout Vietnam' but also that the 'Army claimed 128 Viet Cong were killed'. Vietnamese civilians were to tell reporters that the figure was 567. Distributed through the Washington-based Despatch News Service, the revelations appeared in thirty-five newspapers.[28] On the same day, *The New York Times* carried its own story, 'Officer Kept in Army in Inquiry into Killing of Vietnam Civilians'.[29] Hersch's article included an interview with Lieutenant Calley, leader of the unit of Charlie Company responsible for the massacre, who had been formally charged with murdering 109 'Oriental human beings'. Hersh included three further eyewitness accounts in a follow-up story on 20 November in *The Times*, London,[30] which *The New York Times* referenced on the same day.[31] They carried their own story, 'G.I. Says He Saw Vietnam Massacre',[32] and also referenced the fact that on the night of 19 November *The Cleveland Plain Dealer* reproduced photographs of the massacre.[33]

These photographs visualised the atrocity with tremendous effect on the media. *The Cleveland Plain Dealer* printed eight black and white photographs taken from Sergeant Ron Haeberle's transparencies of the terrified villagers and murdered bodies which he took at My Lai as an army photographer. He had handed over black and white photographs taken with his army Leica; but had kept colour transparencies taken on his own Nikon. On the evening of 20 November, CBS's nightly news programme had Walter Cronkite introducing the television audience to the front page of *The Cleveland Plain Dealer* with its black and white images of the horror of My Lai. But even more stunning was an interview on CBS television news on 24 November between Mike Wallace and Paul Meadlo, who had personally killed dozens of Vietnamese under Calley's orders. The interview was reported on the front page of *The New York Times* next day, dwarfed by the lead headline and photos of Apollo 12's splashdown in the Pacific. The transcript of the interview was also included on page 16. Meadlo recalled that the women, children and old men were 'just pushed in a ravine or just sitting, squatting . . . and shot'. In answer to a follow up question, he replied: 'Right, they was [*sic*] begging and saying, "No, no." And the mothers was hugging their children and, but they kept on firing. Well, we kept right on firing. They was waving their arms and begging.'[34]

The use of M-16 rifles and M-60 machine-guns added to the horror for all those who knew the power of these weapons. They ripped bodies apart, severed heads and limbs, and shredded flesh and splintered bone. The horror of the event led Wallace to observe, 'we've raised such a dickens about what the Nazis did, or what the Japanese did . . . in the second world war, the brutalization and so forth'. How then could 'young, capable American boys . . . line up old men, women and children and babies and shoot them down in cold blood'? Meadlo couldn't explain why. This parallel with Nazi atrocities, as in Guernica, Oradour and Lidice, became inescapable in news reports. One example is in *The New York Times* on 20 November, where Hersh's interview with Private Michael Terry published in *The Times* (London) on the same day, is referred to. Terry is quoted: 'They had them in a group standing over a ditch – just like a Nazi-type thing . . . Mostly women and kids . . . A lot of guys feel that they [South Vietnamese civilians] aren't human beings. We just treated them like animals.'[35]

Murder was only one part of My Lai. As many readers of the reports suspected, there were other brutal acts. Scalping, mutilation of sexual organs and severing of body parts had become part of the brutalisation of the Vietnamese by GIs, themselves brutalised by the 'American way of war'. Although there is a long history of these acts within the United States military, the specific problem led General Westmorland to issue a directive on 13 October 1967, which condemned the practice of cutting off ears of Vietnamese as 'contrary to all policy and below standards of human decency'.[36] The other suspicion was sexual assault. Later it was confirmed that women and girls were subjected to multiple rape, sodomy and oral sex before being mutilated and shot.[37] Some of the sexual assaults were publicly hinted at in a further intensification of the media reports of My Lai, most explosively in *Time* and *Life* magazines dated 5 December 1969.[38] *Life* magazine reproduced Haeberle's photographs in colour in a ten-page spread with accompanying article, interviews and reports: 'The Massacre at Mylai: Exclusive pictures, eyewitness accounts'.[39] These colour photographs and text revealed more of the massacre by now twenty-one months in the past.

Life and the power of the visual

This issue of *Life* signifies much about the magazine's envisaged audience and the dominant United States ideology of 'business as usual'. Unlike the covers of *Time* and *Newsweek*, *Life*'s front cover is a photograph of sable African antelope in Kenya with the promise, 'Great Action Pictures by John Dominis'. But before the reader gets to these pictures by Dominis,[40] those action photos by Haeberle completely disrupt any comfortable expectation. Overall, such expectation is encouraged by the full-page consumer advertisements which jostle with an article on Graham Kerr, 'Comedian in the Kitchen',[41] a gossipy piece on 'The Presidency', including a grinning Henry Kissinger, Nixon's 'eligible national security advisor'[42] and the inevitable photo-spread on 'The Go-Go Astronauts of Apollo 12'.[43] In the space between the latter and the My Lai spread, the image of a 'disembodied' ear filling a whole page is used to advertise De Beers's diamonds.[44] A large earring hanging from the ear serves as a reminder of many GIs' own jewellery – necklaces of severed ears strung with bandoliers as evidence of the military's emphasis on 'body count'.

Numbers and bodies were differently articulated in another major news report. The United States media had been dominated by coverage of the Apollo missions since the first moon landing in the summer, where the astronauts left a plaque: 'We came in peace for all mankind.' Faith Ringgold's painting *Flag for the Moon: Die Nigger* (1969) represents critical dissent using the hallowed Stars and Stripes to draw attention to the hypocrisy of the plaque's claim in face of the reality of domestic racism. And the anti-war movement could draw further damning comparisons between 'peace' on the moon and United States racism and imperialism in Indochina. A major problem, however, in raising wider critical consciousness was the media's obsession with one version of American experience, 'for all mankind'. Cracks in this controlled version appeared unexpectedly, bleeding through a tightly bound body of collusion and consent: for example the trusted voice of CBS news, Walter Cronkite, being faced by, and facing millions of viewers with, My Lai massacre photos in *The Cleveland Plain Dealer*, and the coverage of the Apollo 12 splashdown being violently ruptured by Wallace's interview with Meadlo.

Life's regular audience hungry for the magazine's latest illustrated spreads could be satisfied by, for example, pages 10 to 15. First a black and white double-page spread, 'Gallery', with three 'nude' photographs by Christer Hallgren of 'his girlfriend . . . [dancing] to a rock record in his studio', immediately followed by an advertisement for Polaroid cameras with a colour photograph of two United States children taken in front of a Christmas tree (pages 12–13); and on page 15 a colour advertisement for three *Life* 'Journey to the Moon' jigsaw puzzles. This seamless presentation and the remainder of the images and texts is cut through by Haeberle's photographs of other 'girlfriends' and 'children'. On page 37 we see a full-page photo of terrified Vietnamese women, teenagers and children whose fate we learn on page 43:

> Then a soldier asked 'Well, what'll we do with 'em?'
> 'Kill 'em,' another answered.
> 'I heard an M60 go off,' says Roberts [Sergeant Jay Roberts], 'a light machine gun, and when we turned back around, all of them and the kids with them were dead.'

Just before this report, on the same page, there is the sole hint of sexual assault, the full extent of which became clear only in later reports. Referring to the people in the above photograph, Roberts and Haeberle recalled:

> The girl was about 13 and wearing black pyjamas. A GI grabbed the girl and with the help of others started stripping her.
> 'Let's see what she's made out of,' a soldier said.

'VC boom-boom,' another said, telling the 13-year-old girl that she was a whore for the Vietcong.

'I'm horny,' said a third.

As they were stripping the girl, with bodies and burning huts all around them the girl's mother tried to help her, scratching and clawing at the soldiers.

'Q. And babies? A. And babies.'

Members of the AWC/AWP[45] followed the revelations about My Lai with growing outrage. Wishing to find a way of expressing their public protest, they relied on strategies established in previous visual productions and campaigns. These include the collective and interventionist Los Angeles Tower (1966), Angry Arts and *The Collage of Indignation* (1967) and a range of visual manifestations in demonstrations. Examples are the use of body bags obtained from the army for a 'patriotic play' and carried aloft to signify the deaths in Vietnam, long *Guernica* banners, and Lieutenant Calley masks worn on the back of heads as in medieval plays.[46] The latter were the idea of Irving Petlin, who had been a major organiser and creative force drawing upon his experience in France from 1959 to 1964 when French intellectuals were engaged in trying to end the Algerian war. This struggle with colonialism followed on from the protests at French imperialist rule in Indochina which had ended in the 1950s. This colonial role was taken over at first covertly by the United States and during Kennedy's administration entrenched by military invasion.[47]

Petlin's political 'apprenticeship' in France helped to formulate a sense of what he calls 'primitive situational politics' which characterised the early activities of anti-Vietnam-War protests. One major aspect of this was a high degree of 'visualisation' or 'high visual content' that would not only appeal to a broad United States audience becoming used to the proliferation of visual media but also gain the attention of broadcasting companies and thus publicise the protests. With My Lai it became imperative to continue these strategies in ways that cut across both high-art expectations, institutionally and practically, and those of the 'mass media'. The AWC decided on a mass-produced poster that would engage with modern techniques and subvert the normal conditions of production and consumption (Plate 13). Their first choice was to use one of the most disturbing of Haeberle's photographs of the dead strewn along a dirt road. Already shown in *The Cleveland Plain Dealer* and on CBS, this photograph appeared on its own in *The New York Times* on 22 November[48] with a short cover story about Haeberle. The report also stated that *Life* had acquired exclusive rights to the colour reproduction of Haeberle's eighteen photographs and recorded an interview with him, all of which would appear in their 5 December issue, on the newsstands on 1 December.

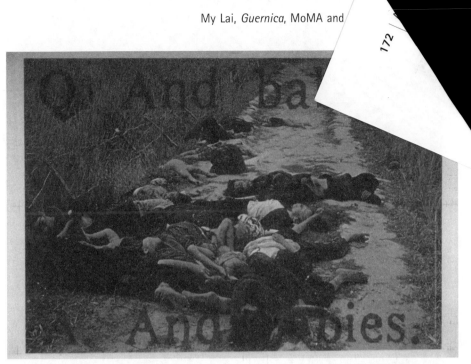

13 Art Workers' Coalition/Peter Brandt/From an interview with Paul Meadlo by Mike Wallace/Photograph R. L. Haeberle, *Q. And babies? A. And babies*, 1970, offset lithographic colour poster, 25 × 38 inches.

Alongside, concerned readers could read a report of the horrified reaction to My Lai in Britain. Charles Wheeler, the BBC's Washington correspondent, remarked on the relatively calm reaction in the United States and said: 'Seen from here, it seems that the conscience of America rests in the House of Commons and Fleet Street.' Not so with the AWC/AWP, concerned by *The New York Times*'s front-page story, which ran and ran: 'MASSACRE REPORT DENIED BY SAIGON'.

Alerted to the possibility of a colour image and recognising the need for an immediate response, the AWC's second choice was made after 24 November. This was to reproduce on the image the literal typeface of a question and answer from the televised Wallace interview with Meadlo as transcribed in *The New York Times*: 'Q. And babies? A. And babies.' But these important choices would have been ineffective gestures without subverting the normal systems of appropriation. If the AWC were to fulfil its ambitious aims, how could its 'situational politics' produce circumstances in which the establishment, here represented by MoMA, unwittingly revealed the contradictions of its own power and assumptions? A major opportunity came on 25 November when there was a scheduled meeting between the AWC, MoMA's Staff Executive (sometimes referred to as 'Ad Hoc Planning') Committee, other members of the staff and seven non-aligned artists invited by the Museum.

To understand the issues at stake at this meeting, it is important to recognise the specific cultural and political implications of the AWC's choices of image and text. One of these was to evoke the effect of ruptures in television networks' news reporting, especially after the Tet offensive which began on 31 January 1968. Prior to this, the reports from Vietnam generally colluded with the ideological assumptions about the moral correctness of United States involvement. Major studies have concluded that the United States news media were dependent upon information provided by the executive branch, placed their faith in the moral authority of the White House and were subject to the military's controlled access to sites in Vietnam. Analyses of broadcasts have also shown that television news stations and those making editorial decisions followed the line of official optimism.[49] This was a form of self-censorship which replicated and colluded with the political 'establishment'. The period after the Tet offensive did lead to the United States media, including television, being more critical of the war and echoing public dissent. The shift can be connected to the Johnson administration's lack of flow of information in the wake of the offensive, which blew apart the government's propaganda line. However, this relative critical edge did not last, nor did it mean that reporting was ever fundamentally *against* United States involvement. When pressure was brought to bear by Nixon's White House machine, the media became dependent again on the government's language, agenda and perspective.

However, despite the control, those images of battlefield carnage that did enter into the homes of everyone with a television had a visual rhetoric which was unsettling, at least potentially. The sheer regularity of the images and their availability in living rooms and bars were received by activists and the 'silent majority' alike. For a young activist and artist like Martha Rosler the contrast between the conservative assumptions and patriarchal relations of United States domestic life, symbolised by the 'living room', and the colonial carnage inflicted in the name of the United States became inescapable, both in political action and in visual representation.[50] The medium of television was one element in artists' and writers' understanding of the importance of representation in cultural control. Petlin recalls that this was a period when the effect of colour in television reports became a vital element. It conveyed both the bloody brutality, literally, of the American way of war and the seamless technological medium designed, in Martha Rosler's words, to make viewers 'audience spectators rather than citizen participants'.[51] The widespread purchase of colour receivers in the United States began in 1964 and by the beginning of 1971 sales of colour receivers in the United States exceeded those of domestically manufactured black and white sets.

In retrospect, there have been different assessments of the effect of media exposure in ending the war. For analysts such as Kevin Williams, it is a myth that 'television coverage of war leads to a loss of public support. There is little evidence to support this view. Television did not provide a regular flow of graphic representations of the Vietnam War.'[52] On the other hand, participants such as Petlin and Rosler were representative of viewers able to cut through the disinformation provided by official television channels at the same time as recognising the power of the media in terms of both 'information' and 'message'. In 1976, General Weyand observed, 'we should have made the realities of war obvious to the American people before they witnessed it on their television screens. The army must make the price of involvement clear *before* we get involved.'[53] The strategy employed by the United States ever since, as with Britain in the Falklands War in the early 1980s, is to deprive camera crews of anything to film other than that which confirms military decisions. Thus journalistic independence and the editorial process is even more curtailed and contained.

The Nixon administration knew the importance of control and dissuasion. On 13 November, the day Hersh's first My Lai reports hit the newspapers, Vice-President Agnew delivered an unprecedented speech accusing the television news medium of bias, particularly in reports on Vietnam.[54] This made the main headline in *The New York Times* on the next day, with the paper including a full transcript of the speech and replies by networks.[55] The administration's intervention was an attempt to police and contain information and comment particularly, as in Agnew's words:

> At least 40 million Americans every night, it's estimated, watch the network news. Seven million of them view A.B.C., the remainder being divided between N.B.C. and C.B.S.
>
> According to Harris polls and other studies, for millions of Americans the networks are the sole source of national and world news.[56]

Agnew's strategy of attempting to intimidate, discipline and contain the network news derives from the climate of fear which was begun during the McCarthy years and encouraged by Nixon when Vice-President during the 1950s. Even *The New York Times*, which rarely departed from the establishment line, reported a parallel: 'There were some who thought that the President was encouraging Mr. Agnew to play the "point of the spear," as Mr. Nixon did in the early years of the Eisenhower Administration.'[57]

Hence, during the disclosures about My Lai and the increasing public protests the television networks were having to defend their already compromised position. The negative effects continued to curtail live coverage of some demonstrations, including that by around half a million anti-war protesters at the Washington Monument on 16 November. The controversy was still live in early December, with the *Life* editorial for the issue containing the My Lai photographs devoted to a defence of the investigatory role of the press against Agnew's attacks. The editorial, 'The Press Faces its Critics', claimed that the whole debate

> deserves more enlightened discussion than has been provided so far either by Vice President Agnew's politically self-serving speeches or by such thin-skinned responses as that of the CBS President, Dr. Frank Stanton, who thinks the press has not been so intimidated by anyone since 1798.[58]

Stanton's critical response to Agnew's speech, given at a luncheon in front of 750 members of the International Radio and Television Society, was also broadcast live over CBS. His attack on Agnew's 'ominous' attempt at 'suppression and harassment' was reported in *The New York Times* on 26 November.[59] Stanton's CBS connection is, as we will see, important because of Walter Paley, President of MoMA's Board of Trustees, who was Head of CBS.

Life's editorial continued to defend the press in a liberal conservative mode, with one of its revealing assertions echoing Stanton's personal admission that the network news covered 'events and personalities that are jolting to many of us'.[60] *Life*, speaking for the 'silent majority', stated that 'At a time of extraordinarily unattractive contentiousness in U.S. public life, millions of Americans doubtless wish that the assortment of hippies, yippies, war protesters and race-rioters on the evening news would simply go away'.[61] No doubt Nixon and his Vice-President felt the same.

MoMA and 'hippies, yippies, war protesters and race-rioters'

Alongside the story of Agnew's attack on television news, *The New York Times* reported on its front page more examples of what Stanton called 'contentiousness'. One was 'F.B.I. CHARGES 4 WITH 8 BOMBINGS HERE SINCE JULY', relating to revolutionary attacks on the establishment heralded by the so-called 'Weatherman Manifesto' of June 1969. Two others were the '"March Against Death" Begun by Thousands in Washington' and 'Nationwide Protest on War Opens With Light Turnout'.[62] The latter was the start of the second Vietnam Moratorium, the former the first of three days of protests planned by the New Mobilization Committee to End the War in Vietnam. The paper carried other stories on protests, including on the 'Yippies',[63] which were in contrast to reports on Nixon's 'extraordinary visits to the House and the Senate', where he was pushing for support of his Vietnam policy.[64] These visits were co-ordinated with news of Agnew's attack on the media and the production of the USIA patriotic film which sought to marginalise the protesters.

Links between the interests of the establishment, particularly those with political and financial interests in the Vietnam War, and the art world – epitomised by MoMA – were made by the AWC and the Guerrilla Art Action Group (GAAG). The latter included Jon Hendricks, who along with Petlin was a driving force in producing the AWC *'And babies'* poster. Drawing upon the traditions of Fluxus, GAAG had already entered MoMA on 31 October 1969, carefully removed Malevich's *White on White* from the gallery walls and replaced it with the group's manifesto of demands to the Museum and affidavit of intent of action.[65] On 10 November GAAG delivered to the Museum 'A Call for the Immediate Resignation of all the Rockefellers From the Board of Trustees of the Museum of Modern Art'.[66] This made explicit claims about the trustees: 'They use art as a disguise, a cover for their brutal involvement in all spheres of the war machine . . . [these people] sterilize art of any form of social protest and indictment of the oppressive forces in society; and therefore render art totally irrelevant to the existing social crisis.' The 'manifesto' went on to make specific sourced connections between the Rockefellers'[67] business interests and the war: the manufacture of napalm; aircraft production and chemical and biological warfare research; arms manufacture and the Pentagon.[68] GAAG followed this up with a communiqué and protest performance in the Museum lobby, which included tearing at each other clothes, bursting bags of blood hidden under their clothes and yelling and screaming gibberish with an occasional cry of 'rape'.

Within the New Left there were several sites for a critique of the establishment, one being the universities. Within the art world a major focus was 'the museum', particularly MoMA which the AWC had picketed, attacked and strategically courted. Reasons for the latter included known disquiet in the institution about the Vietnam War, about the Museum's exclusionary attitudes (in its selection both of art and of staff) and about the lack of union recognition which came to a head in 1970 with the formation of PASTA MoMA.[69] Between 25 November and early January, the relationship between the role of the staff and trustees, the meaning of My Lai, *Guernica*'s symbolic importance and the activities of the art left reached a point of crisis. The issues in this crisis were a microcosm of wider struggles in the United States, struggles which help us to understand the context of Schapiro's choice and what was at stake.[70]

The meeting between the AWC and MoMA staff on 25 November applauded a proposal from Irving Petlin:

> I feel the Museum should issue a vast distribution of a poster so violently outraged at this act [massacre at My Lai, referred to as Songmy] that it will place absolutely in print and in public the feeling that this Museum – its staff, all the artists which contribute to its greatness – is outraged by the massacre at Songmy.[71]

A motion that the AWC should pay for the poster with MoMA handling distribution via other museums in the United States and abroad was, according to the AWC press release, 'voted in'; according to the MoMA release, the 'possibility' was to be pursued. What is agreed in the documentation is that a Poster Committee was formed to oversee the need for rapid execution of the project. Members were Frazer Dougherty, Jon Hendricks and Irving Petlin for the AWC, and Arthur Drexler (Director of the Department of Architecture and Design) and Elizabeth Shaw (Director of Public Information) for the Museum staff. Drexler had an important role here. He was ambitious to fill the then vacant post of Director of MoMA, which had its own internal political problems. But he was ambivalent about the Museum's place in the 'political arena', though according to Wilder Green he was passionate about Vietnam and My Lai.[72] Within the context, too, of MoMA's social history Drexler was uneasy about the effects of his homosexuality on the process of selecting a new Director.

After several delays on the Museum's part, the Poster Committee had its first meeting on 3 December, two days after the edition of *Life* magazine with Haeberle's colour photographs had hit the newsstands. Although 'certain staff members were reluctant to support the documentary nature of the image chosen' (AWC press release), the committee was authorised to use the Museum's name in seeking reproduction rights and a printer. At that meeting, too, the specific photograph, the Wallace/Meadlo quotation, the layout and the edition number were agreed. According to the AWC, Drexler began to have cold feet, and a two-and-a-half-hour meeting was necessary in the afternoon to reconvince him of the importance of the Museum's involvement.

In the meantime the AWC had to negotiate a number of other production problems. Two of these were securing permission to reproduce Haeberle's photograph and, more practically, obtaining a colour negative. Petlin recalls that a source at *Life* told the AWC that Haeberle had agreed only one-time reproduction rights with the magazine. Petlin and Hendricks contacted Haeberle directly to ask for a similar arrangement. Whilst Haeberle was clearly bemused by the whole media explosion around his photographs, he responded positively to the AWC request. A major reason was his wish to do the 'right thing' in making My Lai public. Haeberle, therefore, granted a reproduction right to the AWC without charge on 16 December, and phoned *Life* magazine saying that he had given authorisation for someone to collect the C-print (colour separation). An AWC member went along to *Life* via its source there and picked up the C-print. Enough paper for the fifty thousand edition was supplied by Peter Brandt as a donation.

Another major difficulty – getting the poster printed – reveals much about attitudes to the war and to political action within what is regarded as a normal constituency of the left, the working class. The problematic relationship between the role of intellectuals and working-class struggle and consciousness has been a major debate in Marxist traditions, notably in the writings of Trotsky and Gramsci. For Schapiro, whose political roots were steeped in the 1930s, this relationship was still a concern in the 1960s, as evidenced by his obituary, in 1965, for Alfred Rosmer, whom Schapiro described as 'a model figure of a working-class revolutionary'. In one of his few pieces for *Dissent*, Schapiro writes of Alfred and Marguerite Rosmer being 'alert to all that concerned the well-being and future of the working-class throughout the world, and undiscouraged by the bitter experience of the last twenty-five years'.[73] In practice, the AWC found one branch of the working class, skilled lithographers, less than revolutionary. Many working-class union members were hostile to anti-war protesters and regarded the 'last twenty-five years' from a different consumerist and Cold War perspective.

Petlin recalls that the leader of the Amalgamated Lithographers Union, along with his assistant, was a committed anti-war labour leader. But he led a union, like many other unions at the time, with conservative blue-collar members for whom

> patriotism was a part of their persona and whose families probably had young men involved in the war. And he was aware that there were very few shops that could print that poster with those big four colour presses that would be sympathetic to doing this job. It was not a job that came in the normal way through a commercial enterprise like through a movie company who wanted to print a movie poster or a company advertising cars for posters that are going to go out on the billboards which is the kind of thing they handled. This is why we chose to print it that way. It was going to compete with the stuff that's out there at the same technical level. And so he said to us when we had the poster and we had the paper, he said 'we're going to do this as a union contribution as a union project. We're going to print it for you for nothing. Basically we have to find the most sympathetic shop to do it in so that they don't sabotage it out of anger.' Because this was still early in the anti-war struggle.[74]

The shop chosen was on Hudson Street in the Manhattan printing district which contained large printing firms with floors of around 10,000 square feet necessary to house huge four colour presses capable of printing fifty thousand copies. The Union leaders thought not only that they had the most influence over this shop to print the poster as a Union project but also that it contained a number of workers sympathetic to anti-war protests. However, Petlin recalls that there was a definite split among the print workers. When he and others from the AWC went to colour-proof the poster there was

> incredible hostility in the shop, not by everybody but by quite a few people who were making remarks about 'faggots', 'afraid to go to the war' . . . A lot of very denigrating remarks that you could hear when you were there. Jokes between the workers themselves: 'we're doing this, but these guys will get theirs'.[75]

One reason for this attitude is basic but crucial. Lithographic print workers were very skilled and had worked hard to achieve their levels of technical competence and pay. In the consumerist-induced boom following the Second World War these were workers 'imagining themselves already to be middle class, working middle class . . . They were America's success stories from working class families.' Importantly, as Petlin continues, these 'were people who really thought they had a stake in what was going on and they identified with the government tremendously'. Contradictions within the working class, unable to recognise the sources of their own oppression, and the threat of a right-wing backlash were a deep worry for the Old Left. For example, Irving Howe was concerned in the run up to the Presidential elections of 1968 by some twenty per cent of the American electorate saying that they would consider voting for George Wallace, the right-wing Governor of Alabama:

> just as everything else in modern society becomes bureaucratized, so has backlash. Instead of swarming mobs, there are now trained police. The white workers of Italian or Polish or Slavic origin who have managed to save up enough money to buy themselves little homes in the suburbs aren't likely to organize mobs to invade the black ghettos – at least not yet; but they are inclined, many of them, to vote for George Wallace in the name of 'law and order'.[76]

For the working class, to recognise their own oppression within capitalism would mean joining the contemporary struggles against racism, the Vietnam War, patriarchy and the power of the state. But such action would also mean acknowledging that their relative material improvements within United States post-1945 consumerism were a distraction from and dissuasion to collective action.[77] Consumerism was capitalism's double-edged 'reward' to the working class: for denying their own political consciousness and for expressing disapproval of manifestations of dissent in others. To disapprove of external dissent is to confirm the acceptance of internal denial.

Evidence of domestic conservativism was matched by evidence revealing acceptance of United States violence abroad. For example, a *Time*-Louis-Harris poll published by *Time* magazine in its issue dated 12 January 1970 stated that

> Surprisingly, Americans are not particularly disturbed by the disclosure that U.S. troops apparently massacred several hundred South Vietnamese civilians at My Lai. By a substantial 65% to 22%, the public shrugs off My Lai, reasoning that 'incidents such as this are bound to happen in a war'. It also rejects by a margin of 65% to 24% the charge that My Lai proves that U.S. involvement in the war has been morally wrong all along.[78]

The poll charts a conservative move in opinion between October and December of 1969, with another result significant for my argument here.

In reply to the question 'Do you agree that opposition to the war is led by radicals who don't care what happens to the U.S.?' the results in October were: Agree 37%; Disagree 49%; Not Sure 14%. In December these percentages had shifted to: 44%; 42%; 14%, respectively. This is a move from rejecting to accepting the statement.[79]

One of the several possible reasons for this shift in opinion is suggested by a letter that appeared in *The Nation* on 12 January 1970 under the heading 'hippie as "nigger"'.[80] The letter was written by John Bright, presumably the screenwriter and critic whose reviews appeared frequently in the journal *Frontier*, a radical journal published in Los Angeles.[81] Writing from North Hollywood, California, Bright draws attention to the two instances of 'multiple murder which have shared the front pages in the last month. One is the slaughter of the innocents at Song My in Vietnam . . . The other, the multiple Tate killings in Los Angeles.' On 9 August 1969, the actress Sharon Tate, two other women and three men were brutally murdered in a house rented by Tate and her husband Roman Polanski in a secluded area of Beverly Hills.[82] They were tortured, shot and stabbed, with the word 'Pig' scrawled in blood at the Tate house and, next day, at the Hollywood home of Leno and Rosemary LaBianca who were similarly murdered.[83]

It was not until 1 December that the first arrests of what became known as the Charles Manson 'family' were made. In reports next day on the front page of *The New York Times*, those arrested were described as 'Two members of a nomadic band of hippies'. This significant use of the word 'hippies' came from the Los Angeles Police Chief Edward M. Davis, who 'described the suspects as a "roving band of hippies"' on the same page as the report titled, 'Both Sides in Calley Trial Ask Songmy Publicity Ban' and another on the 'Order of the Draft Drawing'. The latter refers to the birth dates of hundreds of thousands of young men, drawn from a cylinder by an eighteen-year-old member of 'President Nixon's Youth Advisory Council': 12,500 of these were to be drafted the following month.

On 3 December, *The New York Times* carried a photo captioned 'Where "Family" Lived' placed just above before and after photographs of Charles Watson, one of the Manson 'family'.[84] The first image of Watson is of a clean-shaven young man in graduation gown and mortar with the caption: 'Charles D. Watson, student, in photo from 1964 Farmersville, Tex., school yearbook'. The later image is of a casually dressed and long-haired twenty-three-year-old with the caption: 'Mr. Watson, murder suspect in a photograph released by the Los Angeles police'. Both the contrasting visual juxtaposition and the shift from the description 'student' to 'murder suspect' are significant in contemporary discourse and imagination where terms such as 'hippie', 'student', 'radical', 'protester', 'draft dodger' and 'counter-culture' gained particular currency in the government's agenda to deflect criticism of the war. One strategy, supported by White House rhetoric and manifest in many media reports, was to characterise the opposition as a combination of an unpatriotic rabble, militant revolutionary Blacks (as in the Black Panthers) and drug-dependent followers of eastern mystics and gurus. Such characterisations can also be found in the writings of those opposed to the government. Irving Howe in his attack (October 1968) on the strategies of the New Left referred to Herbert Marcuse as 'the current New-Left guru . . . his political conclusions offer a simultaneous rationalization of withdrawal and wildness, copping-out and turning-on'.[85] Later he draws attention to the prevalent view amongst 'millions of ordinary Americans' for whom 'student protest-drugs-hippiedom-Negro rioting forms a stream of detested association'.[86]

The story in *The New York Times* dated 3 December is entitled '3 Suspects in Tate Case Tied to Guru and "Family"' and includes the description: the 'persons accused . . . lived a life of indolence, free sex, midnight motorcycle races and apparently blind obedience to a mysterious guru'. Continuing the report, on page 44 we get a photo of 'Charles Manson, guru of "family" whose members are held in Tate murders'. The 'family' consisted of six men and twelve women, led by Manson, of whom a local is quoted as saying: '"He played the guitar, he sang, he would make love to a girl . . . He preached love and peace and all that, you know. He conditioned the girls to do anything."'[87]

The sequence of images and text on the page of *The New York Times* with the photographs of Watson and of the Manson 'family' home is instructive. At the bottom of the page there is an illustrated story, 'Campus Editors Now Expressing Bold Views', which continues at length on page 39.[88] This reports the radicalisation of campus newspapers and consequent unhappiness among college administrators and conservative students. The introductory story relates to the president of Fichtburg State College cancelling an issue of its newspaper 'after the printer informed him that the issue was to contain an article by Eldridge Cleaver, the Black Panther leader. The text was considered obscene by the printer and president.'[89] The report describes the activist roles of many papers; students on trial on charges of criminal libel against Nixon; the role of radicals among editors and reporters; support for SDS activities; and an incident at Boston University where 'the 53-year-old *News* printed photographs last year of a couple having intercourse, the school is paying the paper $50,000 over two and a half years during which it must move off campus. It will vacate this spring.'[90]

In the context of this combination of utterances, the conclusion to Bright's letter in *The Nation* bears comparison with the findings of the *Time*-Louis-Harris Poll which charts a move to conservatism and a distrust of 'radicals':

> So the legitimacies of the youth revolt, grounded in the inequities of our
> society, is somehow transmogrified – by public ignorance and fear – into
> something sinister . . . the Tate tragedy has made of the hippie the 'new
> nigger', menacing and frightening. An already existing bigotry has been
> sustained.[91]

It should be remembered, too, that this was at a time when the police
took brutal action against the Panthers. *The New York Times* carried a
report on 6 December of the police killing of Fred Hampton, the Illinois
chairman of the Black Panther party and Mark Clark, a Panther leader
from Peoria, in an apartment in Chicago. Four others were injured. One
local alderman is reported as calling the killings ' "an assassination" and
saying that the shooting was part of a "systematic extermination" of the
organization's leadership'. The executive director of the Illinois division
of the American Civil Liberties Union stated that ' "The Chicago raid and
killings seem a part of a nationwide pattern of police action against the
Panthers" '.[92]

Many members of the Old Left were impatient and angry with what
they regarded as political terrorism and hysteria on the part of the New
Left, including the Weathermen, 'Yippies' and Black Panthers. Much of
this came to a head with the trial of the 'Chicago Eight' (to become the
'Chicago Seven') which began in September 1969 and ended with the
conviction of five, including Jerry Rubin and Abbie Hoffman, two members of the Youth International Party ('Yippies'). They were charged
with conspiring to cross state lines and with intent to riot at the Democratic National Convention in Chicago in 1968. Irving Howe can be taken
as a measure of such opinion. Arguing for democratic socialism and the
traditional channels of organising, unionising and campaigning, he claimed
to be 'impatient with the maudlin claim that the young have "tried everything" '.[93] This observation was included in his highly critical article
reviewing the previous month's activities by the left and their small-
circulation magazines in *The New York Times Magazine* in April 1970. In
this he makes an explicit connection between the morality of young
political radicals and the Manson 'family':

> The moral consequences for the lives of the young terrorists are already
> clear. Bernadine Dohrn a Weatherman leader, is quoted by a New Left paper,
> The Guardian, as saying that the Weathermen 'dig' Charlie Manson, accused
> leader of the gang that allegedly murdered several people in Beverly Hills.
> 'Dig it, first they killed the pigs, then they ate dinner in the same room with
> them, then they shoved a fork into a victim's stomach! Wild!' is how The
> Guardian quotes Miss Dohrn.[94]

Howe concludes with an observation which would have found favour
amongst members of the *Dissent* constituency:

what matters is the quality and discipline of the life one leads at a given moment, and what one sees at the outer edges of the New Left . . . is at least as discouraging as what one sees in American society at large.

The bomb-thrower and the jailer are brothers under the skin.[95]

For Howe, confrontation politics and the violent activities of parts of the New Left smacked of what Lenin identified as 'Left-Wing Communism: An Infantile Disorder'.[96]

Corporate power and repetitive compulsions

There were several issues which paradoxically united representatives of the Old Left with those agents of corporate United States who subscribed to an official modernist culture, as represented by museums, such as MoMA, and a 'free press', however compromised, as represented by Walter Cronkite and CBS news. One of these issues was a fear of losing what were perceived as liberal-democratic gains in culture and education if 'left-wing' protesters with 'an infantile disorder' were allowed to go unchecked. However, the fear and impatience of the constituency for Howe's journal *Dissent* was always in danger of playing into the hands of those with real power. The real power of those who actually ran the corporations, feeding off and fuelling the views of, in Howe's words, 'millions of ordinary Americans' for whom 'student protest-drugs-hippiedom-Negro rioting forms a stream of detested association'.[97] Continuing the story of the *'And babies'* poster provides a specific example of this dilemma and one in which an Old Leftist such as Schapiro became enmeshed.

On 18 December the colour-plate for the poster was completed and the print shop awaited MoMA's approval of the final credit line as jointly sponsored by the AWC and MoMA. Whilst the Museum staff still supported MoMA's participation, Arthur Drexler, along with Wilder Green, decided that they had better check with the trustees. Both of the press releases make clear that they took the final mock-up of the poster to Walter S. Paley, President of the Board of Trustees, and head of CBS. Petlin recalls that the Rockefellers were also involved. Drexler returned after a few minutes with the trustees 'white faced', saying that the joint project was off and asking all from the AWC to go away. Nelson Rockefeller and Paley had 'hit the ceiling'. MoMA's press release states that

> The Museum's Board and staff are comprised of individuals with diverse points of view who have come together because of their interest in art, and if they are to continue effectively in this role, they must confine themselves to questions related to their immediate subject.
>
> Mr. Paley said that he could not commit the Museum to any position on any matter not directly related to a specific function of the Museum, and that the use of the Museum's name on this poster was a policy matter to be decided by a full Board [of Trustees].[98]

Whilst Paley offered to do this during its next meeting on 8 January there was 'little likelihood of the proposal being accepted'. Besides the AWC feeling betrayed so late in the day, there are important issues here about Paley's and the Rockefellers' power and their view of the function of the museum amidst contemporary events. This function, as an art citadel, was paradoxically not dissimilar to the view held by leftist intellectuals critical of the New Left assault on institutions.

Paley and David and Nelson Rockefeller carried the greatest weight amongst the trustees (following his $5 million donation to the Museum's fund-raising drive, Paley was elected President of the Board of Trustees in 1968). All three were used to exercising their authoritarian power in business and culture and protecting themselves by delegating any tasks that would reflect adversely upon them.[99] Not so when it came to sacking Bates Lowry as Director of MoMA in May 1969 after ten months in the job and four months of responding to demonstrations and protests by artists, such as the AWC. The precise reasons for his dismissal are disputed, though according to Grace Glueck in *The New York Times* a small group of trustees was unhappy with Lowry's proposal 'to establish a series of committee hearings at which the museum and the artists would engage in a "dialogue"'.[100] One repeated reason was Paley's and the Rockefellers' view that financial matters were completely out of control. Important for my discussion, though, are the power dynamics amongst the trustees as they inform their rejection of the 'And babies' poster a few months later.

Paley and the Rockefellers decided that Lowry had to go. They enlisted Walter Bareiss, a fellow trustee, to negotiate a 'settlement' and Lowry's 'resignation'. All the arrangements were sewn up prior to the formal meeting of the Board of Trustees. However, two trustees, John de Menil and Ralph Colin, were outraged by the lack of consultation and the treatment of the Board as a rubber stamp for the decisions of a small powerful group. Colin publicly attacked Paley in the meeting, accusing him of bad faith. Bareiss recalls that nobody who crossed Bill Paley expected to get away scot-free. Soon after, Paley summoned Colin to his office at CBS to inform Colin that he had decided to replace him as his personal attorney after more than forty years. Subsequently Paley's CBS replaced Colin's firm as its lead legal council with considerable negative effects on the firm. At a meeting a few months later Colin told Paley that he was upset that their friendship of more than forty years had suffered. Paley is reported to have replied, 'Ralph, you were never my friend, you were my lawyer.' This all became common knowledge.

The story of Bates Lowry's sacking makes it clear why Arthur Drexler would have come away from Paley and the Rockefellers so ashen-faced clutching the 'And babies' mock-up. As far as the Vietnam issue was concerned, Paley and Stanton were 'firm supporters of U.S. intervention'.[101]

And whilst Paley's loyalties were with Nelson Rockefeller rather than with Nixon in the 1968 campaign for the Republican Presidential nomination, he felt that after Nixon's election his many years of loyal service to the Party might have been rewarded with the patronage prize of appointment as ambassador to the Court of St James.[102] After this didn't materialise he devoted himself to being MoMA's ambassador and 'chief executive'.

Was it politics that made Paley and the Rockefellers 'hit the ceiling' over the My Lai image? Paley defended his CBS news network by supporting Stanton's speech against intervention and intimidation by Nixon's administration. However, in practice this period marked a renewal of media self-censorship: even with the expansion of the war into Laos and Cambodia there was less war coverage and more caution in the reporting: '64 percent of TV film reports of the anti-war movement after the invasion of Cambodia in 1970 contained no discussion of the war. In only 16 per cent of reports of marches were extracts from speeches used . . . the media, in particular television, were far more comfortable with dissent from within the establishment.'[103]

For Paley and the Rockefellers politics was part of official business, but there had to be a boundary, however fictitious, between it and 'art'. Though they might operate at MoMA as they did in their other areas of interest, the trustees wished to maintain the image that 'art', museums and galleries were a salvation from everyday life. Petlin offers this view: 'I think it had to do with [Nelson] Rockefeller's idea of the Museum of Modern Art as a temple apart, as a citadel apart, which doesn't deal in the dirty business of the world. Certainly he knew plenty about the dirty business of the world.'[104]

The AWC press release ended by characterising MoMA's withdrawal of support for the poster 'as bitter confirmation of this institution's decadence and/or impotence'. On 26 December, the poster was published sponsored by the AWC alone and distributed through an informal network of artists, students and peace movement workers throughout the world. About a hundred volunteers went to the loading bay at the printers and broke up the large pallets of fifty thousand posters into smaller packages to get them into cars and vans. As Petlin recalls: 'People carried them under their arm to California . . . they appeared in rallies in Berkeley a few days later . . . It was posted all over the New York subway system almost the day after it was printed. It was like a blitz . . . *The New York Post* had a photo of subway workers tearing it down.'[105]

On Saturday 3 January 1970, My Lai, MoMA and *Guernica* again became a public nexus of protest, intervention and performance:

> performers, witnesses and members of G.A.A.G., D.I.A.S., and A.W.C. infiltrated the Museum of Modern Art of New York, gathering on the third floor in front of Picasso's *Guernica*.

Some artists had smuggled wreaths and flowers in. At 1 p.m., members of the Guerrilla Art Action Group quietly went up to the painting, *Guernica*, and placed four wreaths against the wall underneath the painting. At this moment, Joyce Kozloff, carrying her 8-month-old baby, Nikolas, sat on the floor in front of the wreaths. Father Stephen Garmey came forward and began reading a memorial service for dead babies.[106]

Garmey was an Episcopalian minister and a chaplin at Columbia University where Schapiro was a professor. His service interposed extracts from the Bible with extracts from the My Lai article in *Life* and finished with a poem by Denise Levertov. Supporters held copies of the *'And babies'* poster and at another demonstration the AWC used the poster as a sandwich board.[107]

On 8 January, the date of the full Board of Trustees meeting, the AWC staged a 'lie-in' before *Guernica* and asked to speak with the trustees. They were refused and, in the words of Grace Glueck in 'Yanking the Rug From Under' in *The New York Times*, 'at the meeting's end the trustees scurried off, unconfronted'.[108] Although Glueck recognised that there was a central ' "hot" political issue', for her 'the real issue is staff vs. trustees: analogous to the "troubles" at certain universities, in which administrators mandated by their boards to deal with dissident students had the rug yanked from under them when it was felt they exceeded their authority'.[109] Glueck's analogy indicates a set of regressive relationships, with Drexler and Shaw treated by their Board as 'administrators' dealing with the AWC as 'dissident students'.

Schapiro's 'I will not'

The months of January and February continued to carry news stories about My Lai and anti-war protests. In this context, the AWC/AWP pursued their parallel between Guernica and My Lai and decided to seek Picasso's assistance. Schapiro could have chosen not to reply to their petition, but his written refusal raises particular issues with contemporary significance.[110] One of them is a concern with the AWC/AWP's claim that the hanging of *Guernica* in MoMA 'implies that our establishment has the moral right to be indignant about the crimes of others – and ignore our own crimes'. Schapiro found this statement 'unwarranted and even nonsensical', going on to suggest that museums do not hang pictures as 'protests' against the crimes which those pictures represent or depict:

In hanging *Guernica* the Museum no more protests against the crime of Guernica than the Metropolitan Museum protests against the crucifixion of Christ in hanging a painting of that subject. Is Franco's eagerness to hang *Guernica* in the Prado a protest against the bombing?

Following this question Schapiro states that he will not sign the AWC/ AWP letter. In a further comment, he draws attention to Picasso's refusal to return to Spain with *Guernica* until it is again a democratic republic:

> The Museum is not like the Prado an institution of dictatorship; the United States is a democratic republic as much as was Spain in the years before the Franco regime . . . however ignorant and immoral may be the views of the majority that support the policy of our government in Vietnam.

Schapiro reminds his friends that the United States has a 'free press', though he must have been aware of the collusion of the press with the establishment and its general ideological adherence to the Cold War.[111] This was especially the case with United States reports on Vietnam. In a long article in *The New York Review of Books* on 23 February 1967, in which Schapiro also had a long review to which I will return, Noam Chomsky details the government's propaganda apparatus and the collusion of intellectuals and journalists in what we now call 'disinformation'.[112] Whilst Schapiro correctly stresses in his letter to the AWC/AWP that in the United States 'individuals and organized groups may criticize, resist and act to change what they believe is wrong', he does not acknowledge the cultural power of those who can consciously or unconsciously manipulate the assumptions of readers and viewers. And with the AWC/AWP, here was an organised group inviting Schapiro to support its members to 'criticize, resist and act to change what they believe is wrong'. Though Schapiro does not provide alternatives, he may have had in mind similar choices provided a few weeks later by Howe, his colleague at *Dissent*: 'help Sam Brown organize the Moratorium against the war; join Cesar Chavez in unionizing grape pickers and Leon Davis in unionizing hospital workers; campaign for Allard K. Lowenstein's re-election to Congress; work with Ralph Nader for consumer rights and Philip Stern for tax reforms.'[113] Howe saw these as 'far more useful, *far more radical*, than the posture of bomb throwing'. Whilst he meant this literally, Schapiro may have seen the AWC/AWP letter as a metaphorical bomb throwing at a target, MoMA, for which he must have had ambivalent feelings.

Schapiro ends his letter of refusal with a charge of moralism that journals such as *Dissent* had levelled against the New Left. By all means, he says, ask Picasso to voice his protest against the war in Vietnam:

> but do not urge him to remove his picture from the Museum as a sign that he condemns the hypocrisy of 'our establishment' which fails to protest with you. That is a piece of self-righteous moralism that the community of protesting artists would find it hard to live up to in their own daily collaboration with museums, schools, galleries and collectors.

The phrase 'self-righteous moralism' shouts out of this paragraph. Schapiro is right to draw attention to the contradictions faced by protesting artists claiming to bite the hand that feeds them. But is there more to all this?

In 1969 and early 1970, *Dissent* was bubbling away about the New Left, direct action, Nixon, Vietnam and My Lai. In the September–October 1969 issue, Irving Howe's 'The Agony of the Campus' appeared.[114] Whilst he remembers 'what we owe the students . . . undogmatic young people who in 1963–4 began to assault the injustices of American society', he thinks that by now 'it's mostly gone bad'. For him, the New Left is entangled with 'musty authoritarian dogmas and a nasty cult of violence'.[115] Is this how Schapiro viewed the actions of the AWC and GAAG since early 1969? Howe goes on to talk of the SDS convention in summer 1969 'putting to shame the early Communist sects in the twenties' and recalls meeting the SDS in the early 1960s, some of whom he found admirable but 'others, like Tom Hayden, the most gifted of the group, already had the bearing of an *apparatchik* about them'.[116] He warns against the 'kamikaze-style politics of the desperado-totalitarian left'[117] and attacks students' claims that 'the campus is caught up with the war machine, it serves imperialism . . . because we live in a capitalist society, the university *cannot* be significantly autonomous'.[118] Howe calls this 'quatsch-Marxism, an insult to Marx'[119] and attacks recent direct action as a 'mixture of Guevarist fantasia, residual Stalinism, anarchist braggadocio, and homemade tough-guy methods. This is not the path for serious radicals.'[120] Schapiro's letter to the AWC/AWP has all of the bearing of a serious radical for whom the universities and the museums have a scholarly and civilising autonomy that has to be defended against illogicality or moralism. Howe's final sentence echoes through Schapiro's letter: in institutions the need 'to persist in our devotion to rational discourse, democratic procedures, and radical change'.[121]

In the issue of *Artnews* for January 1970, Schapiro responded to a questionnaire about the Metropolitan Museum, New York. He argues for the need to democratise the board of trustees by admitting representatives of the membership, 'including women', limiting the present seven-year term of office and inviting a more active representation of the city. In doing so the Metropolitan will 'enter its second hundred years with the promise of a more vital role in the art of the nation'.[122] But first Schapiro refers his readers to a lengthy book review he published twenty-five years earlier, in 1945, in the *Art Bulletin*.[123] In the latter he takes Francis Taylor, Director of the Metropolitan, to task for criticising the intellectualism and dominance of German scholarship for the 'failure' of the American museum. Schapiro is also scathing about Taylor's alternative for reform of the museums and fulfilment of their democratic mission: 'Taylor would have them converted into exhibitions of social and cultural history, illustrating the universal progress of man towards Democracy.'[124] Schapiro sees a political danger in this attitude, and in Taylor's uncritical defence of trustees, general inconsistency and negative attitude to modern art. Schapiro quotes Taylor's reproach of Picasso in *Guernica* for 'failing to evoke the heroism of Guernica itself' and follows up with a parenthesis: 'One wonders if Mr. Taylor knows what happened at Guernica.'[125] He also observes that Taylor 'speaks of modern artists as neurotics, degenerates, and "utterly confused" souls in a way which would have pleased Goebbels'.[126]

In the final paragraph Schapiro concludes with a view which prefigures Irving Howe's criticisms of the New Left: '[Taylor's] false ideas . . . are more likely to be heard with respect than the considered opinions of the scholars whom he attacks under cover of the present public feeling against an enemy nation.' In 1945 the enemy nation was Germany, during the Cold War the Soviet Union; in 1970 for the student public it was the United States itself. Schapiro continues his criticism of Taylor: 'What is especially to be regretted is that the low state of self-criticism among students of art makes possible such treatment of our problems.' To draw this long review from 1945 to the attention of readers in January 1970 is to make a particular scholarly and political point consistent with Howe's views about institutions and the 'errors' of the New Left.

Three days before Schapiro wrote his refusal to the AWC/AWP, a report by Grace Glueck appeared in *The New York Times*: 'Metropolitan Museum to Study its Role in City's Communities'.[127] Schapiro may have seen this move by the Museum as partly the result of the long series of replies to the Metropolitan questionnaire by various scholars in *Artnews*. Did he regard this as a preferable process to the activities of the AWC and GAAG at MoMA? He may have had mixed feelings about this, especially in the light of the AWC's effective campaign since 1969 to persuade the Museum of Modern Art to have a free admission day. *The New York Times* reported the first of these, held on Monday 9 February 1970, on an experimental basis: 'Museum's Attendance Triples on Free Day'.[128] The 7,000 visitors also outstripped the average of 4,500 on Saturdays and Sundays: 'the crowd, as a Museum guard observed, was "younger and less white" than usual, and included many family groups. Also on hand "to celebrate" were 30 members of the Art Workers Coalition.'[129]

On the previous Sunday, *The New York Times* devoted a large amount of space to an article by Hilton Kramer, 'About MoMA, The AWC and Political Causes', which was partly in response to a long letter, published alongside, from Frazer Dougherty, Hans Haacke and Lucy Lippard on behalf of the AWC.[130] The latter was written in response to Kramer's earlier article, 'Do You Believe in the Principle of Museums?', in the same paper on 18 January. Alongside the letter from the AWC is one from Alex Gross, also a member of the group, welcoming Glueck's recent article, which included a detailed account of the production of the My Lai poster[131] but drawing attention to MoMA's aggressive response to the AWC since 1969. Significantly, too, Gross's letter is followed by one from Lynn H. Schafran, Project Associate, Department of Exhibitions at MoMA. She claims that the majority of MoMA staff (totalling over five hundred) did not have any knowledge of the Songmy [My Lai] poster prior to its publication: 'our own Department of Public Information had to issue a release on its history for the benefit of our silent majority'. This latter phrase had a contemporary political significance, as we have seen.

The interchange between Kramer and the AWC raises several issues. One of them, of concern to Schapiro, was the relationship between protest, moralism and practicalities. Kramer offers his opinion that the AWC is, at the present moment, 'the only professional art group in this country that is addressing itself to the fundamental social and political problems that currently afflict the visual arts both as a profession and as a cultural enterprise'.[132] But he is critical of the group for arguing that MoMA 'is already serving political interests' because the money made by the trustees, some of which is donated to the Museum, is politically 'tainted' as much of it comes from the 'profits of the Vietnam War'. Kramer does not believe that this fact results in the 'conservative politicization of the museum' as the trustees are nominated because of their economic rather than their political standing. That the trustees may intervene in the Museum's affairs in accord with their conservative social values and economic interest (for example, to safeguard the market value of their private art collections), Kramer sees as 'undeniable as well as distasteful'. Raising several ideological questions, Kramer does not see such activities as evidence of politicisation.[133] On the other hand, he sees the AWC's 'call upon the museum to serve political causes' as suggesting a 'society totally governed by political tests – in other words, a totalitarian society'. Here we have Kramer raising the spectre of Stalinism when political action is mentioned.

The trauma of Stalinism for the left and the press's equation of political radicalism with Communism continually led commentators to defend a system of gradual reform of the status quo. This in fact meant a deeper entrenchment of existing power and repressive ideologies. African-American and Puerto-Rican artists as well as feminists even became critical of the AWC because, they argued, the agenda of its radicalism was set by the existing system; the ideological constraints and interests produced by a system which sustains the power base of rich cultural managers and, as Chomsky argues, intellectuals and journalists whose assumptions are moulded by the Cold War.[134]

In an attempt to find a way around this process and the role of the establishment press, *The New York Element* was founded in 1968. Published every two months, it started out as a publication of the Arts Section of the Peace and Freedom Party opposed to the Vietnam War and American foreign and domestic policy. The paper carried reports on the relationship between art and politics, charting the activities of groups such as the AWC and those of the early feminist and women's liberation movements. However, to many, its initial support for Eldridge Cleaver and the Black Panthers marked it out as part of what Howe and *Dissent* regarded as the destructive element of the New Left. Grace Glueck drew readers attention to *The Element* in an article in *The New York Times*, 'Keeping Art on the Streets', on 28 September 1969,[135] at a time when splits within the left were threatening. I want to point to one with a direct bearing on Schapiro's letter of refusal.

In his article of 8 February, Kramer contrasts the AWC's engagement with 'social and political problems' with those of other professional groups:

> the art dealers, the art historians, the art critics, the art educationists, the museum directors, the museum memberships, and the older, mostly somnolent organizations of artists have chosen, for the most part, to remain silent, indifferent, or simply superior in the face of these problems.[136]

They were not always silent, nor predictable in their allegiances. In June 1969, artists associated with Abstract Expressionism and its generation came out attacking the AWC and defending MoMA. Here, again, the issues of moralism, hypocrisy and self-seeking became part of the attack. During the course of MoMA's exhibition *The New American Painting and Sculpture: The First Generation* (18 June to 5 October), the AWC had printed ten thousand handbills entitled 'Errata'. These were distributed and mailed, to participants in the show among others, with a covering letter dated 8 June.[137] Basically, the AWC had a two fold objection to the way the exhibition had been organised. First, it regarded the show as an example of the Museum's self-centred interest in wanting to have the world's major collection of that period and to be the prime source of information with little regard for the artists themselves. Second,

> As the present exhibition was organized, the Museum purchased one work by those living artists not previously in the collection, but considered necessary to the show. Donations were also solicited from the estates of dead artists. The burden of the exhibition was left, therefore, on those living artists whose work was already represented, often unsatisfactorily, in the Museum's collection . . . the request for donations from the artists constitutes a subtle form of blackmail.[138]

Responses to the AWC were immediate; three of them dated 11 June. First, a biting letter from Barnett Newman, addressed 'To whom it may concern'.[139] He declares that he has been 'critical' of MoMA but is 'shocked' by the AWC's attack on the Museum concerning the forthcoming exhibition. Newman accuses the AWC of being 'insincere' and of a 'self-serving attack on their fellow artists. Their letter says very openly that what they want the Museum to do is that [*sic*] it buy their own work.'[140] Newman finds the AWC's concern with 'the morality of artists'

> truly offensive. After all such moral superiority can only be understood as careerism . . . It is the easiest thing in the world to build a career by constantly taking care of everyone else's morality except one's own. We have had too much of that already. Let's let lie the sleeping watchdog ghosts of Ad Reinhardt and Anthony Comstock.[141]

The second response, also critical of the AWC, was a joint letter addressed to William Rubin, Senior Curator of Painting and Sculpture and organiser of the exhibition. It is signed by Herbert Ferber, Adolph Gottlieb, Peter Grippe, Philip Guston, Seymour Lipton, Robert Motherwell, Theodore Roszak, Mark Rothko and Mrs Ad Reinhardt. Louise Bourgeois, David Hare and Richard Pousette-Dart are cited as 'in complete agreement with this group in refuting the notion that any form of coercion was involved' though they wish to 'make their own statements'.[142] This letter states that 'the various allegations and innuendoes to the effect that we have been pressured or coerced into donating our works is false'. The nine authors of the letter share Newman's position in that they do not 'agree with everything the Museum of Modern Art (or any other institution) does' but applaud the work of MoMA, and of Rubin: 'the program that you are instituting, of recognition for post World War II modern American art, is far sighted and constructive, and can only be of great benefit to artists and public'.[143] This view was clearly at total odds with that of the AWC. Although most of the Abstract Expressionists were anti-war, these letters reveal the paradoxical or contradictory predicament in which this episode positioned them.

The third response was from MoMA itself, with a press release containing a defence of its policy. The controversy reached the press with an article by Grace Glueck, 'Modern Museum's Policy on Artists' Gifts Assailed' in *The New York Times* of 12 June, which reported the joint letter and, in the same paper on the following day, 'Artist Defends Modern Museum In a Dispute Over Soliciting Art'.[144] On 15 June the AWC replied publicly, including copies of all the relevant letters and publications. The Coalition's two-page reply is, not surprisingly, critical of the responses I have quoted. The AWC concludes:

> The AWC does not begrudge the success of the artists in this show, to whom we all owe a major esthetic debt, nor are we judging the esthetic content of the exhibition. We are all too aware of the conditions in which these artists have existed for years under the present system, and it is this system we would like to change. We have no intention of letting the 'watchdog' ghost of Ad Reinhardt lie. In the 1960s large sections of the world's population have realized what Reinhardt realized in the art world long before, that sins of omission and commission, crimes of silence and rhetoric, are equally indefensible.[145]

Judging from Schapiro's letter of February 1970, he would most likely have distanced himself from the AWC's position and identified more with the letters from Newman and the group of dissenting artists including Rothko and Motherwell. Schapiro had long associated himself with a particular reading of Abstract Expressionism, as exemplified by 'The Liberating Quality of Avant-Garde Art' (1957).[146] Historically, this essay was a product of a Marxist intellectual writing to support a critical version of the avant garde in the face of the great traumas of Stalinism, the Holocaust and McCarthyism. Within his reading the work of Mark Rothko was as important as that of any abstract artist of the 1950s.

In 1974 Schapiro spoke in the 'Rothko trial', placing him with Pollock and de Kooning as 'not only the outstanding American painters but also in world painting at the moment'.[147] Two days before Schapiro dated his letter of refusal to the AWC/AWP petition, Rothko committed suicide. There were reports in *The New York Times* on 26 February.[148] Did this act and its personal and cultural significance affect Schapiro? The metaphors of suicide and loss were powerful in the rhetoric of criticisms of the New Left whose attacks were often seen as self-destructive and as throwing away those gains in America that had been struggled for since the 1930s.

Rothko, Chambers, Hiss, Nixon

In the 1930s and 1940s, MoMA was regarded as an oasis of progressive modernist culture amongst many leftist intellectuals even though it was recognised as economically reliant on families such as the Rockefellers. There was something to defend in MoMA's support of modern art even though by the late 1960s it was widely regarded as formalist and the epitome of the selective tradition with all its exclusive mechanisms. Was Schapiro keen to preserve that element of MoMA's modernism which could be lost in the strategies and aims of that constituency centred on the AWC, GAAG and *The New York Element*? At the same time he shared the New Left's disappointment with how the United States had developed in the Cold War years, especially now under President Nixon. Nixon had been hated by the Old Left ever since his rise to political prominence on the back of McCarthyite witchhunts.[149]

There are two areas for speculation here and one of firmer fact. The latter is the story of Petlin's attempts to get the letters of petition to Picasso, and Barr's role in trying to prevent this happening. One area for speculation is why Schapiro sent a copy of his refusal, with a covering letter, to Barr at MoMA. This was as much a definite act of solidarity as his letter to the AWC/AWP was an act of rejection. A second is the long-term legacy of the Whittaker Chambers and Alger Hiss case in many leftists' view of the politics of the United States since the late 1940s. This case and the controversial role of freshman Congressman Richard Nixon, whose political career was launched by actions he made in the case, is vital to an understanding of Cold War America. In 1948 before the House Committee on Un-American Activities (HUAC), Whittaker Chambers stated that he had been a functionary of the Communist Party (CP) and named Alger Hiss, his younger brother and six other former officials from the New Deal of the 1930s as members of a covert group organised by the CP in the 1930s. Hiss, a prominent former United States, State Department official and president of the Carnegie Endowment for International Peace, appeared before the HUAC to deny the accusations. In the climate of Republican-fuelled anti-Communism, not least Nixon's campaign to generate headlines about treason, Hiss was indicted for perjury. In January 1950, after two trials and on the basis of flimsy evidence, Hiss was convicted of perjury in testifying that he had not passed State Department documents to Chambers in 1938 and that he had not seen Chambers since 1 January 1937. The day after Hiss was sentenced to five years in prison, Nixon gave a four-hour House speech, 'Lessons of the Hiss Case', which proposed a five-point programme to combat subversives and Communism. The agenda was taken up, almost word for word, by Senator McCarthy, and publication of Nixon's speech became a platform for his campaign to become Vice-President in 1952.

Schapiro was a friend of Chambers, helped him to gain work and was a witness in the actual trial. He had a long and sensitive memory about friendships, political struggle and scholarship. The latter is evidenced by his reference to his own review from 1945 in his response to *Artnews* in January 1970. Rothko's suicide may have not only signified a loss of a major figure in Schapiro's own cultural commitments but also reminded him of Chambers's suicide in 1961. One reason for raising this possibility is the figure of Nixon, whose election in 1968 and subsequent actions were regarded as a catastrophe by those who knew his career and political history. On the day that news of Rothko's suicide appeared in *The New York Times*, the front page carried yet another story critical of the President, 'Senators Assail Policy of Nixon on War in Laos', which drew attention to the administration's secrecy and hidden agendas. On the same day, there was more news of revelations about My Lai, as there had been all through January and February. And on the day Schapiro dated his letter, *The New York Times* carried a front-page story of another atrocity in Vietnam, where five marines were accused of 'murdering 11 South Vietnamese women and 5 children on February 19th'.[150]

The continuation of atrocities in Vietnam served as a reminder to those who lived through the historic shift of American attitudes in the late 1940s. In this shift, John Cabot Smith argues, 'the defeat of world Communism was given a higher priority than the pursuit of world peace ... it was soon to become the majority view and to furnish support for the policies of the Cold War and shooting wars in Korea, Vietnam and Cambodia'.[151] Smith goes on to argue that the Hiss case became a dramatic turning point in America's rejection of Roosevelt and acceptance of the Cold War:

> It was precisely because Roosevelt and his policies could be attacked through Hiss that Richard Nixon made such a spectacle of Hiss before the HUAC and hounded him into jail. Nixon and his supporters made Hiss a symbol of what the public feared, because the symbol suited their purposes, although it did fit the man.[152]

What was Schapiro's view of the political effects of the Hiss case? In 1967 he wrote a long review of a psychoanalytic analysis of Chambers and Hiss, illustrated by two of Schapiro's drawings from summer 1923.[153] The review is highly critical of the book, and its detail deserves closer analysis than possible here. Schapiro leaves the reader with little doubt that he believes Hiss to be guilty of being associated with Communism. However, it also reads as though Schapiro is avoiding contradictions which Conor Cruise O'Brien picked up in his subsequent letters of criticism.

Schapiro's role in the trials was this. As a schoolmate and old friend of Chambers he gave corroborative evidence for Chambers's allegation that he had bought four oriental rugs in late 1936. According to Chambers, one of the rugs was to be given to Hiss on Colonel Bykov's instructions as a token of the Soviet Union's gratitude for the help he had already given. Hiss acknowledged he owned an oriental rug but was this the one? If it was the rug Chambers's alleged he gave to Hiss in early 1937, it suggested that Hiss was lying when he claimed that he had lost contact with Chambers in 1936. Chambers stated that in late 1936 he had asked Schapiro to buy some oriental rugs on his behalf with the promise that he would reimburse him. At the trials, over a decade later, Schapiro produced his cancelled cheque for $600, dated 23 December 1936, and a receipt confirming his receipt of the rugs on 29 December of the same year.

At the end of his review, in 1967, Schapiro makes some revealing and surprising observations about privileged status and political idealism. He observes that both Hiss and Chambers had reached the top of their respective professions. Whilst they had

> therefore presumably no strong incentive to rebel against a society in which they had the prospect of enjoying the greatest benefits, [they] were nevertheless attracted by the Communist movement and engaged in secret work of a criminal nature. They could justify it inwardly by the thought that they were contributing in this way to the struggle for a good society, more in keeping with their idealism than the society in which they had lost confidence though it offered them a privileged status.[154]

This claim is at odds with much of Schapiro's earlier analyses of capitalism published since the 1930s. Is he saying that only the poor, underprivileged and oppressed will genuinely and understandably be drawn to Communism? That those with privileged status and benefits will be tempted only by idealism? This seems too stereotypical. Schapiro continues, perhaps in a classic case of projection, to talk of the 'young minds of the 1930s'. The whole passage deserves to be quoted:

> Their rationality, their critical attitude to dogmas, their moral seriousness, were not proof against the seductions of a corrupt party propaganda at a time of general economic disarray and threatening chaos. By 1949 those who had broken with the Communist movement were more ready to believe Chambers's story; it confirmed so much in their own experience and justified a break that had been a painful recantation of passionately held ideas and commitments. To those who had not come so close to the Left but had supported in a liberal spirit many causes of humane appeal advanced by the Communist front-organizations and had looked to Russia as a promising source of progress in spite of the reported repressions and intolerance, the revelations of Chambers, so welcome to Nixon and McCarthy, seemed merely an attack on that liberal spirit and its trust in a future unity of the liberal and radical.[155]

Communism was clearly a word of pain and betrayal for Schapiro. Was a 'trust in a future unity of the liberal and radical' part of Schapiro's own consciousness after the great trauma of Stalinism? Did he later misunderstand the AWC/AWP petition? If so, was it because he saw their call for the removal of *Guernica* more as an attack on MoMA, which he regarded as a symbolic monument for the achievements of the 'liberal and radical' aesthetics of modernism, rather than as a protest at the My Lai atrocity? Such a question is prompted by a reply to Schapiro from Rudolf Baranik on behalf of the AWC. Baranik ends by pointing to what he sees as Schapiro's mistake: 'you believe that we protested against the Museum of Modern Art, while our protest was against the Guernica in Vietnam – My Lai'.[156]

Letters, phone calls and subversion

MoMA believed that the AWC/AWP protest was directed at the Museum. For instance, on 24 February 1969, Walter Bareiss wrote to Wilder Green from Germany, where he had business interests, alerting him to an article which he had recently seen in a German newspaper. Bareiss enclosed a copy of the article, which details the AWC's attempt to petition Picasso about *Guernica*. Although he had heard hints about this when in the United States, he had not read anything about 'the problem'. Bareiss advises Green to inform John Hightower, Director elect of MoMA, who 'is supposedly taking care of our relations with the Art Workers Coalition . . . I do not think it is serious but as these people are completely irresponsible or rather the extremist storm troops are, you never know to what length they might go.'[157]

Bareiss's politicised phrase 'extremist storm troops' reveals a particular attitude to the protests of late 1969 and early 1970 which I have discussed. He may also have had in mind parallels with, for example, the Chicago Seven and the Black Panthers. On 19 February, *The New York Times* carried a report on the result of their trial: 'Chicago 7 Cleared of Plot; 5 Guilty on Second Count'.[158] Seven of the charged were acquitted of plotting to incite a riot during the Democratic National Convention in 1968 but five were 'convicted of seeking to promote a riot through individual acts'. Stories of the Panthers were also common – for example 'Panther Hearings Halted Over Defendants' Conduct' on the front page of *The New York Times* of 26 February.

Presumably Alfred Barr felt the same as Bareiss about protests and protesters as they affected MoMA, at least, and was glad of weighty support. In his reply to Schapiro's letter he states that 'Your opinion is important and I hope the A.W.C. can be swayed. I shall take the liberty to show your letter to some of my colleagues.'[159]

In 1967, with the Angry Arts Petition to Picasso,[160] Barr had acted directly to prevent its success. He wrote to Kahnweiler on 14 April, 1967, and after a reply, dated 18 April, Barr wrote to Picasso on 21 April.[161] These letters bear some examination as, according to Petlin, Barr telephoned him in 1970 to persuade him against the advisability of the AWC/AWP petition.[162] In his letter to Kahnweiler, Barr enclosed a copy of the Angry Arts petition which he says 'is organized by a number of serious but perhaps naive artists who did not think twice about the importance of *Guernica*, which Picasso painted as a demonstration against "brutality and war"'. Barr had used the word 'naive' over a decade earlier, in 1955, to describe Picasso's politics. In a memo to Elizabeth Shaw on a right-wing article in the *American Legion Magazine*, Barr refers to Picasso's *Seated Woman*, which 'was painted 17 years before Picasso became a Communist. Picasso is politically naive and foolish, but the Soviet authorities have not accepted his art.'[163]

Barr was very concerned with the connection between art and Communism during the early Cold War years. Picasso's politics was a central issue. An indication of the depth of concern can be found in the files on Picasso in the Barr Papers, MoMA Archives.[164] For example, there is correspondence between Barr and Richard Hunt, National Committee for a Free Europe, with a copy of information on 'attacks on Picasso [by Communists]', from its Information and Reference Department, and gathered from the scriptwriters for Radio Free Europe. The term 'Reds' is used consistently in the extracts from United States papers. And, as an example of personal connections, there is Roland Penrose's letter to Barr, from Paris, dated 16 December 1956. He details Picasso's worry about events in Hungary, the artist's happiness at reproductions of *Massacre in Korea* being shown in the streets there, and Picasso's signature on the open letter to *L'Humanité* in which intellectuals departed from the Party line. Penrose was keen to publicise all of this in his forthcoming book *Portrait of Picasso*. In his reply to Penrose, Barr says:

> Of course I am pleased that he signed the open letter to *L'Humanité*, but can't help feeling a certain sense of disgust that it should have taken him so long to declare what has been so painfully obvious to the rest of the world, namely that the Communist press everywhere is a great deal more corrupt than the non-Communist press.[165]

As Herbert Mitgang details, the FBI maintained a voluminous secret dossier on Picasso. Its officials were concerned about the effect of the artist, and his Communism, on opinion in the United States and how to use him for propaganda purposes.[166] Picasso's 'name continued to appear in FBI references up through 1971, when he was nearly 90 years old'.[167]

In 1967, Kahnweiler made clear to Barr his opposition to the war in Vietnam but was against the petition. One reason for this has to be art-market considerations and the role of MoMA in maintaining the aesthetic status not only of Picasso but also of other artists with whom the Kahnweiler–Leiris Gallery was connected. He advised Barr to write to Picasso, which he did immediately, saying: 'As you know, millions of American people are profoundly disturbed and anxious about the Vietnam War. However, . . . [*Guernica's*] withdrawal would, I believe, appear to be a misunderstood retreat.'[168] Unlike Kahnweiler, Barr does not indicate whether he is for or against the Vietnam War. To be 'disturbed and anxious' is non-committal politically. No doubt Presidents Johnson and Nixon and General Westmorland were also 'disturbed and anxious about the Vietnam War'. Again it is instructive to see Barr's use of such words in earlier more explicitly politicized contexts. In a letter to Nelson Rockefeller of 3 May 1947, Barr offered some suggestions for a letter that Rockefeller might write to Secretary Marshall about the State Department exhibition 'recently withdrawn from circulation under pressure from Congress and (I guess) the President . . . I believe that we should not indicate any kind of censure but simply serious concern and interest.'[169]

Given these precedents, it is neither a surprise to see Barr welcome Schapiro's letter of refusal nor that he intervened in the 1970 petition. Petlin had been selected to carry the letters to Paris and then to Picasso because he knew people close to the artist, such as the painter Edouard Pignon, who was an old friend from the PCF days, his wife Hélène Parmelin, who had modelled for Picasso for many years, and Michel Leiris, writer and Kahnweiler's son-in-law. Bearing in mind the great discretion with which artists and writers had been approached to sign the petition, Petlin was surprised to receive a phone call from Alfred

Barr a few days before he was due to leave for Paris. Petlin recalls Barr saying that 'we may all agree with the sentiment involved here and with the sense that there is something terrible going on [in Vietnam]. But, we feel that it would be terrible to petition Picasso to remove the *Guernica* because it would have such terrible ramifications, for both the Museum of Modern Art and for Picasso himself.'[170]

When Petlin said to Barr that he did not understand why it would cause such a reaction, the response was

> 'People who normally contribute large sums of money to the Museum would shy away from doing so because the Museum has been identified with an anti-government gesture.' That's Alfred Barr. 'The Museum would suffer, art would suffer, younger artists in turn would suffer because they would suddenly be identified with a side and the punishment for the Museum would be severe.'

Petlin declined Barr's invitation to meet to discuss the matter as their views were so diametrically opposed. But Petlin asked

> 'How did you know to call me, Mr. Barr?' He said, 'Oh, the art world' but I know differently because I know in retrospect that my phone was tapped and that Alfred Barr was informed whether directly or indirectly. And not only was Alfred Barr informed but Roland Penrose was informed and not only was Roland Penrose informed but Michel Leiris was informed.

Petlin learned that his phone was tapped from his younger brother who, because he was a commodities broker in Chicago, had a secure Watts telephone line. There was a legal requirement to inform him of any tapping on lines with which he had been in contact when his telephone line was cleared. Petlin's number was on the list of information provided.

By the time Petlin got going on his journey to Paris and Picasso, 'Roland Penrose had contacted Leiris and told Leiris to basically sabotage the event'. Leiris took the package of letters and assured Petlin that he would try to bring this petition to Picasso, as they were in constant contact, and would phone him within the week. No phone call, though Petlin tried to contact Leiris without success. In frustration Petlin went to seek the assistance of Picasso's old friend, Pignon. Upon hearing the story, Pignon immediately said that Penrose and Leiris were probably working against this thing. Even when Hélène Parmelin phoned Picasso's home in the south of France, she was prevented from speaking to him by Jacqueline Picasso, who let it be known that she knew all about the petition but that 'we're [in the *plural*] going to keep it from Picasso'. Parmelin tried for days to contact Picasso but without success. When Leiris finally contacted Petlin he declared that he hadn't had a chance to contact Picasso. Petlin, furious, knew differently. He felt particularly betrayed because Leiris had demonstrated that he was a friend of political action from his signature, alongside other French intellectuals, on the telegram of support for the Tower in Los Angeles in February 1966. The telegram supporting the Artists' Protest Committee was sent direct to Petlin.[171] This precedent prompted members of Artists and Writers Protest to enlist Leiris in attempts to convey to Picasso their '1000 American Artists Petition' in April 1967, urging the artist to withdraw *Guernica* from the Museum of Modern Art as an act of protest against United States bombing in Vietnam. A telegram was sent to Leiris on 27 April, containing the main text of the petition, asking for his agreement to present the petition personally to Picasso. Sent by Cecilia Clarac-Serou on behalf of the Artists and Writers Protest, the telegram was signed by Bill Copley, Walter de Maria, Leon Golub, Max Kozloff and Irving Petlin.[172] An apologetic telegram was received from Leiris on 13 June 1967, saying that he had not been able to see Picasso but had sent the petition by express letter.[173] Three years later, Petlin tried again to enlist Leiris's assistance. This time he made a personal rather than a telegraphic attempt. However, the earlier sympathetic if delayed response was now met with obstruction. Leiris, it seems, shared the views expressed by Barr and Bareiss about the relationship between politics and the art market.

To begin to understand the context in which Schapiro made his choice in February 1970 is to recover the contradictions in a crucial period in the history of the art left. In an important sense it also assists us to reflect upon the capacity for amnesia within the United States, then and since: 'My Lai is now almost completely forgotten, erased almost entirely from the national consciousness. What was once an image of incandescent horror has become at most a vague recollection of something unpleasant that happened during the Vietnam War.'[174] We can, though, choose a different recollection: a recollection that avoids repetitive compulsions driving individuals and groups back into a conservativism and a dominant ideological account of the past. We know from psychoanalysis that there are unconscious resistances, compulsions and repetitions within individuals. Within social interaction similar processes are manifest in the erasure of collective memory.

Notes

1 An earlier version of this chapter appeared as a two-part article: 'Meyer Schapiro's Choice: My Lai, *Guernica*, MoMA and the Art Left, 1969–70' (Part 1), *Journal of Contemporary History*, 30:3 (July 1995), 481–511; 'Meyer Schapiro's Choice: My Lai, *Guernica*, MoMA and the Art Left, 1969–70 – Part 2', *Journal of Contemporary History*, 30:4 (October 1995), 705–28.

2 I am indebted to the following for allowing me to interview them: Dore Ashton, Rudolf Baranik, Mark di Suvero, Jon Hendricks, Max Kozloff, Leon Golub, Arthur Hughes, Lucy Lippard, Irving Petlin, Nancy Spero, Therese Schwartz, May Stevens.

3   John P. Diggins makes useful distinctions between the 'Lyrical Left', the 'Old Left' and the 'New Left' in *The Rise and Fall of the American Left* (New York and London, Norton, [1973] 1992), especially pp. 154–7 and pp. 231–8.

4   There are numerous references for an understanding of Schapiro's contribution to intellectual and political life in the United States. See the special issue of the *Oxford Art Journal*, 17:1, 1994; my *Pollock and After: The Critical Debate* (New York and London, Harper and Row, 1985); Hélène Epstein, 'Meyer Schapiro: "A Passion to Know and to Make Known"', *Art News*, 82:5 (May 1983), 60–85, and 82:6 (June 1983), 84–95; Alan Wallach, 'Marxism and Art History', in Bertell Ollman and Edward Vernoff (eds), *The Left Academy* (New York, Praeger, 1984).

5   In '265 LETTERS TO PICASSO REQUEST REMOVAL OF *GUERNICA* AS WAR PROTEST', AWC/AWP Press Release (13 March 1970) in Lucy R. Lippard Papers, PAD/D archive (Museum of Modern Art Library). The press release without the accompanying 'list of those who have signed' has been published in Ellen C. Oppler (ed.), *Picasso's Guernica* (New York and London, Norton, 1988), pp. 239–40.

6   Interview with the author (7 June 1993).

7   Copy of letter in the Museum of Modern Art Archives, Alfred H. Barr Jnr, Papers [Archives of American Art (AAA) Roll 2196, Frames 247–8] and in the *Guernica* file, Department of Painting and Sculpture (Museum of Modern Art, New York). Letter reprinted, almost in full, in Oppler, *Picasso's Guernica*, pp. 242–3.

8   Barr's early role in theorising a dominant account of modern art and in its institutionalised entrenchment at MoMA is well known. So, too, Schapiro's incisive critique of Barr's *Cubism and Abstract Art*, 1936, in 'Nature of Abstract Art', *Marxist Quarterly*, 1:1 (January–March 1937), 77–98. On this see my *Pollock and After: The Critical Debate*, especially pp. 3–20.

9   See Museum of Modern Art Archives, Alfred H. Barr Jnr, Papers, [Archives of American Art (AAA) Roll 2196, Frames 245–6] and *Guernica* file, Department of Painting and Sculpture (Museum of Modern Art, New York). Many thanks to Rudolf Baranik for a copy of his unpublished letter to Schapiro.

10 Alloway, 'Art', *The Nation*, 23 February 1970, 221–2. Later that year Alloway, who was close to many of the activists amongst artists and writers, wrote a brief overview of their campaigns: *The Nation*, 19 October 1970, 381–2.

11 Alloway, 'Art', *The Nation*, 23 February 1970, 221.

12 *Ibid.*

13 *The New York Times*, 26 February 1966, 20.

14 ANGRY ARTS letter asking for artists to donate a work of art for sale, Dore Ashton Papers, PAD/D archive (Museum of Modern Art Library).

15 Copy of blank petition in Rudolf Baranik Papers, PAD/D archive (Museum of Modern Art Library). Oppler, *Picasso's Guernica*, p. 242, claims that Schapiro signed the 1967 petition.

16 'The New "Confrontation Politics" is a Dangerous Game', *The New York Times Magazine*, 20 October 1968, 27–9, 133–40, and 'Political Terrorism: Hysteria on the Left', *The New York Times Magazine*, 12 April 1970, 25–7, 124–8. On Schapiro and on Howe see Alan Wald, *The New York Intellectuals: The Rise and Fall of the Anti-Stalinist Left from the 1930s to the 1980s* (Chapel Hill and London, University of North Carolina Press, 1987), especially pp. 210–17 and chapter 10. On Howe and *Dissent* see Maurice Isserman, *If I Had a Hammer: The Death of the Old Left and the Birth of the New Left* (Urbana and Chicago, University of Illinois Press, 1993), especially chapter 3. Another example of Schapiro's activism is his speech, along with a Professor of Physics, at an anti-war demonstration at Columbia University in 1968.

17 On the anti-war protests in general, see Tom Wells, *The War Within: America's Battle Over Vietnam* (Berkeley, Los Angeles and London, University of California

Press, 1994); on the relationship between artists and the anti-war movement see Lucy R. Lippard, *A Different War: Vietnam in Art* (Seattle, Whatcom Museum of History and Art and The Real Comet Press, 1990).

18   *Le Monde*, 24 October 1969, 3.

19   *Le Monde*, 14 November, 1969, 2.

20   *The New York Times*, 29 October 1969, 32.

21   *Ibid.*

22   On this, see my later discussion. Also: Serge Guilbaut, 'Postwar Painting Games: The Rough and the Slick', in Guilbaut (ed.), *Reconstructing Modernism: Art in New York, Paris and Montreal, 1945–1964* (Cambridge, Mass., and London, MIT Press, 1990), pp. 30–79; and my 'The Politics of Representation', in Paul Wood, Francis Frascina, Jonathan Harris and Charles Harrison, *Modernism in Dispute: Art Since the Forties* (New Haven and London, Yale University Press, 1993), pp. 77–169.

23   Michael Bilton and Kevin Sim, *Four Hours in My Lai* (New York and London, Penguin, 1992), p. 26. Asphalt was a metaphor in Greenberg's famous condemnation of *Guernica*: 'With its bulging and buckling, it looks not a little like a battle scene from a pediment that has been flattened out under a defective steam roller', 'Picasso at Seventy-Five', *Arts*, 33 (October 1957), 45.

24   Baranik's posters of a napalmed and bandaged child were widely distributed: 'Angry Arts: Against the War in Vietnam' and 'For This You've Been Born?', 1967, Baranik file, PAD/D Archive (Museum of Modern Art Library). Baranik also worked on such images in paintings called the *Napalm Elegy*: see for example: *Rudolf Baranik, Napalm Elegies and Other Works* (Dayton, Ohio, Wright State University Art Galleries, 1977) and *Rudolf Baranik, Elegies: Sleep; Napalm; Night Sky* (Columbus, Ohio, Ohio State University Gallery of Fine Art, 1987). Leon Golub produced a series of paintings entitled *Napalm* and wrote 'The Artist as an Angry Artist: The Obsession with Napalm', *Arts Magazine*, April 1967, 48–9.

25   'Vietnam Myths and American Military Realities', *Commander's Call* (July/August 1976), quoted in Bilton and Sim, *Four Hours in My Lai*, p. 15.

26   '265 LETTERS TO PICASSO REQUEST REMOVAL OF *GUERNICA* AS WAR PRO-TEST', AWC/AWP Press Release (13 March 1970).

27   The official Peers Commission Report, 1970, states that the precise number of Vietnamese killed cannot be determined but was at least 175; subsequent researchers have put the figure at around five hundred. For discussion of the variously claimed numbers and of the context, including military censorship, of the Peers Report see Bilton and Sim, *Four Hours in My Lai*.

28   My references are to 'Lieutenant Accused of Murdering 109 Civilians', *St Louis Post-Dispatch*, 13 November 1969, 1, 19. The *Alabama Journal* had its own story the previous afternoon.

29   *The New York Times*, 13 November 1969, 1, 7.

30   *The Times*, London, 20 November 1969, 1. Also see pages 10 and 11.

31   *The New York Times*, 20 November 1969, 14.

32   *Ibid.*, 1, 14.

33   *Ibid.*, 14.

34   *The New York Times*, 25 November 1969, 16.

35   *The New York Times*, 20 November, 1969, 14.

36   Quoted in Bilton and Sim, *Four Hours in My Lai*, p. 367. See pp. 366–7 on public disclosures of similar events by United States military.

37   See Bolton and Sim, *Four Hours in My Lai*, chapters 4 and 5, for a comprehensive account of these atrocities. Seymour Hersh in his 'My Lai 4: A Report on the Massacre and its Aftermath', *Harper's Magazine*, May 1970, 53–84, details some of the rapes and mutilations, as does the Peers Report even though subjected to military censorship.

38 *Time*, 5 December 1969, carried, on its cover, a colour-key transfer image of Calley's head and shoulders in military uniform with the question 'THE MASSACRE Where does the Guilt lie?'. Inside, the magazine carried various analyses: 'My Lai: An American Tragedy', 23–4, 26, 28–32; 'An Average American Boy?', 25; 'On Evil: The Inescapable Fact', 27; 'On the Other Side: Terror as Policy', 29; 'The Legal Dilemmas', 32–4. Whilst *Time* included some of Haeberle's photographs, it was *Life* which carried the most horrifying photos; it was the latter that had the greatest impact on the constituency that I am considering here. The cover of *Newsweek*, 8 December 1969, also carried a head and shoulders photograph of Calley in military uniform. Inside was a lengthy report 'The Killings at Song My: A Single Incident in a Brutal War Shocks the American Conscience', 33–4, 36, 41, with one of Haeberle's photos from *The Cleveland Plain Dealer*, and an examination of 'The "War Crime" Issue: Some Nagging Questions' drawing a parallel with Lidice, 35.

39 'The Massacre at Mylai: Exclusive Pictures, Eyewitness Accounts', *Life*, 5 December 1969, 36–45.

40 *Life*, 5 December 1969, 74–85.

41 *Ibid.*, 51–6.

42 *Ibid.*, 6.

43 *Ibid.*, 72–3.

44 *Ibid.*, 63.

45 For information on the Art Workers' Coalition, including participants, see: AWC, *Open Hearing* (New York, Art Workers Coalition, 1969) and AWC, *Documents I* (New York, Art Workers Coalition, 1969) and Lucy Lippard, 'The Art Workers' Coalition: Not a History', *Studio International*, 180:927 (November 1970), 171–4. Generally see Therese Schwartz, 'The Politicization of the Avant-Garde', Part I, *Art in America*, 59:6 (1971), 97–105; Part II, *Art in America*, 60:2 (1972), 70–9; Part III, *Art in America*, 61:2 (1973), 69–71; Part IV, *Art in America*, 62:1 (1974), 80–4.

46 Author's interviews with Rudolf Baranik (24 November 1991); Therese Schwartz (24 October 1992); Irving Petlin (27 October 1992).

47 For this and what follows I draw on my interview with Petlin (27 October 1992). On the early context of French and United States involvement see Noam Chomsky, *Rethinking Camelot: JFK, the Vietnam War, and US Political Culture* (London, Verso, 1993) and Howard Zinn, 'The Impossible Victory: Vietnam', *The Twentieth Century: A People's History* (New York, Harper and Row, 1984).

48 *The New York Times*, 22 November, 3.

49 See, for example: Todd Gitlin, *The World Is Watching* (Berkeley, University of California Press, 1980); Daniel Hallin, *The Uncensored War: The Media and Vietnam* (Oxford, Oxford University Press, 1986); Kevin Williams, 'The Light at the End of the Tunnel: The Mass Media, Public Opinion and the Vietnam War', in Glasgow University Media Group, John Eldridge (ed.), *Getting the Message: News Truth and Power* (London and New York, Routledge, 1993), pp. 305–28; Chester J. Pach, Jr, 'And That's the Way it Was: The Vietnam War on the Network Nightly News', in David Farber (ed.), *The Sixties: From Memory to History* (Chapel Hill and London, University of North Carolina Press, 1994), pp. 90–118.

50 Interview with the author (24 November 1991). See Rosler's series of 20 photomontages *Bringing the War Home* (*Bringing the War Home: House Beautiful*, 15 photomontages, and *Bringing the War Home: Vietnam*, 5 photomontages), 1967–72, originally disseminated in underground newspapers and flyers. For example, see the newspaper versions of *Tron* (*Amputee*) and *Vacation Getaway*, both from *Bringing the War Home: House Beautiful*, in *Goodbye to All That*, newspaper for San Diego Women, 13 October 1970.

51 Rosler, *Bringing the War Home: House Beautiful*. See, too, Martha Rosler, 'War in My Work', *Camera Austria International*, 47/48 (1994), 69–78 and Catherine de Zegher (ed.), *Martha Rosler: Positions in the Life World* (Birmingham, Vienna, Cambridge Mass., and London, Ikon Gallery, Generali Foundation and the MIT Press, 1998).

52 Williams, 'The Light at the End of the Tunnel', p. 325.

53 'Vietnam Myths and American Military Realities'.

54 Speech delivered in Des Moines, Iowa, before the Mid-West Regional Republican Committee and released in Washington. Agnew urged television viewers to register 'their complaints' by writing to the networks and telephoning local stations.

55 *The New York Times*, 14 November 1969, 24.

56 From transcript of speech, *The New York Times*, 14 November 1969, 24.

57 *The New York Times*, 14 November 1969, 24.

58 'The Press Faces its Critics', *Life*, 5 December 1969, 46.

59 *The New York Times*, 26 November 1969, 1, 91.

60 Stanton as reported in *The New York Times*, 26 November 1969, 91.

61 'The Press Faces its Critics', 46.

62 *The New York Times*, 14 November 1969, 1.

63 *Ibid.*, 20–1.

64 *Ibid.*, 1, 21.

65 See Jon Hendricks and Jean Toche, *GAAG: The Guerilla Art Action Group 1969–1976 A Selection* (New York, Printed Matter, 1978), 'Number 2' (unpaginated).

66 *Ibid.*, 'Number 3'. Participants were Hendricks, Toche, Poppy Johnson and Silvianna, the artist/film-maker and member of the AWC. The 'Call' was supported by the Action Committee for Art Workers Coalition.

67 The Rockefellers' art interests had been much in the news in 1969. In May Governor Nelson Rockefeller announced that he intended to transfer his collection of primitive art from the Museum of Primitive Art, of which he was the founder and President, to the Metropolitan Museum of Art. Hilton Kramer reported Rockefeller's decision to 'leave 25 "key works" from his private collection of modern art to the Museum of Modern Art', *The New York Times*, 27 May 1969, 42. See, too, Kramer, 'Art and "Everything Else"', *The New York Times*, 15 June 1969, 25. On the evening of 26 May 1969, twenty-five members of the AWC picketed the museum during a preview exhibition of the Rockefeller collection.

68 In their call, GAAG state the following sources:

'1. According to Ferdinand Lundberg in his book, *The Rich and the Super-Rich*, the Rockefellers own 65% of the Standard Oil Corporations. In 1966, according to Seymour M. Hersh in his book, *Chemical and Biological Warfare*, the Standard Oil Corporation of California which is a special interest of David Rockefeller (Chairman of the Board of Trustees of the Museum of Modern Art) – leased one of its plants to United Technology Centre (UTC) for the specific purpose of manufacturing *napalm*.

'2. According to Lundberg, the Rockefeller brothers own 20% of the McDonnell Aircraft Corporation (manufacturers of the Phantom and Banshee jet fighters which were used in the Korean War). According to Hersh, the McDonnell corporation has been deeply involved in *chemical and biological warfare* research.

'3. According to George Thayer in his book, *The War Business*, the Chase Manhattan Bank (of which David Rockefeller is Chairman of the Board) – as well as the McDonnell Aircraft Corporation and North American Airlines (another Rockefeller interest) – are represented on the committee of the Defense Industry Advisory Company (DIAC) which serves as a liaison group between the *domestic arms manufacturers* and the International Logistics Negotiations (ILN) which reports directly to the International Security Affairs Division in the *Pentagon*.'

69 On PASTA MoMA see Museum of Modern Art Archives, John B. Hightower Papers, Box 5.

70 Major sources for what follows are: my interviews with Irving Petlin (27 October 1992 and 7 June 1993) and Jon Hendricks (10 October 1992); 'THE MUSEUM AND THE PROTEST POSTER', MoMA press release (8 January 1970), Museum of Modern Art Library: AWC file; 'DOES MoMA APPROVE OF THE SONG MY [My Lai] MASSACRE?, undated AWC press release (soon after 26 December 1969), copy in John Hightower Papers, MoMA Archives Box 3, file 1.II.a., 'Art Workers Coalition II'.

71 Quoted in 'THE MUSEUM AND THE PROTEST POSTER', 1.

72 *MoMA Oral History Project: Interview with Wilder Green*, conducted by Sharon Zane, (New York, October/November 1991), p. 121.

73 'Notebook: Alfred Rosmer (1877–1964)', *Dissent*, 12:1 (winter 1965), 75–6.

74 Petlin, in interview with the author (7 June 1993).

75 *Ibid.*

76 'The New "Confrontation Politics" is a Dangerous Game', 134–5.

77 Right-wing Republicans were well aware of demographic and consumerist shifts during the decade. In a blueprint for Nixon, Kevin Phillips claimed, in *The Emerging Republican Majority*, that 'The great political upheaval of the 1960s is not that of Senator Eugene McCarthy's relatively small group of upper middle class and intellectual supporters, but a populist revolt of the American masses who have been elevated by prosperity to middle class status and conservatism'. Quoted in a review of Phillips's book by Paul Cowan, 'Blue Print for Nixon: The Crabgrass Future', *The Village Voice*, 1 January 1970, 5.

78 'The War: New Support for Nixon' *Time*, 12 January 1970, 10–11.

79 *Although* only 39% of those polled supported Agnew's charges against the press and television networks (29% unable to make any judgement on them at all), approval of Nixon's handling of the war went up from 40% in October (50% disapproving) to 54% in December (40% disapproving).

80 John Bright, letter title 'hippie as "nigger"', *The Nation*, 12 January 1970, 2. Later in the year, Alex Gross wrote an article entitled 'The Artist as Nigger', *The East Village Other*, 22 December 1970.

81 For example, in the January 1966 issue of *Frontier*, 17:3, Bright wrote an enthusiastic review of Claude Brown's memoirs of Harlem, *Manchild and the Promised Land*, 17–19, advertised on the front cover as 'How it is with the Negro'.

82 Reported in *The New York Times*, 10 August 1969, 1, 60.

83 Readers of *The New York Times* were reminded of this in the reports of arrests, 2 December 1969, 76 (see next paragraph).

84 *The New York Times*, 3 December 1969, 37.

85 Howe, 'The New "Confrontation Politics" Is a Dangerous Game', 133.

86 *Ibid.*, 135.

87 Images of Manson and discussion of 'hippie' and 'cult' continued to appear in the news through December. So, too, images of Calley and Vietnam deaths. For example, on 15 December *The New York Times* carried on its cover a story on 'The Hippie Mystique' beneath a lead story on 'G.I.'s Kill 53 of the Enemy In a Battle Near Songmy'. The latter was accompanied by a large photo of American soldiers looking at the bodies of North Vietnamese soldiers on a site 'two miles southeast of Songmy, scene of alleged massacre of South Vietnamese civilians'. Both stories continued inside with 'The Hippie Mystique' accompanied by a photo of 'Charles Manson, leader of cult' at the age of fourteen (page 42). Here there was a psychiatrist's description of 'a mirror image of the hippie': 'demonic' and 'beatific' characteristics. Such reporting paralleled the contrasts made in descriptions of those involved in the My Lai massacres where manichean moralistic polarities about persons over-shadowed deeper social and political causes for these events.

88 In the same issue of *The New York Times*, 3 December 1969, 3, there is a report on the reaction of the world's press, 'Much of World Views Songmy Affair as an American Tragedy' with a photograph of a workman removing a swastika from the Monument to President Kennedy at Runnymede, England. The report noted that many people linked the My Lai massacre 'to what they saw as the inherent evil of the Vietnam war'.

89 *The New York Times*, 3 December 1969, 37.

90 *Ibid.*, 39.

91 John Bright, 'hippie as "nigger"'.

92 'Inquiry Into Slaying of 2 Panthers Urged in Chicago', *The New York Times*, 6 December 1969.

93 Howe, 'Political Terrorism: Hysteria on the Left', 128.

94 *Ibid.* As is well-known, dissident groups including the 'Yippies' were under constant state surveillance.

95 *Ibid.*

96 See his 'The New "Confrontation Politics" Is a Dangerous Game', 139–40.

97 *Ibid.*, 135.

98 'THE MUSEUM AND THE PROTEST POSTER', MoMA press release (8 January 1970), Museum of Modern Art Library: AWC file.

99 Major sources for what follows are: William S. Paley, *As It Happened: A Memoir* (New York, Doubleday, 1979); Sally Bedell Smith, *In All His Glory: The Life of William S. Paley* (New York, Simon and Schuster, 1990); *The Museum of Modern Art Oral History Project: Interview with Walter Bareiss*, conducted by Sharon Zane (September, October 1991); *The Museum of Modern Art Oral History Project: Interview with Wilder Green*, conducted by Sharon Zane (October, November 1991); Russell Lynes, *Good Old Modern: An Intimate Portrait of The Museum of Modern Art* (New York, Atheneum, 1973); Museum of Modern Art Archives, Bates Lowry Papers; Museum of Modern Art Archives, Alfred H. Barr Jnr, Papers [Archives of American Art (AAA) Roll 2196].

100 3 May 1969, reprinted in AWC, *Documents 1*, p. 116. See too Glueck's article in *The New York Times*, 12 May 1969, for further revelations about the trustees' actions.

101 Bedell Smith, *In All His Glory*, p. 445.

102 *Ibid.*, pp. 472–3.

103 Williams, 'The Light at the End of the Tunnel', p. 324, quoting statistics from Hallin, *The Uncensored War: The Media and Vietnam*.

104 Interview with the author (7 June 1993).

105 *Ibid.*

106 'Guerilla Art Action in Front of *Guernica* on 3 January 1970', in Hendricks and Toche, *GAAG: The Guerilla Art Action Group 1979–1976 A Selection*, 'Number 6' (unpaginated). See, too, 'Ars Gratia Artis?', *Newsweek*, 9 February 1970, 80.

107 On six 'framings' of Haeberle's 'photograph' see Amy Schlegel, 'My Lai: "We Lie, They Die" Or, a Small History of an "Atrocious" Photograph', *Third Text*, 31 (summer 1995), 47–66.

108 Sunday 25 January 1970, Section D, 25.

109 *Ibid.*

110 All following quotations from Schapiro's letter to the AWC/AWP, 27 February 1970.

111 See for example James Aronson, *The Press and the Cold War* (New York, Monthly Review Press, [1970] 1990).

112 Noam Chomsky, 'A Special Supplement: The Responsibility of Intellectuals', *The New York Review of Books*, 8:3 (23 February 1967), 16–26, and letters in subsequent issues: 23 March 1967, 28; 20 April 1967, 30–5; 9 November 1967, 35–6.

113 Howe, 'Political Terrorism: Hysteria on the Left', 27.

114 Howe, 'The Agony of the Campus', *Dissent* (September–October 1969), 387–94.

115 *Ibid.*, 387.

116 *Ibid.*, 388.

117 *Ibid.*, 391.

118 *Ibid.*, 393.

119 *Ibid.*, 394.

120 *Ibid.*, 392.

121 *Ibid.*, 394.

122 Schapiro, 'Democratize the Board of Trustees' one of fourteen contributions on 'The Metropolitan Museum, 1870–1970–2001', *Artnews*, 68:9 (January 1970), 29.

123 Schapiro, book review of Francis H. Taylor, *Babel's Tower. The Dilemma of the Modern Museum* (New York 1945), in *Art Bulletin*, 27:4 (December 1945), 272–6.

124 *Ibid.*, 273.

125 *Ibid.*, 275.

126 *Ibid.*, 276.

127 *The New York Times*, 24 February 1970, 51.

128 *The New York Times*, 11 February 1970, 42.

129 *Ibid.*

130 *The New York Times*, 8 February 1970, Section D, 23; AWC letter, 23–4.

131 *The New York Times*, 25 January 1990, Section D, 25.

132 *The New York Times*, 8 February 1970, Section D, 23.

133 As is well known, Kramer's politicisation of his own writings became explicit when he became editor of the right-wing *The New Criterion*, financed by equally right-wing sponsors. His hysterical attack on the left in that journal, especially during the 1980s, is notorious.

134 See for example *Manifesto WSABAL, Women Students and Artists for Black Art Liberation A Student Organisation of Black Art Workers* (June 1970) organised by Michele Wallace, and other press releases; *The Puerto Rican Art Worker's Coalition Indicts the Metropolitan Museum of Art* (18 June 1970). In Museum of Modern Art Archives, Hightower Papers Box 5/8, File III.2.15, 'Black and Puerto Rican Artists'.

135 *The New York Times*, 28 September 1969, Section 2, D, 35.

136 *The New York Times*, 8 February 1970, Section D, 23.

137 For relevant documents see AWC, 'AN EXCHANGE BETWEEN THE ART WORKERS' COALITION, THE ARTISTS PARTICIPATING IN THE EXHIBITION, AND THE MUSEUM OF MODERN ART' (15 June 1969), Museum of Modern Art Library, AWC file.

138 'Errata', AWC, dated 15 June 1969, though this should read 5 June as the covering letter sent to all artists in the exhibition is dated 8 June.

139 Letter in Museum of Modern Art Library, AWC file.

140 *Ibid.*

141 *Ibid.*

142 Letter in Museum of Modern Art Library, AWC file. See also letter in the same file supporting MoMA from Louise Bourgeois, 12 June 1969, to the editor of *The New York Times*.

143 *Ibid.*

144 *The New York Times*, 12 June 1969, 50, and 13 June 1969, 40.

145 'AN EXCHANGE BETWEEN THE ART WORKERS' COALITION, THE ARTISTS PARTICIPATING IN THE EXHIBITION, AND THE MUSEUM OF MODERN ART'.

146 *Artnews*, 56:4 (summer 1957), 36–42. On this text see David Craven, 'Abstract Expressionism, Automatism and the Age of Automation', *Art History*, 13:1 (March 1990), 72–103, and Nancy Jachec, '"The Space Between Art and Political Action":

Abstract Expressionism and Ethical Choice in Postwar America', *The Oxford Art Journal*, 14:2 (1991), 18–29.

147 Quoted in Lee Seldes, *The Legacy of Mark Rothko: An Exposé of the Greatest Art Scandal of Our Century* (London, Secker and Warburg, 1978), p. 257.

148 *The New York Times*, 26 February 1970: articles by Grace Glueck, 1, 39, and by Hilton Kramer, 39.

149 For *Dissent*'s view of Nixon see Irving Howe, 'A Note on Vietnam: Duplicity, Murk and Blood', November–December 1969, 469–70.

150 'Vietnam Murders Laid to 5 Marines', *The New York Times*, 27 February 1970, 1, 2. Earlier stories would have echoed in the memory.

151 John Cabot Smith, *Alger Hiss The True Story* (New York, Holt, Rinehart and Winston, 1976), p. 439. I am indebted to Dore Ashton for reminding me of the importance of the Hiss case for an understanding of Schapiro's subsequent development.

152 *Ibid.*, 440. Also see Ronald Seth, *The Sleeping Truth: The Hiss–Chambers Affair Reappraised* (New York, Hart Publishing Company, 1968) and Edith Tiger (ed.), *In Re Alger Hiss* (New York, Hill and Wang, 1979). Hiss's own view coincides with Cabot Smith's: 'The unjust Verdict, thus left uncorrected, spawned consequences far more momentous than my continued imprisonment. It facilitated Nixon's election to the presidency and the ongoing attacks on both the New Deal and Roosevelt's foreign policies.' Alger Hiss, *Recollections of a Life* (New York, Henry Holt and Co., 1988), p. 160.

153 Meyer Schapiro, 'Dangerous Acquaintances', review of *Friendship and Fratricide, An Analysis of Whittaker Chambers and Alger Hiss*, by Meyer A. Zeligs, M.D. (New York, Viking, 1967), *The New York Review of Books*, 8:3 (23 February 1967), 5–9. See letters from Conor Cruise O'Brien and Schapiro's replies in *The New York Review of Books*, 8:6 (6 April 1967), 35, and 8:8 (4 May 1967), 37. I am indebted to David Craven for drawing my attention to Schapiro's review.

154 Schapiro, 'Dangerous Acquaintances', 8–9.

155 *Ibid.*, 9.

156 Letter (3 March 1970), copy kindly provided by Rudolf Baranik.

157 Letter from Bareiss to Green (24 February 1970); article by Robert Von Berg, 'Entfernt GUERNICA aus dem Museum! Eine Aktion der amerikanischen Art Worker's Coalition', *MÜNCHNER KULTURBERICHTE* (original and in a typed translation). All in *Guernica* File, Department of Painting and Sculpture, Museum of Modern Art.

158 *The New York Times*, 19 February 1970, 1; the five were David Dellinger, Rennie Davis, Thomas Hayden, Abbie Hoffman and Jerry Rubin.

159 Letter (7 April 1970), Museum of Modern Art Archives: Alfred H. Barr Jnr Papers [Archives of American Art (AAA) Roll 2196, Frame 245] and in *Guernica* File, Department of Painting and Sculpture, Museum of Modern Art.

160 Copy in Rudolf Baranik Papers, PAD/D Archive (Museum of Modern Art Library).

161 Copies of all three letters in *Guernica* File, Department of Painting and Sculpture, Museum of Modern Art.

162 Interview with the author (7 June 1993).

163 Memorandum from Barr to Shaw (8 October 1955) Museum of Modern Art Archives: Alfred H. Barr Jnr Papers [Archives of American Art (AAA) Roll 3155, Frame 1239].

164 The Museum of Modern Art Archives: Alfred H. Barr Jnr, Papers, 'Picasso Papers', Box II.C, 'Communists and Picasso 1950s'.

165 Penrose to Barr (16 December 1956); Barr to Penrose (1 January 1957). Both in Museum of Modern Art Archives: Alfred H. Barr Jnr, Papers, 'Picasso Papers', Box II.C, 'Communists and Picasso 1950s'.

166 Herbert Mitgang, 'When Picasso Spooked the F.B.I.', *The New York Times*, 11 November 1990, Section 2, 1, 39.

167 *Ibid.*, 39.

168 Letter (21 April 1967) in *Guernica* File, Department of Painting and Sculpture, Museum of Modern Art.

169 Museum of Modern Art Archives: Alfred H. Barr Jnr, Papers [Archives of American Art (AAA) Roll 3157, no frame number].

170 This and subsequent quotations by Petlin from an interview with the author (7 June 1993).

171 Telegram, 12.03 p.m. Pacific Standard Time (26 February 1966) to Petlin, 520 Strand, Santa Monica. Copy of the telegram kindly provided by Charles Brittin.

172 Telegram in Petlin's possession. Text of the French version in Golub Papers, [Archives of American Art (AAA) Roll N/69 22, Frame 0019].

173 Telegram in Petlin's possession.

174 Michael Bilton and Kevin Sim, *Four Hours in My Lai*, p. 4. Twenty-five years after the disclosures, 'historians, military strategists, journalists, and even witnesses, disagree about the facts of the massacre and its legacy'. So observes Scott Shepard in his report on a major conference on My Lai at Tulane University ending on 3 December 1994: 'US tries to Exorcise the Ghosts of My Lai', *The Guardian*, 5 December 1994, 11. Only just prior to the thirtieth anniversary of My Lai, 16 March 1998, was US Army Warrant Officer Hugh C. Thompson, the helicopter pilot who intervened to halt the massacre and to evacuate survivors, at last honoured. He was presented with the Soldiers' Medal at the Vietnam Veterans' Memorial in Washington on 6 March 1998. In the seventy-fifth Anniversary Issue of *Time*, 9 March 1998, a 'history' of its seventy-five years included an entry on 'The War' for the period 1960–73. Two extracts were used to characterise these years. Significantly, one was from *Time*, 28 November 1969, on the 'My Lai Massacre' when it became public.

Conclusion: culture wars and the American left

Those who ignore the past will be forced to relive it.

(H. Cruz)

Not to know is bad; not to wish to know is worse.

(Nigerian Proverb)[1]

The four main chapters of this book, case studies of specific events in the 1960s, have necessitated consideration of the processes of memory and amnesia. Some aspects of subsequent representations of that decade within particular branches of art history have, inevitably, been part of that consideration – but only in so far as they reveal a selective tradition that has confined parts of the past to the margins or to a place of loss. It has not been my intention to survey retrospective texts, nor to offer a comprehensive revised history of the period. The latter would be a huge task given the paradoxes and contradictions revealed by non-canonical accounts which also unpick the seams of the canon's ideological disguise.

Museums and galleries enshrine symbolic objects to remind visitors of 'the past', often without acknowledging whose past, whose selections, whose constituency. The positive functions of such institutions – conserving, educative, archival – are reliant on absent others and a process of selection produced by ideas, values and beliefs that normally remain opaque to scrutiny: opaque until a paradigmatic rupture or an action reveals unanswered basic questions. In the United States, such questions were revealed by various 'counter-cultural' critiques associated with '1968', that 'moment' with a broader chronology. The success of the counter-culture was as critique, questioning the patterns and values of the 'American way of life', almost breaking, as James Farrell puts it, 'the silence of the silent majority'.[2] In New York, the Museum of Modern Art became a focal point for artists' version of a counter-culture. MoMA's image as, for many, an oasis of modernist culture was fractured by realisations that it was not only a major manipulator of that culture but also a site of power where, for example, the trustees' love of art dissembled the sources and relations that guaranteed their economic capital. Other museums, including the Whitney and the Metropolitan, were also sites for resistance and demonstration both during the 'Art Strike' in 1970 and from that year on by women artists' groups such as Women Artists and Revolution

(WAR), the Ad Hoc Women Artists' Committee and Women Students and Artists for Black Art Liberation (WSABAL).[3]

Critical judgements, purchasing power, rhetorics of display, curatorial careers and the accumulation of museums' internal archives have traditionally intertwined to preserve unquestioned givens about the role and function of art and its defining objects. Such preservation can lead and has led to institutional self-censorship by exclusion and omission, if not by deliberate acts of excision. Since the late 1960s, the Museum of Modern Art has come under heavy scrutiny by historians. Rattled in 1969 and 1970 by direct action and since then discomforted by texts, the participants in MoMA as institution have continued to support its expansion both in size and in its central cultural concerns. An example of the latter has been the development of the Museum's production of classic catalogues, defining moments in the paradigmatic discipline of modern art history and criticism, into larger publishing ventures redefining and redefending the source of official history.[4] The 'catalogue' has spawned the symposia publication[5] and the 'studies' series, with MoMA competing with other institutions, particularly European enterprises such as the Pompidou Centre in Paris.[6] In the counter-revisionist decade of the 1990s, the fourth and fifth of MoMA's 'Studies in Modern Art' have been devoted to reinvesting in positive representations of itself, its activities and major figures in its history.[7] Essays by Michael Kimmelman, in particular, Lynn Zelevansky and Helen Franc attempt to redress the critiques of MoMA, its touring exhibitions and the International Programme and Council as connected in various ways to Cold War ideology.[8] These critiques started to be published in the early 1970s with Max Kozloff's 'American Painting During the Cold War', which was not so much about MoMA as it was a reflective analysis of the relationship between the culture and politics of a period in which Kozloff was himself an active contributor. Published in *Artforum* in 1973, after Phil Leider had relinquished his editorship, it inaugurated a number of articles, including within *Artforum* itself, which developed the hypotheses Kozloff's article raised.[9]

'1968'

The early years of the 1970s were characterised also by a mixture of a reinvigorated museum culture exemplified by the opening of the John Paul Getty Museum, Malibu, in 1974; political deception and corruption, not least about the Vietnam War, resulting in President Nixon's resignation in August 1974; and differing reflections on the effects of Sixties 'counterculture'. A flavour of the latter can be conveyed by an extract from a text published in 1974 by Christopher Gray, an expelled member of the

Situationist International. Alhough only referencing the United States within comments on other manifestations of 1968, he draws attention to a characteristic set of events in the six years up to 1974:

> May 1968 and France on the verge of anarchy . . . an atmosphere of martial law in Paris and hundreds of factories occupied . . . 140 American cities in flames after the killing of Martin Luther King . . . German and English Universities occupied . . . Hippie ghettoes directly clashing with the police state . . . The sudden exhilarating sense of how many people felt the same way . . . The new world coming into focus . . . The riots a great dance in the streets . . .
>
> Today – nothing. The Utopian image has faded from the streets. Just the endless traffic, the blank eyes that pass you by, the nightmarish junk we're all dying for. Everyone seems to have retreated into themselves, into closed occult groups. The revolutionary excitement that fuelled the sixties is dead. The 'counter-culture' a bad joke. No more aggression, no more laughter, no more dreams. 'To talk of life today is like talking of rope in the house of a hanged man'.[10]

Gray's text suggests a profound sense of loss and pessimism. In contrast, other authors in 1974 produced works that render Gray's 'Today – nothing' problematic. In that year Juliet Mitchell's *Psychoanalysis and Feminism* was published.[11] It was an attempt both to critique the patriarchy of the Marxist left of the 1960s and to reforge a radical combination of the social and psychoanalytic for the historical, theoretical and practical work of those who identified with the 'women's movement'. A year before, in 1973, T. J. Clark, who had been a member of the Situationist International,[12] published two books on the abortive Revolution of 1848, *Image of the People: Gustave Courbet and the 1848 Revolution* and *The Absolute Bourgeois: Art and Politics in France 1848–51*,[13] which have been acclaimed as major landmarks in the 'social history of art' and in various accounts of 'the new art history'. Were publications such as those by Mitchell and Clark examples of what Christopher Gray calls 'talking of rope in the house of a hanged man [of 1968]', or major contributions towards empowerment? Were they both critical responses, implicit or explicit, to '1968' and paradigms for work in the context of its various legacies?

To consider such questions is to enter into unresolved debates. For instance, as David Caute demonstrates, to recover the grounds and context of '1968' is to become immersed in the broader base of the years 1967–70 and in a series of differences that characterise the particular situations in, for example, cities in the United States which should not be used to explain conditions and events in, say Paris, Prague or London.[14] Further, the perspective of twenty-five years enabled Theodore

Roszak to produce a critical review of the successes and disappointments of the generation for whom *The Making of a Counter Culture*, first published 1969, represented their experiences.[15] More militantly, Michele Wallace in 'Reading 1968: The Great American Whitewash' argues that there is a 'tendency for "history" in the major sense to corroborate a racist, phallocentric hegemony' even by historians of the New Left in their examinations of the 'phenomenon of 1968'.[16] Feminists have also produced a variety of historical perspectives on the events and struggles both in the late 1960s and since.[17] This is not all, as thirty years later there are evaluations of groups and events, such as the Weather Underground, that sought to dismantle the very processes by which such evaluations can be made.[18]

For many commentators, a major strand in the matrix of causal conditions for '1968' was a 'counter-culture' that established critical alternatives to the social, economic, sexual and visual conventions of postwar capitalist reconstruction. For example, in the late 1950s and 1960s, on the West Coast of the United States artists, poets, musicians, photographers, and novelists were concerned with cultural, social, and sexual critiques of Cold War America. Many of them regarded their country as largely racist, homophobic, xenophobic and obsessed with a cocktail of consumerism, colonialism, military superiority and repression of all kinds. Two major centres were San Francisco and Los Angeles, where communities of 'alternative' artists and intellectuals produced a range of work often characterised as 'Beat Culture'. The lifestyle and works of Wallace Berman were highly influential on contemporaries, particularly those concerned with a subcultural identity and a constituency that was 'other' to established rules of social decorum and official institutions. Berman's first exhibition at the 'avant-garde' Ferus Gallery, Los Angeles, in 1957 was closed by the police on the grounds of obscenity. Reluctant to re-enter the world of galleries, dealers and the commodification of the art object, he continued to produce issues of *Semina*, posted to members of his cultural community. Was the series of nine issues an attempt to evade the forces and pressures of capitalism and commodification in the postwar United States? can these 'magazines' be regarded as a politicised project in terms of Marx's distinction between *productive labour* and *unproductive labour*? or were they the product of a self-indulgent, drug-induced subculture obsessed with utopian fantasy? Richard Cándida Smith identifies the paradoxes. Berman the citizen demonstrated in favour of Civil Rights and protection of the environment and marched in opposition to the Vietnam War in the mid-1960s. With him he carried a banner displaying the photograph of a black person's hand giving the finger[19] which he had juxtaposed with a Jack Kerouac lyric in *Semina* 8: 'I am that noise which / must against their / common paraphrase / charge deceit.' Cándida-Smith continues:

In 1971 he won a Linus Pauling Peace Prize for the best visual art promoting world peace. Yet to the degree that Berman the artist could be said to be a social critic at all, his stance was irresponsible and defeatist, as he warned of the dangers of active involvement in public life. Rather than commenting on the social events of the day, Berman used *Semina* 8 to reaffirm his belief that poets find their success in the private rather than the public realm.[20]

The proliferation of experimental and collaborative writing in little magazines, from San Francisco to New York, during the 1960s demonstrates that Berman was not alone in such a belief.[21] The paradoxes, however, of dissent and critique within a dominant consumerist culture, reliant on manufacturing a desire for spectacular novelty, remained entrenched.[22]

Wall Street *culture*

Two decades later, during the Reagan and Bush presidencies, there erupted renewed intense battles in the United States about economics and power as they are encoded in public questions of ethnicity, sexuality, morality, obscenity and freedom of artistic expression. From 1989 such battles centred most famously on work by Robert Mapplethorpe, Andres Serrano and Sally Mann. Many of those involved in the battles were unaware of the history of the period since McCarthy. One reason for this lack of awareness was a dominant consumerist cultural attitude which Oliver Stone critically exemplified and represented in the film *Wall Street*. Released in December 1987, shortly after the financial crash of the New York Stock Exchange on 19 October, *Wall Street* is set in 1985, a moment of capitalist frenzy.[23] In these years, the art market was booming. Revamped apartments and loft conversions for a new class, described as 'Yuppies', were characterised by investment in conspicuous signifiers of interior design and works of art.[24] The main villain of the film, Gordon Gekko, is an investor whose amoral capacity is matched by his appetite for purchasing works of art that adorn his office and home. In a dramatic interchange, at a party at Gekko's home, Darien Taylor, interior designer, and Bud Fox, a broker, discuss the purchase of a painting in terms of its significance as cultural capital and/or economic investment.

The year 1985 was also the year in which the Guerrilla Girls were formed, in the context not only of the preoccupation with fame and money that Stone's moral tale critiques but also as a counter to the effects of the institutionalised denial of the earlier work of women artists' groups such as WAR, the Ad Hoc Women Artists' Committee and WSABAL. In the spring of 1985 MoMA produced an exhibition entitled *An International Survey of Painting and Sculpture* which was designed to contain the most important contemporary manifestations. However, of the 169 artists only thirteen were women. This outraged many, including those who formed the Guerrilla Girls, a collective of women artists and art-world professionals who retain their anonymity by wearing gorilla masks (hence the pun) and taking the names of dead women artists and writers. One of them, 'Käthe Kollwitz' recalls: 'Even fewer were artists of colour and none [of these] were women. That was bad enough but the curator, Kynaston McShine, said any artist who wasn't in the show should rethink "his" career.'[25] There is a particular irony here. As we have seen, McShine had been, fifteen years earlier, the organiser of the *Information* exhibition at MoMA in 1970. In its engagement with several contemporary social issues, *Information* was arguably the Museum's most explicitly politicised exhibition. Now in 1985, the yet-to-form Guerrilla Girls were annoyed by McShine, whom they regarded as 'extremely prejudiced'. Women demonstrated in front of the Museum with the placards and picket line, so effective in the early 1970s, but with little impact on passers-by in 1985 or on MoMA, which had just completed a massive multi-million-dollar building expansion in 1984.[26] Amnesia and apathy confronted them.

Although the past tells us that such battles are nothing new, it is important to be aware of contemporary ideological struggle manifest in cultural forms and debates. Those who wish to know about the constituent parts of recent instances of permissibility and control require resources and information to allow any possible critical corrective to the production of stereotypes. Here the role of the state and the manifestations of official culture continue to be major determinants despite claims for the emancipatory power of a post-colonial condition of plural identities. That the latter may be true for certain individuals and communities does not negate the pervasive and conditioning power of entrenched notions of culture which affect our whole way of life.[27] Collected documents in Richard Bolton's *Culture Wars* provide a specific instance of issues and debates raised by a particular controversy about government funding of the arts in the United States.[28] What Bolton calls 'wars' can be alternatively theorised in Voloshinov's terms as an instance of differently orientated social accents intersecting in an arena of class and fractional struggle.[29]

One major side in these 'culture wars' represents a brand of puritanism which has been a substantial strand in the paradoxes and contradictions of the 'American experience'. Since the Second World War the various strands of this experience have been entwined within an umbilical cord connecting the elements of United States imperialism abroad and at home: no Cold War without McCarthyism, no Vietnam War without segregation, no CIA foreign intervention without Watergate and J. Edgar Hoover's FBI, no Gulf War without what Noam Chomsky calls cultural commissars. It is now widely accepted that all of these elements necessitated assumptions, unconscious and conscious, about the production and/or use of cultural forms as strategic resources and symbols. These range from the worldwide distribution of Hollywood movies to MoMA's international travelling exhibitions, from the CIA's funding of, for example, a tour of the Boston Symphony Orchestra to Paris in 1952 to the activities of the United States Information Agency (USIA) and the Voice of America in the dissemination of American values. One example is *The Voice of America Forum Lectures: The Visual Arts* broadcast worldwide in 1960–1 and including, amongst the eighteen lectures, Greenberg's 'Modernist Painting' in 1961. The audience for such broadcasts was between thirty and fifty million each day. For those on the left a major problem has been how to produce an oppositional art which escapes the determining effect of the interests that sustain United States imperialism and the powerful resentment of its representatives.

Since 1989 a newly invigorated right wing has been particularly outraged. One focus of rage has been the use of 'taxpayers' money' in grants awarded by the National Endowment for the Arts (NEA), a federal agency chartered in 1965 'to support the best of all forms that reflect the American heritage in its full range of cultural and ethnic diversity and to provide national leadership on behalf of the arts'. Part of Johnson's 'Great Society', the NEA was established at a time when artists were demonstrating against government agencies for destroying cultural and ethnic diversity abroad. In 1989 the budget for the NEA was $169.09 million. In May of that year in the Senate, Republican Senator D'Amato tore up a copy of the NEA Awards in the Visual Arts catalogue which reproduced Andres Serrano's *Piss Christ* (1987). He denounced the NEA award of $15,000 dollars to the artist and declared, in rhetorical terms that echo the attacks on Kienholz's work by Warren M. Dorn and Kenneth Hahn in 1966:

> This so-called piece of art is a deplorable, despicable display of vulgarity . . . This is not a question of free speech. This is a question of the abuse of taxpayers' money . . . If people want to be perverse, in terms of what they recognize as art or culture, so be it, but not with my money, not with the taxpayers' dollars, and certainly not under the mantle of this great Nation. This is a disgrace.[30]

Besides Serrano's *Piss Christ*, other works denounced in similar attacks include Robert Mapplethorpe's *X Portfolio* of 1977–8. Both represent an interest in the body, including its fluids, and sexual and social taboos. Serrano's work is a cibachrome photograph of a mass-produced wood and plastic crucifix submerged in urine. In April 1989 Donald Wildmon, Executive Director of the American Family Association (AFA) sent out a letter about *Piss Christ* suggesting blasphemy and claiming that the 'bias and bigotry against Christians, which has dominated television and movies for the past decade or more, has now moved over to the art museums'.[31]

Cancellation, erasure, denial

Mapplethorpe's photographs of intimate acts from a gay subculture formed a part of an exhibition, *Robert Mapplethorpe: The Perfect Moment*, planned to be shown at the Corcoran Gallery of Art, Washington, DC in 1989. In June the Corcoran trustees cancelled their plans, reportedly because of the growing sexual and political controversy about Mapplethorpe's work. They were anxious that to proceed with the show would threaten congressional reauthorisation of the NEA, which had partly funded the exhibition. Their anxiety had been fuelled by the puritanical rhetoric and social mobilisation of the forces of order and control both in the United States Senate and in the network of religious, moral and political groups throughout the country. Such rhetoric and mobilisation and the acts of cancellation, erasure and denial are not new in the cultural history of the United States. One of the best known was the cancellation of *Sport in Art* and *100 American Artists of the Twentieth Century* in 1956 because of claims, particularly from conservative religious groups, that some of the artists were pro-Communist.[32] Both exhibitions were to travel abroad under the sponsorship of the United States government through the federal agency of the USIA. Time, Inc. was the publisher of *Sports Illustrated*, which sponsored *Sport in Art* and jointly selected artists with the American Federation of Arts. This exhibition shown in the Dallas Museum was planned to travel to Australia during the Olympic Games. The second exhibition, to tour Europe, was the result of the USIA asking the American Federation of Arts to select one hundred American paintings of the twentieth century from realist to non-objective. First, *Sport in Art* was attacked because it was claimed that four of the artists had long associations with Communist front organisations: Yasuo Kuniyoshi, Leon Kroll, Ben Shahn and William Zorach. The attacks were prompted, not least, by Haroldson Lafyette Hunt's *Facts Forum* radio and television broadcasts, expressing extreme right-wing views over the previous five years, and a monthly magazine entitled *Facts Forum News* which went to sixty thousand people. Hunt, one of the richest citizens in the United States, was a supporter of Senator McCarthy and the House Un-American Activities Committee.[33] *Facts Forum* was broadcast on 246 radio stations and 67 television stations. He also sent out sample 'polls' on public opinion, weighted by his ultra-conservative views, to 1,800 newspapers and five hundred radio and television stations.

In the wake of the attacks on *Sport in Art*, the USIA asked the American Federation of Arts to withdraw ten of the chosen artists work from *100 American Artists of the Twentieth Century* because they were regarded as 'social hazards'. When the trustees of the Federation voted unanimously not to comply with this request, the USIA cancelled the exhibition. Theodore Streibert, Director of USIA, was in a dilemma. In a letter to John Hay Whitney, Chairman of the Board at MoMA, of 23 May 1956, he writes that the established policy of the USIA was that it would sponsor and support the exhibition of works of art provided that the artists were not Communists or had close associations with Communist fronts or groups. This policy was for him a matter of public and congressional relations.[34] The cases against the artists in *Sport in Art* were not proven and, as Whitney pointed out to Streibert, seemed in conflict with President Eisenhower's statement on freedom of arts made at MoMA's twenty-fifth anniversary ceremonies.[35] Streibert was aware that to cancel the exhibition was to court criticism of America from abroad and from museum directors at home who were aware that defending 'freedom of expression' was crucial in keeping McCarthyism and the rabid criticisms of Representative George A. Dondero away from their activities.[36] But to allow works associated with the suspicion of 'guilt' was to face Congressional criticism: using taxpayers' money to send work by political suspects abroad. Finally the decision was to cancel and to cease further government-sponsored overseas exhibitions of works of art after 1917.[37] In the wake of the controversy Hunt surprisingly put his pet political project *Facts Forum* out of existence in November 1956, reportedly because he had become tired with his project 'accomplishing nothing'.[38] Hunt was incorrect. Throughout the decade, at least, museum curators, critics and academics were anxious about interference, subtle censorship or withdrawal of support by the USIA or the State Department in cultural activities. With its large budget, enormous influence and organisational power, the USIA could not be ignored or dealt with easily.

There were at least three legacies of overt and covert censorship in the 1940s and 1950s and of the ideas, values and beliefs of those associated with McCarthyism. Those with conservative moral, political and religious views were encouraged by their success; artists and writers whose work dealt with critical and transgressive issues were subject either to self-censorship – not risking exposure – or to attacks and prosecution if venturing into the public domain; third, work and events could be censored through omission, by being ignored by journals, critics, institutions. In previous sections we have seen instances such as Berman at Ferus, Connor Everts in Los Angeles in 1964, Kienholz and Ginzburg in 1966, Radich and Morrel in 1967 and MoMA's withdrawal of support for the AWC's '*And babies*' poster at the end of 1969. In the wake of the latter, the Guggenheim cancelled its Hans Haacke exhibition in 1971 because of the political implications of his social systems pieces uncovering malpractice amongst New York landlords.[39] Generally, and unsurprisingly, issues of sexuality, the body and pornography cause pandemonium but *are* addressed in journals and magazines. Issues of politics such as 'Communism', American values – including the symbolism of the 'flag' – and protests at the exercise of state power, are addressed differently.[40] It is possible to trace a similar process in other institutional representations of the past in which difficult politicised work is dealt with by omission. An instance of a French institution excising explicitly political work from a major representation of the art of the late 1940s and 1950s is *L'Art en Europe: les Années Décisives 1945–53* (Musée d'art moderne de Saint-Etienne, December 1987–February 1988).[41] An instance of another French museum following a widespread and totalising modernist theory in its account of 'political engagement' is the refusal by curators and organisers at the Centre Georges Pompidou of particular works produced by Leon Golub for their exhibition *Face à l'Histoire (1933–1990)*, December 1996 to April 1997. Organisers of this exhibition, devoted to the reaction of modern artists to historical events including political engagement, selected six portraits and a *Napalm Flag* by Golub. They refused to show any of Golub's *Gigantomachies* and *Napalms* from 1965–9, *Vietnam* paintings from 1972–4 or the *Mercenary* and *Interrogation* paintings of the 1980s. Golub declined to participate in the face of what he described as the Pompidou's 'prohibitions'.[42]

Golub's paintings engage with the human body as political metaphor: the body as napalmed, as destroyer and as abused, as tortured and torturing. In these senses he deals with the dark and punitive aspects of human nature and the body as site for non-rational acts. He also deals with a particular society's capacities for brutality, oppression and the denial of freedom of expression whether that be social, political or sexual. In the United States all of these areas were deeply uncomfortable for representatives of the State – those involved in, for example, brutal activities from Vietnam to Nicaragua – and those for whom particular American values were God-given. In 1984 Golub's participated in Andres Serrano's photographic work *Heaven and Hell*. Serrano invited Golub to pose after they had met as a result of the Artists' Call Against US Intervention in Latin America. Golub posed in red cardinal's robes turned away from a woman (Lisa Pukalski) who is nude to the waste, streaked with blood with her head thrown back and her hands tied above her head as though hung from a ceiling. Among the several possible readings of the image, the relationships between the Catholic Church, woman as tortured victim or sexual pawn, and contemporary activities by the United States in Latin America are strong candidates. The use of Golub, well known in the worlds of art and political activism, as a 'cardinal' also indexes the photograph to particular associations and commitments. Serrano's work, therefore, is addressed to a series of prohibitions and references that were of major concerns to figures inside and outside the 'art world'.

Obsessive prohibitions

In the United States, an indication of the depth and character of obsessive prohibitions from outside of the gallery system can be gained from the words of the Reverend Donald Wildmon, a profoundly influential figure in the 1980s and 1990s. In the light of successful campaigns against sponsors of television programmes and advertisements, on claimed religious and sexual grounds, Wildmon says that he is 'involved in a great spiritual struggle for the heart and mind and soul of our society. It's very much a cultural battle . . . It has taken fifty years or longer to reduce our culture to its present sorry state. We are just beginning to swing the pendulum back the other way.'[43] His project included attacks on Martin Scorsese's *The Last Temptation of Christ* (1988), succeeding in persuading the House of Representatives to pass a resolution (on 9 August 1988) urging Universal Studios to cancel the release of the film because it offended the Christian community by supposedly exceeding acceptable bounds of decency nationwide. Similarly Madonna's *Like a Prayer* video (1989) was regarded by the right as offensive and openly sexual in its use of religious imagery. The American Family Association called for a one-year boycott of all Pepsi products because of advertisements for its products featuring Madonna and her songs. The boycott was called off after Pepsico, Inc. withdrew its $5 million commercial contract with Madonna in April 1989.

For Wildmon the 'other way' is 'to put into a political frame of reference the ideals of Jesus Christ'[44] consistent with the ideological reconstruction of American values which were to the right of the Reagan and Bush administrations. The strength with which such views were held is clear from the candidacy of Pat Buchanan for the Republican presidential nomination in 1991–2. Buchanan was a syndicated journalist and television commentator who was closely linked to Wildmon and Senator Jesse Helms. Helms was responsible for an amendment, passed by the Senate in 1989, to the Interior Department's Appropriations Bill. The amendment's purpose was to 'prohibit the use of appropriated funds for the dissemination, promotion, or production of obscene or indecent materials denigrating a particular religion'.[45] This amendment had originally been designed to undermine the work of the NEA, particularly its Visual Arts Programme, because of its grants to, for example, the ICA in Philadelphia which organised *Robert Mapplethorpe: The Perfect Moment* and Southeastern Centre for Contemporary Art (SECCA) in Winston-Salem, North Carolina, which had awarded a $15,000 fellowship to Andres Serrano.

Issues of art and 'freedom of expression' raise questions about power, class and elitism. For example, in an interview Amy Adler, a New York lawyer specialising in issues of free speech, considers the relationship between laws on obscenity, debates about the representation of children and censorship in the United States:

> There is a history of suppressing and controlling what people see, based on elitist fears of mass access. Censorship is often motivated by class anxiety,

and the fear that the [so-called] lower classes will be out of control if they have access to the same things as the upper classes. This is an argument that I think the Left could use to counter the Right's accusations of cultural elitism. I think this is a real problem; I think elitism is an unanswered charge in the culture war.[46]

Representations – visual, verbal, oral – retain the possibility of transgression; the possibility of providing critical knowledge, awareness and insights about, and interventions in, the conditions that produce social, political and psychological marginalisation and repression.

A major question, therefore, to consider is the relationship between Wildmon's and others' 'cultural battle' and the United States government's aims to restore corporate profitability and impose some discipline on a turbulent world, at home and abroad. The political programme of a broad elite consensus in the 1970s and 1980s produced a disciplinary process which Chomsky has analysed as 'deterring democracy':

> The natural domestic policies were transfer of resources to the rich, partial dismantling of the limited welfare system, an attack on unions and real wages, and expansion of the public subsidy for high-technology industry through the Pentagon system, which has long been the engine for economic growth and preserving the technological edge.[47]

This process was spectacularly symbolised on domestic and international television, largely via Cable News Network (CNN), during the Gulf War where an enormous financial investment in technological death machines provided viewers with a mega 'super-Nintendo' experience. The astounding and orchestrated televisual display of destruction fed the induced consumerist need for computer games and the state's long-term desire to erase the negative memory of 'Vietnam' as 'US defeat'. Such elements of the culture industry captivating its alienated and monadic audience are not in need of NEA grants. Funding comes from elsewhere. The 'Holy War' to control oil supplies, to reinvigorate the order books of the arms industry and to confirm a 'New World Order' was mirrored by a 'Holy War' to regain the 'heart and mind and soul' of America supposedly corrupted by blasphemy, feminism, gays and sexual liberation. And worse, in the eyes of the 'moral majority' the NEA was funding artists such as Serrano, Mapplethorpe and Karen Finley, to produce their 'corrupting' representations. What the Pentagon was funding from 'taxpayers' money' did not get the same attention. In all of this we should not forget the power of agencies such as CNN in forging a perception of United States culture as a global norm. Andrew Ross has argued that a

> perception of the national culture is the primary shaping principle behind CNN's own house style for editing and broadcasting world news across the major league of nations. Performing the global function once served by the BBC in the age of radio, CNN's decentred corporate populism has effectively

replaced the voice of paternal imperialism that used to issue from Europe's metropolitan centres.[48]

A 'perception of the national culture' clearly drives many of the authors of texts in Richard Bolton's *Culture Wars*. And the ability of groups such as the American Family Association, a right-wing Christian organisation whose director was the Revd Donald Wildmon, to utilise computer data bases to saturate a targeted constituency with mail shots or to command broadcasting time is a domestic equivalent of the 'decentred corporate populism' of CNN.

Notions of 'the national culture' and the role of the arts had conflicting aspects in twentieth-century America. The view that art can act to limit social unrest by means of a comforting dissuasion were evident from the WPA onwards. During the 1960s the role of television media was also a central component of a broader cultural ambition. For example, as we have seen, Walter Paley, President of MoMA's Board of Trustees, was Head of CBS. In 1962, President Kennedy appointed August Heckscher special consultant on the arts. In research published in *The Public Happiness* (1962), Heckscher reported:

> With urban malaise spreading, a small group of business leaders, men like David Rockefeller, Arnold Gingrich of *Esquire*, George Weissman of Philip Morris and Dr. Frank Stanton of CBS, recognized and promulgated an important concept – that a so-called amenity, such as the arts, was in reality the very lifeblood needed to inject hope, purpose and beauty into a troubled society.[49]

Alternatively, for adherents to the views espoused by Representative George A. Dondero, modern art, inherently dangerous and potentially an ally of Communism, was a cause of general malaise. In Dallas in the 1950s Haroldson Lafyette Hunt subscribed to such views, supporting McCarthy in his pursuit of radicals within culture. The relationship between art, as possibly subversive, and television, as a medium for spreading a message about anti-Communism, had powerful potential for such citizens. In the 1980s and 1990s, this potential has been reinvigorated by the religious right and its use of existing technology, such as television broadcasts, and new technology, such as computer databases and Internet sites.

Repetitive syndromes

It is with this perspective that documents and analyses such as those in Bolton's *Culture Wars* make possible the construction of a contemporary archaeology of knowledge. However, such knowledge is symbolic of a profound problem in which the United States left has often found itself since the Second World War. The effects of forgetting and amnesia as they relate to repression are problematic and painful enough in the individual, but in the body politic they have more fundamental and far-reaching disciplinary consequences. A major element in the contradictions endemic to 'art and politics' in the United States since the Second World War is the American left's failure to recognise that it is caught in the repetitive syndrome of reinventing itself. As the artist Irving Petlin, a driving force in the Los Angeles Tower and the AWC during the 1960s, recalls: 'The Civil Rights movement, the anti [Vietnam] war movement and even the environmental movement literally had to invent themselves, adopt methods and invent strategies that were outside traditional politics in order to attract the attention of a larger public.'[50]

Without internalising the struggles of the past, radical groups are forced to relive them while believing that 'the present crisis' is somehow unique. The history of the left cannot be understood without an awareness of this process of repetition which has contributed to the United States management of its corporate public image, domestic puritanism, consumerist soma and technological 'efficiency'. In Culture Wars, a chronology detailing 'selected examples of major cases of censorship and controversy in American culture'[51] begins only in 1962, and the first example of actual censorship is the cancellation of the Haacke exhibition in 1971. It is significant that earlier instances from the late 1940s to the 1950s are forgotten. For example, in 1946 Advancing American Art a state-sponsored exhibition to tour Europe and Latin America came under attack from Dondero-inspired right-wing newspapers and magazines, including those owned by Randolph Hearst. In mixing an antipathy for modern art with a hostility to any radical political associations, attacks were made against the inclusion of 'left-wing painters who are members of Red Fascist organizations'.[52] Eventually, under such pressure the exhibition was terminated while on tour in 1947 by the State Department. A year later, the State Department auctioned the paintings purchased for the exhibition, with the Hearst organisation buying five for the Los Angeles County Art Museum, which was heavily endowed by Hearst publications.[53] This latter irony and the outrage at state censorship by the art museum community which, paradoxically, had increased its stock of art objects, are two aspects of the event. However, a more significant lesson for the political right was that a precedent had been set for censoring art and exhibitions through attacks on artists as left-wing or Communist: guilt by association became a recurrent strategy. Dondero's views were shared by other Republicans, including the young Richard Nixon. In a letter to Charles Plant, Mill Valley, California, who objected to what he regarded as Communist art in his Federal Building, Nixon expressed sympathy for Plant's views and those of Dondero with whom Nixon had consulted. Nixon believed that an investigating committee of Congress needed to be established with a view to removing from government buildings all art that was found to be inconsistent with American ideals and principles.[54] Nixon maintained his allegiances to Dondero throughout the period. For example, he was present when Dondero was awarded a Gold Medal from the International Fine Arts Council in February 1957 (the first non-artist to be so honoured). In his address, the Council President talked of Dondero's exposure of 'subversive elements in the field of art' and the connections between art and 'communism which undoubtedly and unquestionably is anti-God'. He continued: 'Present here is the greatest foe to communism, the very epitome of anti-communism, our very great Vice-President, Richard M. Nixon. To have him on your side is the best stamp of approval of all your efforts. Also, the Hon. Frances E. Walters the Chairman of the Un-American Activities Committee.'[55]

These early examples are important in so far as they reveal close connections between the interests which underpinned Dondero's rhetoric and those which determine utterances by Wildmon, Buchanan, Helms, D'Amato and so on. A major reason for the left's neglect of the roots of its current problems is the persistent legacy of the era of McCarthyism and the early Cold War which has encouraged the process of denying or erasing that which still acts as a determining force. The cutting away of roots and associations became a pathological process in the 1950s and subsequently internalised as amnesia into the American experience.

Two glosses on this. At a panel discussion in New York in October 1992, the numerous collective activities of artists protesting in the late 1960s against the Vietnam War and the systems of state power were retold and illustrated by original activists including Max Kozloff, Irving Petlin and Therese Schwartz. Startlingly, these marches, events and strikes were largely unknown to the audience and to representatives of the newest collective group of the early 1990s, Women's Action Coalition (WAC).[56] One reason for this is the lack of official record, though there have been numerous publications to consult ranging from catalogues and books such as *ABC No Rio Dinero: The Story of a Lower East Side Art Gallery* and *Cultures in Contention* (both 1985)[57] to publications such as *Heresies* and *Upfront*, a publication of Political Art Documentation Distribution (PAD/D). PAD/D, initiated by Lucy Lippard in 1979 as an international archive of socially concerned art, was an attempt to provide a usable resource to counter a lack of continuity and awareness.[58] Paradoxically, the PAD/D Archive is now housed within the Library of the Museum of Modern Art, New York.[59] A second gloss is the way in which 'views from the margin' are treated by the official culture. Terry Eagleton ironically concluded in a review of Edward Said's *Culture and Imperialism* that Said's views 'as he well knows are no more than the resentful whinings of those with a chip on their shoulder, when measured against the disinterested discourse of academics in the pay of the White House'.[60]

Importantly, the influence of this 'disinterested discourse' has not deterred Said or Chomsky from making their lucid analyses of imperialism and totalitarianism from *within* the United States. However, it should be realised that, for Chomsky at least, the major constituency is defined by those who read publications such as *The Nation* and *Z Magazine*.

Bolton, though, at the end of his excellent introduction to *Culture Wars* draws on political theorists and cultural commentators, from outside the United States: Ernesto Laclau and Chantal Mouffe. He quotes their argument, from *Hegemony and Socialist Strategy*, that the political logic of totalitarianism in the name of the 'nation', or whatever, is one in which the state seeks to 'control all the networks of sociability. In the face of the radical indeterminacy which democracy opens up, this involves an attempt to reimpose an absolute center, and to re-establish the closure which will thus restore unity.'[61]

For Bolton, Laclau's and Mouffe's argument can be applied to describe 'the logic behind the attack on NEA', as it does many other manifestations of control in nations and groups: 'censorship of the arts reveals the failure of democratic institutions to articulate and defend the complexity and diversity of the American public'.[62] This is part of the NEA's founding remit. But are United States institutions 'democratic' in any real sense? The evidence largely says no and even more so recently. Therese Schwartz was editor of *The New York Element* in the late 1960s and early 1970s and active in demonstrations against MoMA and the Metropolitan in the late 1960s and early 1970s. In retrospect she believes that whilst these institutions were seriously rattled by protests such as those by the AWC, Guerrilla Art Action Group, WAR, the Ad Hoc Women Artists' Committee and WSABAL, the power base of such institutions in the 1990s produces at best indifference and at worst contempt for manifestations of criticism and dissent.[63]

Evidence supports Schwartz's view about the moment of '1968' which ruptured the dominant post-1945 process influentially articulated by George Kennan in *Policy Planning Study* 23, 1948:

> We have about 50% of the world's wealth, but only 6.3% of its population . . . Our real task in the coming period is to devise a pattern of relationships which will permit us to maintain this position of disparity without positive detriment to our national security. To do so, we will have to dispense with all sentimentality and day-dreaming; and our attention will have to be concentrated everywhere on our immediate national objectives. We need not deceive ourselves that we can afford today the luxury of altruism and world-benefaction . . . We should cease to talk about vague – and for the Far East – unreal objectives such as human rights, the raising of living standards, and democratization. The day is not far off when we are going to have to deal in straight power concepts. The less we are then hampered by idealistic slogans, the better.[64]

Has the left, particularly since '1968', been unable not only to resist the implementation and affects of this process, including its participating institutions, but also to find a sustainable tradition for the articulation and defence of the 'complexity and diversity of the American public'? To attempt the latter at a specific historical moment, as exemplified by *Culture Wars*, is to be open to the requirements of a non-doctrinaire strategy in the face of the political logic of totalitarianism. This is an interventionist strength derived from a Brechtian realist critique. However, to attempt this without an awareness of the left's traditions, struggles, failures and consequent lessons is to perpetuate the broader problems identified by Irving Petlin. The danger is to relive the past, yet again, leaving the dominant structures and assumptions intact.

One reason for the existence of these problems is the effect of the powerful public image of self-proclaimed democratic and progressive institutions such as museums, research centres and philanthropic funding foundations. The construction of this image, underpinned by the proliferation of such institutions during the postwar consumerist boom, has hidden the reality of the fragmentation of actual democratic possibilities. Again, the evidence of the 1950s is instructive, especially if we look at the cultivated liberal intelligentsia, who were in positions of cultural power, such as Alfred H. Barr Jnr at MoMA, Lloyd Goodrich, Associate Director at the Whitney, those associated with the American Federation of Arts (AFA) and regional museum directors and supporters of modernism in art. Many of them were caught in a dilemma which encouraged paranoid tendencies, especially in the light of attacks in and out of Congress.[65] They wished to preserve what they regarded as the progressiveness of cultural modernism (including that later enshrined in the NEA as 'the complexity and diversity of the American public') which for them largely meant the ideology of the aesthetic and autonomous art. But their ideas, and they themselves, were under attack from those licensed by Dondero's hostility to modern art in general. The attack on the Dallas Museum and its exhibition of *Sport in Art* in 1956 demonstrates the connection between Dondero-derived ideas, right-wing financial interests and a puritan fundamentalism.

Barr retained comprehensive files on everything he regarded as a threat to his belief in modern art, as defined by MoMA. But equally, he and others, such as Goodrich, were nervous of any support for artists who could be shown to have Communist sympathies. Their nervousness at explicit political commitment in art became translated into hostility and condemnation: Picasso, a member of the PCF who produced *Massacre in Korea* (1951), was described by Barr in 1955 as 'politically naive and foolish',[66] and the work of Rivera characterised by Goodrich, in 1952, as 'political propaganda, and as such in my opinion has no place in a governmental exhibition sent abroad'.[67] In a letter to Smith (President of the AFA) Barr upheld the 'American tradition of freedom of expression' but recommended that 'we ought to take the greatest care not to include works of art which can reasonably be considered subversive in any overtly political manner'.[68] Goodrich similarly countenanced 'genuine works of art which contain social criticism or protest' not least because 'exhibition abroad of such works does a great deal of good, counteracting the common impression that Americans are materialistic, standardized, sentimental and pollyannaish; and by proving our democratic freedom and diversity of viewpoints'.[69]

United States artists, writers, critics and film-makers with Communist connections, actual or inferred, were similarly marginalised. This situation led many of the liberal intelligentsia to denounce those whom they suspected of Communist sympathies. One of the most extraordinary examples in relation to the art world was the publication by Dondero of letters by Clement Greenberg and Granville Hicks at a time when there was controversy over Communist infiltration of political news magazines such as *The Nation*. An anti-Communist group, The American Committee for Cultural Freedom, of which Greenberg was a member, attempted to expose Soviet sympathisers in *The Nation*, for which Greenberg had been a contributor and Art Editor from 1943 to 1949.[70] Many members of the Marxist left of the 1930s and of the liberal intelligentsia, particularly supporters of modernism, united in their libertarian allegiances by becoming associated with anti-Communism as members of the American Committee for Cultural Freedom, affiliated to the Congress for Cultural Freedom. Members included Alfred Barr, and Clement Greenberg was on the Executive Committee.[71] In the 1960s it was revealed that the Congress for Cultural Freedom was CIA funded as part of Cold War attrition,[72] which was a subtle confirmation of Kennan's 'real task': 'to deal in straight power concepts. The less we are then hampered by idealistic slogans, the better.'

Dilemmas

The legacy of the dilemmas of the cultivated liberal intelligentsia, particularly those in powerful positions in supposed 'democratic' institutions, still haunts the United States and helps us to understand some of the events documented in *Culture Wars*. I want to split this into two related areas. The first is the example of what I'll call the *Tilted Arc* problem. Serra's massive 'public' sculpture was commissioned in 1979 by the General Services Administration for New York's Federal Plaza and installed in 1981. Dominating the architectural space and that of the viewing subject, the curved and tilted slab of Corten steel, 120 feet long and more than 12 feet high, caused a heated public controversy during the 1980s. Calls for its removal culminated in a public hearing where

many artists, critics, curators and dealers spoke up for the integrity of
the sculpture and warned against attacks on the freedom of the arts and
the risks of censorship.[73] Should not critically ratified 'progressive' artists in a proclaimed free society be left alone to produce whatever they
wish in a public space, thereby preserving the autonomy of art? A
problem with such a question is that in the postwar United States, the
concept of autonomy had been deprived of its oppositional political
credentials and subsumed within a formalist aesthetic, however that was
radically elaborated in the 1970s and 1980s.[74]

For supporters of Serra's sculpture, which Frank Stella regarded as an
example of a 'benign, civilising effort',[75] the contemporary version of
autonomous art overrode the interests of those who worked in and around
Federal Plaza. To these supporters, social and human accountability somehow smacked of idealistic slogans and those political aspects of art which
had long been institutionally suppressed and in their terms 'discredited'.
In contrast, for those who were critical of *Tilted Arc* and its rhetoric of
power the reality of the curving and leaning slab cutting across the Plaza
was that it destroyed and dehumanised a public space in which workers
relaxed and ate their lunch. The viewing subject's body was dominated
by a rusting coldsteel slab which signified corporate masculine power
and the authority of an alienating 'autonomy'. Danny Katz, who worked
in the building as a clerk, perceptively observed that the blame for the
whole event – planning, production, reception and now public hearing –
fell on everyone for forgetting 'the human element'.[76] Unlike many of
the other speakers, he did not think that the issue should be regarded as
a 'dispute between the forces of ignorance and art, or art versus government'. Whilst he did not expect much from government, he did expect a
lot more from the artists who spoke in favour of *Tilted Arc*:

> I didn't expect to hear them rely on the tired and dangerous reasoning that
> the government has made a deal, so let the rabble live with the steel because
> it's a deal. That kind of mentality leads to wars. We had a deal with Vietnam.
> I didn't expect to hear the arrogant position that art justifies interference
> with the simple joys of human activity in a plaza. It's not a great plaza by
> international standards, but it is a small refuge and place of revival for people
> who ride to work in steel containers, work in sealed rooms, and breathe
> recirculated air all day.[77]

Katz saw the problem in the position and location of 'the work', which
could be 'moved to a place where it will better reveal its beauty'. Many
defenders and Serra himself regarded the site-specificity as an essential
element of 'the work'. After bitter documented controversy, Serra's sculpture was removed in 1989. Was this a gross act of censorship? Was the
art world's defence of *Tilted Arc*, from Rubin to Krauss, a continuation
of the classic dilemma of the United States liberal intelligentsia since the

1950s?[78] Did the defence of autonomy in the midst of Reaganomics leave the ground open for right-wing attacks on art works such as *Piss Christ* and Mapplethorpe's *X Portfolio*? Did these attacks in turn deflect attention from and marginalise projects on social activism and multiculturism?[79] In 1966 the critical function of the Tower in Los Angeles was partly reliant on its site-specificity but artists' rights and freedom of expression were differently articulated to those around *Tilted Arc*. The social and political significance of the Artists' Protest Committee's project were not addressed by the art establishment, whose concerns were more comfortably and conveniently addressed by the Kienholz controversy at the Los Angeles County Art Museum. Importantly, too, Katz's evocation of a mentality that can be indexed to the Vietnam War and what he calls 'the human element' have strong roots in the paradoxes and contradictions evident in the practice of art and criticism in 1966.

The second related area I want to outline connects to recent concerns with the body as a metaphor for the struggle for identity and difference. A major part of the puritan outrage contained in the documents in *Culture Wars* relates to the representation of the body, its fluids and its private parts in unratified contexts: Serrano's piss covering an image of Christ's semi-naked body; Mapplethorpe's photographs of, for example, a hooded 'Jim' pissing into the mouth of 'Tom' or of a male arm, or a bull whip, deep into the anus of another male. These images and their reception raise issues that have centred on the 'discourse of the body'. There are at least two sides to this. One is the development of radical approaches in the United States and Europe in which concerns with metaphor and power may coexist with an insouciance and ignorance of socialist struggles. As Eagleton has argued, there 'is a privileged, privatized hedonism about such discourse, emerging as it does at just the historical point where less exotic forms of politics found themselves suffering a setback'.[80] The second side is the fascination with and fear of the body as a symbol of wholeness and power. This is profoundly masculine in the rhetoric of cultural life in the United States both as a personal obsession and as a national idea. For example: 'perfectibility', signified by the enormous plastic surgery industry; 'policing', signified by the culture of political and racial surveillance and surgical strikes; 'puritanism', signified by groups dedicated to pro-life, the emphases on procreation rather than erotic pleasure and the homophobic denial of sexual difference; and so on.

Powerful aspects of control are embedded in the ideology that insists on the libido as attracted only to unities. Many of Mapplethorpe's photographs confound this ideology with close-ups of parts of the male body, a process conventionally devoted to the patriarchal fetishisation of parts of the female body, in film and photography. The ideology of perfectibility produces a powerful anxiety in various utterances and actions, many of which are rooted in the history of the post-war United States, particularly that which is erased in official representations. For example, this ideology can help to explain the repeated cases of United States troops' castration of the corpses of the 'Vietcong'. As we have seen in Chapter 4, dismemberment was a sign of a loss of sexuality, and to mutilate, to ruin, the oriental 'other' was to confirm the GI's notion of acceptability as 'Western man' in the eyes of his peers. This went together with the GI's fear of fragmentation-bomb wounds to every part of the body including genitals, buttocks, hands and legs. At the same time the United States war machine had developed napalm and cluster bombs which dismembered and fragmented the bodies of the Vietnamese. There is also evidence, as we have seen, that American troops cut off the ears of warm corpses, stringing them around the neck as a sign of previous kills.[81] In the Gulf War, dismemberment of the Iraqis, systematically devalued in media rhetoric, was mostly achieved at a technological distance. But advance fear of fragmentation led some of the United States troops to place their frozen sperm in 'banks' so that a whole version of themselves could be reproduced in the unerotic process of clinical fertilisation.[82] No wonder Mapplethorpe's photographs produced a shudder of rage.

Bolton's *Culture Wars* is an important resource of knowledge about instances of political struggles fought out within culture. But its value will be lost if its historical place and symbolic meaning are forgotten. As I have argued, cultural and political amnesia enables the United States to police or manage dissent and at the same time to make a few more bucks by encouraging the production of commodities and media spectacles in the market of ideas. This market not only poses little actual threat to capitalism but also provides the system's guardians and cultural commissars with interesting information on what the actual and fantasised oppositions are thinking. For them there is nothing better than to encourage dissent, with its novel forms ripe for commodification, when its more troublesome manifestations are contained and fragmented. However, those who know their history can resist the process which forces them to relive the past.

Notes

1   Both quoted in Willie Birch, *Knowing Our History, Teaching Our Culture* (1992), mixed media, wood, papier maché, four parts, exhibited at the Arthur Roger Gallery, New York (October to November 1992). See Birch's essay with the same title in Mark O'Brien and Craig Little, *Reimaging America: The Arts of Social Change* (Philadelphia, New Society Publishers, 1990), pp. 137–43. Earlier versions of some arguments in this conclusion appeared as a review article in Frascina, 'American Culture Wars: Prisoners of the Past', *Art History*, 16:3 (September 1993), 485–90.

2   James J. Farrell, *The Spirit of the Sixties: The Making of Postwar Radicalism* (New York and London, Routledge, 1997), p. 228.

3   See documents collected in Jacqueline Skiles and Janet McDevitt (eds), *A Document-ary Herstory of Women Artists in Revolution* (New York, WAR, 1971).

4   On paradigms, Alfred Barr's *Cubism and Abstract Art* (1936) and the early theorising of modern art see the introduction to my *Pollock and After: The Critical Debate* (London and New York, Harper and Row, 1985), pp. 3–20.

5   One example is *Picasso and Braque: A Symposium* (New York, MoMA, 1992) to consolidate the exhibition *Picasso and Braque: Pioneering Cubism*, 1989, at MoMA, which had its own hefty catalogue. For a critique of the methods and approaches in the symposium see Patricia Leighten, 'Cubist Anachronisms: Ahistoricity, Crypto-formalism, and Business-as-Usual in New York', *Oxford Art Journal*, 17:2 (1994), 91–102.

6   See MoMA's 'Studies in Modern Art' series, a publishing vehicle for the Museum's Research and Scholarly Publications Programme. On the Pompidou Centre [Beaubourg] and its early catalogues see: 'Beaubourg: The Containing of Culture in France' by the Cultural Affairs Committee of the Parti Socialist Unifé, *Studio International*, 194 (January–February 1978), 27–36.

7   *The Museum of Modern Art at Mid-century, At Home and Abroad*, 'Studies in Modern Art 4', (New York, MoMA, 1994); *The Museum of Modern Art at Mid-century, Con-tinuity and Change*, 'Studies in Modern Art 5' (New York, MoMA, 1995). In particular, Michael Kimmelman's 'Revisiting the Revisionists: The Modern, Its Critics and the Cold War' attempts to rebut the substance of critical texts that have appeared since the late 1960s (in 'Studies in Modern Art 4', pp. 38–55).

8   All in 'Studies in Modern Art 4'.

9   For a selection see my *Pollock and After: The Critical Debate*, especially section II and the introduction to that section, pp. 91–106.

10 Christopher Gray, ' "Those who make half a Revolution only dig their own graves": The Situationists since 1969', in *Leaving the 20th Century: The Incomplete Work of the Situationist International*, translated and edited by Christopher Gray (London, Free Fall Publications, 1974), p. 165. Gray's commentary was written in 1972 or 1973.

11 London, Allen Lane, 1974. In 1994, the Freud Museum in London organised a con-ference to mark the twentieth anniversary and to consider the legacy of the issues raised by the book on the range of feminist politics. The previous ten years were a time when many of the achievements of differing feminisms were subject to a backlash.

12 For his reflection on long-ago conflicts see T. J. Clark and Donald Nicholson-Smith, 'Why Art Can't Kill the Situationist International', *October*, 79 (winter 1997), 15–31.

13 Both London, Thames and Hudson, 1973.

14 David Caute, 'Introduction', *Sixty-Eight: The Year of the Barricades* (London, Hamish Hamilton, 1988), pp. vii–x.

15 Berkeley, University of California Press, 1995.

16 Michele Wallace, 'Reading 1968: The Great American Whitewash', in *Invisibility Blues: From Pop to Theory* (London, Verso, 1990), pp. 187–98. See, too, Mary Schmidt Campbell (ed.), *Tradition and Conflict: Images of a Turbulent Decade, 1963–73* (New York, Studio Museum in Harlem, 1985).

17 For example: Alice Echols, *Daring to Be Bad: Radical Feminism in America 1967–1975* (Minneapolis and London, University of Minnesota Press, 1989); Sheila Rowbotham, *The Past Before Us: Feminism in Action since the 1960s* (London, Pandora, 1989); Monica Threlfall (ed.), *Mapping the Women's Movement: Feminist Politics and Social Transformation in the North* (London, Verso, 1996). See also Randy Rosen and Catherine Brawer (eds), *Making Their Mark: Women Artists Move into the Main-stream, 1970–85* (New York, Abbeville Press, 1989); Norma Broude and Mary D. Garrard, *The Power of Feminist Art: Emergence, Impact and Triumph of the American Feminist Movement* (London, Thames and Hudson, 1994); Amelia Jones, 'Power and Feminist Art (History)', *Art History*, 17:4 (September 1995), 435–43; Amelia Jones

(ed.), *Sexual Politics: Judy Chicago's* Dinner Party *in Feminist Art History* (Berkeley, UCLA/Hammer/California University Press, 1996); Lisa Tickner, 'The Body Politic: Female Sexuality and Women Artists since 1970', *Art History*, 1:2 (June 1978), 236–51; Rozsika Parker and Griselda Pollock (eds), *Framing Feminism: Art and the Women's Movement 1970–1985* (London, Pandora, 1987) and Pollock, 'Screening the Seventies: Sexuality and Representation in Feminist Practice – a Brechtian Perspective', *Vision and Difference: Femininity, Feminism and the Histories of Art* (London, Routledge, 1988).

18 For example, Ron Jacobs, *The Way the Wind Blew: A History of the Weather Underground* (London and New York, Verso, 1997).

19 See photograph from the Berman papers, Archives of American Art, reproduced in Richard Cándida-Smith, *Utopia and Dissent: Art Poetry and Politics in California* (Berkeley, University of California Press, 1995), p. 276.

20 *Ibid.*, pp. 276–7.

21 See the extensive exhibition *A Secret Location on the Lower East Side: Adventures in Writing 1960–1980* (New York, The New York Public Library, January–July 1998).

22 Guy Debord, *The Society of the Spectacle*, first published in 1967, is still the most powerful analysis of the process (see translation by Donald Nicholson-Smith, New York, Zone Books, 1994). On attempts to maintain a radical critique through 'art' see Lucy R. Lippard, 'Trojan Horses: Activist Art and Power', in Brian Wallis (ed.), *Art After Modernism: Rethinking Representation* (New York, New Museum of Contemporary Art New York and Godine, 1984), pp. 340–58.

23 See Norman K. Denizen, 'Reading "Wall Street": Postmodern Contradictions in the American Social Structure', in Bryan S. Turner, *Theories of Modernity and Postmodernity* (London, Sage Publications, 1990), pp. 31–44.

24 For an incisive account, see Sharon Zukin, *Loft Living: Culture and Capital in Urban Change* (Baltimore, Johns Hopkins University Press, 1982). Whilst *Wall Street* represents developments in the United States, 'yuppies' were an international phenomenon associated in England with the controversial redevelopment of London's 'docklands'. For artists' critique of the latter, via the public sites of billboards, see Peter Dunn and Loraine Leeson, 'The Changing Picture of Docklands', in Douglas Kahn and Diane Neumaier (eds), *Cultures in Contention* (Seattle, Real Comet Press, 1985), pp. 14–35.

25 Guerrilla Girls, *Confessions of the Guerrilla Girls* (New York, Harper Collins, 1995), p. 13.

26 For an overview, see Alan Wallach, 'The Museum of Modern Art: the Past's Future', in Francis Frascina and Jonathan Harris (eds), *Art in Modern Culture: An Anthology of Critical Texts* (London, Phaidon Press, 1992), pp. 282–91. Discussion of plans for yet another massive expansion can be found in *Imagining the Future of The Museum of Modern Art*, 'Studies in Modern Art 7' (New York, MoMA, 1998).

27 On this, see Homi K. Bhabha, *The Location of Culture* (London, Routledge, 1994) and Terry Eagleton's review 'Goodbye to the Enlightenment' in *The Guardian*, 2, 18 February 1994, 12.

28 Richard Bolton (ed.), *Culture Wars: Documents from the Recent Controversies in the Arts* (New York, New Press, 1992). See too, Carol Vance, 'The Pleasures of Looking: The Attorney General's Commission on Pornography Versus Visual Images', in Carol Squiers, *The Critical Image: Essays on Contemporary Photography* (London, Lawrence and Wishart, 1991), pp. 38–58.

29 V. N. Voloshinov, *Marxism and the Philosophy of Language*, translated by L. Matejka and I. R. Tutunik (Cambridge, Mass., and London, Harvard University Press, 1986). On this see my 'Realism and Ideology: An Introduction to Semiotics and Cubism', in Charles Harrison, Francis Frascina, and Gill Perry, *Primitivism, Cubism, Abstraction* (New Haven and London, Yale University Press, 1993), pp. 87–183.

30 Sen. Alphonse D'Amato in debate in Senate, 18 May 1989, in Bolton, *Culture Wars*, pp. 28–9.

31 April 5 1989, reprinted in Bolton, *Culture Wars*, p. 27.

32 See Charlotte Devree, 'The U.S. Government Vetoes Living Art', *Art News*, 55:5 (September 1956), 34–5, 54–6. Also William Hauptman, 'The Suppression of Art in the McCarthy Decade', *Artforum*, 12:2 (October, 1973), 48–52. Generally, see Jane de Hart Mathews, 'Art and Politics in Cold War America', *American Historical Review*, 81 (October 1976) ,762–87.

33 Hunt maintained close personal privacy. Brief details about him and his oil base wealth emerged in articles such as 'The World's Richest Men', *The New York Times Magazine*, 20 October 1957, 35, 37–8.

34 Copy of letter from Streibert to Whitney (23 May 1956) Museum of Modern Art Archives, Alfred H. Barr Jnr, Papers [Archives of American Art (AAA) Roll 3156, Frame 710].

35 See letter from Whitney to Streibert (16 May 1956), Museum of Modern Art Archives, Alfred H. Barr Jnr, Papers [Archives of American Art (AAA) Roll 3156, Frame 709].

36 The best known is Dondero's speech in the US House of Representatives, 'Modern Art Shackled To Communism', *Congressional Record*, 81st Congress, 95:9 (16 August 1949), 11584–11587. An earlier text on what he calls Communist front organisations, such as the Artists Equity Association, names Yasuo Kuniyoshi and Ben Shahn, as well as Frank Klienholtz, Philip Evergood, Max Weber, Robert Gwathmey, Leon Kroll, Hudson Walker, Rockwell Kent and, inevitably, Diego Rivera: see 'Communists Manoeuvre to Control Art in the United States', *Congressional Record*, 81st Congress, 95:3 (25 March 1949), 3233–3235.

37 Detailed memos and cuttings related to the events can be found in the Museum of Modern Art Archives, Alfred H. Barr Jnr, Papers [Archives of American Art (AAA) Rolls 3155 and 3156].

38 William H. A. Carr, 'Why Oilman Hunt Killed Facts Forum', *New York Post*, 13 November 1956, 5–6. Also to be found in the Museum of Modern Art Archives, Alfred H. Barr Jnr, Papers [Archives of American Art (AAA) Rolls 3155, Frames 1278 and 1279 and 3156]. This and many other documents on 'political controversies' were systematically collected by Barr.

39 See Haacke, 'Catalogue of Works: 1969–1986', in B. Wallis (ed.), *Hans Haacke: Unfinished Business* (New York, New Museum of Contemporary Art, 1986), pp. 88–97; 'Gurgles Around the Guggenheim', *Studio International*, 181:934 (1971), 246–50.

40 See for example the continuing dilemmas around the American 'flag': Steven C. Dubin, 'Rally 'Round the Flag', *Arresting Images: Impolitic Art and Uncivil Actions* (London and New York, Routledge, 1992).

41 The works of several artists in the PCF were not included in the exhibition, though some are discussed in the catalogue. For a critique see Frascina, ' "L'Art en Europe" at St. Etienne', *Art Monthly*, 116 (May 1988), 17–20.

42 Correspondence between Marc Bormand, Curator at the Pompidou Centre, and Leon Golub in Golub's personal files.

43 Wildmon in Connaught Marshner, 'How Don Wildmon Is Beating the Princes of Porn', *Conservative Digest*, March 1988, 80, quoted in Bolton, *Culture Wars*, p. 9.

44 Quoted in Bolton, *Culture Wars*, p. 9.

45 Debate in Senate and excerpts from the amendments in Bolton, *Culture Wars*, pp. 73–86.

46 'Age of Innocence', *Frieze* January 1996, 34.

47 *Deterring Democracy* (London, Vintage, 1992), p. 81.

48 Ross, 'The Private Parts of Justice', in Toni Morrison (ed.), *Race-ing Justice, Engendering Power: Essays on Anita Hill, Clarence Thomas, and the Construction of Social Reality* (London, Chatto and Windus, 1993), p. 41.

49 Heckscher, *The Public Happiness* (New York, Athenaeum, 1962), p. 222, quoted in Zukin, *Loft Living*, p. 107.

50 Interview with the author (26 October 1992).

51 Bolton, *Culture Wars*, pp. 331–63.

52 Editorial in Baltimore *American*, October 1946, quoted in both Hauptman, 'The Suppression of Art in the McCarthy Decade', 49, and de Hart Mathews, 'Art and Politics in Cold War America', 777. Also see Taylor D. Lyttleton and Maltby Sykes, *Advancing American Art: Painting, Politics, and Cultural Confrontation at Mid-century* (Tuscaloosa and London, University of Alabama Press, 1989).

53 Hauptman, 'The Suppression of Art in the McCarthy Decade', 49.

54 Letter from Nixon to Plant (18 July 1949) in Hudson Walker Papers, [Archives of American Art (AAA) Roll 0352, Frame 666]. Also see correspondence between Plant and Dondero on such issues, from 1950 to 1956, in Dondero Papers [Archives of American Art (AAA) Roll 722, Frames 1–4,12–15,28,57].

55 Dr Harry Cohen, President (14 February 1957), Dondero Papers [Archives of American Art (AAA) Roll 722, Frame 264].

56 An attempt to locate some of the roots was made briefly in Nina Felshin's 'Introduction' to her anthology of essays by a variety of contributors in *But Is It Art? The Spirit of Art as Activism* (Seattle, Bay Press, 1995). Also see *WAC Stats: The Facts About Women* (New York, Women's Action Coalition, 1992).

57 *ABC No Rio Dinero: The Story of a Lower East Side Art Gallery* (New York, ABC No Rio and Collaborative Projects, 1985); Kahn and Neumaier (eds), *Cultures in Contention*.

58 It was not universally appreciated. In 1983 the NEA Chair vetoed a panel-approved grant to the Heresies Collective and PAD/D that would have funded a series of public forums featuring Hans Haacke, Martha Rosler, Suzanne Lacy and Lucy Lippard.

59 See the exhibition *Political Art Documentation & Distribution: The PADD Archives* (New York, Museum of Modern Art, June 1993 to May 1994), and accompanying Library Bulletin, no. 86 (Museum of Modern Art Library, winter 1993/94).

60 *The Guardian 2*, 9 February 1993, 10.

61 Laclau and Mouffe, *Hegemony and Socialist Strategy: Towards a Radical Democratic Politics* (London, Verso, 1985), p. 188, quoted in Bolton, *Culture Wars*, p. 24.

62 Botton, *ibid*.

63 Interview with the author (24 October 1992).

64 Quoted in Chomsky, 'Visions of Righteousness', in John Carlos Rowe and Rick Berg (eds), *The Vietnam War and American Culture* (New York, Columbia University Press, 1991), pp. 46–7.

65 See for example Museum of Modern Art Archives, Alfred H. Barr Jnr, Papers [Archives of American Art (AAA) Rolls 3155 and 3156]; *Lloyd Goodrich Reminisces*, as recorded in talks with Dr Harlan B. Phillips (Archives of American Art (AAA) Brandeis University, 1963).

66 Memo from Barr to Elizabeth Shaw (8 October 1955), Museum of Modern Art Archives, Alfred H. Barr Jnr, Papers [Archives of American Art (AAA) Roll 3155 Frame 1239].

67 Lloyd Goodrich, letter to Lawrence Smith, President of the AFA (3 April 1952) copied to Barr in the Museum of Modern Art Archives, Alfred H. Barr Jnr, Papers [Archives of American Art (AAA) Roll 3155, Frame 1149].

68 Letter (11 April 1952), Museum of Modern Art Archives, Alfred H. Barr Jnr, Papers [Archives of American Art (AAA) Roll 3155, Frame 1146].

69 Lloyd Goodrich, letter to Lawrence Smith (3 April 1952).

70 See Annette Cox, *Art-as-Politics: The Abstract Expressionist Avant-Garde and Society* (Ann Arbor, UMI Research Press, 1982), p. 142. Dondero, 'How the Magazine *The Nation* is Serving Communism', *Congressional Record*, 82nd Congress, 97:16 (4 May 1951), 4920–4925.

71 See Museum of Modern Art Archives, Alfred H. Barr Jnr, Papers [Archives of American Art (AAA) Roll 2178, Frames 139–339] for documents and correspondence related to the American Committee for Cultural Freedom, affiliated to the Congress for Cultural Freedom.

72 Reports on the CIA's support for the Congress for Cultural Freedom through dummy foundations made public in *The New York Times*, 27 April 1966, followed by Christopher Lasch, 'The Cultural Cold War: A Short History of the Congress for Cultural Freedom', in Barton J. Bernstein (ed.) *Towards a New Past: Dissenting Essays in American History* (New York, Pantheon Books, 1968), pp. 322–59. Good retrospective overview in Alan M. Wald, *The New York Intellectuals: The Rise and Fall of the Anti-Stalinist Left from the 1930s to the 1980s* (Chapel Hill and London, University of North Carolina Press, 1987), chapter 9, pp. 267ff. Also, Christopher Lasch, *The Agony of the American Left* (New York, Vintage, 1968); Peter Coleman, *The Liberal Conspiracy: The Congress for Cultural Freedom and the Struggle for the Mind of Postwar Europe* (New York, Free Press, 1989). Even in Barbara Rose's 'The Politics of Criticism IV: The Politics of Art, Part I', *Artforum*, 6:6 (February 1968), she opens with a reference to 'indiscriminate CIA subsidy', 31.

73 See 'Transcript: The Storm in the Plaza', excerpts from the General Services Administration hearing on the *Tilted Arc*', *Harper's*, 21:1622 (July 1985), 27–33; Clara Weyergraf-Serra and Martha Buskirk (eds), *The Destruction of 'Tilted Arc': Documents* (Cambridge, Mass., and London, MIT Press, 1991); Robert Storr, '*Tilted Arc* Enemy of the People', in Arlene Raven (ed.), *Art in the Public Interest* (Ann Arbor and London, UMI Research Press, 1989), pp. 269–86; Casey Nelson Blake, 'An Atmosphere of Effrontery: Richard Serra, *Tilted Arc*, and the Crisis of Public Art', in Richard Wrightman Fox and T. J. Jackson Lears (eds), *The Power of Culture* (Chicago and London, University of Chicago Press, 1993), pp. 247–89. Richard Serra, 'Art and Censorship', in W. J. T. Mitchell, *Art and the Public Sphere* (Chicago and London, University of Chicago Press, 1992), pp. 226–33; Anna Chave, 'Minimalism and the Rhetoric of Power', *Arts Magazine*, 64:5 (January 1990), 44–63.

74 See Chapter 3.

75 Stella in 'Transcript: The Storm in the Plaza', 32; Weyergraf-Serra and Buskirk (eds), *The Destruction of 'Tilted Arc'*, p. 100.

76 Katz in 'Transcript: The Storm in the Plaza', 33. The Katz statement does not appear in Weyergraf-Serra and Buskirk (eds), *The Destruction of 'Tilted Arc'*.

77 *Ibid*.

78 For examples of such defences see Serra's own defence, 'Art and Censorship', and Thomas Crow, 'Site-specific Art: The Strong and the Weak', in *Modern Art in the Common Culture* (New Haven and London, Yale University Press, 1996), pp. 130–50. For an incisive discussion of the issues and contradictions, see Casey Nelson Blake, 'An Atmosphere of Effrontery: Richard Serra, *Tilted Arc*, and the Crisis of Public Art'.

79 See, for example: *If You Lived Here: The City in Art, Theory and Social Activism, A Project by Martha Rosler*, edited by Brian Wallis (Seattle, Bay Press, 1991); Michele Wallace, *Invisibility Blues: From Pop to Theory* (London, Verso, 1990); Lucy Lippard, *Mixed Blessings: New Art in a Multicultural America* (New York, Pantheon, 1990).

80 *The Ideology of the Aesthetic* (Oxford and Cambridge, Blackwell, 1990), p. 7.

81 See Chapter 4 and David Haward Bain, *Aftershocks: A Tale of Two Victims* (New York, Methuen, 1980); Maurice Berger, *Representing Vietnam 1965–1973: The Antiwar Movement in America* (New York, Hunter College Art Gallery, 1988); Susan Jeffords, 'Tattoos, Scars, Diaries, and Writing Masculinity' in Berg and Rowe (eds), *The Vietnam War and American Culture*, pp. 208–25.

82 A fact extraordinarily incorporated in Tony Harrison's long poem 'A Cold Coming', first published in *The Guardian* (18 March 1991) in which he refers to marines from Seattle who had banked their sperm in nitrogen before leaving for the Gulf. See Tony Harrison, *A Cold Coming: Gulf War Poems* (Newcastle-Upon-Tyne, Bloodaxe Books, 1991), pp. 7–16.

Index

ABC No Rio Dinero: The Study of a Lower East Side Art Gallery 223

Abstract Expressionism 6, 65, 84, 85, 133, 161, 190, 191, 192

Ad Hoc Women Artists' Committee 112, 136, 210, 213, 224

Adler, Amy 219

Adorno, Theodore 71, 139–40, 161
'Commitment' 139

Advancing American Art (exhibition) 222

Aerojet General 26

Agnew, Spiro 173, 174

Air Force 34
Space Technology Laboratory 26

Albers, Josef 41

Alloway, Lawrence 162

Altamont 147

Altoon, John 26, 27

Amalgamated Lithographers Union 177

American Civil Liberties Union (ACLU) 67, 72, 121, 181

American Committee for Cultural Freedom, The 226

American Family Association 219, 221

American Federation of Arts (AFA) 216, 225
100 American Artists of the Twentieth Century (exhibition) 216

American Flag 119, 120–2

American Legion Magazine 196

Analytic Services (ANSER) 35

Andre, Carl 141

Anger, Kenneth 90
Scorpio Rising 90

Angry Arts 85, 125–6, 128, 170
petition to Picasso 161–6, 196

Angry Arts Week 6, 64, 114, 115–20

anti-Capital Punishment movement 86

Apollo 12 mission 167, 169

Appel, Karel 17, 65, 116

Arendt, Hannah 71

Arensbergs 26

Arnold, General H. H. 'Hap' 34

Art Bulletin 187

Art of Assemblage, The (exhibition) 46

Art Gallery Row, North La Cienega Boulevard 4

Art in America 68, 135

Art International 83

Art Strike (1970) 209

Art Workers' Coalition (AWC) 6, 8, 111, 112, 135–7, 139, 141, 174–6, 182–92, 222, 224
petition to Picasso 161–6, 185–7, 196

Artforum 6, 15, 16, 19, 28, 39, 46–7, 61, 82–7, 88, 108, 113, 114, 124, 126, 132, 138, 140–6, 148, 210

Artists and Writers Dissent 21

Artists and Writers Protest 6, 23, 64, 85, 114, 115, 121, 161
1000 American Artists Petition 199
Artists' Call Against US Intervention in Latin America 218
Artists Civil Rights Assistance Fund, Inc. (ACRAF) 84
Artists Protest 21
Artists' Protest Committee 4, 15–47, 57–8, 70, 73, 74, 85
formation 20–6
RAND, 'Dialogue on Vietnam' and 34–41, 44
'We Dissent' 29–34
see also Artists' Tower of Protest
Artists' Tower of Protest 2, 3, 4–6, 13, 16–17, 57–96, 114, 135, 170, 222, 228
appeal for panels 63–6
Artforum and 82–7
autonomy and commitment 81–2
building and safety approval 61–3
installation 66–8
intellectual reaction 74–81
origins of 18, 20–6
reception 68–74
site 59–61
Artnews 86, 87, 187, 188, 193
Arts Magazine 128
ARVN 79, 80
Ashton, Dore 114
Aspen Times, The 137
Assembly of Men and Women in the Arts Concerned with Vietnam 85
Atomic Energy Commission 34
Audry, Colette 71
autonomous art, politics of 137–42

Baer, Jo 141
Ban-the-Bomb 86
Baranik, Rudolf 21, 63, 115, 116, 162, 165, 195
Bareiss, Walter 183, 195, 196, 199
Barr, Alfred H., Jr 46, 47, 112, 162, 192, 196, 197–8, 199, 225–6
Barr, Jerry Lee 72
Bataille, Georges 131
Beat Culture 6, 19, 26, 46, 58, 66, 212
Beauvoir, Simone de 71
Bell, Larry 26, 27, 28, 39, 43, 83, 84, 85
Bellinger, David 138
Bellows, Georg 41
Bengston, Billy Al 26, 27, 32, 43
Benjamin, Walter 71, 161
Berghaus, Günter 123
Berman, Wallace 6, 19, 26, 27, 58, 66, 89, 212, 213, 217
Semina 6, 212
Wallace Berman: Support the Revolution 19
Bingham, Lois 42
Bischoff, Werner: Life in Vietnam 125
Black Mask group 116
Black Panthers 111, 147, 180–1, 190, 196
Blackwell, Patrick 68
Blazys, John 120
Blum, Irving 26, 28, 31
Bly, Robert 126
Bolton, Richard: Culture Wars 214, 221, 222, 224, 225, 226, 228, 229
Bonelli, Supervisor 92–3
Borchgrave, Arnaud de 77–8
Boston Symphony Orchestra 215
Bourgeois, Louise 191
Brandt, Peter 176
Bread and Puppet Theatre 117, 126, 130

Brecht, Bertold 147
Breton, André 71
Bright, John 179, 180
Brittin, Charles 30, 66, 68, 71, 72,
   85
Brodie, Bernard 33, 39
Brown, Sam 186
Buchanan, Pat 219, 223
Buchloh, Benjamin 110
Burrell, Ed 67
Bush, President George 80, 213
   administration 219
Butor, Michael 71
Buzzanco, Robert 81
Bykov, Colonel 194

Cable News Network (CNN) 220
Calder, Alexander 41
California Institute of Technology
   (Cal Tech) 26, 94
'Call from the Artists of Los
   Angeles, A' (poster) 21, 22
Calley, Lieutenant 112, 147, 166,
   167, 170
Calvin Klein 9, 12
Camnitzer, Luis 148
   April 1970 148
Camus, Albert 24
Caro, Anthony 146
Carter, Edward W. 91
Castelli, Leo 130
Caute, David 211
CBS 221
Centre for the Study of
   Democratic Institutions 18
Centre Georges Pompidou 218
César 17, 65
Chamberlain, John 42
Chambers, Whittaker 192, 193,
   194, 195
Chase Manhattan Bank 111
Chave, Anna 148
   'Minimalism and the Rhetoric
   of Power' 146

Chavez, Cesar 186
Chessman, Caryl 87
Chicago, Judy *see* Gerowitz, Judy
Chicago Art Institute 63
Chicago Seven 181, 196
Chinouard Institute of Art 91
Chomsky, Noam 76, 85, 186, 189,
   214, 220, 224
CIA 19, 71, 76, 214
Civil Rights Act (1964) 80
Civil Rights movement 4, 16, 23,
   30, 45, 57, 58, 73, 84, 86,
   110, 119, 138, 163, 212, 222
Clarac, Matta 71
Clarac, Max 71
Clarac-Serou, Cecilia 199
Clark, Mark 181
Clark, T. J. 211
   *Absolute Bourgeois, The:
   Art and Politics in France
   1848–51* 211
   *Image of the People: Gustave
   Courbet and the 1848
   Revolution* 211
Cleaver, Eldridge 180, 190
Cleveland Plain Dealer, The 167,
   169, 170
Clinton, President Bill 13
CNN 220–1
Cold War 12, 18, 214
Colin, Ralph 183
Collage of Indignation, The 6, 16,
   108, 115–16, 120, 121, 124,
   125, 126–30, 135, 170
Collins, Jess 66
Collins, Judy 68
Committee of the Professions 115
Comstock, Anthony 191
Conceptual Art 108, 110, 142, 143
Cone, Jane Harrison 142
Congress for Cultural Freedom 226
Congress of Industrial
   Organisation 82
Conner, Bruce 46, 58

Constructivism 147
Coplans, John 28, 83, 84, 86
Copley, Bill 199
Corcoran Gallery of Art,
    Washington, DC 216
Cowles, Charles 46, 47
Crane, Diane 136
Crawford, Ralston 41
Cronkite, Walter 167, 169, 182
Crow, Thomas: *Rise of the Sixties,*
    The 19
Cultures in Contention 223

D'Amato, Senator 215, 223
D'Arcangelo, Allan 82, 115, 118
Dada 19, 58, 108, 136
Dallas Museum 225
Davis, Police Chief Edward M.
    179
Davis, Mike 26
    City of Quartz 15
Davis, Stuart 41
De Feo, Jay 6, 58, 66
de Kooning, Elaine 17, 23, 64, 65,
    86
de Kooning, Willem 41, 192
de Maria, Walter 199
de Menil, John 183
Debs, Ernest E. 93
DeLap, Tony 84
Demagny, Oliver 71
Deming, Barbara 138
Depp, Johnny 9
Dewasne, Jean 65
di Suvero, Mark 6, 17, 20, 59, 62,
    63, 66, 67, 83, 115–16
Dillon, Dejon 28
Dillon, Kenneth H. 17, 61, 62
Dine, Jim 42
Disney, Walt 91
Dissent 163, 177, 181, 182, 186,
    187, 190
Dohrn, Bernadine 181
'Dollard' 39

Dondero, George A. 217, 221,
    222–3, 225, 226
Donovan, Headley 85
Dorn, Warren, M. 90, 91, 92 93,
    95, 96, 215
double agency 123
Dougherty, Frazer 176, 188
Douglas Aircraft Company 34
Drama Review, The (TDR) 122
Drexler, Arthur 176, 182, 183,
    185
Dreyfus, Harold 39, 60
Duchamp, Marcel 26
Duncan, Master-Sergeant Donald
    4, 16, 71, 72, 78–80
Duncan, Robert 39
Dwan Gallery 27, 28–9, 31, 59,
    83, 87, 140

Eagleton, Terry 223, 228
East Timorese National Liberation
    Front 76
Edward Scissorhands 9
Edwards, Melvin 66, 67
Eisenhower, President 45, 217
Eisenhower Administration 173
Elementary and Secondary
    Education Act 80
Ellsberg, Daniel 39, 40
Embid, Florentino 164
Eros magazine 90
Esquire 221
Evergood, Philip 17, 65
Everts, Conner 217
    Studies in Desperation 91

Face à l'Histoire (exhibition) 218
Facts Forum News 216
Falklands War 173
Fall, Bernard F. 118
Farman 136
Farrell, James 209
FBI 71, 109, 214
Feminist Art Journal 141

Ferber, Herbert 17, 65, 191
Ferus Gallery 6, 18, 26–9, 61, 89, 212
Finley, Karen 220
Fiore, Quentin 129
  Medium is the Message, The 129–30
First American Artists Congress 161
Flag Day 120
Flavin, Dan 142, 148, 149
Fluxus 122, 130, 136
Ford Foundation 3, 35
Foster, Hal 147, 148
  'Crux of Minimalism, The' 146
  'Return of the Real, The' 135
Franc, Helen 210
Francis, Sam 17, 65
Franco, General 163, 164, 185
Frankfurt School 71
Frasconi, Antonio 115
Freedom House 25
Fried, Michael 83, 84, 110, 113, 114, 124, 144, 146
  'Art and Objecthood' 108, 109, 110, 114, 132, 142, 145, 146
  Three American Painters: Kenneth Noland, Jules Olitski, Frank Stella 84, 85
Friedman, Martin 42
Friedman, Saul 34
Frontier 28, 31, 47, 76, 85, 179
Fulbright, J. William 78
Fuller, Buckminster 67

Galerie du Dragon 64, 65
Gallagher, Jim 72, 73
Garmey, Father Stephen 185
Gavin, Lieutenant-General James 78
Geneva Accord (1954) 24, 44, 79
Gerowitz, Judy (Judy Chicago) 6, 17, 65, 66, 67, 83
Getty *Calender* (winter 1995–6) 3

Getty Center for the History of Art and the Humanities 2–3
Gingrich, Arnold 221
Ginzburg, Ralph 90, 217
Glueck, Grace 20, 183, 185, 188, 190, 191
Goldberg, Helen 42
Goldstein, J. R. 37
Goldstein, Malcolm: *State of the Nation* 131
Golub, Leon ~~17~~, ~~25~~, 39, 40, ~~63~~, ~~64, 65, 82~~, ~~108~~, ~~116~~, ~~126~~, ~~128–30~~, 147, 165, 199, 218
  Burnt Man 116
  Gigantomachies 218
  Interrogation 218
  Mercenary 218
  Napalm Flag 218
  Napalms 218
  Vietnam 218
Goodman, Mitchell 21
Goodman, Paul 138
Goodrich, Lloyd 225, 226
Gottlieb, Adolph 191
Graff, Henry F. 38
Gramsci, Antonio 176
Graves, Nancy 116
Gray, David 84
Gray, Christopher 211
  'Today – nothing' 211
Great Society 16, 80–1, 215
Green, Wilder 176, 182, 195
Greenberg, Clement 58, 83, 84, 88, 108, 110, 138, 143, 144, 145, 147, 148, 162, 226
  Art and Culture 142
  'Modernist Painting' 84, 142, 109, 215
  'Recentness of Sculpture' 146
'Greenberg and the Group' (Barbara Reise) 88, 142
Greene, Balcomb 116
Greenwich Village Peace Centre 115, 117

Grippe, Peter 191
Grosberg, Carol 115, 117, 132
Gross, Alex 188
Grosz, George 128
Guerrilla Art Action Group
    (GAAG) 111, 130, 136,
    174–5, 184, 185, 188, 224
Guerrilla Girls 213, 214
Guggenheim Museum, New York
    217
Gulf War (1991) 10, 164, 214,
    220, 229
Guston, Philip 191

Haacke, Hans 188, 217, 222
    MoMA-Poll 111, 113
Haeberle, Ron 10, 112, 167, 168,
    170, 176
Hahn, Kenneth 90, 91, 93, 215
Hallgren, Christer 169
Hampton, Fred 181
Hamrol, Lloyd 17, 39, 65, 67
Hannon, Michael 73
Hansen, Al 130, 131
Hanson, Hardy 21, 47, 64
    'Call from the Artists of Los
    Angeles, A' 63
Hare, David 191
Hartgan, Grace: *Essex Market* 41
Hayden, Tom 109, 187
Hearst, Randolph 222
Heckscher, August: *Public
    Happiness, The* 221
Heizer, Michael: *Double Negative*
    148
Helion, Jean 17, 65
Helms, Jesse 219, 223
Henderson, David 119
Henderson, Jim 39
Hendrick, Wally 58
Hendricks, Bici 131
Hendricks, Jon 116, 130, 175, 176
Heresies 136
Herman, Edward, S. 76

Herms, George 58
Hersh, Seymour 166, 167, 168, 173
Hess, Thomas B. 86
Hesse, Eva 65
Hicks, Granville 226
Higher Education Act 80
Hightower, John 112, 113, 195
Hiss, Alger 192, 193, 194
Ho Chi Minh 45, 68, 165
Hoffman, Abbie 181
Hofmann, Hans 41
Hollywood Ten 59
Hook, Sydney 161
Hoover, J. Edgar 214
Hopkins, Bud 115
Hopper, Dennis 42
Hopper, Edward 41
Hopps, Walter 17–18, 26, 27, 28,
    41–2, 43, 47, 85
Horkheimer, Max 71, 161
Housing and Urban Development
    Act 80
Howe, Irving 161, 162, 163, 178,
    180, 181–2, 186, 188, 190
    'Agony of the Campus, The'
    187
Hudson Institute 40
Huet, Henri 85
Hughes Aircraft 26
Hunt, Haroldson Lafyette 221
    Facts Forum 216, 217
Hunt, Richard 196
Huot, Robert 141

ICA 219
ICBM (Inter Continental Ballistic
    Missile) programme 35
imagists 63
Indonesian Communist Party (PKI)
    76
Information (exhibition) 111–13,
    214
Institute for Policy Studies,
    Washington, The 17

Inter-American Foundation for the Arts 132
International Fine Arts Council 223
International Survey of Painting and Sculpture, An (exhibition) 213
Irascibles 66
Irwin, Robert 26, 27, 43, 83, 85
Iwo Jima statue 120

Janss, Ed 18
Jess (Collins) 6, 58
Jet Propulsion Laboratory 26
John, Pope 116
John Paul Getty Museum 1, 2, 4, 8, 13, 210
John Paul Getty Trust 2
Johns, Jasper 41, 42
  Flag 8
Johnson, Eddie 115, 116
Johnson, President L. B. 25, 29, 38, 76, 80, 81, 116, 118, 131, 197, 215
  administration 16, 36, 37, 42, 43, 71, 78, 80, 94, 172
Johnson, Poppy 130
Jonas, Joan 148
Judd, Donald 27, 43, 84, 85, 137, 138, 139, 140, 141, 145, 147, 148
  'Imperialism, Nationalism and Regionalism' 148
Judd, Julie 137
Judson Gallery 130
  '12 Evenings of Manipulations' 130, 131, 132
Judson Publications Manifesto 130, 131
Just Seventeen 8

Kahn, Herman 33, 40, 70
  On Escalation 33
  Thinking the Unthinkable 33

Kahnweiler, Daniel-Henri 196, 197
Katz, Danny 227
Kauffman, Craig 27, 28, 39
Kauffmann, William 33
Kefauver, Estes 41
Kennan, Ambassador George 78, 224
Kennedy, Harold W. 91
Kennedy, John F. 11, 221
  administration 37, 170
Kent State 147
Kerouac, Jack 212
Kerr, Graham 168
Kesey, Ken, and his 'Merry Pranksters' 6, 68, 69–70
Kienholz, Ed 6, 26, 27–8, 46, 87–96, 215, 217, 228
  Back Seat Dodge – '38 27, 89, 92, 93, 95
  Barney's Beanery 87, 88
  Birthday, The 27, 95
  Eleventh Hour Final 28, 89
  Five Dollar Billy 92, 93
  History as a Planter 88
  Illegal Operation, The 27, 95
  National Banjo on the Knee Week 27
  Nativity, The 95
  Portable War Memorial, The 28, 120
  Psycho-Vendetta case 87
  Roxy's 89, 92, 95
  While Visions of Sugar Plums Danced on their Heads 27
Kimmelman, Michael 210
King, Martin Luther 118, 119, 211
Kirby, Michael 122
Kissinger, Henry 168
Klix, Richard 28
Klonsky, Mark 59
Kohler, Foy D. 41
Kolkowicz, Roman 35, 38
Kollwitz, Käthe 128, 214
Koppelman, Dorothy 115

Koppleman, Chaim 116
Kozloff, Joyce 185
Kozloff, Max 16, 19, 39, 40, 64,
83, 108, 113, 114, 126–9,
132, 199, 223
'American Painting During the
Cold War' 19, 210
Renderings 16
Kozloff, Nikolas 185
Kramer, Hilton 20, 112–13, 188,
189, 190
Krauss, Rosalind 83, 84, 110, 142,
144, 227
Kroll, Leon 216
Kuniyoshi, Yasuo 216
Kunkin, Art 44, 68, 71, 72

*L'Art en Europe: les Années
Décisives 1945–53*
(exhibition) 218
L'Humanité 197
LaBianca, Leno 179
LaBianca, Rosemary 179
Laclau, Ernesto 224
'ladder of escalation' 31, 33–4
Land Art 108, 142, 143
Landau, Felix 31
Lasch, Christopher 19
Le Witt, Sol 141, 142
Leary, Dr Timothy 69–70
Leen, Nina 66
Leibowitz, René 71
Leider, Philip 28, 31, 47, 82–7,
94, 95, 108, 109, 141–5, 147,
210
Leiris, Michel 71, 161, 197, 199
Lenin, Vladimir Illyich 182
Leopold, Herb 115
Levertov, Denise 21, 185
Levine, Jack 86, 116
Lewin, Si 116
Liberation 137–8
Lichtenstein, Roy 17, 41, 65, 68,
116

Life magazine 10, 38, 66, 82, 85,
163, 168–70, 185
Lippard, Lucy 83, 86, 87, 141,
144, 188, 223
*Different War, A: Vietnam in
Art* 141
Lipton, Seymour 191
Loeb Student Centre 6–7, 125
Los Angeles Committee Against
Censorship 90
Los Angeles County Museum of
Art (LACMA) 4, 6, 29, 31,
32, 85, 87–96
*New York School, The: the First
Generation – Paintings of the
1940s and 1950s* (exhibition)
85
Los Angeles Free Press 5, 6, 20,
21, 28, 30, 31, 32, 36, 39, 40,
44, 47, 57, 59, 62, 66, 67, 68,
71, 72, 73, 77, 90, 91, 93, 94
Los Angeles Herald Examiner 88,
89–90, 92, 93
Los Angeles Peace Centre 18, 65
Los Angeles Times, The 38, 89, 90,
92, 93
Louis, Morris 42
Lowell, Robert 145
Lowenstein, Allard K. 186
Lowry, Bates 136, 183
Lynch, Allen 27
Lynd, Staughton 138

MacArthur, General Douglas A.
92
*Machine as Seen at the End of the
Mechanical Age, The*
(exhibition) 135, 164
Madonna: *Like a Prayer* 219
Malevich, Kasimir: *White on
White* 175
Mall, Albert 39, 40
'Manifesto of 121' 25, 72
Mann, Sally 213

Manson, Charles 59, 179, 180, 181
Mapplethorpe, Robert 213, 216, 220
  Robert Mapplethorpe: The Perfect Moment 89, 216, 219
  X Portfolio 215, 228
Marcuse, Herbert 71, 180
Marmor, Dr Judd 39
Marshall, (Secretary) 197
Marx, Karl 63, 212
Marxist Quarterly 161
Mason, John 27
Masson, André 71
Matta 116, 121
Mattox, Charles 28
Mauriac, François 24
McCarthy, Senator 193, 195, 216, 221
McCarthyism 13, 58, 70, 109, 123, 134, 192, 214, 217
McClure, Michael 39
McCracken, John 84
McLuhan, Marshall 129
  Medium is the Message, The 129–30
McNamara, Robert Strange 36, 37, 38, 78, 81, 165
McShine, Kynaston L. 111, 214
Meadlo, Paul 167, 169, 171
Medicaid 80
Medicare 80
Meltzer, David 27
Mesches, Arnold 65, 67
Mexican Muralists 128
Michelson, Annette 39
Midler, Jay 115
Miller, Dorothy 46
Minimalism 108, 114, 137, 142, 143, 145, 146–9
Mishkin, Edward 90
Mitchell, Juliet: *Psychoanalysis and Feminism* 211
Mitgand, Herbert 197

Modernism (Greenbergian) 83, 88, 95, 108, 109, 110, 132, 140, 142, 143, 144, 146
Morrel, Marc 6, 82, 120, 125, 217
Morris, Philip 221
Morris, Robert 137, 141, 142, 145, 147
Morrison, Norman 57
Moses, Ed 27
Moss, Kate 8, 9, 12
Mothers Union for a Clean Society 92
Motherwell, Robert 17, 41, 65, 86, 191, 192
Mouffe, Chantal 224
Mullican, Lee 17, 65
Museum Associates (MoMA) 92
Museum of Modern Art (MoMA) 8, 41, 46, 110, 112, 124, 129, 164, 174–99, 209–10
  corporate power of 182–5
  criticism of 209–10
  Information exhibition 111–13, 214
My Lai massacre 10, 111–12, 147, 160, 161, 162, 165–8, 178, 184, 195

Nadeau, Maurice 71
Nader, Ralph 186
Naifeh, Steven 136
NASA 34
Nation, The 16, 19, 20, 21, 75, 76, 108, 113, 126, 127, 162, 179, 180, 224, 226
National Committee for a SANE Nuclear Policy 25
National Endowment for the Arts (NEA) 80, 215, 216, 219
National Endowment for the Humanities 80
National Science Foundation 37
National Security Action Memorandum (NSAM) 23

Neel, Alice 116
Nelson, Rolf 39
Nemser, Cindy 141
Nevelson, Louise 65
New American Painting and Sculpture, The: The First Generation (exhibition) 190
New Deal 81
New Images of Man (exhibition) 64, 129
New York Artists' Strike Against Racism, Sexism, Repression and War 110
New York Element, The 135, 189, 190, 224
New York Post, The 184
New York Review of Books 186
New York Times, The 20, 21, 23, 24, 25, 27, 34, 38, 40, 41, 65, 66, 73, 90, 94, 96, 112, 115, 148, 166, 167, 168, 170, 171, 173, 179–80, 183, 185, 188, 190, 191, 196
New York Times Magazine, The 38, 163
New York University (NYU) Students for a Democratic Society 115
New Yorker, The 132
Newman, Barnett 27, 43, 85, 190–1, 192
Newsweek 77, 168
Nichols, Robert 117
Nixon, President Richard 10–13, 80, 111, 141, 172, 174, 180, 184, 192–5, 197, 222–3
  administration 163, 173
  resignation 210
  'silent majority' of 165–8
Nochlin, Linda 83
Noland, Ken 42, 84, 85, 146

O'Brien, Conor Cruise 194
Oldenburg, Claes 17, 42, 65

Olitski, Jules 146
Operation Ranch Hand 164
Operation Rolling Thunder 76
Organizations of American States 29
Orr, Eric 67
Ortiz, Ralph 130
  'Brainwash' 131
  'Destruction Room' 131

Pageant Players 118, 126
Paley, Walter S. 112, 174, 182, 183–4, 221
Parker, Chief of Police 44
Parmelin, Hélène 197, 198
Partisan Review 86, 161
Pasadena Art Museum 17, 18
Pauker, Guy 39
Paula Cooper Gallery 141
Pauling, Linus 36, 43, 70
Peace and Freedom Party, Arts Section 189
Peace Parade Committee Commitment 124
'Peace Tower' *see* Artists' Tower of Protest
Penrose, Roland 196, 198
Pepper, William F. 118
Pepsico, Inc 219
Perreault, John 135
Petlin, Irving 4, 6, 16, 18, 20, 21, 25–9, 32, 33, 35–40, 57, 59, 63–5, 67, 71–4, 78, 80, 84, 87, 115, 161, 162, 170, 172, 173, 175–8, 184, 192, 196–9, 222, 223, 225
  'L. B. J. Infant People Burner, Long May You Roast in History's Hell' 121
Picard, Lil 130
Picasso, Jacqueline 198
Picasso, Pablo 24, 161–2, 166, 192, 196, 225
  Guernica 128, 161, 162, 163–5, 166, 175, 184–6, 195, 196, 198

Massacre in Korea 197, 225
Seated Woman 196
Pignon, Edouard 197
Pilger, John 76
Plagens, Peter 15
   'Los Angeles: The Ecology of
     Evil' 15
   *Sunshine Muse: Contemporary
     Art on the West Coast* 15
Plant, Charles 222
Platoon 9
Polanski, Roman 179
Policy Planning Study 23 78
Political Art Documentation
   Distribution (PAD/D) 223
Pollock, Jackson 192
   Number One, 1948 8
Pompidou Centre 210
Poons, Larry 27, 43, 84
Pop Art 6, 65, 135, 143, 145
Popular Front 134
Port Huron Statement 109
Pousette-Dart, Richard 191
Price, Ken 27, 84
Project RAND 34
Protest and Hope (exhibition) 124,
   133, 134
Puerto Rican Art Workers'
   Coalition 112
Pukalski, Lisa 218

Q. *'And babies?'*; A. *'And babies'*
   poster 111, 171, 175, 182,
   183, 185, 217

Radich, Stephen 121, 217
Radio Free Europe 196
Ramparts 4, 13, 37, 44, 78, 118
RAND (Research And
   Development) Corporation 3,
   4, 6, 33–41, 70, 114
Rand Institute 26
Rauschenberg, Robert 19, 42, 46, 86
   Urban 41

Reagan, Ronald 80, 90, 213
   administration 219
*Reconsidering the Art Object:
   1965–1975* (exhibition) 111
Refregier, Anton 115
Reinhardt, Ad 17, 23, 41, 65, 81,
   82, 86, 116, 191
Reinhardt, Mrs Ad 191
Reitz, Robert 115
Ringgold, Faith: *Flag for the
   Moon: die Nigger* 169
Rivera, Diego 225
Rivers, Larry 17, 41, 65
Roberts, Sergeant Jay 169
Rockefeller, David 112, 113, 183,
   221
Rockefeller, Nelson 111, 182, 183,
   184, 197
Rockefeller family 192
Rodia, Sabatino (Simon; Sam) 45,
   46, 47
Rolf Nelson Gallery 84
Roosevelt, President 81, 194
Rose, Barbara 42, 83, 84, 88, 147
Rosenberg, Harold 58, 132–3, 135,
   143–4
   Anxious Object, The 143
Rosenblum, Robert 83
Rosenquist, James 17, 65, 68, 116,
   126, 128
   F-111 86, 143
   Homage to the American Negro 86
Rosler, Martha 172, 173
Rosmer, Alfred 177
Rosmer, Marguerite 177
Ross, Andrew 220
Roszak, Theodore 191, 211–12
   *Making of a Counter Culture,
     The* 212
Rothko, Mark 17, 41, 65, 191,
   192–5
Rubin, Jerry 181, 227
Rubin, William 112, 191
Ruscha, Ed 27

Rusk, Dean 38
Russell, Bertrand 70, 76
Ryman, Robert 141

Sacco, Nico 46, 88
Safiello, Anthony 67
Said, Edward 224
    Culture and Imperialism 223
Sandford, Mariellen 122, 123
Santa Barbara Museum of Art 67
Saar, Betye 66
Sartre, Jean-Paul 24, 71
Saxton, Al 91
Schafran, Lynn H. 189
Schapiro, Meyer 58, 132, 160–3,
    175, 176, 177, 182, 185–92,
    194, 195
    'Liberating Quality of Avant-
        garde Art, The' 109, 139, 161
    'Nature of Abstract Art' 161
    'Social Bases of Art, The' 161
Schechner, Richard 122
Schneemann, Carolee 12, 123–4,
    130, 131–2
    Divisions and Rubble 131
    Fuses 123
    Meat Joy 123
    Ordeals 131
    Snows 6, 122, 123, 124, 131
    Viet-Flakes 124, 131, 132
Schneider, Rebecca 123
Schumann, Peter 117, 126, 130
Schwartz, Therese 68, 223, 224
    'Politicization of the Avant-
        Garde, The' 135
Scorsese, Martin: *Last Temptation
    of Christ, The* 219
Segal, George 17, 65
    Execution, The 124, 134
Seitz, William 46
Selz, Peter 64, 129
Serra, Richard 84, 116, 137, 141,
    226, 227
    Tilted Arc 227, 228

Serrano, Andres 213, 219, 220
    Heaven and Hell 218
    Piss Christ 215, 228
Shahn, Ben 82, 128, 216
Shaw, Elizabeth 176, 185, 196
Sidney Janis Gallery 83
Situationist International 211
Sloman, Joel 118
Smith, John Cabot 193–4
Smith, Lawrence (President of the
    AFA) 225
Smith, David 146
Smith, Richard Cándida 212
Smithson, Nancy 148
Smithson, Robert 141, 142, 148
    Spiral Jetty 148
Soby, James 112
Social Realists 82
Solomon, Alan 27, 42
Sonenberg, Pheobe 116
Sontag, Susan 4, 16, 74–5, 76, 78,
    80
Sony Corporation 12
Southeastern Centre for
    Contemporary Art (SECCA)
    219
Southern Christian Leadership
    Conference (SCLC) 30
Soyer, Moses 65
Soyer, Raphael 116
Spero, Nancy 25, 63, 66, 116
Spiegel, C. D. 120
Spock, Dr Benjamin 118
Sport in Art (exhibition) 216, 217,
    225
Sports Illustrated 216
Spring Mobilization to End the
    War in Vietnam 125–6
Stalinism 134, 189, 193, 194, 195
Standard Oil Company 111, 118
Stanton, Dr Frank 174, 183, 184,
    221
Steiner, Mike 28
Steinitz, Kate 46

Stella, Frank 17, 27, 42, 43, 65 73, 84, 85, 143, 227
Stellenrad, Ellen 121
Stellenrad, Johan 121
Stern, Philip 186
Stern, Seymour 90
Stern, Sol 37
Sterne, Hedda 66
Stevens, May 63, 66, 116
Stone, Oliver 213
    Wall Street 8
'Stop Escalation' symbol 31, 32
Streibert, Theodore 216, 217
Stuart, David 32
Student Mobilization Against the War 141
Student Nonviolent Coordinating Committee (SNCC) 23, 30
Students for a Democratic Society (SDS) 23, 59, 109
Subcommitte on Internal Security 71
Sugarman, George 17, 64, 65
Surrealism 19, 58, 64, 128
Systems Development Corporation (SDC) 35

Takis (Takis Vassilakis) 135–6, 164
    Tele-Sculpture 135
Tate, Sharon 179
Tatlin, Vladimir 47
Taylor, Francis 187–8
Taylor, General Maxwell 78
Tenney, James 123, 124
Terry, Michael 168
Tillim, Sidney 83, 87, 88, 142
Time 77, 78, 163, 167, 168
Toche, Jean 130
Toney, Anthony 23
Trotsky, Leon 176
Trotskyism 133
TRW 26
Tuchman, Maurice 87–8

Un-American Activities Committee of the United States Congress 25, 71
United Aircraft 118
United Nations 29, 36
United States Information Agency (USIA) 18, 41, 42, 215
United Technology Centre (UTC) 118
Universal Studios 219
US Armed Forces Recruiting Centre 12

Vanzetti, Bartolomeo 46, 88
Vicente, Esteban 86
Vietnam Day Committee 94
Vietnam War 4, 7, 11, 16
Villa dei Papiri 2
Village Voice, The 115, 121, 135
Vogue 8
Voice of America 215
Voice of America Forum Lectures, The: The Visual Arts 215
Voloshinov, Valentin, N. 214
von Meier, Kurt 67, 70, 71, 72
Voting Rights Act 80
Voulkos, Peter 27

Wall Street 213
Wallace, George 178
Wallace, Michele 212
Wallace, Mike 167, 169, 171
Walters, Frances E. 223
War on Poverty 80
War Resisters' League, The (WRL) 137, 138, 148
Warhol, Andy 26, 41, 113, 135
Watergate scandal 11, 214
Watson, Charles 179, 180
'Watts Riots' 16, 44, 47
Watts Tower 45, 46, 47
Weatherman Manifesto 174
Weathermen 147, 181, 212

Weber, John 27, 28, 36, 83, 84
Weissman, George 221
Wesselmann, Tom 65
Westmorland, General 38, 81, 165, 168, 197
Weyand, General Fred C. 165, 173
What's Eating Gilbert Grape? 9
Wheeler, Charles 171
White, Theodore H. 38
Whitney, John Hay 217
Wilcock, John 68
Wildmon, Revd Donald 215, 219, 220, 221, 223
Williams, Kevin 172
Williams, Raymond 2
Willoughby 136
Wilner, Tyler (Twila) 60
WIN (Workshop in Non-Violence) 137
Wirein, A. L. 73, 74
Wolin, Ron 141
Women Artists and Revolution (WAR) 112, 136, 210, 213, 224
Women Strike for Peace 23

Women Students and Artists for Black Art Liberation (WSABAL) 112, 136, 210, 213, 224
Women's Action Coalition (WAC) 223
Woodstock Music and Art Fair 11
Woodward, Stanley 41
Woodward Foundation of Washington 41
women's movement 110
Works Progress Administration (WPA) 6, 65, 128, 221
Writers and Artists Protest 21

Yippies (Youth International Party) 130, 174, 181
'Museum of the Streets' 130
Youngerman, Jack 116

Z Magazine 224
Zajac, Jack 17, 65
Zelevansky, Lynn 210
Zerbe, Karl 41
Zora Gallery 91
Zorach, William 216